The American Record

Images of the Nation's Past
Volume Two: Since 1865

The
American
Record

Images of the Nation's Past
Volume Two: Since 1865

THIRD EDITION

EDITED BY

William Graebner
State University of New York,
College at Fredonia

Leonard Richards
University of Massachusetts,
Amherst

McGraw-Hill, Inc.

New York   St. Louis   San Francisco   Auckland   Bogotá   Caracas
Lisbon   London   Madrid   Mexico City   Milan   Montreal   New Delhi
San Juan   Singapore   Sydney   Tokyo   Toronto

This book was set in Palatino by Ruttle, Shaw & Wetherill, Inc.
The editor was Peter Labella;
the production supervisor was Friederich W. Schulte.
The cover was designed by John Hite.
Project supervision was done by Ruttle, Shaw & Wetherill, Inc.
R. R. Donnelley & Sons Company was printer and binder.

Cover Art
Paul Meltsner, Ohio, Bellevue, Ohio.
National Archives and Records Administration.

THE AMERICAN RECORD
Images of the Nation's Past
Volume Two: Since 1865

This book is printed on acid-free paper.

4 5 6 7 8 9 0 DOC DOC 9 0 9

ISBN 0-07-023988-6

Library of Congress Cataloging-in-Publication Data

(Revised for vol. 2)

The American record.

    Includes bibliographical references (p.   ).
    Contents: v. 1. To 1877 — v. 2. Since 1865.
      1. United States—History.   2. United States —History—
Sources.   I. Graebner, William.   II. Richards, Leonard L.
E178.6.A4145   1995   973   94-26793
ISBN 0-07-023987-8 (v. 1)
ISBN 0-07-023988-6 (v. 2)

About the Editors

WILLIAM GRAEBNER is Professor of History at the State University of New York at Fredonia. He received the Frederick Jackson Turner Award from the Organization of American Historians for *Coal-Mining Safety in the Progressive Period: The Political Economy of Reform*. Another book, *A History of Retirement: The Meaning and Function of an American Institution, 1885-1978*, was published in 1980. He is also the author of *The Engineering of Consent: Democracy and Authority in Twentieth-Century America* (1987); *Coming of Age in Buffalo: Youth and Authority in the Postwar Era* (1990); and *The Age of Doubt: American Thought and Culture in the 1940s* (1991). In 1993, he was Fulbright Professor of American Studies at the University of Rome. He currently serves on the editorial boards of *American Studies* and *The Historian*.

LEONARD RICHARDS is Professor of History at the University of Massachusetts at Amherst. He was awarded the 1970 Beveridge Prize by the American Historical Association for his book *"Gentlemen of Property and Standing": Anti-Abolition Mobs in Jacksonian America*. Professor Richards is also the author of *The Advent of American Democracy* and *The Life and Times of Congressman John Quincy Adams*. He is planning another book on the "Slave Power" thesis.

Contents

Chapter 14   Culture Wars   345

PREFACE

During the past two or three decades, the study of history in the United States has become in many ways more sophisticated and, we think, more interesting. Until the mid-1960s the dominant tradition among American historians was to regard the historian's domain as one centered on politics, economics, diplomacy, and war. Now, in the mid-1990s, historians are eager to address new kinds of subjects and to include whole sections of the population that were neglected in the traditional preoccupation with presidential administrations, legislation, and treaties. Women and children, the poor and economically marginal, gays and native Americans, have moved nearer the center of the historians' stage. We have become almost as eager to know how our ancestors dressed, ate, reared their children, made love, and buried their dead as we are to know how they voted in a particular presidential election. In addition, ordinary Americans now appear on the stage of history as active players who possess the power to shape their lives, rather than as passive victims of forces beyond their control. The result is a collective version of our national past that is more inclusive, more complicated, and less settled.

The third edition of *The American Record* continues the effort begun in the first and second editions. We have attempted to bridge the gap between the old history and the new, to graft the excitement and variety of modern approaches to history on an existing chronological and topical framework with which most of us feel comfortable. Most of the familiar topics are here. We have included essays on the early colonial settlements, the Revolutionary War, the Founding Fathers, immigration, Progressivism, and the Great Depression. But by joining these essays to primary sources, we have tried to make it possible for teachers and students to see links between the Puritan social order and the lessons children learned from their primers; between the Revolutionary War and the colonial class structure; between the Founding Fathers and the physical layout of the nation's capital; between immigration and the prairie houses of Frank Lloyd Wright; between Progressivism and the proclamation of Mother's Day; and between the Great Depression and the murals that were painted on post office walls across the nation in the mid-1930s. The third edition also takes up issues and themes that are not so universally familiar, but which are beginning to re-shape our understanding of the American past, among them the rise of a con-sumer society, the history of the environment, and the late–20th century conflict over "culture." This is a book that teaches the skill of making sense out of one's whole world.

Throughout, we have attempted to incorporate materials with *texture:* doc-uments that are not only striking but can be given more than one interpretation; photographs that invite real examination and discussion; tables and maps that have something new and interesting to contribute; and essays, such as James H. Merrill's account of the "new world" as it appeared to the Catawba Indians, and Lizabeth Cohen's study of how Chicago workers experienced mass culture, that are at once superb examples of recent historical scholarship and accessible to undergraduates.

From the beginning, we realized that our approach to American history would require some adjustment for many students and teachers. It was one thing to expect a student to place an address by Teddy Roosevelt in the context of turn-of-the-century imperialism, yet quite another to expect students to do the same with Edgar Rice Burrough's *Tarzan of the Apes.* For this reason, we have offered a good deal of guidance. Introductions to primary and secondary mate-rials are designed not just to provide basic background information, but to sug-gest productive avenues of interpretation. Interpretive essays and questions are intended to create a kind of mental chemistry in which students will have enough information to experience the excitement of putting things together, and yet not so much guidance that conclusions become obvious.

We remain indebted to R. Jackson Wilson, who inspired the first edition of this book. We also wish to thank our editors at Alfred A. Knopf and McGraw-Hill—first David Follmer and Chris Rogers, later Niels Aaboe and Peter La-bella—for their patient supervision of a difficult project. And we are especially grateful to the teachers and students who used the first and second editions of *The American Record* and showed us how to make the book better.

McGraw-Hill and the authors would like to thank the following reviewers for their many helpful comments and suggestions: Jeffrey Adler, University of Florida; Bruce Cohen, Worcester State College; Peter Filene, University of North Carolina; Benjamin McArthur, Southern College of Seventh Day Adventists; Sonya Michel, University of Illinois at Urbana-Champaign; and David Sloan, University of Arkansas.

William Graebner

Leonard Richards

The American Record

Images of the Nation's Past
Volume Two: Since 1865

CHAPTER 1

Reconstruction

When it was first coined in the crisis months between the election of Lincoln and the beginnings of the Civil War, the term "Reconstruction" meant simply the re-unification of the nation. By the time the war ended in 1865, the idea of Reconstruction was more complicated: it now meant more than simple political re-establishment of the Union; it meant reconstructing the south, refashioning its social and economic life to some degree or other. For the freedmen—many only days removed from slavery—Reconstruction would soon come to represent freedom itself. Even in 1865, most southern blacks realized that without thoroughgoing Reconstruction, in which freedmen obtained land as well as the right to vote, freedom would mean only a new kind of economic oppression.

Twelve years later, in 1877, many people, north and south, realized that Reconstruction had ended. But by then the term had taken on intense moral meanings. To most white southerners, it was a term of resentment, the name of a bleak period during which vindictive Yankee politicians had tried to force "black rule" on a "prostrate south." Tried and finally failed, for the south had in the end been "redeemed" by its own leaders. Slavery had ended, but white supremacy had been firmly re-established. To perhaps a majority of whites in the north, Reconstruction had over the years become a nuisance, and they were glad to let go of it, to reaffirm the value of the Union, and to let the bitter past die. There were other northerners, however, who looked back from 1877 to twelve years of moral failure, of lost opportunities to force freedom and equality on an unrepentant south.

There were hundreds of thousands of freedmen who experienced this "moral failure" in very real ways. Instead of farming their own land, they farmed the lands of whites as tenants and sharecroppers. Far from benefiting from meaningful voting rights, most blacks were denied the franchise, and those who continued to exercise it did so in a climate of hostility hardly conducive to political freedom. Nonetheless, it was possible for blacks to look back positively at the Reconstruction experience. The 1866 Civil Rights Act granted blacks both citizenship and all the civil rights possessed by whites. When the

1

constitutionality of that statute seemed in doubt, Congress made ratification of the Fourteenth Amendment (accomplished in 1868) a precondition for southern restoration to the Union. In theory, that amendment made the federal government the protector of rights that might be invaded by the states. Under "Radical" reconstruction, carried out by Congress after 1867, hundreds of thousands of southern blacks voted, and many held high elective office. And in 1875, when whites had re-established their authority throughout most of the region, a new civil rights act "guaranteed" blacks equal rights in theaters, inns, and other public places. If in the end it proved impossible to maintain these gains, Reconstruction still remained the bright spot in the lives of many former slaves.

INTERPRETIVE ESSAY

Elizabeth Rauh Bethel

Promised Land

Most accounts of the Reconstruction period have been written largely from the perspective of powerful white men such as presidents, northern congressmen, or southern "redeemers." As a result, students often get the impression that all decisions were made by whites, and blacks were idly sitting on their hands, just the beneficiaries or victims of white actions. That was not the case. Throughout the south black men and women, even though they were just months away from slavery, actively shaped their own futures and challenged the power and prejudices of their white neighbors. Most wanted to own land and become family farmers. The odds against them were immense, and many struggled valiantly only to see their hopes dashed by their lack of money, or by political decisions made in distant Washington, or by white terrorists such as the Ku Klux Klan. But some, as Elizabeth Rauh Bethel documents in the following selection, overcame great obstacles and established tightly knit communities. What do you think accounts for the courage and determination of the families Bethel describes? Do you think the course of American history would have been changed if most black families during Reconstruction had obtained a forty-acre farm? In what respect?

The opportunity to acquire land was a potent attraction for a people just emerging from bondage, and one commonly pursued by freedmen throughout the south. Cooperative agrarian communities, instigated in some cases by the invading Union Army and in other cases by the freedmen themselves, were scattered across the plantation lands of the south as early as 1863. Collective land purchases and cooperative farming ventures developed in the Tidewater area of Virginia, the Sea Islands of South Carolina and Georgia, and along the Mississippi River as refugees at the earliest contraband camps struggled to establish economic and social stability.

These initial land tenure arrangements, always temporary, stimulated high levels of industrious labor among both those fortunate enough to obtain land and those whose expectations were raised by their neighbors' good fortunes. Although for most freedmen the initial promise of landownership was never realized, heightened expectations resulted in "entire families laboring together, improving their material conditions, laying aside money that might hopefully be used to purchase a farm or a few acres for a homestead of their own" during the final years of the war.

The desire for a plot of land dominated public expressions among the freed-

From Elizabeth Rauh Bethel, *Promiseland: A Century of Life in a Negro Community*, Temple University Press, Philadelphia, 1981, pp. 5–8, 17–21, 23, 25–33, 39–40. © 1981 by Temple University. Reprinted by permission of Temple University Press.

men as well as their day-to-day activities and behaviors. In 1864 Secretary of War Stanton met with Negro leaders in Savannah to discuss the problems of re-settlement. During that meeting sixty-seven-year-old freedman Garrison Frazier responded to an inquiry regarding living arrangements by telling Stanton that "we would prefer to 'live by ourselves' rather than 'scattered among the whites.'" These arrangements, he added, should include self-sufficiency established on Negro-owned lands. The sentiments Frazier expressed were not unusual. They were repeated by other freedmen across the south. Tunis Campbell, also recently emancipated, testified before the congressional committee investigating the Ku Klux Klan that "the great cry of our people is to have land." A delegate to the Tennessee Colored Citizens' Convention of 1866 stated that "what is needed for the colored people is land which they own." A recently emancipated Negro representative to the 1868 South Carolina Constitutional Convention, speaking in support of that state's land redistribution program, which eventually gave birth to the Promised Land community, said of the relationship between landownership and the state's Negro population: "Night and day they dream" of owning their own land. "It is their all in all."

At Davis Bend, Mississippi, and Port Royal, South Carolina, as well as similar settlements in Louisiana, North Carolina, and Virginia, this dream was in fact realized for a time. Freedmen worked "with commendable zeal . . . out in the morning before it is light and at work 'til darkness drives them to their homes" whenever they farmed land that was their own. John Eaton, who supervised the Davis Bend project, observed that the most successful land experiments among the freedmen were those in which plantations were subdivided into individually owned and farmed tracts. These small farms, rather than the larger cooperative ventures, "appeared to hold the greatest chance for success." The contraband camps and federally directed farm projects afforded newly emancipated freedmen an opportunity to "rediscover and redefine themselves, and to establish communities." Within the various settlements a stability and social order developed that combined economic self-sufficiency with locally directed and controlled schools, churches, and mutual aid societies. In the years before the Freedmen's Bureau or the northern missionary societies penetrated the interior of the south, the freedmen, through their own resourcefulness, erected and supported such community institutions at every opportunity. In obscure settlements with names like Slabtown and Acreville, Hampton, Alexandria, Saxtonville, and Mitchelville, "status, experience, history, and ideology were potent forces operating toward cohesiveness and community." . . .

. . . In South Carolina, perhaps more intensely than any of the other southern states, the thirst for land was acute. It was a possibility sparked first by General William T. Sherman's military actions along the Sea Islands, then dashed as quickly as it was born in the distant arena of Washington politics. Still, the desire for land remained a goal not readily abandoned by the state's freedpeople, and they implemented a plan to achieve that goal at the first opportunity. Their chance came at the 1868 South Carolina Constitutional Convention.

South Carolina was among the southern states that refused to ratify the

Fourteenth Amendment to the Constitution, the amendment that established the citizenship of the freedmen. Like her recalcitrant neighbors, the state was then placed under military government, as outlined by the Military Reconstruction Act of 1867. Among the mandates of that federal legislation was a requirement that each of the states in question draft a new state constitution incorporating the principles of the Fourteenth Amendment. Only after such new constitutions were completed and implemented were the separate states of the defeated Confederacy eligible for readmission to the Union.

The representatives to these constitutional conventions were selected by a revolutionary electorate, one that included all adult male Negroes. Registration for the elections was handled by the army with some informal assistance by "that God-forsaken institution, the Freedman's Bureau." Only South Carolina among the ten states of the former Confederacy elected a Negro majority to its convention. The instrument those representatives drafted called for four major social and political reforms in state government: a statewide system of free common schools; universal manhood suffrage; a jury law that included the Negro electorate in county pools of qualified jurors; and a land redistribution system designed to benefit the state's landless population, primarily the freedmen.

White response to the new constitution and the social reforms that it outlined was predictably vitriolic. It was condemned by one white newspaper as "the work of sixty-odd Negroes, many of them ignorant and depraved." The authors were publicly ridiculed as representing "the maddest, most unscrupulous, and infamous revolution in history." Despite this and similar vilification, the constitution was ratified in the 1868 referendum, an election boycotted by many white voters and dominated by South Carolina's 81,000 newly enfranchised Negroes, who cast their votes overwhelmingly with the Republicans and for the new constitution.

That same election selected representatives to the state legislature charged with implementing the constitutional reforms. That body, like the constitutional convention, was constituted with a Negro majority; and it moved immediately to establish a common school system and land redistribution program. The freedmen were already registered, and the new jury pools remained the prerogative of the individual counties. The 1868 election also was notable for the numerous attacks and "outrages" that occurred against the more politically active freedmen. Among those Negroes assaulted, beaten, shot, and lynched during the pre-election campaign months were four men who subsequently bought small farms from the Land Commission and settled at Promised Land. Like other freedmen in South Carolina, their open involvement in the state's Republican political machinery led to personal violence.

Wilson Nash was the first of the future Promised Land residents to encounter white brutality and retaliation for his political activities. Nash was nominated by the Republicans as their candidate for Abbeville County's seat in the state legislature at the August 1868 county convention. In October of that year, less than two weeks before the general election, Nash was attacked and shot in the leg by two unidentified white assailants. The "outrage" took place in the barn on his rented farm, not far from Dr. Marshall's farm on Curltail Creek. Wilson Nash was thirty-three years old in 1868, married, and the father of three small children. He had moved from "up around Cokesbury" within Abbeville County, shortly after emancipation to the rented land further west. Within months after the Nash family was settled on their farm, Wilson Nash joined the many Negroes who affiliated with the Republicans, an alliance probably instigated and encouraged by Republican promises of land to the freedmen. The extent of Nash's involvement with local politics was apparent in his nomination for public office; and this same nomination brought him to the forefront of county Negro leadership and to the attention of local whites.

After the attack Nash sent his wife and young children to a neighbor's home, where he probably believed they would be safe. He then mounted his mule and fled his farm, leaving behind thirty bushels of recently harvested corn. Whether Nash also left behind a cotton crop is unknown. It was the unprotected corn crop that worried him as much as his concern for his own safety. He rode his mule into Abbeville and there sought refuge at the local Freedman's Bureau office where he reported the attack to the local bureau agent and requested military protection for his family and his corn crop. Captain W. F. DeKnight was sympathetic to Nash's plight but was powerless to assist or protect him. DeKnight had no authority in civil matters such as this, and the men who held that power generally ignored such assaults on Negroes. The Nash incident was typical and followed a familiar pattern. The assailants remained unidentified, unapprehended, and unpunished. The attack achieved the desired end, however, for Nash withdrew his name from the slate of legislative candidates. For him there were other considerations that took priority over politics.

Violence against the freedmen of Abbeville County, as elsewhere in the state, continued that fall and escalated as the 1868 election day neared. The victims had in common an involvement with the Republicans, and there was little distinction made between direct and indirect partisan activity. Politically visible Negroes were open targets. Shortly after the Nash shooting young Willis Smith was assaulted, yet another victim of Reconstruction violence. Smith was still a teenager and too young to vote in the elections, but his age afforded him no immunity. He was a known member of the Union League, the most radical and secret of the political organizations that attracted freedmen. While attending a dance one evening, Smith and four other League members were dragged outside the dance hall and brutally beaten by four white men whose identities were hidden by hoods. This attack, too, was an act of political vengeance. It was, as well, one of the earliest Ku Klux Klan appearances in Abbeville. Like other crimes committed against politically active Negroes, this one remained unsolved.

On election day freedmen Washington Green and Allen Goode were precinct managers at the White Hall polling place, near the southern edge of the Marshall land. Their position was a political appointment of some prestige, their reward for affiliation with and loyalty to the Republican cause. The appointment brought them, like Wilson Nash and Willis Smith, to the attention of local whites. On election day the voting proceeded without incident until midday, when two white men attempted to block Negroes from entering the polling site. A scuffle ensued as Green and Goode, acting in their capacity as voting officials, tried to bring the matter to a halt and were shot by the white men. One freedman was killed, two others injured, in the incident that also went unsolved. In none of the attacks were the assailants ever apprehended. Within twenty-four months all four men—Wilson Nash, Willis Smith, Washington Green, and Allen Goode—bought farms at Promised Land.

Despite the violence surrounding the 1868 elections, the Republicans carried the whole of the state. White Democrats refused to support an election they deemed illegal, and they intimidated the newly enfranchised Negro electorate at every opportunity. The freedmen, nevertheless, flocked to the polls in an unprecedented exercise of their new franchise and sent a body of legislative representatives to the state capitol of Columbia who were wholly committed to the mandates and reforms of the new constitution. Among the first legislative acts was one that formalized the land redistribution program through the creation of the South Carolina Land Commission.

The Land Commission program, as designed by the legislature, was financed through the public sale of state bonds. The capital generated from the bond sales was used to purchase privately owned plantation tracts that were then subdivided and resold to freedmen through long-term (ten years), low-interest (7 percent per annum) loans. The bulk of the commission's transactions occurred along the coastal areas of the state where land was readily available. The labor and financial problems of the rice planters of the low-country were generally more acute than those of the up-country cotton planters. As a result, they were more eager to dispose of a portion of the landholdings at a reasonable price, and their motives for their dealings with the Land Commission were primarily pecuniary.

Piedmont planters were not so motivated. Many were able to salvage their production by negotiating sharecropping and tenant arrangements. Most operated on a smaller scale than the low-country planters and were less dependent on gang labor arrangements. As a consequence, few were as financially pressed as their low-country counterparts, and land was less available for purchase by the Land Commission in the Piedmont region. With only 9 percent of the commission purchases lying in the up-country, the Marshall lands were the exception rather than the rule.

The Marshall sons first advertised the land for sale in 1865. These lands, like others at the eastern edge of the Cotton Belt, were exhausted from generations of cultivation and attendant soil erosion; and for such worn-out land the price was greatly inflated. Additionally, two successive years of crop failures, low cotton prices, and a general lack of capital discouraged serious planters from purchasing the lands. The sons then advertised the tract for rent, but the land stood idle. The family wanted to dispose of the land in a single transaction rather than subdivide it, and Dr. Marshall's farm was no competition for the less expensive and more fertile land to the west that was opened for settlement after the war. In 1869 the two sons once again advertised the land for sale, but conditions in Abbeville County were not improved for farmers, and no private buyer came forth.

Having exhausted the possibilities for negotiating a private sale, the family considered alternative prospects for the disposition of a farm that was of little use to them. James L. Orr, a moderate Democrat, former governor (1865 to 1868), and family son-in-law, served as negotiator when the tract was offered to the Land Commission at the grossly inflated price of ten dollars an acre. Equivalent land in Abbeville County was selling for as little as two dollars an acre, and the commission rejected the offer. Political promises took precedence over financial considerations when the commission's regional agent wrote the Land Commission's Advisory Board that "if the land is not bought the (Republican) party is lost in this district." Upon receipt of his advice the commission immediately met the Marshall family's ten dollar an acre price. By January 1870 the land had been subdivided into fifty small farms, averaging slightly less than fifty acres each, which were publicly offered for sale to Negro as well as white buyers.

The Marshall Tract was located in the central sector of old Abbeville County and was easily accessible to most of the freedmen who were to make the lands their home. . . .

The farms on the Marshall Tract were no bargain for the Negroes who bought them. The land was only partially cleared and ready for cultivation, and that which was free of pine trees and underbrush was badly eroded. There was little to recommend the land to cotton farming. Crop failures in 1868 and 1869 severely limited the local economy, which further reduced the possibilities for small farmers working on badly depleted soil. There was little credit available to Abbeville farmers, white or black; and farming lacked not only an unqualified promise of financial gain but even the possibility of breaking even at harvest. Still, it was not the fertility of the soil or the possibility of economic profit that attracted the freedmen to those farms. The single opportunity for landownership, a status that for most Negroes in 1870 symbolized the essence of their freedom, was the prime attraction for the freedmen who bought farms from the subdivided Marshall Tract.

Most of the Negroes who settled the farms knew the area and local conditions well. Many were native to Abbeville County. In addition to Wilson Nash, the Moragne family and their in-laws, the Turners, the Pinckneys, the Letmans, and the Williamses were also natives of Abbeville, from "down over by Bordeaux" in the southwestern rim of the county that borders Georgia. Others came to their new farms from "Dark Corner, over by McCormick," and another nearby Negro settlement, Pettigrew Station—both in Abbeville County. The Redd family lived in Newberry, South Carolina before they bought their farm; and James and Hannah Fields came to Promised Land from the state capitol, Columbia, eighty miles to the east.

Many of the settlers from Abbeville County shared their names with prominent white families—Moragne, Burt, Marshall, Pressley, Frazier, and Pinckney. Their claims to heritage were diverse. One recalled "my grandaddy was a white man from England," and others remembered slavery times to their children in terms of white fathers who "didn't allow nobody to mess with the colored boys of his." Others dismissed the past and told their grandchildren that "some things is best forgot." A few were so fair skinned that "they could have passed for white if they wanted to," while others who bought farms from the Land Commission "was so black there wasn't no doubt about who their daddy was."

After emancipation many of these former bondsmen stayed in their old neighborhoods, farming in much the same way as they had during slavery times. Some "worked for the marsters at daytime and for theyselves at night" in an early Piedmont version of sharecropping. Old Samuel Marshall was one former slave owner who retained many of his bondsmen as laborers by assuring them that they would receive some land of their own—promising them that "if you clean two acres you get two acres; if you clean ten acres you get ten acres" of farmland. It was this promise that kept some freedmen on the Marshall land until it was sold to the Land Commission. They cut and cleared part of the tract of the native pines and readied it for planting in anticipation of ownership. But the promise proved empty, and Marshall's death and the subsequent sale of his lands to the state deprived many of those who labored day and night on the land of the free farms they hoped would be theirs. "After they had cleaned it up they still had to pay for it." Other freedmen in the county "moved off after slavery ended but couldn't get no place" of their own to farm. Unable to negotiate labor or lease arrangements, they faced a time of homelessness with few resources and limited options until the farms became available to them. A few entered into labor contracts supervised by the Freedman's Bureau or settled on rented farms in the county for a time.

The details of the various postemancipation economic arrangements made by the freedmen who settled on the small tracts at Dr. Marshall's farm, whatever the form they assumed, were dominated by three conscious choices all had in common. The first was their decision to stay in Abbeville County following emancipation. For most of the people who eventually settled in Promised Land, Abbeville was their home as well as the site of their enslavement. There they were surrounded by friends, family, and a familiar environment. The second choice this group of freedmen shared was occupational. They had been Piedmont farmers throughout their enslavement, and they chose to remain farmers in their freedom.

Local Negroes made a third conscious decision that for many had long-range importance in their lives and those of their descendants. Through the influence of the Union League, the Freedman's Bureau, the African Methodist Church, and each other, many of the Negroes in Abbeville aligned politically with the Republicans between 1865 and 1870. In Abbeville as elsewhere in the state, the alliance was established enthusiastically. The Republicans promised land as well as suffrage to those who supported them. If their political activities became public knowledge, the freedmen "were safe nowhere"; and men like Wilson Nash, Willis Smith, Washington Green, and Allen Goode who were highly visible Negro politicians took great risks in this exercise of freedom. Those risks were not without justification. It was probably not a coincidence that loyalty to the Republican cause was followed by a chance to own land.

. . . The Land Commission first advertised the farms on the Marshall Tract in January and February 1870. Eleven freedmen and their families established conditional ownership of their farms before spring planting that year. They were among a vanguard of some 14,000 Negro families who acquired small farms in South Carolina through the Land Commission program between 1868 and 1879. With a ten-dollar down payment they acquired the right to settle on and till the thin soil. They were also obliged to place at least half their land under cultivation within three years and to pay all taxes due annually in order to retain their ownership rights.

Among the earliest settlers to the newly created farms was Allen Goode, the precinct manager at White Hall, who bought land in January 1870, almost immediately after it was put on the market. Two brothers-in-law, J. H. Turner and Primus Letman, also bought farms in the early spring that year. Turner was married to LeAnna Moragne and Letman to LeAnna's sister Francis. Elias Harris, a widower with six young children to raise, also came to his lands that spring, as did George Hearst, his son Robert, and their families. Another father-son partnership, Carson and Will Donnelly, settled on adjacent tracts. Willis Smith's father, Daniel, also bought a farm in 1870.

Allen Goode was the wealthiest of these early settlers. He owned a horse, two oxen, four milk cows, and six hogs. For the other families, both material resources and farm production were modest. Few of the homesteaders produced more than a single bale of cotton on their new farms that first year; but all, like Wilson Nash two years earlier, had respectable corn harvests, a crop essential to "both us and the animals." Most households also had sizable pea, bean, and sweet potato crops and produced their own butter. All but the cotton crops were destined for household consumption, as these earliest settlers established a pattern of subsistence farming that would prevail as a community economic strategy in the coming decades.

This decision by the Promised Land farmers to intensify food production and minimize cotton cultivation, whether intentional or the result of other conditions, was an important initial step toward their attainment of economic self-sufficiency. Small-scale cotton farmers in the Black Belt were rarely free agents. Most were quickly trapped in a web of chronic indebtedness and marketing restrictions. Diversification of cash crops was inhibited during the 1870s and 1880s not only by custom and these economic entanglements but also by an absence of local markets, adequate roads, and methods of transportation to move crops other than cotton to larger markets. The Promised Land farmers, generally unwilling to incur debts with the local lien men if they could avoid it, turned to a modified form of subsistence farming as their only realistic land-use option. Through this strategy many of them avoided the "economic nightmare" that fixed the status of other small-scale cotton growers at a level of permanent peonage well into the twentieth century.

The following year, 1871, twenty-five more families scratched up their ten-dollar down payment; and upon presenting it to Hollinshead obtained conditional titles to farms on the Marshall Tract. The Williams family, Amanda and her four adult sons—William, Henry, James, and Moses—purchased farms together that year, probably withdrawing their money from their accounts at the Freedman's Savings and Trust Company Augusta Branch for their separate down payments. Three of the Moragne brothers—Eli, Calvin, and Moses—joined the Turners and the Letmans, their sisters and brothers-in-law, making five households in that corner of the tract soon designated "Moragne Town." John Valentine, whose family was involved in A.M.E. organizational work in Abbeville County, also obtained a conditional title to a farm, although he did not settle there permanently. Henry Redd, like the Williamses, withdrew his savings from the Freedman's Bank and moved to his farm from Newberry, a small town about thirty miles to the east. Moses Wideman, Wells Gray, Frank Hutchison, Samuel Bulow, and Samuel Burt also settled on their farms before spring planting.

As the cluster of Negro-owned farms grew more densely populated, it gradually assumed a unique identity; and this identity, in turn, gave rise to a name, Promised Land. Some remember their grandparents telling them that "the Governor in Columbia [South Carolina] named this place when he sold it to the Negroes." Others contend that the governor had no part in the naming. They argue that these earliest settlers derived the name Promised Land from the conditions of their purchase. "They only promised to pay for it, but they never did!" Indeed, there is some truth in that statement. For although the initial buyers agreed to pay between nine and ten dollars per acre for their land in the original promissory notes, few fulfilled the conditions of those contracts. Final purchase prices were greatly reduced, from ten dollars to $3.25 per acre, a price more in line with prevailing land prices in the Piedmont.

By the end of 1873 forty-four of the fifty farms on the Marshall Tract had been sold. The remaining land, less than seven hundred acres, was the poorest in the tract, badly eroded and at the perimeter of the community. Some of those farms remained unsold until the early 1880s, but even so the land did not go unused. Families too poor to consider buying the farms lived on the state-owned property throughout the 1870s. They were squatters, living there illegally and rent-free, perhaps working a small cotton patch, always a garden. Their condition contrasted sharply with that of the landowners who, like other Negroes who purchased farmland during the 1870s, were considered the most prosperous of the rural freedmen. The freeholders in the community were among the pioneers in a movement to acquire land, a movement that stretched across geographical and temporal limits. Even in the absence of state or federal assistance in other regions, and despite the difficulties Negroes faced in negotiating land purchases directly from white landowners during Reconstruction, by 1875 Negroes across the south owned five million acres of farmland. The promises of emancipation were fulfilled for a few, among them the families at Promised Land.

Settlement of the community coincided with the establishment of a public school, another of the revolutionary social reforms mandated by the 1868 constitution. It was the first of several public facilities to serve community residents and was built on land still described officially as "Dr. Marshall's farm." J. H. Turner, Larkin Reynolds, Iverson Reynolds, and Hutson Lomax, all Negroes, were the first school trustees. The families established on their new farms sent more than ninety children to the one-room school. Everyone who could be spared from the fields was in the classroom for the short 1870 school term. Although few of the children in the landless families attended school regularly, the landowning families early established a tradition of school attendance for their children consonant with their new status. With limited resources the school began the task of educating local children.

The violence and terror experienced by some of the men of Promised Land during 1868 recurred three years later when Eli and Wade Moragne were attacked and viciously beaten with a wagon whip by a band of Klansmen. Wade was twenty-three that year, Eli two years older. Both were married and had small children. It was rumored that the Moragne brothers were among the most prominent and influential of the Negro Republicans in Abbeville County. Their political activity, compounded by an unusual degree of self-assurance, pride, and dignity, infuriated local whites. Like Wilson Nash, Willis Smith, Washington Green, and Allen Goode, the Moragne brothers were victims of insidious political reprisals. Involvement in Reconstruction politics for Negroes was a dangerous enterprise and one that addressed the past as well as the future. It was an activity suited to young men and those who faced the future bravely. It was not for the timid.

The Republican influence on the freedmen at Promised Land was unmistakable, and there was no evidence that the "outrages" and terrorizations against them slowed their participation in local partisan activities. In addition to the risks, there were benefits to be accrued from their alliance with the Republicans. They enjoyed appointments as precinct managers and school trustees. As candidates for various public offices, they experienced a degree of prestige and public recognition that offset the element of danger they faced. These men, born slaves, rose to positions of prominence as landowners, as political figures, and as makers of a community. Few probably had dared to dream of such possibilities a decade earlier.

During the violent years of Reconstruction there was at least one official attempt to end the anarchy in Abbeville County. The representative to the state legislature, J. Hollinshead—the former regional agent for the Land Commission—stated publicly what many local Negroes already knew privately, that "numerous outrages occur in the county and the laws cannot be enforced by civil authorities." From the floor of the General Assembly of South Carolina Hollinshead called for martial law in Abbeville, a request that did not pass unnoticed locally. The editor of the *Press* commented on Hollinshead's request for martial law by declaring that such outrages against the freedmen "exist only in the imagination of the legislator." His response was probably typical of the cavalier attitude of southern whites toward the problems of their former bondsmen. Indeed, there were no further reports of violence and attacks against freedmen carried by the *Press*, which failed to note the murder of County Commissioner Henry Nash in February 1871. Like other victims of white terrorists, Nash was a Negro.

While settlement of Dr. Marshall's farm by the freedmen proceeded, three community residents were arrested for the theft of "some oxen from Dr. H. Drennan who lives near the 'Promiseland.'" Authorities found the heads, tails, and feet of the slaughtered animals near the homes of Ezekiel and Moses Williams and Colbert Jordan. The circumstantial evidence against them seemed convincing; and the three were arrested and then released without bond, pending trial. Colonel Cothran, a former Confederate officer and respected barrister in Abbeville, represented the trio at their trial. Although freedmen in Abbeville courts were generally convicted of whatever crime they were charged with, the Williamses and Jordan were acquitted. Justice for Negroes was always a tenuous affair; but it was especially so before black, as well as white, qualified electors were included in the jury pool. The trial of the Williams brothers and Jordan signaled a temporary truce in the racial war, a truce that at least applied to those Negroes settling the farms at Promised Land.

In 1872, the third year of settlement, Promised Land gained nine more households as families moved to land that they "bought for a dollar an acre." There they "plow old oxen, build log cabin houses" as they settled the land they bought "from the Governor in Columbia." Colbert Jordan and Ezekiel Williams, cleared of the oxen stealing charges, both purchased farms that year. Family and kinship ties drew some of the new migrants to the community. Joshuway Wilson, married to Moses Wideman's sister Delphia, bought a farm near his brother-in-law. Two more Moragne brothers, William and Wade, settled near the other family members in "Moragne Town." Whitfield Hutchison, a jack-leg preacher, bought the farm adjacent to his brother Frank. "Old Whit Hutchison could sing about let's go down to the water and be baptized. He didn't have no education, and he didn't know exactly how to put his words, but when he got to singing he could make your hair rise up. He was a number one preacher." Hutchison was not the only preacher among those first settlers. Isaac Y. Moragne, who moved to Promised Land the following year, and several men in the Turner family all combined preaching and farming.

Not all of the settlers came to their new farms as members of such extensive kinship networks as the Moragnes, who counted nine brothers, four sisters, and an assortment of spouses and children among the first Promised Land residents. Even those who joined the community in relative isolation, however, were seldom long in establishing kinship alliances with their neighbors. One such couple was James and Hannah Fields, who lived in Columbia before emancipation. While still a slave, James Fields owned property in the state capital, which was held in trust for him by his master. After emancipation Fields worked for a time as a porter on the Columbia and Greenville Railroad and heard about the upcountry land for sale to Negroes as he carried carpet bags and listened to political gossip on the train. Fields went to Abbeville County to inspect the land before he purchased a farm there. While he was visiting, he "run up on Mr. Nathan Redd," old Henry Redd's son. The Fieldses' granddaughter Emily and Nathan were about the same age, and Fields proposed a match to young Redd. "You marry my granddaughter, and I'll will all this land to you and her." The marriage was arranged before the farm was purchased, and eventually the land was transferred to the young couple.

By the conclusion of 1872 forty-eight families were settled on farms in Promised Land. Most of the land was under cultivation, as required by law; but the farmers were also busy with other activities. In addition to the houses and barns that had to be raised as each new family arrived with their few possessions, the men continued their political activities. Iverson Reynolds, J. H. Turner, John and Elias Tolbert, Judson Reynolds, Oscar Pressley, and Washington Green, all community residents, were delegates to the county Republican convention in August 1872. Three of the group were landowners. Their political activities were still not received with much enthusiasm by local whites, but reaction to Negro involvement in politics was lessening in hostility. The *Press* mildly observed that the fall cotton crop was being gathered with good speed and "the farmers have generally been making good use of their time." Cotton picking and politics were both seasonal, and the newspaper chided local Negroes for their priorities. "The blacks have been indulging a little too much in politics but are getting right again." Iverson Reynolds and Washington Green, always among the community's Republican leadership during the 1870s, served as local election managers again for the 1872 fall elections. The men from Promised Land voted without incident that year.

Civic participation among the Promised Land residents extended beyond partisan politics when the county implemented the new jury law in 1872. There had been no Negro jurors for the trial of the Williams brothers and Colbert Jordan the previous year. Although the inclusion of Negroes in the jury pools was a reform mandated in 1868, four years passed before Abbeville authorities drew up new jury lists from the revised voter registration rolls. The jury law was as repugnant to the whites as Negro suffrage, termed "a wretched attempt at legislation, which surpasses anything which has yet been achieved by the Salons in Columbia." When the new lists were finally completed in 1872 the *Press*, ever the reflection of local white public opinion, predicted that "many of [the freedmen] probably have moved away; and the chances are that not many of them will be forthcoming" in the call to jury duty. Neither the initial condemnation of the law nor the optimistic undertones of the *Press* prediction stopped Pope Moragne and Iverson Reynolds from responding to their notices from the Abbeville Courthouse. Both landowners rode their mules up Five Notch Road from Promised Land to Abbeville and served on the county's first integrated jury in the fall of 1872. Moragne and Reynolds were soon followed by others from the community—Allen Goode, Robert Wideman, William Moragne, James Richie, and Luther (Shack) Moragne. By 1874, less than five years after settlement of Dr. Marshall's farm by the new Negro landowners began, the residents of Promised Land remained actively involved in Abbeville County politics. They were undaunted by the *Press* warning that "just so soon as the colored people lose the confidence and support of the North their doom is fixed. The fate of the red man will be theirs." They were voters, jurors, taxpayers, and trustees of the school their children attended. Their collective identity as an exclusively Negro community was well established. . . .

The representatives to the 1868 South Carolina Constitutional Convention who formulated the state's land redistribution hoped to establish an economically independent Negro yeomanry in South Carolina. The Land Commission intended the purchase and resale of Dr. Marshall's farm to solidify the interests of radical Republicanism in Abbeville County, at least for a time. Both of these designs were realized. A third and unintended consequence also resulted. The land fostered a socially autonomous, identifiable community. Drawing on resources and social structures well established within an extant Negro culture, the men and women who settled Promised Land established churches and schools and a viable economic system based on landownership. They maintained that economic autonomy by subsistence farming and supported many of their routine needs by patronizing the locally owned and operated grist mills and general store. The men were actively involved in Reconstruction politics as well as other aspects of civil life, serving regularly on county juries and paying their taxes. Attracted by the security and prestige Promised Land afforded and the possible hope of eventual landownership, fifty additional landless households moved into the community during the 1870s, expanding the 1880 population to almost twice its original size. Together the eighty-nine households laid claim to slightly more than four square miles of land, and within that small territory they "carved out their own little piece of the world."

SOURCES

The Meaning of Freedom

*What did it mean to be free? As Bethel's account of the settlers of Promised
Land indicates, there were many obstacles in the path of every freedman and
only a few succeeded in becoming independent small farmers. Some twentieth-
century writers have argued that the gains for most blacks were minuscule,
that being a poor tenant farmer or share-cropper was often even worse than
being a slave. But these writers, of course, never experienced the change from
slavery to freedom. Here is a man who did.*

Dayton, Ohio, August 7, 1865

To My Old Master, Colonel P. H. Anderson,
Big Spring, Tennessee

Sir: I got your letter and was glad to find you had not forgotten Jourdon, and
that you wanted me to come back and live with you again, promising to do better for me than anybody else can. I have often felt uneasy about you. I thought
the Yankees would have hung you long before this for harboring Rebs they
found at your house. I suppose they never heard about your going to Col. Martin's to kill the Union soldier that was left by his company in their stable. Although you shot at me twice before I left you, I did not want to hear of your
being hurt, and am glad you are still living. It would do me good to go back to
the dear old home and see Miss Mary and Miss Martha and Allen, Esther, Green,
and Lee. Give my love to them all, and tell them I hope we will meet in the better world, if not in this. I would have gone back to see you all when I was working in the Nashville hospital, but one of the neighbors told me Henry intended
to shoot me if he ever got a chance.

I want to know particularly what the good chance is you propose to give
me. I am doing tolerably well here; I get $25 a month, with victuals and cloth-
ing; have a comfortable home for Mandy (the folks here call her Mrs. Anderson),
and the children, Milly, Jane and Grundy, go to school and are learning well; the
teacher says Grundy has a head for a preacher. They go to Sunday-School, and
Mandy and me attend church regularly. We are kindly treated; sometimes we
overhear others saying, "Them colored people were slaves" down in Tennessee.
The children feel hurt when they hear such remarks, but I tell them it was no
disgrace in Tennessee to belong to Col. Anderson. Many darkies would have
been proud, as I used to was, to call you master. Now, if you will write and say
what wages you will give me, I will be better able to decide whether it would be
to my advantage to move back again.

As to my freedom, which you say I can have, there is nothing to be gained

From Lydia Maria Child, ed., *The Freedmen's Book*, Boston, 1865, pp. 265–267.

on that score, as I got my free-papers in 1864 from the Provist-Marshal-General of the Department at Nashville. Mandy says she would be afraid to go back without some proof that you are sincerely disposed to treat us justly and kindly—and we have concluded to test your sincerity by asking you to send us our wages for the time we served you. This will make us forget and forgive old scores, and rely on your justice and friendship in the future. I served you faithfully for thirty-two years and Mandy twenty years. At $25 a month for me, and $2 a week for Mandy, our earnings would amount to $11,680. Add to this the interest for the time our wages has been kept back and deduct what you paid for our clothing and three doctor's visits to me, and pulling a tooth for Mandy, and the balance will show what we are in justice entitled to. Please send the money by Adams Express, in care of V. Winters, esq., Dayton, Ohio. If you fail to pay us for faithful labors in the past we can have little faith in your promises in the future. We trust the good Maker has opened your eyes to the wrongs which you and your fathers have done to me and my fathers, in making us toil for you for generations without recompense. Here I draw my wages every Saturday night, but in Tennessee there was never any pay day for the negroes any more than for the horses and cows. Surely there will be a day of reckoning for those who defraud the laborer of his hire.

In answering this letter please state if there would be any safety for my Milly and Jane, who are now grown up and both good-looking girls. You know how it was with poor Matilda and Catherine. I would rather stay here and starve and die if it comes to that than have my girls brought to shame by the violence and wickedness of their young masters. You will also please state if there has been any schools opened for the colored children in your neighborhood, the great desire of my life now is to give my children an education, and have them form virtuous habits.

P.S.—Say howdy to George Carter, and thank him for taking the pistol from you when you were shooting at me.

From your old servant,
Jourdon Anderson

The Cartoonist's View of Reconstruction

Thomas Nast was America's foremost political cartoonist. He also was a Radical Republican who had no love for the white south or the Democratic party. The touchstone cause of Radical Republicans was black civil rights—particularly the right to vote—and conflict with the Democrats and the white south often focused on this issue. Nast's drawings in Harper's *Weekly, as you will notice, illustrated vividly this ongoing battle. The high point for Nast came when Hiram Revels, a black, occupied the Senate seat from Mississippi once held by Jefferson Davis. The low point came shortly afterward. What effect do you think each cartoon had on the electorate? Were any more compelling than the others?*

PARDON.

Columbia—"Shall I Trust These Men,

FRANCHISE.

And Not This Man?"
Thomas Nast, *Harpers Weekly, August 5, 1865. Courtesy of The Research Libraries,
The New York Public Library, Astor, Lenox, and Tilden Foundations.*

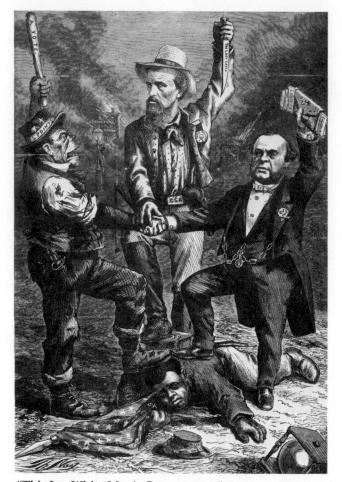

"This Is a White Man's Government."
"We regard the Reconstruction Acts (so called) of Congress as usurpations, and unconstitutional, revolutionary,
and void."—*Democratic Platform. Thomas Nast, Harper's
Weekly, September 5, 1868, Courtesy of The Research Libraries,
The New York Public Library, Astor, Lenox and Tilden Foundations.*

"TIME WORKS WONDERS."

IAGO.(JEFF DAVIS.) "FOR THAT I DO SUSPECT THE LUSTY MOOR
HATH LEAP'D INTO MY SEAT: THE THOUGHT WHEREOF
DOTH LIKE A POISONOUS MINERAL GNAW MY INWARDS." — OTHELLO.

*Thomas Nast, Harper's Weekly, April 9, 1870. Courtesy of The
Research Libraries, The New York Public Library, Astor, Lenox
and Tilden Foundations.*

The Commandments in South Carolina.
"We've pretty well smashed that; but I suppose, Massa
Moses, you can get another one." *Thomas Nast, Harper's
Weekly, September 26, 1874. Courtesy of The Research Li-
braries, The New York Public Library, Astor, Lenox and Tilden
Foundations.*

Thomas Nast, Harper's Weekly, October 24, 1874. Courtesy of The Research Libraries, The New York Public Library, Astor, Lenox and Tilden Foundations.

The Target

" * * They (Messrs. Phleps & Potter) seem to regard the White League as innocent as a Target Company."—Special Dispatch to the "N.Y. Times", from Washington, Jan. 17, 1875. Thomas Nast, Harper's Weekly, February 6, 1875. Courtesy of The Research Libraries, The New York Public Library, Astor, Lenox and Tilden Foundations.*

"To Thine Own Self Be True."

Thomas Nast, Harper's Weekly, April 24, 1875. Courtesy of The Research Libraries, The New York Public Library, Astor, Lenox and Tilden Foundations.

"These Few Precepts in Thy Memory"
Beware of entrance to a quarrel; but, being in,
Bear it that the opposer may beware of thee.
Give every man thine ear, but few thy voice:
Take each man's censure, but reserve thy judgment.
Costly thy habit as thy purse can buy,
But not express'd in fancy; rich, not gaudy:
For the apparel oft proclaims the man.

This above all,—To thine own self be true;
And it must follow, as the night the day,
Thou canst not then be false to any man.

Shakespeare

The "Civil Rights" Scare Is Nearly Over.

The game of (Colored) fox and (White) goose. Thomas Nast, Harper's Weekly, May 22, 1875. Courtesy of The Research Libraries, The New York Public Library, Astor, Lenox and Tilden Foundations.

"Is *This* a Republican Form of Government? Is *This* Protecting Life, Liberty, or Property? Is *This* the Equal Protection of the Laws?"

Mr. Lamar (Democrat, Mississippi). "In the words of the inspired poet, 'Thy gentleness has made thee great.'" [Did Mr. Lamar mean the colored race?] *Thomas Nast, Harper's Weekly, September 2, 1876. Courtesy of The Research Libraries, The New York Public Library, Astor, Lenox and Tilden Foundations.*

The South Redeemed

As Nast's cartoons indicate, the crusade for black voting rights and other civil rights ran into stiff opposition and eventually failed. By 1877, white supremacy was firmly re-established throughout the south, and black political voices were almost completely stilled. The south, according to many white southerners, had been "redeemed" by its white leaders. But the white south did not get back everything it wanted. Black men had refused to work as gang laborers, and black families had refused to let women and children work long hours in the field. Grudgingly, while land owners had let blacks work the land in family plots, usually as either tenant farmers or share-croppers. Thus, despite "redemption," the southern landscape would look startlingly different from Reconstruction. Here are maps of the same Georgia plantation in 1860 and in 1880. What, in your judgment, were the important features in the new and the old landscape? Do the changes match up with the kinds of attitudes discussed in Bethel's essay? How many of the 1880 families, would you guess, once lived in the old slave quarters?

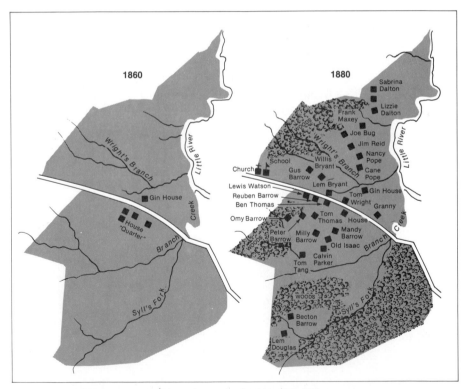

Adapted from Scribner's Monthly, vol. 21, April 1881, 832–833.

CHAPTER 2

The Gilded Age

Nineteenth-century Americans were obsessed with change, progress, development, and growth. And this obsession reached a new peak during the decades after the Civil War. An American who had matured in the 1850s or 1860s could look backward from 1890 or 1900 and remember a lifetime filled with what seemed to be the most astonishing kinds of transformations.

The facts were there to support such memories of change. The population more than doubled between 1870 and 1900. The telegraph, the telephone, the electric light, and the Linotype were only four of the dozens of inventions that made life—and work—remarkably different. In 1850, most workers were artisans, plying their crafts in small shops under employers working beside them on similar tasks. By 1900, larger industrial enterprises were employing thousands of workers; employers seldom had any personal knowledge of their employees; and much of the skill had been removed from the work process. There were new cities, too—six in 1900 with populations of more than 500,000. The United States leapfrogged over England, France, and Germany to become the leading industrial nation of the world. Steel production increased 2000 percent between the Civil War and the end of the century. Many firms for the first time supplied national and urban markets rather than local and rural ones. This meant new opportunities, more intense competition, and, finally, the emergence of the big corporations that have become the hallmark of the American economy. Change was a whirling, accelerating affair that altered the horizons of experience in every decade.

Above the whirl, a kind of official opinion developed, an orthodox opinion that change was "progress." Presidents and senators, newspaper editors and magazine writers, preachers and book publishers—all the molders of what was coming to be thought of as "public opinion"—voiced a belief that industrialization was creating a better life for the republic. Within this view, industrial growth meant opportunity. Competition meant success. All the inventions created leisure and material comfort. The great new factories meant a sort of democracy of well-being for the workers in them. And, in national terms, industrial growth meant the potential triumph in the world of American principles of freedom and equality.

But the awareness of change also generated problems and anxieties. For the wealthy and the sophisticated, there was the possibility that industrialization might lead to a world of materialism, greed, and speculation, a world with only a thin and false veneer of culture and moral values. This fear was a theme of the book that gave a name to the period, Mark Twain and Charles Dudley Warner's *Gilded Age*, published in 1873.

What became known as the "labor question" or the "labor problem" was really a collection of doubts and anxieties. Could the United States absorb the huge pool of immigrants who were attracted to the industrializing cities and towns? Would the new industrial work force tolerate long hours, factory conditions, and gross disparities of wealth, or would they form labor unions and even take to the streets to protest and redress their grievances? Would ordinary Americans continue to believe in the possibilities of success and self-improvement, and so resign themselves to a place in the new order of things? Or would radical ideologies—socialism, communism, anarchism—thrive in the new industrial environment and bring American capitalism crashing down?

INTERPRETIVE ESSAY

Jeremy Brecher

The 1877 Railroad Strike

In the midst of the great economic changes of the latter half of the nineteenth century, most Americans believed that their country could somehow avoid the deep social conflicts and sharp ideological struggles associated with industrialization in Europe. There were, to be sure, disquieting signs. American workers had come together in unions as early as the 1790s, formed workingmen's political parties in the 1820s and 1830s, and, like Philadelphia textile workers in 1844, gone out on strike against their employers. In the decade after the Civil War, national unions, bringing together workers in similar occupations, had grown dramatically in number and influence, led by the iron molders and the railroad "brotherhoods." Yet even as Americans suffered through the depression of the 1870s, it was easy to believe that race and sectionalism, not class and economics, were the nation's most critical problems.

With the fourth year of the depression came the rude awakening known as the 1877 railroad strike. Although less familiar to most students of American history than the Pullman strike and the Homestead strike of the 1890s, the railroad conflict, recounted here by Jeremy Brecher, was arguably more significant.

While reading Brecher's account, consider the following questions. How did the strike begin, and why did it spread? What did the railroad workers— and others who became involved—seek to express through the strike? Did the strikers represent a serious threat to the social stability of the nation, or even to particular communities? Was the government's response to the strike justified? In general, was the strike as significant an event as Brecher seems to think?

In the centers of many American cities are positioned huge armories, grim nineteenth-century edifices of brick or stone. They are fortresses, complete with massive walls and loopholes for guns. You may have wondered why they are there, but it has probably never occurred to you that they were built to protect America, not against invasion from abroad, but against popular revolt at home. Their erection was a monument to the Great Upheaval of 1877.

July 1877 does not appear in many history books as a memorable date, yet it marks the first great American mass strike, a movement that was viewed at the time as a violent rebellion. Strikers stopped and seized the nation's most important industry, the railroads, and crowds defeated or won over first the police, then the state militias, and in some cases even the federal troops. General strikes stopped all activity in a dozen major cities, and strikers took over social authority in communities across the nation.

From Jeremy Brecher, *Strike!*, South End Press, Boston, 1972, pp. 1–22. Reprinted by permission of the publisher.

It all began on Monday, July 16, 1877, in the little railroad town of Martinsburg, West Virginia. On that day, the Baltimore and Ohio Railroad cut wages ten percent, the second cut in eight months. In Martinsburg, men gathered around the railroad yards, talking, waiting through the day. Toward evening the crew of a cattle train, fed up, abandoned the train, and other trainmen refused to replace them.

As a crowd gathered, the strikers uncoupled the engines, ran them into the roundhouse, and announced to B&O officials that no trains would leave Martinsburg till the pay cut was rescinded. The mayor arrived and conferred with railroad officials. He tried to soothe the crowd and was booed; when he ordered the arrest of the strike leaders they just laughed at him, backed up in their resistance by the angry crowd. The mayor's police were helpless against the population of the town. No railroad workers could be found willing to take out a train, so the police withdrew and by midnight the yard was occupied only by a guard of strikers left to enforce the blockade.

That night, B&O officials in Wheeling went to see Governor Matthews, took him to their company telegraph office, and waited while he wired Col. Charles Faulkner, Jr., at Martinsburg, to have his Berkeley Light Guards preserve the peace "if necessary, . . . prevent any interference by rioters with the men at work, and also prevent the obstruction of the trains."

Next morning, when the Martinsburg master of transportation ordered the cattle train out again, the strikers' guard swooped down on it and ordered the engineer to stop or be killed. He stopped. By now, hundreds of strikers and townspeople had gathered, and the next train out hardly moved before it was boarded, uncoupled, and run into the roundhouse.

About 9:00 A.M., the Berkeley Light Guards arrived to the sound of a fife and drum; the crowd cheered them. Most of the militiamen were themselves railroaders. Now the cattle train came out once more, this time covered with militiamen, their rifles loaded with ball cartridges. As the train pulled through the yelling crowd, a striker named William Vandergriff turned a switch to derail the train and guarded it with a pistol. A soldier jumped off the train to reset the switch; Vandergriff shot him and in turn was fatally shot himself.

At this, the attempt to break the blockade at Martinsburg was abandoned. The strikebreaking engineer and fireman climbed down from the engine and departed. Col. Faulkner called in vain for volunteers to run the train, announced that the governor's orders had been fulfilled, dismissed his men, and telegraphed the governor that he was helpless to control the situation.

With this confrontation began the Great Upheaval of 1877, a spontaneous, nationwide, virtually general strike. The pattern of Martinsburg—a railroad strike in response to a pay cut, an attempt by the companies to run trains with the support of military forces, the defeat or dissolution of those forces by amassed crowds representing general popular support—became that same week the pattern for the nation.

With news of success at Martinsburg, the strike spread to all divisions of the B&O, with engineers, brakemen, and conductors joining with the firemen who gave the initial impetus. Freight traffic was stopped all along the line, while the men continued to run passenger and mail cars without interference. Seventy engines and six hundred freight cars were soon piled up in the Martinsburg yards.

The governor, resolved to break the strike, promised to send a company "in which there are no men unwilling to suppress the riots and execute the law." He sent his only available military force, sixty Light Guards from Wheeling. But the Guards were hardly reliable, for sentiment in Wheeling supported the strike strongly. They marched out of town surrounded by an excited crowd, who, a reporter noted, "all expressed sympathy with the strikers"; box and can makers in Wheeling were already on strike and soon people would be discussing a general strike of all labor. When the Guards' train arrived in Martinsburg, it was met by a large, orderly crowd. The militia's commander conferred with railroad and town officials, but dared not use the troops, lest they "further exasperate the strikers." Instead, he marched them away to the courthouse.

At this point the strike was virtually won. But hardly had the strike broken out when the president of B&O began pressing for the use of the U.S. Army against the strikers in West Virginia. "The loss of an hour would most seriously affect us and imperil vast interests," he wrote. With federal troops, "the rioters could be dispersed and there would be no difficulty in the movement of trains." The road's vice-president wired his Washington agent, saying that the governor might soon call for federal troops, and telling him "to see the Secretary of War and inform him of the serious situation of affairs, that he may be ready to send the necessary force to the scene of action at once." Although a newspaperman on the scene of action at Martinsburg reported "perfect order," and other correspondents were unable to find violence to report, the Colonel of the Guards wired the governor:

> The feeling here is most intense, and the rioters are largely cooperated with by civilians. . . . The disaffection has become so general that no employee could now be found to run an engine even under certain protection. I am satisfied that Faulkner's experiment of yesterday was thorough and that any repetition of it today would precipitate a bloody conflict, with the odds largely against our small force.

On the basis of this report, the governor in turn wired the president:

To His Excellency, R. B. Hayes,
President of the U.S.
Washington, D.C.:

Owing to unlawful combinations and domestic violence now existing at Martinsburg and at other points along the line of the Baltimore and Ohio Railroad, it is impossible with any force at my command to execute the laws of the State. I therefore call upon your Excellency for the assistance of the United States military to protect the law abiding people of the State against domestic violence, and to maintain supremacy of the law.

The president of the B&O added his appeal, wiring the president that West Virginia had done all it could "to suppress this insurrection" and warning that "this great national highway [the B&O] can only be restored for public use by the interposition of U.S. forces." In response, President Hayes sent three hundred federal troops to suppress what his secretary of war was already referring to publicly as "an insurrection."

This "insurrection" was spontaneous and unplanned, but it grew out of the social conditions of the time and the recent experience of the workers. The tactics of the railroad strikers had been developed in a series of local strikes, mostly without trade union support, that occurred in 1873 and 1874. In December 1873, for example, engineers and firemen on the Pennsylvania Railroad system struck in Chicago, Pittsburgh, Cincinnati, Louisville, Columbus, Indianapolis, and various smaller towns, in what the *Portsmouth* [Ohio] *Tribune* called "the greatest railroad strike" in the nation's history. Huge crowds gathered in depot yards and supported the strikers against attempts to run the trains. State troops were sent into Dennison, Ohio, and Logansport, Indiana, to break strike strongholds. At Susquehanna Depot, Pennsylvania, three months later, shop and repair workers struck. After electing a "Workingmen's Committee," they seized control of the repair shops; within twenty minutes the entire works was reported "under complete control of the men." The strike was finally broken when 1800 Philadelphia soldiers with thirty pieces of cannon established martial law in this town of 8000.

The strikes were generally unsuccessful; but, as Herbert Gutman wrote, they "revealed the power of the railroad workers to disrupt traffic on many roads." The employers learned that "they had a rather tenuous hold on the loyalties of their men. Something was radically wrong if workers could successfully stop trains for from two or three days to as much as a week, destroy property, and even 'manage' it as if it were their own." And, Gutman continued, "the same essential patterns of behavior that were widespread in 1877 were found in the 1873–1874 strikes. Three and a half years of severe depression ignited a series of local brush fires into a national conflagration."

The more immediate background of the 1877 railroad strike also helps explain why it took the form of virtual insurrection, for this struggle grew out of the failure of other, less violent forms of action.

The wage cut on the B&O was part of a general pattern that had started June 1 on the Pennsylvania Railroad. When the leaders of the Brotherhoods of Engineers, Conductors, and Firemen made no effort to combat the cut, the railroad workers on the Pennsylvania system took action themselves. A week before the cut went into effect, the Newark, New Jersey, division of the Engineers held an angry protest meeting against the cut. The Jersey City lodge met the next day, voted for a strike, and put out feelers to other workers; by the day the cut took effect, engineers' and firemen's locals throughout the Pennsylvania system had chosen delegates to a joint grievance committee, ignoring the leadership of their national union. Nor was the wage cut their only grievance; the committee proposed what amounted to a complete reorganization of work. They opposed the system of assigning trains, in which the first crew into town was the first crew out, leaving them no time to rest or see their families; they wanted regular runs to stabilize pay and working days; they wanted passes home in case of long layovers; they wanted the system of "classification" of workers by length of service and efficiency—used to keep wages down—abolished.

But the grievance committee delegates were easily intimidated and cajoled by Tom Scott, the masterful ruler of the Pennsylvania Railroad, who talked them into accepting the cut without consulting those who elected them. A majority of brakemen, many conductors, and some engineers wanted to repudiate the committee's action; but, their unity broken, the locals decided not to strike.

Since the railroad brotherhoods had clearly failed, the workers' next step was to create a new, secret organization, the Trainmen's Union. It was started by workers on the Pittsburgh, Fort Wayne, and Chicago. Within three weeks, lodges had sprung up from Baltimore to Chicago, with thousands of members on many different lines. The Trainmen's Union recognized that the privileged engineers "generally patched things up for themselves," so it included conductors, firemen, brakemen, switchmen, and others besides engineers. The union also realized that the various railroad managements were cooperating against the workers, one railroad after another imitating the Pennsylvania with a ten percent wage cut. The union's strategy was to organize at least three-quarters of the trainmen on each trunk line, then strike against the cuts and other grievances. When a strike came, firemen would not take engineers' jobs, and men on nonstriking roads would not handle struck equipment.

But the union was full of spies. On one railroad the firing of members began only four days after the union was formed, and others followed suit: "Determined to stamp it out," as one railroad official put it, the company has issued orders to discharge all men belonging to "the Brotherhood or Union." Nonetheless, on June 24, forty men fanned out over the railroads to call a general railroad strike for the following week. The railroads learned about the strike through their spies, fired the strike committee in a body, and thus panicked part of the leadership into spreading false word that the strike was off. Local lodges, unprepared to act on their own, flooded the union headquarters with telegrams asking what to do. Union officials were denied use of railroad telegraphs to reply, the companies ran their trains, and the strike failed utterly.

Thus, the Martinsburg strike broke out because the B&O workers had discovered that they had no alternative but to act completely on their own. Not only were their wages being cut, but, as one newspaper reported, the men felt they were "treated just as the rolling stock or locomotives"—squeezed for every drop of profit. Reduced crews were forced to handle extra cars, with lowered pay classifications, and extra pay for overtime eliminated.

A similar spontaneous strike developed that same day in Baltimore in response to the B&O wage cut, but the railroad had simply put strikebreakers on the trains and used local police to disperse the crowds of strikers. What made Martinsburg different? The key to the strike, according to historian Robert Bruce, was that "a conventional strike would last only until strikebreakers could be summoned." To succeed, the strikers had to "beat off strikebreakers by force, seize trains, yards, roundhouses . . ." This was possible in Martinsburg because the people of the town so passionately supported the railroad workers that they amassed and resisted the state militia. It was now the support of others elsewhere that allowed the strikers to resist the federal troops as well.

On Thursday, three hundred federal troops arrived in Martinsburg to quell the "insurrection" and bivouacked in the roundhouse. With militiamen and U.S. soldiers guarding the yards, the company was able to get a few trains loaded with regulars through the town. When one hundred armed strikers tried to stop a train, the sheriff and the militia marched to the scene and arrested the leader. No one in Martinsburg would take out another train, but with the military in control, strikebreakers from Baltimore were able to run freights through unimpeded. The strike seemed broken.

But the population of the surrounding area also now rallied behind the railroad workers. Hundreds of unemployed and striking boatmen on the Chesapeake and Ohio Canal lay in ambush at Sir John's Run, where they stoned the freight that had broken the Martinsburg blockade, forced it to stop, and then hid when the U.S. regulars attacked. The movement soon spread into Maryland, where at Cumberland a crowd of boatmen, railroaders, and others swarmed around the train and uncoupled the cars. When the train finally got away, a mob at Keyser, West Virginia, ran it onto a side track and took the crew off by force—while the U.S. troops stood helplessly by. Just before midnight, the miners of the area met at Piedmont, four miles from Keyser, and resolved to go to Keyser in the morning and help stop trains. Coal miners and others—"a motley crowd, white and black"—halted a train guarded by fifty U.S. regulars after it pulled out of Martinsburg. At Piedmont a handbill was printed warning the B&O that 15,000 miners, the united citizenry of local communities, and "the working classes of every state in the Union" would support the strikers. "Therefore let the clashing of arms be heard . . . in view of the rights and in the defense of our families we shall conquer, or we shall die."

The result was that most of the trains sent west from Martinsburg never even reached Keyser. All but one, which was under heavy military escort, were stopped by a crowd of unemployed rolling-mill men, migrant workers, boatmen, and young boys at Cumberland, Maryland, and even on the one that went through a trainman was wounded by a gunshot. When two leaders of the crowd were arrested, a great throng went to the mayor's house, demanded the release of the prisoners, and carried them off on their shoulders.

Faced with the spread of the strike through Maryland, the president of the B&O now persuaded Governor Carrol of Maryland to call up the National Guard in Baltimore and send it to Cumberland. They did not reckon, however, on the reaction of Baltimore to the strike. "The working people everywhere are with us," said a leader of the railroad strikers in Baltimore. "They know what it is to bring up a family on ninety cents a day, to live on beans and corn meal week in and week out, to run in debt at the stores until you cannot get trusted any longer, to see the wife breaking down under privation and distress, and the children growing up sharp and fierce like wolves day after day because they don't get enough to eat."

The bells rang in Baltimore for the militia to assemble just as the factories were letting out for the evening, and a vast crowd assembled as well. At first they cheered the troops, but severely stoned them as they started to march. The crowd was described as "a rough element eager for disturbance; a proportion of mechanics [workers] either out of work or upon inadequate pay, whose sullen hearts rankled; and muttering and murmuring gangs of boys, almost outlaws, and ripe for any sort of disturbance." As the 250 men of the first regiment marched out, 25 of them were injured by the stoning of the crowd, but this was only a love-tap. The second regiment was unable even to leave its own armory for a time. Then, when the order was given to march anyway, the crowd stoned them so severely that the troops panicked and opened fire. In the bloody march that followed, the militia killed ten and seriously wounded more than twenty of the crowd, but the crowd continued to resist, and one by one the troops dropped out and went home, and changed into civilian clothing. By the time they reached the station, only 59 of the original 120 men remained in line. Even after they reached the depot, the remaining troops were unable to leave for Cumberland, for a crowd of about two hundred drove away the engineer and firemen of the waiting troop train and beat back a squad of policemen who tried to restore control. The militia charged the growing crowd, but were driven back by brickbats and pistol fire. It was at that stage that Governor Carrol, himself bottled up in the depot by the crowd of 15,000, in desperation wired President Hayes to send the U.S. Army.

Like the railroad workers, others joined the "insurrection" out of frustration with other means of struggle. Over the previous years they had experimented with one means of resistance after another, each more radical than the last. First to prove their failure had been the trade unions. In 1870, there were about thirty-three national unions enrolling perhaps five percent of non-farm workers; by 1877, only about nine were left. Total membership plummeted from 300,000 in 1870 to 50,000 in 1876. Under depression conditions, they were simply unable to withstand the organized attack levied by lockouts and blacklisting. Unemployment demonstrations in New York had been ruthlessly broken up by police. Then the first major industrial union in the United States, the Workingmen's Benevolent Association of the anthracite miners, led a strike that was finally broken by the companies, one of which claimed the conflict had cost it $4 million. Next the Molly Maguires—a secret terrorist organization the Irish miners developed to fight the coal operators—were infiltrated and destroyed by agents from the Pinkerton Detective Agency, which specialized in providing spies, agents provocateurs, and private armed forces for employers combatting labor organizations. Thus, by the summer of 1877 it had become clear that no single group of workers—whether through peaceful demonstration, tightly knit trade unions, armed terrorism, or surprise strikes—could stand against the power of the companies, their armed guards, the Pinkertons, and the armed forces of the government.

Indeed, the Great Upheaval had been preceded by a seeming quiescence on the part of workers. The general manager of one railroad wrote, June 21: "The experiment of reducing the salaries has been successfully carried out by all the Roads that have tried it of late, and I have no fear of any trouble with our employees if it is done with a proper show of firmness on our part and they see that they must accept it cheerfully or leave." The very day the strike was breaking out at Martinsburg, Governor Hartranft of Pennsylvania was agreeing with his adjutant general that the state was enjoying such a calm as it had not known for several years. In less than a week, it would be the center of the insurrection.

Three days after Governor Hartranft's assessment, the Pennsylvania Railroad ordered that all freights eastward from Pittsburgh be run as "double-headers"—with two engines and twice as many cars. This meant in effect a speed-up—more work and increased danger of accidents and layoffs. The trains were likely to break and the sections collide, sending fifty or sixty men out of work. Then Pennsylvania trainmen were sitting in the Pittsburgh roundhouse listening to a fireman read them news of the strike elsewhere when the order came to take out a "double-header." At the last minute a flagman named Augustus Harris, acting on his own initiative, refused to obey the order. The conductor appealed to the rest of the crew, but they too refused to move the train. When the company sent for replacements, twenty-five brakemen and conductors refused to take out the train and were fined on the spot. When the dispatcher finally found three yard brakemen to take out the train, a crowd of twenty angry strikers refused to let the train go through. One of them threw a link at a scab, whereupon the volunteer yardmen gave up and went away. Said flagman Andrew Hice, "It's a question of bread or blood, and we're going to resist."

Freight crews joined the strike as their trains came in and were stopped, and a crowd of mill workers, tramps, and boys began to gather at the crossings, preventing freight trains from running while letting passenger trains go through. The company asked the mayor for police, but since the city was nearly bankrupt the force had been cut in half, and only eight men were available. Further, the mayor was elected by the strong working-class vote of the city, and shared the city's upper crust's hatred for the Pennsylvania Railroad and its rate discrimination against Pittsburgh. At most the railroad got seventeen police, whom it had to pay itself.

As elsewhere, the Trainmen's Union had nothing to do with the start of the strike. Its top leader, Robert Ammon, had left Pittsburgh to take a job elsewhere, and the president of the Pittsburgh Division didn't even know that trouble was at hand; he slept late that morning, didn't hear about the strike until nearly noon—his first comment was "Impossible!"—and he busied himself primarily at trying to persuade his colleagues to go home and keep out of trouble.

The Trainmen's Union did, however, provide a nucleus for a meeting of the strikers and representatives of such groups as the rolling-mill workers. "We're with you," said one rolling-mill man, pledging the railroaders support from the rest of Pittsburgh labor. "We're in the same boat. I heard a reduction of ten percent hinted at in our mill this morning. I won't call employers despots, I won't call them tyrants, but the term capitalists is sort of synonymous and will do as well." The meeting called on "all workingmen to make common cause with their brethren on the railroad."

In Pittsburgh, railroad officials picked up the ailing sheriff, waited while he gave the crowd a *pro forma* order to disperse, and then persuaded him to appeal for state troops. That night state officials ordered the militia called up in Pittsburgh but only part of the troops called arrived. Some were held up by the strikers, others simply failed to show up. Two-thirds of one regiment made it; in another regiment not one man appeared. Nor were the troops reliable. As one officer reported to his superior, "You can place little dependence on the troops of your division; some have thrown down their arms, and others have left, and I fear the situation very much." Another officer explained why the troops were unreliable. "Meeting an enemy on the field of battle, you go there to kill. The more you kill, and the quicker you do it, the better. But here you had men with fathers and brothers and relatives mingled in the crowd of rioters. The sympathy of the people, the sympathy of the troops, my own sympathy, was with the strikers proper. We all felt that those men were not receiving enough wages." Indeed, by Saturday morning the militiamen had stacked their arms and were chatting with the crowd, eating hardtack with them, and walking up and down the streets with them, behaving, as a regular army lieutenant put it, "as though they were going to have a party." "You may be called upon to clear the tracks down there," said a lawyer to a soldier. "They may call on me," the soldier replied, "and they may call pretty damn loud before they will clear the tracks."

The *Pittsburgh Leader* came out with an editorial warning of "The Talk of the Desperate" and purporting to quote a "representative workingman": " 'This may be the beginning of a great civil war in this country, between labor and capital. It only needs that the strikers . . . should boldly attack and rout the troops sent to quell them—and they could easily do it if they tried. . . . The workingmen everywhere would all join and help. . . . The laboring people, who mostly constitute the militia, will not take up arms to put down their brethren. Will capital, then, rely on the United States Army? Pshaw! These ten or fifteen thousand available men would be swept from our path like leaves in the whirlwind. The workingmen of this country can capture and hold it if they will only stick together. . . . Even if so-called law and order should beat them down in blood . . . we would, at least, have our revenge on the men who have coined our sweat and muscles into millions for themselves, while they think dip is good enough butter for us.' "

All day Friday, the crowds controlled the switches and the officer commanding the Pittsburgh militia refused to clear the crossing with artillery because of the slaughter that would result. People swarmed aboard passenger trains and rode through the city free of charge. The sheriff warned the women and children to leave lest they be hurt when the army came, but the women replied that they were there to urge the men on. "Why are you acting this way, and why is this crowd here?" the sheriff asked one young man who had come to Pittsburgh from Eastern Pennsylvania for the strike. "The Pennsylvania has two ends," he replied, "one in Philadelphia and one in Pittsburgh. In Philadelphia they have a strong police force, and they're with the railroad. But in Pittsburgh they have a weak force, and it's a mining and manufacturing district, and we can get all the help we want from the laboring elements, and we've determined to make the strike here." "Are you a railroader?" the sheriff asked. "No, I'm a laboring man," came the reply.

Railroad and National Guard officials, realizing that the local Pittsburgh militia units were completely unreliable, sent for six hundred fresh troops from its commercial rival, Philadelphia. A Pittsburgh steel manufacturer came to warn railroad officials not to send the troops out until workingmen were back in their factories. "I think I know the temper of our men pretty well, and you would be wise not to do anything until Monday. . . . If there's going to be firing, you ought to have at least ten thousand men, and I doubt if even that many could quell the mob that would be brought down on us." These words were prophetic. But, remembering the 2000 freight cars and locomotives lying idle in the yards, and the still-effective blockade, the railroad official replied, "We must have our property." He looked at his watch and said, "We have now lost an hour and a half's time." He had confidently predicted that "the Philadelphia regiment won't fire over the heads of the mob." Now the massacre he counted on—and the city's retaliation—was at hand.

As the imported troops marched toward the 28th Street railroad crossing, a crowd of 6000 gathered, mostly spectators. The troops began clearing the tracks with fixed bayonets and the crowd replied with a furious barrage of stones, bricks, coal, and possibly revolver fire. Without orders, the Philadelphia militia began firing as fast as they could, killing twenty people in five minutes as the crowd scattered. Meanwhile, the local Pittsburgh militia stood on the hillside at carry arms and broke for cover when they saw the Philadelphians' Gatling gun come forward. Soon they went home or joined the mob.

With the crossing cleared, the railroad fired up a dozen double-headers, but even trainmen who had previously declined to join the strike now refused to run them, and the strike remained unbroken. Their efforts in vain, the Philadelphia militia retired to the roundhouse.

Meanwhile, the entire city mobilized in a fury against the troops who had conducted the massacre and against the Pennsylvania Railroad. Workers rushed home from their factories for pistols, muskets and butcher knives. A delegation of six hundred workingmen from nearby Temperanceville marched in with a full band and colors. In some cases the crowd organized itself into crude armed military units, marching together with drums. Civil authority collapsed in the face of the crowd; the mayor refused to send police or even to try to quiet the crowd himself.

The crowd peppered the troops in the roundhouse with pistol and musket fire, but finally decided, as one member put it, "We'll have them out if we have to roast them out." Oil, coke, and whiskey cars were set alight and pushed downhill toward the roundhouse. A few men began systematically to burn the yards, despite rifle fire from the soldiers, while the crowd held off fire trucks at gunpoint. Sunday morning, the roundhouse caught fire and the Philadelphia militia were forced to evacuate. As they marched along the street they were peppered with fire by the crowd and, according to the troops' own testimony, by Pittsburgh policemen as well. Most of the troops were marched out of town and found refuge a dozen miles away. The few left to guard ammunition found civilian clothes, sneaked away, and hid until the crisis was over. By Saturday night, the last remaining regiment of Pittsburgh militia was disbanded. The crowd had completely routed the army.

Sunday morning, hundreds of people broke into the freight cars in the yards and distributed the goods to the crowds below—on occasion with assistance from police. Burning of cars continued. (According to Carroll D. Wright, first U.S. commissioner of labor, "A great many old freight cars which must soon have been replaced by new, were pushed into the fire by agents of the railroad company," to be added to the claims against the country.) The crowd prevented firemen from saving a grain elevator, though it was not owned by the railroad, saying "it's a monopoly, and we're tired of it," but workers pitched in to prevent the spread of the fire to nearby tenements. By Monday, 104 locomotives, more than 2000 cars, and all of the railroad buildings had been destroyed.

Across the river from Pittsburgh, in the railroad town of Allegheny, a remarkable transfer of authority took place. Using the pretext that the governor was out of the state, the strikers maintained that the state militia was without legal authority, and therefore proposed to treat them as no more than a mob. The strikers armed themselves—by breaking into the local armory, according to the mayor—dug rifle pits and trenches outside the Allegheny depot, set up patrols, and warned civilians away from the probable line of fire. The strikers took possession of the telegraph and sent messages up and down the road. They took over management of the railroad, running passenger trains smoothly, moving the freight cars out of the yards, and posting regular armed guards over them. Economic management and political power had in effect been taken over by the strikers. Of course, this kind of transfer of power was not universally understood or approved of, even by those who supported the strike. For example, a meeting of rolling-mill men in Columbus, Ohio, endorsed the railroad strikers, urged labor to combine politically and legislate justice, but rejected "mobbism" as apt to destroy "the best form of republican government."

The strike spread almost as fast as word of it, and with it the conflict with the military. In Columbia, Meadville, and Chenago, Pennsylvania, strikers seized the railroads, occupied the roundhouses, and stopped troop trains. In Buffalo, New York, the militia was stoned on Sunday but scattered the crowd by threatening to shoot. Next morning a crowd armed with knives and cudgels stormed into the railroad shops, brushed aside militia guards, and forced shopmen to quit work. They seized the Erie roundhouse and barricaded it. When a militia company marched out to recapture the property, a thousand people blocked and drove them back. By Monday evening, all the major U.S. roads had given up trying to move anything but local passenger trains out of Buffalo. Court testimony later gave a good picture of how the strike spread to Reading, Pennsylvania. At a meeting of workers on the Reading Railroad, the chairman suggested that it would not be a bad idea to do what had been done on the B&O. "While it is hot we can keep the ball rolling," someone chimed in. After some discussion, men volunteered to head off incoming trains. Next day a crowd of 2000 assembled while twenty-five or fifty men, their faces blackened with coal dust, tore up track, fired trains, and burned a railroad bridge. That evening seven companies of the National Guard arrived. As they marched through a tenement district to clear the tracks, the people of the neighborhood severely stoned them, wounding twenty with missiles and pistol shots. The soldiers opened fire without orders and killed eleven. As in Pittsburgh, the population grew furious over the killings. They plundered freight cars, tore up tracks, and broke into an arsenal, taking sixty rifles. Next day the companies that had conducted the massacre marched down the track together with newly arrived troops; the crowd stoned the former and fraternized with the latter. When the hated Grays turned menacingly toward the crowd, the new troops announced that they would not fire on the people, turned some of their ammunition over to the crowd, and told the Grays, "If you fire at the mob, we'll fire at you."

Such fraternization between troops and the crowd was common. When the governor sent 170 troops to Newark, Ohio, they were so unpopular that the county commissioners refused to provide their rations. Thereupon the strikers themselves volunteered to feed them. By the end of the day strikers and soldiers were fraternizing in high good humor. Similarly, when the governor of New York sent six hundred troops to the railroad center of Hornellsville, in response to the strike on the Erie, the troops and strikers fraternized, making commanders doubtful of their power to act. When the entire Pennsylvania National Guard was called up in response to the Pittsburgh uprising, a company in Lebanon, Pennsylvania, mutinied and marched through town amidst great excitement. In Altoona, a crowd captured a westbound train carrying five hundred militiamen. The troops gave up their arms with the best of will and fraternized with the crowd. The crowd refused to let them proceed, but was glad to let them go home—which one full company and parts of the others proceeded to do. A Philadelphia militia unit straggling home decided to march to Harrisburg and surrender. They entered jovially, shook hands all around, and gave up their guns to the crowd.

Persuasion worked likewise against would-be strikebreakers. When a volunteer started to take a freight train out of Newark, Ohio, a striking fireman held up his hand, three fingers of which had been cut off by a railroad accident. "This is the man whose place you are taking," shouted another striker. "This is the man who works with a hand and a half to earn a dollar and a half a day, three days in the week, for his wife and children. Are you going to take the bread out of his mouth and theirs?" The strikebreaker jumped down amidst cheers.

By now, the movement was no longer simply a railroad strike. With the battles between soldiers and crowds drawn from all parts of the working population, it was increasingly perceived as a struggle between workers as a whole and employers as a whole. This was now reflected in the rapid development of general strikes. After the burning of the railroad yards in Pittsburgh, a general strike movement swept through the area. At nearby McKeesport, workers of the National Tube Works gathered early Monday morning and marched all over town to martial music, calling fellow workers from their houses. From the tube workers the strike spread first to a rolling mill, then a car works, then a planing mill. In mid-morning, 1000 McKeesport strikers marched with a brass band to Andrew Carnegie's great steel works, calling out planing-mill and tin-mill workers as they went. By mid-afternoon the Carnegie workers and the Braddocks car workers joined the strike. At Castle Shannon, five hundred miners struck. On the South Side, laborers struck at Jones and Laughlin and at the Evans, Dalzell & Co. pipe works.

In Buffalo, New York, crowds roamed the city trying to bring about a general strike. They effectively stopped operations at planing mills, tanneries, car works, a bolt and nut factory, hog yards, coal yards, and canal works. In Harrisburg, Pennsylvania, factories and shops throughout the city were closed by strikes and crowd action. In Zanesville, Ohio, three hundred unemployed men halted construction on a hotel, then moved through town shutting down nearly every factory and foundry and sending horse-cars to the barns. Next morning a meeting of workingmen drew up a schedule of acceptable wages. In Columbus, a crowd growing from 300 to 2000 went through town spreading a general strike, successfully calling out workers at a rolling mill, pipe works, fire clay works, pot works, and planing mill. "Shut up or burn up" was the mob's slogan. An offshoot of a rally to support the railroad workers in Toledo, Ohio, resolved to call a general strike for a minimum wage of $1.50 a day. Next morning a large crowd of laborers, grain trimmers, stevedores, and others assembled and created a committee of safety composed of one member from every trade represented in the movement. Three hundred men formed a procession four abreast while a committee called on the management of each factory; workers of those not meeting the demands joined in the strike.

In Chicago, the movement began with a series of mass rallies called by the Workingman's Party, the main radical party of the day, and a strike by forty switchmen on the Michigan Central Railroad. The switchmen roamed through the railroad property with a crowd of five hundred others, including strikers from the east who had ridden in to spread the strike, calling out other workers and closing down those railroads that were still running. Next the crowd called out the workers at the stockyards and several packinghouses. Smaller crowds spread out to broaden the strike; one group, for example, called out five hundred planing-mill workers, and with them marched down Canal Street and Blue Island Avenue closing down factories. Crews on several lake vessels struck. With transportation dead, the North Chicago rolling mill and many other industries closed for lack of coke and other supplies. Next day the strike spread still further: streetcars, wagons and buggies were stopped; tanneries, stoneworks, clothing factories, lumber yards, brickyards, furniture factories, and a large distillery were closed in response to roving crowds. One day more and the crowds forced officials at the stockyards and gasworks to sign promises to raise wages to $2.00 a day, while more dock and lumber yard workers struck. In the midst of this, the Workingman's Party proclaimed: "Fellow Workers . . . Under any circumstances keep quiet until we have given the present crisis a due consideration."

The general strikes spread even into the south, often starting with black workers and spreading to whites. Texas and Pacific Railroad workers at Marshall, Texas, struck against the pay cut. In response, black longshoremen in nearby Galveston struck for and won pay equal to that of their white fellow workers. Fifty black workers marched down the Strand in Galveston, persuading construction men, track layers, and others to strike for $2.00 a day. The next day committees circulated supporting the strike. White workers joined in. The movement was victorious, and $2.00 a day became the going wage for Galveston. In Louisville, Kentucky, black workers made the round of sewers under construction, urging a strike for $1.50 a day. At noon, sewer workers had quit everywhere in town. On Tuesday night a march of five hundred stoned the depot of the Louisville and Nashville Railroad, which was refusing a wage increase for laborers. By Wednesday, most of Louisville's factories were shut down by roving crowds, and Thursday brought further strikes by coopers, textile and plow factory workers, brickmakers, and cabinetworkers.

The day the railroad strike reached East St. Louis, the St. Louis Workingman's Party marched five hundred strong across the river to join a meeting of 1000 railroad workers and residents. Said one of the speakers, "All you have to do, gentlemen, for you have the numbers, is to unite on one idea—that the workingmen shall rule the country. What man makes, belongs to him, and the workingmen made this country." The St. Louis General Strike, the peak of the Great Upheaval, for a time nearly realized that goal.

The railroad workers at that meeting voted for a strike, set up a committee of one man from each railroad, and occupied the Relay Depot as their headquarters. The committee promptly posted General Order No. 1, forbidding freight trains from leaving any yard.

That night, across the river in St. Louis, the Workingman's Party called a mass meeting, with crowds so large that three separate speakers' stands were set up simultaneously. "The workingmen," said one speaker, "intend now to assert their rights, even if the result is shedding of blood. . . . They are ready to take up arms at any moment."

Next morning, workers from different shops and plants began to appear at the party headquarters, requesting that committees be sent around to "notify them to stop work and join the other workingmen, that they might have a reason for doing so." The party began to send such committees around, with unexpected results. The coopers struck, marching from shop to shop with a fife and drum shouting, "Come out, come out! No barrels less than nine cents." Newsboys, gasworkers, boatmen, and engineers struck as well. Railroadmen arrived from East St. Louis on engines and flatcars they had commandeered, moving through the yards enforcing General Order No. 1 and closing a wire works.

That day, an "Executive Committee" formed, based at the Workingman's Party headquarters, to coordinate the strike. As one historian wrote, "Nobody ever knew who that executive committee really was; it seems to have been a rather loose body composed of whomsoever chanced to come in and take part in its deliberations."

In the evening, 1500 men, mostly molders and mechanics, armed themselves with lathes and clubs and marched to the evening's rally. To a crowd of 10,000 the first speaker, a cooper, began, "There was a time in the history of France when the poor found themselves oppressed to such an extent that forbearance ceased to be a virtue, and hundreds of heads tumbled into the basket. That time may have arrived with us." Another speaker called upon the workingmen to organize into companies of ten, twenty, and a hundred, to establish patrols to protect property, and to "organize force to meet force." Someone suggested that "the colored men should have a chance." A black steamboatman spoke for the roustabouts and levee workers. He asked the crowd would they stand behind the levee strikers, regardless of color? "We will!" the crowd shouted back.

The general strike got under way in earnest the next morning. The employ-ees of a beef cannery struck and paraded. The coopers met and discussed their objectives. A force of strikers marched to the levee, where a crowd of steam-boatmen and roustabouts "of all colors" forced the captains of boat after boat to sign written promises of fifty percent higher pay. Finally everyone assembled for the day's great march. Six hundred factory workers marched up behind a brass band; a company of railroad strikers came with coupling pins, brake rods, red signal flags, and other "irons and implements emblematic of their calling." Strikers' committees went out ahead to call out those still working, and as the march came by, a loaf of bread on a flag-staff for its emblem, workers in foundries, bagging companies, flour mills, bakeries, chemical, zinc, and white lead works poured out of their shops and into the crowd. In Carondolet, far on the south side of the city, a similar march developed autonomously, as a crowd of iron workers closed down two zinc works, the Bessemer Steel Works, and other plants. In East St. Louis, there was a parade of women in support of the strike. By sundown, nearly all the manufacturing establishments in the city had been closed. "Business is fairly paralyzed here," said the *Daily Market Reporter.*

But economic activities did not cease completely; some continued under control or by permission of the strikers. The British consul in St. Louis noted how the railroad strikers had "taken the road into their own hands, running the trains and collecting fares"; "it is to be deplored that a large portion of the general public appear to regard such conduct as a legitimate mode of warfare." It was now the railroad managements that wanted to stop all traffic. One official stated frankly that by stopping all passenger trains, the companies would cut the strikers off from mail facilities and prevent them from sending committees from one point to another along the lines. Railroad officials, according to the *St. Louis Times,* saw advantage in stopping passenger trains and thus "incommod-ing the public so as to produce a revolution in the sentiment which now seems to be in favor of the strikers." From the strikers' point of view, running non-freights allowed them to coordinate the strike and show their social responsi-bility.

The strikers had apparently decided to allow the manufacture of bread, for they permitted a flour mill to remain open. When the owner of the Belcher Sugar Refinery applied to the Executive Committee for permission to operate his plant for forty-eight hours, lest a large quantity of sugar spoil, the Executive Committee persuaded the refinery workers to go back to work and sent a guard of two hundred men to protect the refinery. Concludes one historian of the strike, "the Belcher episode revealed . . . the spectacle of the owner of one of the city's largest industrial enterprises recognizing the *de facto* authority of the Ex-ecutive Committee."

But the strikers here and elsewhere failed to hold what they had conquered. Having shattered the authority of the status quo for a few short days, they faltered and fell back, unsure of what to do. Meanwhile, the forces of law and order—no longer cowering in the face of overwhelming mass force—began to organize. Chicago was typical: President Hayes authorized the use of federal regulars; citizens' patrols were organized ward by ward, using Civil War veterans; 5000 special police were sworn in, freeing the regular police for action; big employers organized their reliable employees into armed companies—many of which were sworn in as special police. At first the crowd successfully outmaneuvered the police in the street fighting that ensued, but after killing at least eighteen people the police finally gained control of the crowd and thus broke the back of the movement.

Behind them stood the federal government. "This insurrection," said General Hancock, the commander in charge of all federal troops used in the strike, must be stifled "by all possible means." Not that the federal troops were strong and reliable. The army was largely tied down by the rebellion of Nez Percé Indians, led by Chief Joseph. In the words of Lieutenant Philip Sheridan, "The troubles on the Rio Grande border, the Indian outbreak on the western frontier of New Mexico, and the Indian war in the Departments of the Platte and Dakota, have kept the small and inadequate forces in this division in a constant state of activity, almost without rest, night and day." Most of the enlisted men had not been paid for months—for the Congress had refused to pass the Army Appropriations Bill so as to force the withdrawal of Reconstruction troops from the south. Finally, the army included many workers driven into military service by unemployment. As one union iron molder in the army wrote, "It does not follow that a change of dress involves a change of principle." No mutinies occurred, however, as the 3000 available federal troops were rushed under direction of the War Department from city to city, wherever the movement seemed to grow out of control. "The strikers," President Hayes noted emphatically in his diary, "have been put down by *force*." More than one hundred of them were killed in the process.

The Great Upheaval was an expression of the new economic and social system in America, just as surely as the cities, railroads, and factories from which it had sprung. The enormous expansion of industry after the Civil War had transformed millions of people who had grown up as farmers and self-employed artisans and entrepreneurs into employees, growing thousands of whom were concentrated within each of the new corporate empires. They were no longer part of village and town communities with their extended families and stable, unchallenged values, but concentrated in cities, with all their anonymity and freedom; their work was no longer individual and competitive, but group and cooperative; they no longer directed their own work, but worked under control of a boss; they no longer controlled the property on which they worked or its fruits, and therefore could not find fruitful employment unless someone with property agreed to hire them. The Great Upheaval grew out of their intuitive sense that they needed each other, had each other's support, and together were powerful.

This sense of unity was not embodied in any centralized plan or leadership, but in the feelings and action of each participant. "There was no concert of action at the start," the editor of the *Labor Standard* pointed out. "It spread because the workmen of Pittsburgh felt the same oppression that was felt by the workmen of West Virginia and so with the workmen of Chicago and St. Louis." In Pittsburgh, concludes historian Robert Bruce, "Men like Andrew Hice or Gus Harris or David Davis assumed the lead briefly at one point or another, but only because they happened to be foremost in nerve or vehemence." In Newark, Ohio, "no single individual seemed to command the . . . strikers. They followed the sense of the meeting, as Quakers might say, on such proposals as one or another of them . . . put forward. Yet they proceeded with notable coherence, as though fused by their common adversity."

The Great Upheaval was in the end thoroughly defeated, but the struggle was by no means a total loss. Insofar as it aimed at preventing the continued decline of workers' living standards, it won wage concessions in a number of cases and undoubtedly gave pause to would-be wage-cutters to come, for whom the explosive force of the social dynamite with which they tampered had now been revealed. Insofar as it aimed at a workers' seizure of power, its goals was chimerical, for the workers as yet still formed only a minority in a predominantly farm and middle-class society. But the power of workers to virtually stop society, to counter the forces of repression, and to organize cooperative action on a vast scale was revealed in the most dramatic form.

It was not only upon the workers that the Great Upheaval left its mark. Their opponents began building up their power as well, symbolized by the National Guard Armories whose construction began the following year, to contain upheavals yet to come.

Certain periods, wrote Irving Bernstein, bear a special quality in American labor history. "There occurred at these times strikes and social upheavals of extraordinary importance, drama, and violence which ripped the cloak of civilized decorum from society, leaving exposed naked class conflict." Such periods were analyzed before World War I by Rosa Luxemburg and others under the concept of mass strikes. The mass strike, she wrote, signifies not just a single act but a whole period of class struggle.

> Its use, its effects, its reasons for coming about are in a constant state of flux . . . political and economic strikes, united and partial strikes, defensive strikes and combat strikes, general strikes of individual sections of industry and general strikes of entire cities, peaceful wage strikes and street battles, uprisings with barricades—all run together and run alongside each other, get in each other's way, overlap each other; a perpetually moving and changing sea of phenomena.

The Great Upheaval was the first—but by no means the last—mass strike in American history.

SOURCES

Victorian America

Although the term "Victorian" derives from the reign of Queen Victoria of England (1837–1901), when American historians use the term they are refer-ring to the values, beliefs, and assumptions shared by middle-class and upper-class Americans in the late nineteenth century. A contrasting term, mod-ernism, refers to a different set of values and beliefs that had made inroads within the same social classes by the turn of the century. The materials assem-bled in this section—a selection from a book on etiquette published in 1885 and some illustrations and photographs that depict the home life and leisure activ-ities of Victorian Americans—are designed to suggest and reveal certain as-pects of Victorian thought. From these materials, how would you define or characterize a "Victorian"? For example, what did Victorian Americans think about the home? About the roles of men and women? How did they furnish their homes, and what might these furnishings tell us about the people who lived in and used these rooms? What hopes or anxieties might have motivated late nineteenth-century Americans to pay so much attention to the advice dis-pensed in etiquette books? At bottom, would you describe Victorian Americans as secure and self-confident, or insecure and fearful?

Frontispiece to John H. Young, *Our Deportment,* (1885)

John H. Young

Manners, Conduct, and Dress

INTRODUCTORY

Knowledge of etiquette has been defined to be a knowledge of the rules of society at its best. These rules have been the outgrowth of centuries of civilization, had their foundation in friendship and love of man for his fellow man—the vital principles of Christianity—and are most powerful agents for promoting peace, harmony, and good will among all people who are enjoying the blessings of more advanced civilized government. In all civilized countries the influence of the best society is of great importance to the welfare and prosperity of the nation, but in no country is the good influence of the most refined society more powerfully felt than in our own, "the land of the future, where mankind may plant, essay, and resolve all social problems." These rules make social intercourse more agreeable, and facilitate hospitalities, when all members of society hold them as binding rules and faithfully regard their observance. They are to society what our laws are to the people as a political body, and to disregard them will give rise to constant misunderstandings, engender ill-will, and beget bad morals and bad manners. . . .

Originally a gentleman was defined to be one who, without any title of nobility, wore a coat of arms. And the descendants of many of the early colonists preserve with much pride and care the old armorial bearings which their ancestors brought with them from their homes in the mother country. Although despising titles and ignoring the rights of kings, they still clung to the "grand old name of gentleman." But race is no longer the only requisite for a gentleman, nor will race united with learning and wealth make a man a gentleman, unless there are present the kind and gentle qualities of the heart, which find expression in the principles of the Golden Rule. Nor will race, education, and wealth combined make a woman a true lady if she shows a want of refinement and consideration of the feelings of others.

Good manners are only acquired by education and observation, followed up by habitual practice at home and in society, and good manners reveal to us the lady and the gentleman. He who does not possess them, though he bear the highest title of nobility, cannot expect to be called a gentleman; nor can a woman, without good manners, aspire to be considered a lady by ladies. Manners and morals are indissolubly allied, and no society can be good where they are bad. It is the duty of American women to exercise their influence to form so high a standard of morals and manners that the tendency of society will be continually upward, seeking to make it the best society of any nation. . . .

John H. Young, *Our Deportment: Or the Manners, Conduct, and Dress of the Most Refined Society*, F. B. Dickerson & Co., Detroit, 1885.

In a society where the majority are rude from the thoughtfulness of ignorance, or remiss from the insolence of bad breeding, the iron rule, "Do unto others, as they do unto you," is more often put into practice than the golden one.
The savages know nothing of the virtues of forgiveness, and regard those who
are not revengeful as wanting in spirit; so the ill-bred do not understand unde
served civilities extended to promote the general interests of society, and to
carry out the injunction of the Scriptures to strive after the things that make for
peace.

Society is divided into sets, according to their breeding. One set may be said
to have no breeding at all, another to have a little, another more, and another
enough; and between the first and last of these, there are more shades than in
the rainbow. Good manners are the same in essence everywhere—at courts, in
fashionable society, in literary circles, in domestic life—they never change, but
social observances, customs and points of etiquette, vary with the age and with
the people. . . .

OUR MANNERS

No one quality of the mind and heart is more important as an element conducive to worldly success than civility—that feeling of kindness and love for
our fellow-beings which is expressed in pleasing manners. Yet how many of our
young men, with an affected contempt for the forms and conventionalities of
life, assume to despise those delicate attentions, that exquisite tenderness of
thought and manner, that mark the true gentleman.

Manners As An Element of Success

History repeats, over and over again, examples showing that it is the bearing of
a man toward his fellowmen which, more than any other one quality of his nature, promotes or retards his advancement in life. The success or failure of one's
plans have often turned upon the address and manner of the man. Though there
are a few people who can look beyond the rough husk or shell of a fellow-being
to the finer qualities hidden within, yet the vast majority, not so keen-visaged
nor tolerant, judge a person by his appearance and demeanor, more than by his
substantial character. Experience of every day life teaches us, if we would but
learn, that civility is not only one of the essentials of high success, but that it is
almost a fortune of itself, and that he who has this quality in perfection, though
a blockhead, is almost sure to succeed where, without it, even men of good ability fail.

A good manner is the best letter of recommendation among strangers. Civility, refinement, and gentleness are passports to hearts and homes, while awk-
wardness, coarseness, and gruffness are met with locked doors and closed
hearts. Emerson says: "Give a boy address and accomplishments, and you give
him the mastery of palaces and fortunes wherever he goes; he has not the trouble of earning or owning them; they solicit him to enter and possess." . . .

Manner An Index of Character

A rude person, though well meaning, is avoided by all. Manners, in fact, are minor morals; and a rude person is often assumed to be a bad person. The manner in which a person says or does a thing furnishes a better index of his character than what he does or says, for it is by the incidental expression given to his thoughts and feelings, by his looks, tones, and gestures, rather than by his words and deeds, that we prefer to judge him, for the reason that the former are involuntary. The manner in which a favor is granted or a kindness done often affects us more than the deed itself. The deed may have been prompted by vanity, pride, or some selfish motive or interest; the warmth or coldness with which the person who has done it speaks to you, or grasps your hand, is less likely to deceive. The manner of doing any thing, it has been truly said, is that which stamps its life and character on any action. A favor may be performed so grudgingly as to prevent any feeling of obligation, or it may be refused so courteously as to awaken more kindly feelings than if it had been ungraciously granted. . . .

The True Gentleman

Politeness is benevolence in small things. A true gentleman must regard the rights and feelings of others, even in matters the most trivial. He respects the individuality of others, just as he wishes others to respect his own. In society he is quiet, easy, unobtrusive, putting on no airs, nor hinting by word or manner that he deems himself better, or wiser, or richer than any one about him. He never boasts of his achievements, or fishes for compliments by affecting to underrate what he has done. He is distinguished, above all things, by his deep insight and sympathy, his quick perception of, and prompt attention to, those small and apparently insignificant things that may cause pleasure or pain to others. In giving his opinions he does not dogmatize; he listens patiently and respectfully to other men, and, if compelled to dissent from their opinions, acknowledges his fallibility and asserts his own views in such a manner as to command the respect of all who hear him. Frankness and cordiality mark all his intercourse with his fellows, and, however high his station, the humblest man feels instantly at ease in his presence.

The True Lady

Calvert says: "Ladyhood is an emanation from the heart subtilized by culture"; giving as two requisites for the highest breeding transmitted qualities and the culture of good training. He continues:

> Of the higher type of ladyhood may always be said what Steele said of Lady Elizabeth Hastings, "that unaffected freedom and conscious innocence gave her the attendance of the graces in all her actions." At its highest, ladyhood implies a spirituality made manifest in poetic grace. From the lady there exhales a subtle magnetism. Unconsciously she encircles herself with an atmosphere of unruffled strength, which, to those who come into it, gives confidence and repose.

Within her influence the diffident grow self-possessed, the impudent are checked, the inconsiderate are admonished; even the rude are constrained to be mannerly, and the refined are perfected; all spelled, unawares, by the flexible dignity, the commanding gentleness, the thorough womanliness of her look, speech and demeanor. A sway is this, purely spiritual. Every sway, every legitimate, every enduring sway is spiritual; a regnancy of light over obscurity, of right over brutality. The only real gains ever made are spiritual gains—a further subjection of the gross to the incorporeal, of body to soul, of the animal to the human. The finest and most characteristic acts of a lady involve a spiritual ascension, a growing out of herself. In her being and bearing, patience, generosity, benignity are the graces that give shape to the virtues of truthfulness.

✳ Here is the test of true ladyhood. Whenever the young find themselves in the company of those who do not make them feel at ease, they should know that they are not in the society of true ladies and true gentlemen, but of pretenders; that well-bred men and women can only feel at home in the society of the well-bred.

Victorian Photographs

The following photographs portray the experience of well-to-do Victorian families. "Bedroom in the Finch House" requires that we ask the meaning of possessions for these late nineteenth-century elites and that we try to come up with some reason why the feeling, or tone, of this room is so different from what we would expect to find in its late twentieth-century equivalent.

"Family Gathering Around a Portrait of Its Patriarch" also tells us something about Victorian family life and especially, of course, about patriarchy (a form of community in which the father is the supreme authority in the family). Was the notion of patriarchy still relevant to the society of the Gilded Age?

Bedroom in the Finch House, 1884.
Minnesota Historical Society, St. Paul; photo by T. W. Ingersoll, St. Paul.

Family Gathering Around a Portrait of Its Patriarch, c. 1890.
Photograph by Charles Currier. *Library of Congress.*

CHAPTER 3

Cities and Immigrants

In 1860 there were only sixteen cities in the United States with populations over 50,000, and only three cities of more than 250,000. By 1900 the corresponding figures were 78 and 15. In the half-century after 1850, the population of Chicago grew from less than 30,000 to more than 1 million. For older, eastern cities, growth meant change in function and structure. Boston, in 1850 a concentrated merchant city of some 200,000 persons, dependent on ocean-going commerce, was by 1900 a sprawling industrial city with a population of more than 1 million.

Entirely new cities arose to meet particular demands of time and place. For George Pullman, of sleeping-car fame, big cities were sordid and disorderly places that spawned crime and violence. He planned and built an entirely new community isolated from disruptive influences where (so he believed) his workers would always be happy (he was mistaken). Western cities also expanded rapidly, usually by virtue of some nearby exploitable resource. Wichita was one of several Kansas towns founded on the cattle trade. Seattle was a timber city. Denver had its origins in the 1857 gold rush, but it remained to service the Great Plains much as Chicago did the midwest.

The new urban residents were often either immigrants from abroad or migrants from the nation's small towns and rural areas. In 1910 perhaps one-third of the total urban population were native Americans of rural origin; another one-quarter were foreign-born. Although the non-urban population increased absolutely in each decade before 1950, it diminished relatively. During and after the Civil War, the widespread adoption of a variety of labor-saving devices, including cultivators, reapers, mowers, threshers, and corn planters, allowed fewer and fewer farmers to feed the urban populace. Certain areas, such as rural New England, showed marked reductions in population. "We cannot all live in cities," wrote Horace Greeley in the 1860s, "yet nearly all seem determined to do so."

The migration into the United States from abroad was, simply put, a major folk migration. There were 4.1 million foreign-born in the United States in 1860, 13.5 million foreign-born in 1910. And to these numbers must be added the children of the foreign-born—15.6 million in 1900, 18.9 million (more than one out of every five Americans) by 1910.

Some cities attracted a disproportionate share of the foreign-born. By 1910, New York City and two older Massachusetts cities, Fall River and Lowell, had more than 40 percent foreign-born. Twelve major cities, including Boston, Chicago, Milwaukee, Detroit, and San Francisco, had between 30 and 40 percent foreign-born. Seventeen other cities, including Seattle, Portland, Omaha, and Oakland, had over 20 percent foreign-born. (Most southern cities had less than 10 percent.)

After 1880, another change of importance occurred. The national origin of the nation's foreign-born population shifted from the northern and western European mix characteristic of previous decades to the southern and eastern European, Jewish and Catholic, mix dominant in 1900. In contrast to the earlier immigrants, a larger proportion of the later immigrants concentrated in the ghettos of northeastern industrial cities. On New York City's Lower East Side, more than 30,000 people were squeezed into half a dozen city blocks.

Ethnic clustering was nothing new, but the unfamiliar languages, customs, and religious practices of the Italians, Russians, Poles, and Slavs seemed to many observers to be associated with slums, unemployment, delinquency, and disease. The later immigrants were also held responsible for the growth of "alien" ideologies—anarchism and socialism—in large American cities in the last quarter of the century. And there was enough truth in this charge to give it some credence. "Red" Emma Goldman, one of the nation's most active anarchists, was Russian-born. Her friend Alexander Berkman, who was born in Poland, made an unsuccessful attempt to kill steel magnate Henry Clay Frick during the 1892 Homestead strike. In Chicago, a center of working-class politics, radical political ideas were especially well represented, and radical leaders were more often than not German-born. Germany, after all, had produced Karl Marx, and Russia, the anarchist Mikhail Bakunin. Europe simply had a more well-developed radical tradition than the United States. Many new immigrants had with them some portion of this tradition when they set foot on American shores.

This chapter explores several aspects of late nineteenth-century urban history. How did urban political structures respond to increased population and to the new immigrants? What was the experience of ethnic groups in the new urban environments? How was the physical city—its streets, parks, and buildings—reshaped in response to new problems and pressures? How did rich and poor get along? How did Americans imagine what their cities were or could be?

INTERPRETIVE ESSAY

Roy Rosenzweig

Middle-Class Parks and Working-Class Play: The Struggle Over Recreational Space in Worcester, Massachusetts, 1870–1910

During the 1877 railroad strike (see chapter 2), business leaders and the federal government had confronted the needs and demands of organized labor with force and violence. Although that response would continue, the spectacle of violence in Pittsburgh, Baltimore, and other cities contributed to a reconsideration of the policy. Increasingly, industrialists and social reformers turned to subtler ways of dealing with a matrix of problems associated with labor, immigration, and urban life. Among these new solutions were efforts to utilize public space in order to shape relations between social groups. Some of these efforts, like New York's Central Park (completed in the early 1860s) and the model industrial community of Pullman, Illinois (1884), were famous. In the following essay, Roy Rosenzweig describes and interprets the complex politics of public space and park development in Worcester, Massachusetts.

In reading the essay, pay special attention to the term social control. *What does* social control *mean, and how persuasive is Rosenzweig in his criticism of the concept? Then, beginning with the last paragraph of the essay, try to explain why Worcester's workers were unable to mount an effective challenge to the city's factory owners. Overall, what was the role of ethnicity in the lives of these workers? Finally, think about how your own community deals with similar problems of parks and public space.*

"You may take my word for it," landscape architect and horticulturalist Andrew Jackson Downing wrote of parks in 1848, "they will be better preachers of temperance than temperance societies, better refiners of national manners than dancing schools and better promoters of general good-feeling than any lectures on the philosophy of happiness." This vision of parks as instruments of social uplift and social control has captured the imagination of social reformers for over a century. Although park advocates have never been motivated solely by a desire to control urban, immigrant workers, social control has been a persistent, and sometimes even dominant, impulse behind their movement. Frederick Law Olmsted, the most distinguished and influential landscape architect of the mid- and late nineteenth century, hoped, according to one recent historian, that his

Roy Rosenzweig, "Middle-Class Parks and Working-Class Play: The Struggle over Recreational Space in Worcester, Massachusetts, 1870–1910," *Radical History Review,* vol. 21, fall 1979, pp. 31–46. Reprinted with the permission of Cambridge University Press.

pastoral landscapes would "inspire communal feelings among all urban classes, muting resentments over disparities of wealth and fashion."

These motives as well as the overt class bias of park and playground advocates have sometimes earned them the disdained condescension of historians. "Thus it was," charges the author of a recent history of playground reform, "that a movement desiring to release the city's young from the harsher aspects of urban life became one which seemed to prepare them to accept their fate uncomplainingly." But, while social control was certainly an important motivation for many reformers, this analysis distorts history in two ways. First, it tends to reduce social reformers and park advocates to rationally calculating social engineers, when their motivations were much more complex. Early park reformers, for example, were also sparked by naturalistic visions of society, fears about urban disease, and infatuations with European public gardens as well as by the desire to uplift and quiet the masses. Second, and more importantly, the social control formula suggests that the object of reform designs—the urban worker—was both inert and totally pliable. It ignores the possibility that workers might have taken an active part in conceiving or advocating parks and assumes that workers uncritically accepted the park programs handed down by an omnipotent ruling class. In an effort to explore the ways in which working people actively shaped their nonworking lives, this essay focuses on the struggles over recreational space and behavior in one industrial city—Worcester, Massachusetts—in the late nineteenth century.

Neither a commercial port nor a company town, Worcester, with a diversified industrial base, a rapid growth rate, and a large immigrant population, was broadly representative of the manufacturing cities where most American workers made their homes in the late nineteenth century. Worcester's factories turned out a wide range of products from corsets to carpets, but its most important manufacturing activity was concentrated in the metal industries, a rather heterogeneous category that embraced such products as wire, grinding wheels, lathes, and looms. Along with the capitalization of the city's industries, which multiplied about eight times between 1870 and 1910 (from about eight to sixty-five million dollars), Worcester's population grew rapidly from 41,000 to 146,000. Generally speaking, the owners of the city's factories came from native American or "Yankee" backgrounds, while the workers in those factories were predominantly first- or second-generation immigrants. In 1900, for example, native-stock Americans made up only six percent of the city's manual laborers. Thus, ethnicity and class loyalties, often analytically counterpoised by historians, were inextricably intertwined in a city such as Worcester. In the late 1870s and 1880s most of these immigrants were Irish. Indeed, perhaps half the city was of Irish heritage in 1880. By 1900, however, substantial numbers of Swedes and French Canadians had entered the city's neighborhoods and factories. And, in the next ten years Worcester began developing sizable Jewish, Italian, Polish, and Lithuanian communities.

Despite the numerical predominance of the immigrant working class, the city's Yankee upper class officially controlled Worcester's parks, as they did the factories and most major political offices. In the park system, this elite was represented by Edward Winslow Lincoln, the secretary and chairman of the Parks Commission for most of the late nineteenth century. So complete was his control of the Commission that his death in 1896 precipitated a total administrative reorganization of the Parks Commission and necessitated, for the first time, the hiring of a full-time park superintendent. A member of a leading Worcester family (his grandfather had been Jefferson's attorney general and a Justice of the Supreme Court, and his father was governor for nine years as well as the city's first mayor), Lincoln spent most of his first forty years seeking a suitable career, first in law and then in journalism. Beginning around 1860, however, he discovered his true vocation in horticulture and devoted most of his subsequent thirty-six years to the Worcester County Horticultural Society and the city's Parks Commission. Lincoln's background and sensibilities placed him closer to the city's old-line "gentry" than to its newer manufactures, but the distinction between the two groups was not always sharp. Lincoln's brother, for example, was president of the Boston and Albany Railroad.

In his elite background, as well as in his career instability and his idiosyncratic personality, Lincoln resembled Frederick Law Olmsted. More importantly, Lincoln seems also to have shared the conservative social assumptions of Olmsted and such other Gilded Age genteel reformers as Henry Adams and E. L. Godkin, who insisted on a well-ordered and tranquil society based on hierarchy and professional leadership. Parks, in this view, would, in the same way as tariff or civil service reform, promote social cohesion and order. The quiet contemplation of a park's rural scenery, Olmsted believed, would calm the "rough element of the city" and "divert men from unwholesome, vicious, destructive methods and habits of seeking recreation." But Olmsted's elegant vision of public parks—and Lincoln's own, less elaborated view—was not centered on controlling the urban worker. Their primary concern was the middle-class urban dweller, whose frayed nerves and exhausted body could be refreshed and renewed by the contemplation of a carefully crafted landscape.

Initially, at least, Lincoln had scant opportunity to implement this Olmstedian vision of the scenic park, for, upon becoming head of the Parks Commission in 1870, he found he had little to rule. Worcester's park land consisted of an "unsightly" eight-acre common and a larger, twenty-eight-acre tract known as Elm Park. Despite the name, the latter primarily served as "a handy dumping ground for the Highway Department . . . [and] the casual job-wagon or wheel barrow." Such inelegant and inadequate public grounds offended Lincoln's horticultural sensibilities; he found them lacking the beauty of the elaborate European public gardens, fountains, and boulevards that he admired so much. Moreover, such grounds failed to accord with Olmsted's view of parks as instruments of conservative social reform that might defuse social tensions.

Influenced by these aesthetic and moral visions, Lincoln fought for and won the appropriations needed to begin to shape Elm Park into a fair approximation of the Olmstedian contemplative ideal. Gradually, the land was cleared and drained; broad stretches of land were planted with artistically arranged rhododendrons, azaleas, rare trees, exotic shrubs; elaborate pools were constructed and arched by intricate wooden bridges.

In pursuit of this ideal, Lincoln sought to banish active uses of Elm Park. Circuses, which had earlier lost their home on the common, were banned in 1875. Three years later, the soon-to-be-familiar "keep off the grass" signs were given legal sanction. Baseball playing was left undisturbed, but Lincoln hoped that this "dreary amusement" would soon be removed from his cherished Elm Park to specially designated playfields in "different sections" of the city. Presumably, these fields would be placed closer to the homes of working-class Worcesterites who lived in the southeastern part of the city, not in the more exclusive West Side where Elm Park was located.

This clash between what environmental historian J. B. Jackson calls "two distinct and conflicting definitions of the park"—"the upper-class definition with its emphasis on cultural enlightenment and greater refinement of manners, and a lower-class definition emphasizing fun and games"—continued throughout Lincoln's park regime. His annual Park Reports provide some guarded hints of this class conflict over park usage. In 1876, for example, he petitioned for police patrol of the common and Elm Park, declaring "this Commission will exact and enforce that decent behavior from all who frequent the Public Grounds, which is not only seemly in itself but is rightfully expected by the community." Repeated complaints describe correct park behavior as "peaceful," "inoffensive," and "quiet," while misbehavior was seen as "rude and boorish," or "disorderly and obscene."

This conflict between different styles of parks design and usage climaxed in the 1880s as two contrasting groups asserted new interests. On the one hand, the city's industrialists worked out new, more utilitarian arguments for park development that went beyond the contemplative ideal of Lincoln and the old gentry elite who made up the Parks Commission. They urged additions to the city's park land for reasons of fire protection, health, civic pride, real estate development, paternalism, and social control. On the other hand, a large and rapidly growing immigrant working class raised its own demands for space suited to its own more active, play-centered park models. Out of this clash emerged a spatial solution that allowed both groups a measure of autonomy within which to develop their own approaches to park usage and play.

In January 1884, 231 members of Worcester's elite, including several ex-mayors and many leading manufacturers, petitioned the City Council to purchase Newton Hill, a sixty-acre tract adjoining Elm Park. Their motivation, however, was not primarily aesthetic or recreational. Rather, they saw Newton Hill as an ideal spot for a reservoir that would provide fire protection for their fashionable West Side homes. Such political muscle could not be easily resisted. But an unlikely political alliance proved capable of at least temporarily obstructing the Newton Hill acquisition. On the one hand, fiscal conservatives on the Board of Aldermen opposed any new expenditures of public funds. On the other hand, representatives of the so-called lower wards, the immigrant and working-class southeastern section of the city, threatened to block the purchase in retaliation for the earlier defeat of their own efforts to secure public park land for their constituents.

Residents of the East Side confronted the problem of finding play space in

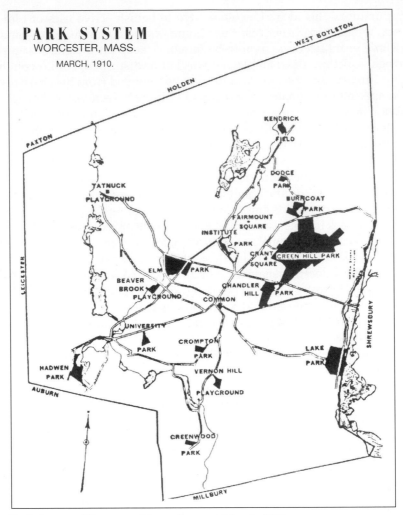

Park System, Worcester, Massachusetts, March, 1910.

a city increasingly crowded by thousands of new immigrants. Quite simply, the expansion of the physical city could not keep pace with such rapid population growth. Before the expansion of streetcar service in the late 1880s and the electrification of the lines beginning in 1891, Worcester workers were sharply limited in their choice of residences. Thus, between 1870 and 1890 the city's population jumped 206 percent, while its platted area grew only 29 percent. Consequently, the number of residents per platted acre increased by over 50 percent, from 43 to 65. Moreover, the effects of this increasing density were felt most strongly in the working-class East Side: most of the city's new residents—the immigrants— moved to that section, while most of the newly laid-out areas of the city were on the West Side.

The class dimensions of such spatial developments were not lost on at least some Worcesterites. James Mellen, the Irish editor of the *Worcester Daily Times* complained repeatedly in his editorials that "the well-to-do-people of the West Side" received "deference" and favored treatment from the city government, while the "workingmen's district" (the "lower wards" or "East Side") remained overcrowded and disease-ridden. "We, east siders," Mellen declared, "want more outside room, we want every inch of space the city can afford us." Not surprisingly, an indigenous movement developed among residents of the Irish working-class fifth (southeastern) ward to demand public play space. In 1882 Richard O'Flynn, an Irish temperance and civic leader, had gathered the signatures of almost 140 neighbors on a petition asking the City Council to acquire a "few acres of land" for "the less-favored children." Desiring recreational space more congenial to active use than Elm Park, the petitioners declared, "there is no public ground in that vicinity (the fifth ward) where children or young men can resort, either for health or amusement."

The signers of the O'Flynn petition contrasted sharply with the elite Newton Hill petitioners. Their only real social relation to these leading Worcesterites was as employees. Seventy-five of the ninety-five signers who could be identified held blue-collar jobs. Even the twenty white-collar signers had little in common with the Newton Hill petitioners: six of them, for example, ran provision or grocery stores and another three kept saloons. While the West Side industrial elite sought a park reservoir, their East Side, Irish employees wanted a play space for themselves and their children. Indeed, so strong was the perception of the class basis of Worcester's spatial inequities that the petition drive united normally antagonistic segments of the Irish working-class community. It was probably the only time that Irish temperance crusader O'Flynn joined politically with the proprietors of the community's working-class saloons. Such classwide support acquires particular significance in a city like Worcester with a traditionally weak labor movement. There, at least, the absence of trade unions and of working-class political parties did not mean the absence of class conflict.

Despite this working-class alliance and another major petition, the bill for an East Side park remained stalled in the Board of Aldermen. Finally, however, the city's two Democratic aldermen, who had been elected largely by the votes of the working-class, Irish eastsiders, decided to hold Newton Hill hostage for the Ward Five park. "If the city is not willing to provide a breathing spot for women and children who are forced to live in the thickly settled tenement houses . . . they (East Siders) shall certainly oppose any addition to the already spacious park areas on the west side where every family has its own door yard and children's playground," reported the *Boston Sunday Herald*.

Thus, the political conflict in the Board of Aldermen reflected the deeper class conflict over the provision, design, and use of public space in Worcester. A letter to the *Worcester Sunday Telegram* contrasted the needs of the city's "wealthy" and its "toilers" and left little doubt about the class basis of the struggle for play space in ward five:

> Our wealthy citizens live in elegant homes on all the hills of Worcester, they have unrestricted fresh air and perfect sewage, their streets are well cleaned and lighted, the sidewalks are everywhere, and Elm Park, that little dream of beauty,

is conveniently near. The toilers live on the lowlands, their houses are close together, the hills restrict the fresh air, huge chimneys pour out volumes of smoke, the marshy places give out offensiveness and poison the air, the canal remains uncovered, the streets are different, the little ones are many. While the families of the rich can go to the mountains or to the sea during the hot months of summer the families of the workers must remain at home.

The temporary resolution of this class conflict was found in a political compromise—the passage of a new Park Act in 1884 and the development of a comprehensive plan for Worcester parks two years later. Of course, other forces, such as real estate development, social uplift, commercial entertainment, and civic boosterism also fostered this new plan. For example, the city's manufacturing elite increasingly saw parks as a means of uplifting and controlling their work force: a way of "cultivating the love of beauty and order" among people of "small means" and even a stimulus to increasing "the excellence of work done" by the city's work people. Other park enthusiasts were more concerned with the general image of the city than with the output of its workshops. "It will not do," Lincoln wrote, comparing Worcester parks with those in New York and Chicago, "to lag in the rear and fall behind our rivals in the race for supremacy."

While a variety of groups backed the new park plan, its real significance lay in its territorial solution to class conflicts over the function and location of Worcester's parks. In effect, if not intent, the Parks Commission opted for a scheme of separate development: the East Side would have its playground, the West Side its scenic parks.

Thus, the 1886 Park Plan represented a spatial victory for Worcester workers. Of the six parcels recommended by the report, the two located on the working-class East Side were specifically designated as playgrounds rather than public gardens. In these play areas, workers would have the space and autonomy to use their leisure time as they pleased. Hence, the enthusiastic working-class support for park reform should not necessarily be seen as an endorsement of the conservative social values of the park reformers. "Even where workingmen made extensive use of the language and concepts of middle-class reformers," labor historian David Montgomery writes in another context, "they infused those concepts with a meaning quite different from what the middle class had in mind."

Despite this working-class victory in the conflict over the location and design of Worcester parks, struggles continued over park maintenance and behavior. The "separate but equal" parks faced the same problems as schools founded under that rubric: in a hierarchical society separate can never be equal. "Most of the park money," charged labor leaders, "has been expended upon parks where the wage workers and their children are least seen, while in East Park, Crompton Park, and the Commons where the most good would be accomplished, the least money is expended and the least improvements made." Even park enthusiasts admitted that Crompton and East Parks were "dumps," and one Republican alderman astutely noted that Worcester had created a system of "class parks." But better maintenance alone could not change this basic inequality, since working-class park users also faced overcrowding. "If you want the use of a baseball diamond at Crompton Park, you must sleep on the ground the night before to secure it," one local resident complained in 1904. Such crowding was largely the structural by-product of an industrial city in which large numbers of workers huddled in a small area, while smaller numbers of manufacturers and managers resided in more spacious surroundings. Paradoxically, the system of "class parks" meant both autonomy and inequality for Worcester workers.

Moreover, Worcester workers also sought to use parks outside their own neighborhoods. And, here, the battle over proper park behavior continued unabated. In the East Side parks, working-class park behavior was usually, but not always, condoned or ignored. But particularly in the parks that drew users from all sections and classes of the city, such as the common, Lake Park, and Green Hill Park, conflict raged over correct park usage and behavior. Since many Worcester industrialists had sold the public on parks on the grounds that they would teach workers "respectable habits" and cultivated manners, they fretted continuously about the obvious persistence of loafing, drinking, and similar habits in these parks. Parks, they feared, were providing a setting for precisely the sort of behavior they were supposed to inhibit.

As the city's most central and visible park space, the common became the object of repeated middle-class complaints about improper use, particularly by working-class patrons. Generally, these commentators grumbled about "dirty unkempt people," "bums," and "idlers" who "loiter," "loaf," and even "sleep off drunks." The implication was that these offenders against public decency were habitual drunks or transient hoboes. While a few probably were homeless drunkards, most seem to have been unemployed workers. During the depression of 1893, for example, one labor sympathizer counted over four hundred jobless men on the common on an average afternoon. Indeed, on at least one occasion, Worcester civil leaders confirmed this picture of the common's patrons. In 1887 as part of a campaign against the building of a new Post Office on the common many prominent citizens proclaimed the common's importance to "the working class" and "the 'plain people' of Abe Lincoln." "This breathing space in the very centre of the city," proclaimed Senator George Frisbe Hoar, Worcester's most prominent political leader, "is the comfort and luxury of the very poorest of the people; women who can snatch a few moments from work . . . men out of and waiting for work." Perhaps, then, the usual complaints about loafing on the common simply reflected middle-class blindness to the large scale, recurrent joblessness of those years. Except when expedient, mid-afternoon relaxation by the unemployed in the city's most visible park space might be defined as unacceptable park behavior—subject to official repression, including the removal of park benches.

Just as idleness was a common experience for nineteenth-century workers, so was drinking an often indispensable part of their popular culture. Not surprisingly, it, too, accompanied them into the parks. Reunions and outings at the lake, for example, were usually lubricated by ale and beer—often donated by brewers eager to advertise their product. To reduce drinking at the lake, the Board of Aldermen on several occasions refused to issue liquor licenses to lakeside establishments. But the main impact seems to have been to encourage whiskey drinking, since flasks were more easily transported and concealed than beer kegs. Even when liquor selling was banned in Worcester, a heavy traffic in beer and whiskey flourished in the woods along the lake shores.

Obviously the parks did not eradicate or reshape deeply embedded behavior patterns. Nor did they Americanize workers—another benefit sometimes promised by enthusiastic park promoters. On the contrary, Worcester parks probably supported existing ethnically based leisure patterns, by providing a convenient location for the outings of ethnic and church organizations. In the early twentieth century, for example, the Chandler Hill and Draper Field sections of East Park seem to have been divided between Swedes and Italians. Chandler Hill, located near the Swedish working-class community of Belmont Hill, was the scene of Swedish temperance rallies. The growing Shrewsbury Street Italian community, on the other hand, dominated the adjoining Draper Field. As recalled by Louis Lomatire, a retired streetcar conductor, it was a "center of activity" for Worcester Italians, with festivals, concerts, fireworks, sledding, skating, and swimming. Green Hill Park offered picnic facilities for a wide array of ethnic groups. However, it was not a place for ethnic intermingling: Worcester immigrant picnickers remained segregated into their own fraternal or church organization. If the parks ever served as a melting pot, it was a rather volatile one. The custodian of the men's bathhouse at the lake, warned against overcrowding the locker rooms: "You take a fellow from French Hill and double him up with a fair haired (Swedish) boy who lives on Belmont Hill, and there will be a fight right away."

The introduction of parks did not "remake" the Worcester working class in the image desired by industrialists and reformers. Neither did it precipitate a new class solidarity or consciousness. Ironically, while the struggle to win an East Side park had transcended some of the divisions within the Irish working-class community, the actual usage of parks revealed greater antagonisms between ethnic working-class communities. Basically, parks provided a leisure space in which workers expressed and preserved their distinct ethnic cultures. And while these immigrant workers carved out a way of life distinct from that prescribed by the native American middle and upper class, they rarely united or directly challenged the economic and political dominance of the city's Yankee elite. Thus, the struggle over recreational space suggests both the strengths and weaknesses of Worcester's working class.

The efforts by workers to reshape the designs of park reformers were not confined to Worcester. Although little work has been done on the relationship between workers and parks in other cities, it seems likely that similar conflicts—and resolutions—can be found in other industrial communities. For example, in 1870 Frederick Law Olmsted designed a system of contemplative parks for Buffalo, New York. But as large numbers of working-class immigrants settled in the vicinity of one of the parks, the complaints of "rowdyism," "vandalism," "disorder," and "improper use of public parks" mounted. Ultimately, the Parks Commission was forced to abandon its efforts to foster park use consistent "with the tasteful embellishment and good housekeeping of the grounds," and to redesign the park in line with working-class usage.

The efforts of reformers to uplift, refine, and control the working class through the provision of parks did not significantly diminish the autonomy Worcester workers exercised over their leisure time and space. On the contrary, workers were able to turn reform efforts to their own advantage and win free space within which to pursue their own conception of leisure activity. Within that unstructured context, working-class communities were able to affirm the distinctive values of the ethnic culture composing them. But, given the nature of economic relationships and power in Worcester society, such recreational autonomy existed only within limited boundaries and under substantial constraints. East Side parks never received the appropriations or care lavished on the West Side equivalents and were, as a result, often poorly maintained and heavily overcrowded. Moreover, although the various attempts to mold working-class recreational behavior were never fully successful, some of these efforts did affect working-class life. Workers could, for example, smuggle liquor to the lake, but that was neither as simple nor as pleasant as purchasing it there. Although not always used, police power stood behind the city's efforts to maintain certain basic middle-class standards of decorum in its parks.

The most fundamental constraint on working-class recreation, however, was work itself. In 1890 the *Worcester Evening Gazette* described in detail how Worcester workers played freely in Institute Park during lunchtime:

> Before the 12:05 whistle blows, the crowd begins to arrive from Washburn and Moen's, the envelope shops, electric light station, and many other establishments north of Lincoln Square. After eating, a good romp is indulged in by the girls, running and racing about, with now and then a scream of laughter when some mishap, a fall perhaps, occurs to one of their number. Some of them wander about in pairs or groups, exchanging girlish confidences, or indulging in good-natured banter with their masculine shop-mates. Occasionally a boat is secured by some gallant youth, who rows a load of laughing maidens about the pond, the envied of their less fortunate friends.

> The younger men try a game of base ball or a little general sport, jumping, running, etc., while their elders sit about in the more shaded spots, smoking their pipes. But when the whistles blow previous to 1 o'clock there is a general stampede to the shops and in a few minutes all of those remaining can be counted on one's fingers.

No matter how much autonomy Worcester workers achieved in their leisure space and time, they still had to confront the factory whistle. Its sound returned them to a sphere of life in which power and control resided outside their class.

SOURCES

Interior Space: The Dumbbell Tenement

By the 1880s, immigrants to New York and other big cities often found themselves living in "dumbbell" tenements, so called because of their shape. Because it was designed as an improvement on existing structures, the dumbbell was, ironically, labeled a "reform." Perhaps it was, but it also had serious deficiencies. Placed side by side, as was the intention, two dumbbells created an airshaft less than five feet wide between the buildings.

From the floor plan reproduced below, imagine what it would have been like to live in a dumbbell tenement. What kinds of experiences would life in such a building promote? And what activities would it inhibit? Speculate on why the building was designed so that the bedrooms in the apartments on the left could be entered from both the living room and the public hallway.

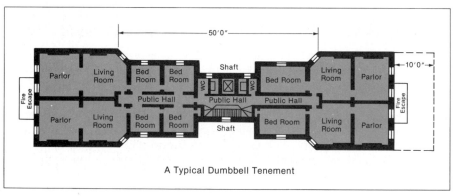

A Typical Dumbbell Tenement

A Typical Dumbbell Tenement.
From Moses Rischin, The Promised City: New York's Jews, 1870–1914, *Harvard University Press, Cambridge, 1962, p. 83. Reprinted by permission.*

Urban Images

By virtue of their size and the new relationships they imposed on their inhabitants, American cities of the late nineteenth century required their residents to live and to communicate in ways unknown just a few decades before. Many of the adjustments that people made—and the institutions they created to facilitate those adjustments—involved attempts to reduce contact where it was felt to be excessive or inappropriate. Which of the following photographs illustrates this kind of effort? This group of illustrations also includes several that might best be understood as mythic images—images that tell us more about what the photographer or illustrator desired or believed than about any existing "reality." Which ones fall in this category, and what does each tell us about how nineteenth-century Americans understood the city?

Central Park, The Drive, Currier and Ives, 1862.
Library of Congress.

World's Columbian Exposition, Chicago, 1893.
Library of Congress.

Frederick C. Robie House, Chicago, Designed by Frank Lloyd Wright.
Library of Congress.

Delmonico's, New York City, 1903.
Library of Congress.

CHAPTER 4

The Farming Frontier

The terms *America* and *the west* had seemed synonymous, from the time of the earliest penetration of the Atlantic coastline down into the nineteenth century. But during the years after the Civil War, a new kind of frontier waited to be conquered by white settlers and surrendered in bitter defeat by the Indians. Beyond the Mississippi lay a vast expanse of plains, known officially as "the Great American Desert." Farther west were the seemingly impenetrable mountains and the real deserts of the southwest. To most Americans, even as late as the 1850s, this half of the continent appeared to be good for little but a permanent reservation for native American tribes.

Amazingly, in little over a generation, the trans-Mississippi west was settled. The first transcontinental railroad was opened shortly after the Civil War. It was followed by others and by a network of rail lines spreading out into Iowa, Missouri, Texas, and the Dakotas. California became a state on the eve of the Civil War, and by the end of the century the process of state making had filled in almost all the continental map. The last effective native American resistance was broken in the 1870s and 1880s, when the old policy of war and extermination was replaced with a new form of aggression, called "assimilation." Mining towns sprang from nothing in Nevada, Colorado, and Montana. Texas and Oklahoma became primary cotton-producing states. Cowboys drove Texas longhorns into the new cow towns of Kansas and Nebraska, where the animals could be loaded onto trains headed for eastern slaughterhouses. New techniques of dry farming created one of the world's most productive wheat belts in the western half of the Great Plains. In 1890, just twenty-five years after Grant had accepted Lee's surrender, the United States Bureau of the Census officially declared that the frontier had ended forever.

The story was not a simple one of geographical expansion. The settlers of the new west were armed with a new technology that helped explain the remarkable rapidity of their success. The repeating rifle and the Gatling gun subdued the native American. The railroad took the wheat and cattle east at heretofore incredible speeds. Miners used steam power and dynamite to pry gold and

silver from the mountains. Farmers—the big ones, at least—had the new mechanical reaper to bring in wheat at a rate that manual labor could not have approached. Californians were tied to the rest of the Union by the railroad and the
new telegraph.

On the surface, then, the experience was one of triumph—at least for the
white society. But there was a dark side to things, too. Even dry farming could
not overcome periodic droughts, and the droughts came. There was competition from Russian and Australian wheat, so prices were very unstable. Some
railroads gouged the farmers. Worst of all, the new technology proved not to be
a blessing at all. The new agriculture was just too efficient. By 1890, one farmer
could produce and get to market what it had taken eight farmers to produce
fifty years before. Together, they produced more food than could be sold. So
prices fell and stayed down, and farmers often could not recoup the cost of their
seed, much less earn the money to pay interest on their mortgages and on the
loans they had made to buy their reapers and plows. Agricultural depression
was so severe and frequent that the whole second half of the nineteenth century—except for the war years—was really one long and chronic economic crisis for farmers, not only in the new west, but everywhere.

Agriculture in the south labored under a different set of burdens. The Civil
War created a long-term capital shortage and, of course, severed the bond that
had held slave labor to the plantation. Southerners responded with two systems. The first, designed to establish a link between free black farm workers and
the plantation, was sharecropping. Under this system, blacks (and poor whites)
agreed to farm the land in return for a share of the crop—usually one-third.
Under the second system, the crop-lien, sharecroppers and tenant farmers borrowed money and received credit for supplies and food from merchants and
landowners, while pledging in return a percentage of their crop. Together,
sharecropping and the crop-lien fostered throughout the south a system of peonage, in which poor whites and blacks were legally bound by debt to work the
lands of others.

Farmers sought to redress their grievances through a variety of protest
movements, each linked to a particular organization. In the 1860s, midwestern
farmers established the Patrons of Husbandry, better known as the Grange. Its
purposes were partly social and partly economic—to lower the costs of shipment and storage of grain. By the 1890s, farmers in the south, the Great Plains,
and the far west had turned to state and national politics. Through the People's
party, or Populists, they sought the aid of the national government in inflating
a depressed currency and in regulating the railroads and other trusts. Populist
influence peaked in 1896, when William Jennings Bryan was the presidential
nominee of both the Democrats and the Populists, but declined after Bryan was
defeated for the presidency by Republican William McKinley.

There were other, less political, ways of coming to grips with the market
revolution, the heritage of slavery, and the dislocation caused by being transplanted, body and soul, onto a remote prairie. Plains farmers brought with them
a weapon that helped them overcome the initial reluctance to move onto the
hard, unyielding sod of Nebraska and the Dakotas. The weapon was *myth:* the

myth that the west was the source of unprecedented opportunity; the myth that climate would respond to the migration of people; the myth that the yeoman farmer—half frontiersman, half man-of-the-soil—could handle anything; the myth that all whites were superior to all native Americans.

If the west was all this to the people who lived there, to the majority of Americans, who lived in cities or just "back east," it was a mirror of what Americans were and wanted to be. Frederick Jackson Turner triggered an ongoing debate on the meaning of the west in 1893, when he read an essay, "The Significance of the Frontier in American History," to an audience of fellow historians assembled in Chicago. Turner read American history as the story of the frontier, a continually receding area of free land that had placed generations of Americans on the cutting edge between civilization and savagery. This experience had shaped the national character. It had made Americans intensely individualistic, nationalistic, and democratic. When he linked his frontier thesis to the announcement in the 1890 federal census that the frontier had ceased to exist, Turner implied that these values were in danger—his way, perhaps, of sharing his sadness that an era had come to an end.

INTERPRETIVE ESSAY

Angel Kwolek-Folland

The Elegant Dugout

Almost every American history textbook contains a photograph that purports to describe life on the late nineteenth-century plains. It usually features a family, sitting stiffly on uncomfortable wooden chairs, their sod house in the background, baking under the prairie sun.

There is a powerful truth in those sod-house photos. But it is a partial truth—an exterior truth, if you will—as the following essay reveals. Using photographs of the interiors of frontier and western homes, Angel Kwolek-Folland describes the remarkable efforts of pioneer women to bring comfort, dignity, and even "civilization" to the Kansas prairies. With its emphasis on the role of women, on space, and on physical culture, the essay is also representative of recent trends in historical writing.

What conclusions should be drawn from the bewildering array of objects that women imported to the prairies? Were the women who did so necessarily satisfied with their lives? Was it really possible to bring Boston to a Kansas sod house?

Most middle-class American women of the late nineteenth century lived out their lives within the domestic realm, performing tasks that had come to be identified as intrinsically female: caring for small children, tending the ill or aged and managing the daily operations of the household. These things have been so closely identified with Victorian American womanhood that it has been possible to overlook the existence of the physical home as an autonomous cultural creation. Historians frequently have focused on the emotional or political content of the set of beliefs and activities called *domesticity* without analyzing the personal or cultural significance of domestic physical space. Yet for the average late Victorian woman who accepted the conventional wisdom of her time—who was neither a reformer nor a reactionary—the home was a constant physical presence, the arena wherein the behavior of day-to-day life helped to define domesticity. In addition to these personal meanings, the material home was a vital symbol within the context of late Victorian culture, and its continuance as a significant part of American life seemed to hinge on whether or not it would adapt to the rapidly changing society of the late nineteenth century.

Late Victorian definitions of what it meant to be an American derived from an awareness of cultural and physical change and the perceived need to standardize American social institutions. Although mobility always had been a fac-

Angel Kwolek-Folland, "The Elegant Dugout: Domesticity and Moveable Culture in the United States, 1870–1900," *American Studies*, vol. 25, no. 2, Fall 1984, pp. 21–37. Reprinted, with author's revisions, from *American Studies*, vol. 25, no. 2, © 1984 Mid-America American Studies Association. Used by permission.

tor in the reality of American political and social institutions, after the Civil War it became a part of the cultural awareness of Americans. The United States Census Bureau, in its documentation of the 1880 census, concentrated almost exclusively on the fact that Americans frequently changed their residence. The attention given by the bureau to this one aspect of American life at the expense of others illustrates that, perhaps for the first time in American experience, the fact of mobility became a conscious part of national self-definition.

Historians writing about the period 1870 to 1900 have discussed this awareness of change as manifested in areas such as the family, business, religion, and politics. Of all these, however, the least-explored is the family and, especially, that construct of feminine experience called "domesticity." The primary purpose of this article is to explore several insistent questions raised by this gap in our knowledge about the late Victorian family. How was domesticity, an essentially conservative construct, reconciled with a mobile society? What was the relationship between women and the mobile physical home? Was personal as well as cultural womanhood bound up with the objects and spaces of the domestic environment? In order to illuminate these questions, I will discuss the behavior of individual women as they created living spaces in both settled and frontier areas of Kansas between 1870 and 1900. Since settlement on the frontier confronted the experience of mobility head on, it magnified phenomena characteristic of the settled life of those who did not choose to become pioneers. Thus, while the pioneer experience was in a certain way unique, in another sense it serves to shed light upon common cultural circumstances.

In addition, this essay will focus on the experience of women settlers, and specifically women's *cultural* role on the frontier in relation to the *physical domestic space* that they occupied and the objects with which they surrounded themselves. The belief in the power of the physical home to transform individual character was an underlying aspect of woman's ideal role in the late nineteenth century. In addition, her ability to create a satisfying domestic environment through the manipulation and placement of domestic objects was an essential part of the late Victorian woman's sense of herself, as well as her awareness of what it meant to be "civilized." The secondary purpose of this article, then, is to explore the cultural role of women in the frontier in relation to the physical arena of domesticity.

I

The settlers of the Kansas frontier of the 1870s and 1880s strove to accommodate rough, make-do living arrangements with ideals of comfort and coziness. The Kansas frontier was not so much conquered as it was domesticated, and women played a leading role in this transformation. The promoters of Kansas settlement expressed their awareness of woman's cultural role when they urged male settlers to cultivate the minds and hearts of the inhabitants by establishing tasteful homes in the new land. "The neat calico dresses and sunshade hats of the ladies, and the cheap but durable raiment of the gentlemen," remarked Evan

Jenkins in 1880, "were in harmony with the times, and with the plain domestic spirit that prevailed in the homestead region."

Kansas women, whether in rural, frontier, or urban areas, attempted to reproduce the visible symbols of home that were an important part of the late Victorian notion of civilization. Frontierswomen brought with them the furniture and books, the pianos and pans, that would recreate the stable family home wherever they went. Some women compared frontier accommodations favorably to their eastern background. When Carrie Robbins moved with her husband to Kansas from Quincy, Illinois, soon after their marriage in 1887, they lived in a sod house in the sagebrush and cactus flats west of Dodge City. At a dinner with some neighbors, she commented on the delicious meal, which was "well cooked and well served. [The] table was really elegant with nice linen and silverware." Despite the fact that Carrie Robbins found herself on the open spaces of western Kansas, with their nearest neighbor a prairie dog colony, she applied her Illinois standards to Kansas homemaking and did not find it wanting.

To understand the significance of the domestic environment for these women, we must first turn to the physical artifacts of the frontier home. Figure 1 shows the interior of a dugout in Ford County, Kansas. Despite the crowding, the homemaker has found a place for everything. Since the photograph was taken as a permanent record of their living arrangements, she probably set out her best items for the benefit of the family history, or to show relatives or friends "back east" the cultured style of dugout life. The illustration [shows] the similarity between her present environment and that she had left behind. She propped the family Bible on the hutch, and on the cloth-covered table in the foreground set an impressive fancy tea service. Pictures and a calendar hang on the walls near the stove, and a birdcage and books are prominently displayed.

FIGURE 1. Interior of Dugout in Ford County, Kansas.
Kansas State Historical Society.

A doll even sits in the infant's chair, in place of a child who would not have remained still for the length of time it took to expose the photograph, but whose presence would help to define a family's rather than an individual's dwelling.

In *The Northern Tier* (1880), Evan J. Jenkins described a Kansas scene that could have taken place in any parlor in the nation: "In one of those dug-outs which I visited on a certain rainy day, an organ stood near the window and the settler's wife was playing 'Home! Sweet Home!' " Jenkins, a surveyor for the Federal Land Office, noted the ability of Kansas women on the western frontier to transmit culture through the objects and arrangement of domestic interiors. He praised the urbane quality of even the most modest Kansas homes and acknowledged that credit for this condition went to women:

> Many of those "dug-outs" . . . gave evidence of the refinement and culture of the inmates. . . . The wife had been reared in the older states, as shown by the neat and tastefully-arranged fixtures around the otherwise gloomy earth walls.

Jenkins' reference to the presence of culture focused on the woman's ability to turn sod walls and a dirt floor into the equivalent of an eastern parlor. The woman who displayed objects that had cultural significance—birdcages, Bibles, tea sets—was able to give her relatives and neighbors visual proof of her lack of privation, and of the identity of her living arrangements to those she had left behind.

The apparent "sloppiness" of the clothing and other objects hanging on the walls of the Ford County dugout is less aberrant when compared with the calculated casualness of other contemporary interior scenes, suggesting that the crowded interior was not caused solely by a lack of space. Studied casualness was intended to communicate comfort, and an expression of comfort was closely tied to the visual impact of material objects. In an 1871 article for *The Ladies' Repository*, Mrs. Willing explained to her readers that one homemaker "had wrought miracles of comfort—a ten cent paper on the wall, fresh and cheery, a bright rag carpet, a white bed spread, groups of engravings from the Repository and some pencil sketches . . . ," when she decorated the family home. In other words, actual comfort in the form of soft chairs, warm blankets, or heated rooms was not as necessary in home decoration as the appearance of comfort communicated through physical objects. Some objects themselves expressed relaxation such as the shawls draped over pictures or the mantle, and the "throw" pillows on chairs or divans. Comfort also could be expressed via a carefully planned jumble, as though the rooms were "lived-in." In the dugout, where space was at a premium and the items were "arranged" for the picture, there is the same sense of studied casualness as in the other rooms. The owner of the dugout expressed the ideal of comfortable, inexpensive, pleasant home surroundings by carefully positioning her visual clues to achieve order in a tight space.

Many photographs of architectural interiors focus on the same imagery as the illustrations in popular magazines and books; others represent a type of iconography that is related to traditional domestic genre scenes. They illustrate the transference of at least some portions of the ideal home to the trans-Missis-

FIGURE 2. View of Kitchen in Unidentified Residence.
Kansas State Historical Society.

sippi west. For example, we can make a further comparison of the intent and content of the Ford County dugout photograph by looking at Figure 2. A table has been set for a meal, in what probably is a lower-middle-class dining room since the chairs do not match one another and the table service is inexpensive ceramic or glass. This type of record occurs often in the family collections of all economic classes. The intent of this type of photograph was to exhibit the abundance of the family and to illustrate the skills of the homemaker who provided this example of the transitory domestic art of table arranging. The preparation of a table for holidays or parties was a "high art" form within the aesthetics of the household; correct positioning in the placement of dishes, silver, and glassware expressed a refined, educated sensibility. While acting as housekeeper of her father's sod house in Rice County, Kansas, Emily Combes prepared an elaborate meal with four kinds of meat, three vegetables, jelly and relishes, dessert, and coffee. She "added to the table that 'charm of civilization' napkins and a white table cloth using for decoration a bowl of wildflowers and green leaves. . . . I was quite proud of myself," she admitted. Even in the upper-class or upper-middle-class household, where the work of setting a holiday or party table might go to a servant, the homemaker received the credit since this function expressed the homemaker's skill in beautifying the home. By executing this function in small town or frontier areas, homemakers linked themselves to other women across the nation.

In addition to their practical uses, certain objects possessed symbolic meanings. Their presence in a home testified that a cultured sensibility pervaded the household. A typical middle-class genre piece of the late nineteenth century [was] a piano, carefully draped by a shawl, with one or more people in attendance. Women appeared most often in such photographs, but occasionally males were present as spectators or vocalists. Mrs. Sweet, who lived on a farm

FIGURE 3. Living Room of the Rob Roy Ranch, c. 1890s.
Kansas State Historical Society.

near Baldwin, Kansas, took piano lessons from a Miss Doyle, who came out once a week to give music lessons and usually stayed for dinner. Small, collapsible pump organs were available in the late nineteenth century, and it probably was this type of instrument that Mr. Jenkins heard in the dugout he visited. A piano or organ was one of the signals that communicated culture and refinement, whether one lived in a dugout, a frame house, or . . . rented rooms. . . .

Books were another signal intended to communicate the degree of a family's culture. Domestic decoration manuals and magazines pictured shelves laden with reading material, as well as vases, plates, and pictures. This juxtaposition of items partially transformed the status of the book to that of a decorative object. Figure 3, an interior view of the living room of the Rob Roy ranch house in western Kansas at the turn of the century, has a typical decorative arrangement, with a plate hung over the mantle and statuary and feathers or shells resting nearby. Photographs and diaries indicate that the emblems of cultivated life transferred to the frontier, although the substance of currently fashionable taste was not perfectly reproduced. Emily Combes had to settle for wildflowers instead of cultivated blooms, and the dugout dweller could fit a collapsible organ but not a full-sized piano into the small space.

This necessity for a certain amount of make-shift in the accommodations of Kansas rural and town dwellings was seen by Kansans as both a virtue and a liability. An almost schizophrenic mingling of attitudes appeared in most public and some private statements about the quality of Kansas life. Kansas boosters somewhat defensively claimed that the rough prairie state was healthier than other areas, as they simultaneously averred that all the advantages of civilization were present in Kansas. This seems to have been a general rural phenomenon rather than a regional one. Sociologist Harry Braverman points out that in the late nineteenth century there were far fewer differences among the lives of people in rural areas around the country than between those in urban and those in rural areas. Despite their distance from the more populous east, the women of late nineteenth-century Kansas or Nebraska, for example, lived much the same sort of life they would have lived in rural or small town areas of Ohio, New York, or Pennsylvania. Braverman notes the persistence of semi-rural and rural areas only a few miles from New York City even as late as 1890.

Newspapers such as *The Rural New Yorker* (which had a large circulation in all farming areas of the country) carried articles or letters to the editor protesting against an image of rural isolation or small-town cultural backwardness. In "A Country Housekeeper's Ideal," Annie L. Jack claimed that it was as easy to lead a "refined" life in the country as in the city. "There need not be any roughness in our amusements; there is every facility for a beautiful and cultivated life, if one can have flowers and books, even if the other surroundings are simple and inexpensive." Emily Combes wrote to her fiancé in April 1871 from Manhattan, Kansas, that "The houses are neat and pretty, many being built of stone and furnished nicely—plenty of books, carpets, pictures, piano. . . . One meets some very cultured people." Other people claimed that being rough around the edges was a positive quality. An article in the Manhattan (Kansas) *Nationalist* on January 13, 1871, claimed that Kansas women were not ignorant of fashion in house furnishings, but that the family and its needs took precedence over the whims of outsiders.

Kansas women generally evidenced great concern for their role as women responsible for maintaining a congenial and civilized home environment, within the constraints of economy. Contrary to the dictates of magazines, however, their attention to home spaces frequently was as much for themselves as for their families. Mrs. Bingham regretted her move from Junction City to a small farm outside town [about 1870]. Her first experience of the tiny farm dwelling, and her realization of its distance from the tree-lined streets of Junction City, shocked and frightened her. "When I went into the little one-room place, with a loft reached by ladder, the tears came to my eyes, thinking of the contrast with the neat new home we had left." Nevertheless, Mrs. Bingham reconciled herself to her new home once her furniture and fixtures were in place. "We finally got things in shape to live. A bed in one corner, the cupboard in another, the stove in another, with chairs and tables between and around." For Mrs. Bingham, the division and distribution of the interior spaces and objects of the home was an important part of creating a livable situation. Her first thought was for the interior of her home, and she carefully arranged her furniture to create a sense of orderliness even in the small space. Mrs. Sweet, who moved to a farm near Ottawa, Kansas, in 1890, spent her first days in her new home freshening and arranging the fixture and furniture. Her diary carefully notes each object, and possessively refers to all of them: "I worked at arranging things and unpacking my white dishes . . . I fixed my safe and unpacked my glass dishes." She put down carpet, hung pictures, put up curtains, papered the walls and painted some of her furniture. With these tasks accomplished, she felt she had transformed a house into her home. Home, in this sense, could be anywhere as long as one had the things that made anywhere into one's special place. Home was transportable, in other words, by transporting objects. The essential ideal of home as a domestic ambiance created by women could be physically moved in the form of household articles or interior arrangements. Thus, the homemaker provided stability for the family not by her person but by her ability to obtain and arrange objects.

The western frontier of the 1870s challenged women's capacity to maintain the quality of the home environment. Carrier Robbins noted in her journal that she was not pleased with her first impressions of frontier dwellings, but she remained undiscouraged. "I had my first look at a sod house, rather low, dark and gloomy looking on the outside, yet with floors, windows, and the walls plastered. They are pleasant and comfortable upon the inside. I think I can make ours seem homelike." The situation frequently was not much better in the towns, where housing was short and women often had to make do with what was available. "I cant [sic] bear the idea of living in the Preston house it is so banged up and there are no conveniences either," lamented Emma Denison in 1873. "It is nothing but a dreary house, pretty enough on the outside but ugly enough inside." Carrie Robbins and Emma Denison mentioned the exterior of their dwellings, but focused sharply on the interiors. For many women, the inside of their homes mattered more to them than the exterior.

The arrangement of the objects in the domestic interior occurred within a time frame that set women's domestic life apart from a clock-regimented society. In the first place, it was tied to the seasonal changes for the household and marked the transitional points of the year in the spring and fall. These changes were the same whether the woman kept house in the city or on a farm, and would not have varied much from New York to Kansas to Oregon. Taking down heavy winter drapes to replace them with lighter summer shades or removing wool carpets in favor of mats or light rag-rugs were seasonal chores that varied little from year to year, but which were always special events in the usual household routine. Susan B. Dimond moved to a farm near Cawker City, Kansas, in 1872. Entry after entry in her diary, beginning when she was in eastern Pennsylvania and continuing while she was in Kansas, simply stated, "Done my usual work," or "Done my housework." Then, in the seasons of change her entries became more detailed, with such comments as "varnished a bedstead" or "commenced to cover our lounge in the evening," "worked on my counterpain, & papered some up stairs and fixed up the chamber."

As further evidence of the importance of this domestic ritual, even women who had regular servants usually reserved the largest part of this seasonal activity for themselves. Mrs. James Horton of Lawrence, Kansas, whose diary almost never mentions her attention to the details of housework unless her servant was ill, noted in April 1874 that she "took up North-chamber carpet & cleaned room." During the course of the month she installed wallpaper in the hall, put down carpets in the bedrooms and on the stairs, removed the blinds so they could be painted, and "arranged Books." Such entries received the same weight as her trips to Leavenworth, her social and literary meetings and her reading habits, which dominate her diary during other months.

For newly married women, the formation of a home was important as the symbol of conjugal happiness. Martha Farnsworth, whose alcoholic and tubercular husband once threatened her life with a shotgun, lived what she described as a "dreary, lonely life in tears." Nevertheless, her home symbolized the happiness they were unable to achieve in their personal relations. When her husband died, she gave away or "burned up" the silverware, blankets, bedstead, and other household items in order not to be reminded of how unhappy she had been. Ridding herself of the physical artifacts of her marriage seemed a way to rid herself of its unpleasant memories. Her second marriage, to Fred Farnsworth, gave her all the happiness she had missed in the first. While living with his parents, she remarked excitedly that she and Fred purchased a "new Gasoline Stove," their *"first purchase . . .* in household furnishing." They later purchased a small home of their own in Topeka.

With virtually no funds, Mrs. Farnsworth set about to create a pleasant ambiance by decorating the rooms.

> I have one pretty Wolf rug, which I placed in front of a Bench, I made myself and covered, then I have a box, covered and two chairs. I got at [the] grocery, common, manila wrapping paper and made window shades, and we have our Piano, and we have music in our home and are happy.

In late summer she put the final touches on the interior of their home by selecting and installing wallpaper. "Got a lovely Terra Cotta Ingrain, with 18 inch border, for the Parlor; a beautiful pink flowered, gilt for the dining-room and Leavender [sic] flowers for the bed-room and we will have a dear 'little nest' when once we get settled." By combining found objects such as grocery wrapping paper, hoarded treasures such as the Wolf rug and the piano, various purchased wallpapers, a rocker, and a home-made bench, Martha Farnsworth created a personal family space to give physical manifestation of her happy marriage. Similarly, in the damp cellar under the Dimond home, where they lived during a particularly cold winter, Susan Dimond assured her family's material and spiritual comfort as well as her own. "We moved our stove and bed down into the basement this afternoon," she noted in her diary on November 28, 1872. "We were over to Dyton['s] to dinner . . .brought some pictures home to hang in our basement." Lacking funds for commercial wallpaper, she used newspapers to cover the earth walls.

In their diaries and letters, homemakers frequently made allusion to themselves as aristocrats or "queens." This may have indicated an awareness on their part that the home could symbolize economic status. Ella Whitney wrote to her cousin Hattie Parkerson in 1872, "How do you like keeping house on your own responsibility. I expect you feel as grand as a queen and step about." Mrs. Bingham felt the crowning touch in her cottonwood shack was two carpets that she had brought with her from New York. When these were down on the floor, she felt "quite aristocratic." It is also possible that the use of words such as these referred to the contemporary cultural metaphor of the home as a castle. Either way, the central position of the physical home is evident. For Mrs. Bingham, her

New York carpets provided links with other homes she had lived in as well as a sense of personal completeness and pride. The objects within the home were inextricably tied to women's concept of self as well as to their cultural role.

II

The vital soul of an ideal Victorian home was the wife and homemaker who transformed an architectural shell into a "Home" by the selection and arrangement of domestic spaces and objects. Most women were committed to the reality of this ideal to the extent that they seemed unable to separate their self-image from the physical domestic environment. When Eva Moll wanted to bring her absent friend Hattie Parkerson to mind in 1898, she conjured up an image of Hattie in her home in Kansas, where "everything impressed itself so deeply upon my memory that if you have made any changes in furnishings or the arrangement of the furniture, I believe I could put everything where it was when I was there." Eva used the image of an unchanged domestic environment to tell Hattie that their friendship endured in spite of distance. Belle Litchfield, in 1899, sent Hattie a photograph of the exterior of her new home in Southbridge, Massachusetts, and then took careful pains to describe the interior: "The room where the corner Bay Window is, is our library. . . . [she then put herself into the picture] where I now sit writing. The chamber above it is my chamber, and the bay window over that is my studio." Her description would not have satisfied an architect, but that was not Belle's intent. She hoped to recreate for her friend a sense of a home—not of a building—where people lived and moved within the various rooms, where the dramas and comedies of the domestic world played on their own timeless stage.

By locating a part of the home's significance in the presence of particular types of objects, Americans attested to the essentially mobile nature of the physical and spiritual home. In addition, the pianos, pictures, and tables set with napkins in the "wilderness," told the world that a cultivated woman was present, one who understood and could communicate her cultural womanhood. Whatever else their ultimate role may have been in providing the institutional marks of culture such as schools and churches, women first "domesticated" the frontier, and linked it to other areas of the nation, by their awareness and use in the home of commonly accepted cultural symbols. Rather than consider a dugout, a rented room, or a damp cellar as temporary living arrangements, and thus not worth improving, they created a stable home by their attention to the domestic interior and the objects that filled it regardless of the size or condition of the dwelling. Like Julia Hand, who began moving her household goods into her sod house before it was finished, the arrangement of domestic space was one of a woman's first considerations in the frontier environment. No doubt a portion of this concern stemmed from the fact that home was a woman's place of work, and organized quarters simplified household tasks. Then too, the objects a woman brought to her new home provided a sense of continuity whether she moved across the nation or across town. Neither of these assumptions, however, explains why Dimond troubled to get pictures to hang in a temporary shelter, or Farnsworth's proud, detailed description of her new wallpaper, or why the anonymous decorator of the Ford County dugout wanted her fancy tea service at center-front for a photograph. In addition to the personal meanings associated with objects, the homemaker also was aware of the cultural significance of domesticity. The [physical] domestic environment, in other words, provided an essential link between personal and cultural womanhood.

SOURCES

Settling the Great Plains: One Couple's Experience

Charles Wooster left his Michigan home in March 1872 to build a new life in the west. He found his way to Nebraska, where his wife joined him nine months later. Their letters to each other reveal a great deal about how one couple of middling means made a beginning on the Great Plains. How did Wooster choose a place to settle? What kinds of possessions did he consider most essential? Do you think that Helen (Nellie) Wooster was about to be pleasantly surprised or disappointed with what her husband had prepared for her? What do the letters tell us about marital relationships in the nineteenth century? Does the experience of this couple support Angel Kwolek-Folland's interpretation of the settlement experience?

Chicago, March 12, 1872
9 P.M.

My Little Wife

I have been here about 24 hours, as you see by the date of this. I found that I could gain no time by starting towards Minnesota before 5 this afternoon. I have been running about town most of the (day) and have learned nothing worth mentioning. I went to the Office of the Prairie Farmer this forenoon. Saw a man there from Minnesota who had been there twenty years and after talking with him and some others and thinking the matter all over again concluded that I would not go to Minnesota at all. This evening I accidentally met a young man who has just returned from southwestern Kansas. He says everything is awful high there and gives a discouraging account generally. Having concluded not to go to Minnesota I have made up my mind to go to Nebraska and shall look for a place with a house and some improvements. I have half a mind to say I will not write again until I find a permanent stopping place, but still I may. I shall leave here within an hour and shall reach Omaha about 10 tomorrow P.M. . . .

Bye Bye

I think of you all the time and hope to see you soon

Charley

From William F. Schmidt, ed., "The Letters of Charles and Helen Wooster: The Problems of Settlement," *Nebraska History*, vol. 46, 1965, pp. 121–137. Reprinted with permission.

Silver Creek, Nebraska
14 6 P.M.

This is a station city or village consisting of the depot, a grocery hotel, and one dwelling house . . .

It [the country] is as much different from anything that you ever saw in Michigan as can possibly be imagined. What I shall do here I can not possibly say. I do not intend to be in a hurry. I shall probably remain here . . . some time and then perhaps [go] to Grand Island . . . You must make up your mind not to get homesick when you come, find what you may. If we find any peace or happiness on this earth, I suppose at least 99 per cent of it will be within our own home . . .

(Unsigned)

Silver Glen, Merrick Co., Nebr.
March 27, 1872

My Little Wife

. . . Although there are Indians to be seen here, almost every day, they are very peaceable and are much more afraid of the whites than the whites are of them. In fact the white people do not fear them at all and I have yet to learn of a woman or child who stands in the slightest dread of them. . . .

When they wish to enter a house they will come and look in at the windows until someone notices them and then if the door is opened they will step right in without further invitation. They most always ask for something to eat, but if one doesn't wish to be troubled with them it is only necessary to refuse and send them on their way.

There is no danger here of raids from wild Indians for the country is settled many miles beyond and the wild Indians are far away . . . So don't give yourself any concern about Indians. You will stand in no more danger of them than in Michigan and when you have been here a little while you will not be a bit afraid of them . . .

Charley

Silver Glen, Neb.
July 28, 1872

My dear little Wife

I do not know what to say to you. You inform me that you are coming this fall. I certainly hope you will do so for it is very unpleasant for me to live alone and do my own house work, no less so perhaps than for you to be without any fixed place in Michigan. But these are only a part of the reasons why we wish to be together. It seems to me however that it would not be very wise for us to undertake to go to keeping house when we have no money even to pay your fare here saying nothing about freight, the cost of enough furniture to enable us to live at all which would be 50$ at least, the incidental expense of living and things which it would be necessary to have to supply our table which the farm will not afford. Fuel would necessarily cost something. How could we live without a cow? A good one would cost 50$—a second rate one might be had for 40$. In the spring if I did not have a team and some farming utensils a little money would be almost a necessity. How should we get the seeds that I had intended to, for hedge plants, fruits and forest trees? True my corn crop ought to be worth 200$, but whether I could realize anything on it would be a very doubtful question. . . . You can estimate our resources and the necessary expenses of settling up here as well as I can.

If I said I could live cheap here alone, it has been proved that I was correct for since the 26 day of April, living, fuel, cooking utensils and all probably has not cost me 10$. I have had no butter for two months and I do not use more than a pound of pork in a week. . . . The more I see of some other places the more I think of my own. I can prove up on it next spring and then I could raise money on it if I wish to, though I do not wish to if possible to avoid it. As heretofore I shall *try* to get along as well as possible but, if in so doing my feet should slip from under me and I should slide into hell, I should endeavor to endure the fry with all fortitude. . . .

Bye bye
Charley

Silver Glen, Neb.
August 28, 1872

My dear little Wife

. . . I think I shall get a yoke of oxen and a second-hand wagon. I think of going down about Columbus to look for them. I can not go till I do four or five days more in haying. I do not want to pay over 150$ for them both. It will be better for me to get them at first if I get them at all as I shall need several days team work preparatory to building. The material for the house will cost altogether 150$, and I am in hopes that I shall be able to do so much of the work myself that it will not be necessary to pay out much for work.

I have bought the heifer I spoke of in my last [letter] and shall pay for her— 40$—in a day or two . . . I would not have bought the heifer now, but I was afraid some one else would get her. She is the only one I have seen that pleased me and is, I think, the best one I have seen or heard of.

Charley

Silver Glen, Neb.
Nov. 24, 1872

Little Wife,

Thursday I went to the station partly in hopes of meeting you. I did not know but you would come notwithstanding my letter. Friday night I went again and instead of yourself I found a letter from you. I am sorry you were feeling out of gear. I am sure I have tried to do the best I could. I wanted you here, but what could I do? My means were insufficient, and whenever I did get money it was not enough to meet demands. My expenses have been greater than I anticipated and now I find myself with a house but not a dollar to furnish it. A few days ago I had 60$ with which I intended to get furniture, but unexpectedly I was obliged to get about 20$ worth of stuff for the house when I supposed I had enough. The charges on the goods were upwards of 18$ and yesterday I went to Columbus . . . and spent 27$ or thereabouts for a pump, inside doors, door hangings, etc.

. . . You see then that we have no money and no prospect of getting any for an indefinite length of time unless it can be borrowed. It seems as though some of your brothers or all of them might have money the[y] should be glad to lend . . . and wait till we could pay. If not we must work in some other direction. As I told you . . . I can prove up on my place and give that as security if it's considered necessary, and that would be worth many times all we shall need to borrow.

. . . It is perhaps useless for me to say more. I am sorry for you, sorry for myself and sorry for the devil . . .

. . . Come now if you can. Let us enjoy again each other's love. The future must provide for itself.

Charley

Silver Glen, Neb.
Dec. 3, 1872

Little Wife

. . . The floor is nearly laid now and two or three days work ought to be sufficient, especially if the pantry is not finished before you come, and it probably will not be as I wish you to have it done after your own heart. If I had money, I could be ready for you in three days and so I can in two or three days at any time after getting money. . . .

I have not opened the melodeon, barrel, chest or box of clothes. In the large box I found one of the large jars of quinces was broken probably from the hilt of the sabre pressing upon the top of it . . .

Your little chickens are no more for this world, some skunks dug in while I was away and eat them all, their mother, two or three other hens and two or three other chickens. I caught one of the skunks in a trap and am trying to catch another . . .

What fine times we shall have when you come.

Bye bye
Charley

Hillsdale, Mich.
Dec. 9, 1872

My dear Boy

I'm now soon coming to you and am not going to be fooled out of it much longer, for although I have had a pretty hard time to find money, I have succeeded *at last* just as I gave up all hope and had gone to bed with a nervous sick headache. You must be pleased and not frown at me for taking the money in the way I have for it is all the way I can get any at present.

[My father] signed a note with me to get the money from Lawt Thompson. I should not have known that Lawt had any but Cousin Mart unbeknown to me asked him if he had some and would let you have it with pa for a signer and he said he would. So this morning pa came up to Lawts with me, and Lawt drew the note and I signed Chas. Wooster to it and pa signed H. P. Hitchcock . . . He had only 70$ to let so I took that for six months at 10 per ct. and now you will be pleased than other wise won't you? and don't for Gods sake send it back. . . .

I am going to start a week from tomorrow (Tuesday) so prepare for my coming and don't you write and say that the floor is not quite laid yet, for if it isn't I can soon hammer it down . . .

Write to me as soon as you get this for I want one more letter from you before I go so I can carry it in the cars for company . . .

Bye bye, for now I'm surely coming even if you write me the house is burned to ashes. Bye.

Nellie

Westward Bound: Images

The journey westward was an experience that real people had. But it was also a popular vehicle for artists and photographers, who tried to capture the reality of that journey while adding to it their own notions about the meaning of the American West. Compare these two versions of the westward movement. Why do you suppose they are so different? Would the artist of Emigrants Crossing the Plains *have agreed with Frederick Jackson Turner that the frontier was the source of individualism and self-reliance? Or would he have claimed some other quality as the West's peculiar contribution to the national character? Also compare these images with the letters of Charles and Nellie Wooster. Which image best expresses the Woosters' particular reality?*

Emigrants Crossing the Plains. Photocopy of engraving by H. B. Hall, Jr., after drawing by F. O. C. Darley.
Library of Congress.

Westward Bound.
Library of Congress.

The Populist Challenge
The Election of 1892

By the 1890s, the individualism of a Charles Wooster had yielded to the cooperative enthusiasm of the Farmers' Alliance and, finally, to the formation of a political party. In November 1892, the People's (or populist) party elected governors in Kansas, North Dakota, and Colorado as well as an estimated 1500 county officials and state legislators. James Weaver, the party's presidential candidate, received more than 1 million votes.

From the following items—the text of most of the 1892 populist party platform and a map that shows the voting pattern in the presidential election of 1892—evaluate the challenge that the populist party leveled at the Republicans and Democrats. Geographically, where did the populists succeed, and where did they fail? Does it appear that the People's party was successful in reaching debt-ridden sharecroppers in the cotton belt? Industrial workers in the urban north? Do you think that the platform strengthened or weakened the party's appeal to either of these groups or to the general public? According to the platform, what issues did the populists emphasize? Several of the measures suggested in the platform, including the provisions dealing with currency and coinage, were designed to produce some measure of inflation (prices fell during

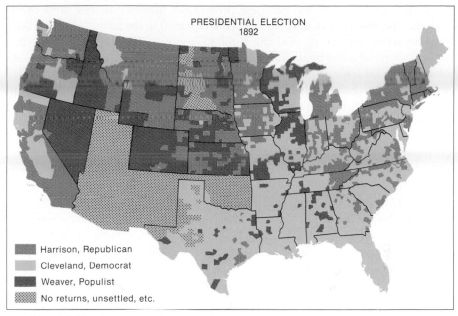

Presidential Election, 1892.
From Atlas of the Historical Geography of the United States, *ed. Charles O. Paullin, (New York: Carnegie Institution of Washington and the American Geographical Society of New York, 1932), copyright Carnegie Institution of Washington.*

most of the late nineteenth century). Assuming that most farmers were debtors, how would they have benefited from an inflationary economy? In general, was the populist response to the market revolution (see the introduction to this chapter) a reasonable one?

The People's Party Platform, 1892

PREAMBLE

The conditions which surround us best justify our co-operation; we meet in the midst of a nation brought to the verge of moral, political, and material ruin. Corruption dominates the ballot-box, the Legislatures, the Congress, and touches even the ermine of the bench. The people are demoralized; most of the States have been compelled to isolate the voters at the polling places to prevent universal intimidation and bribery. The newspapers are largely subsidized or muz-

Donald Bruce Johnson, ed., *National Party Platforms*, vol. 1: *1840–1956*, rev. ed., University of Illinois Press, Urbana, 1978.

zled, public opinion silenced, business prostrated, homes covered with mortgages, labor impoverished, and the land concentrated in the hands of capitalists. The urban workmen are denied the right to organize for self-protection; imported pauperized labor beats down their wages, a hireling standing army, unrecognized by our laws, is established to shoot them down, and they are rapidly degenerating into European conditions. The fruits of the toil of millions are boldly stolen to build up colossal fortunes for a few, unprecedented in the history of mankind; and the possessors of these, in turn despise the Republic and endanger liberty. From the same prolific womb of governmental injustice we breed the two great classes—tramps and millionaires.

The national power to create money is appropriated to enrich bond-holders; a vast public debt payable in legal tender currency has been funded into gold-bearing bonds, thereby adding millions to the burdens of the people.

Silver, which has been accepted as coin since the dawn of history, has been demonetized to add to the purchasing power of gold by decreasing the value of all forms of property as well as human labor, and the supply of currency is purposely abridged to fatten usurers, bankrupt enterprise, and enslave industry. A vast conspiracy against mankind has been organized on two continents, and it is rapidly taking possession of the world. If not met and overthrown at once, it forebodes terrible social convulsions, the destruction of civilization, or the establishment of an absolute despotism.

We have witnessed for more than a quarter of a century the struggles of the two great political parties for power and plunder, while grievous wrongs have been inflicted upon the suffering people. We charge that the controlling influence dominating both these parties have permitted the existing dreadful conditions to develop without serious effort to prevent or restrain them. Neither do they now promise us any substantial reform. They have agreed together to ignore, in the coming campaign, every issue but one. They propose to drown the outcries of a plundered people with the uproar of a sham battle over the tariff, so that capitalists, corporations, national banks, rings, trusts, watered stock, the demonetization of silver, and the oppressions of the usurers may all be lost sight of. They propose to sacrifice our homes, lives, and children on the altar of mammon; to destroy the multitude in order to secure corruption funds from the millionaires.

Assembled on the anniversary of the birthday of the nation, and filled with the spirit of the grand general and chief who established our independence, we seek to restore the government of the Republic to the hands of "the plain people," with which class it originated. . . .

We declare that this Republic can only endure as a free government while built upon the love of the whole people for each other and for the nation; that it cannot be pinned together by bayonets; that the civil war is over and that every passion and resentment which grew out of it must die with it, and that we must be in fact, as we are in name, one united brotherhood of freemen.

Our country finds itself confronted by conditions for which there is no precedent in the history of the world; our annual agricultural productions amount to billions of dollars in value, which must, within a few weeks or months be exchanged for billions of dollars' worth of commodities consumed in their production; the existing currency supply is wholly inadequate to make this exchange; the results are falling prices, the formation of combines and rings, the impoverishment of the producing class. We pledge ourselves that, if given power, we will labor to correct these evils by wise and reasonable legislation, in accordance with the terms of our platform.

We believe that the power of government—in other words, of the people— should be expanded (as in the case of the postal service) as rapidly and as far as the good sense of an intelligent people and the teachings of experience shall justify, to the end that oppression, injustice and poverty, shall eventually cease in the land. . . .

PLATFORM

We declare, therefore,

First—That the union of the labor forces of the United States this day consummated shall be permanent and perpetual; may its spirit enter into all hearts for the salvation of the Republic and the uplifting of mankind.

Second—Wealth belongs to him who creates it, and every dollar taken from industry without an equivalent is robbery. "If any will not work, neither shall he eat." The interests of rural and civic labor are the same; their enemies are identical.

Third—We believe that the time has come when the railroad corporations will either own the people or the people must own the railroads, and should the government enter upon the work of owning and managing all railroads, we should favor an amendment to the Constitution by which all persons engaged in the government service shall be placed under a civil service regulation of the most rigid character, so as to prevent the increase of the power of the national administration by the use of such additional government employees.

Finance—We demand a national currency, safe, sound, and flexible, issued by the general government only, a full legal tender for all debts, public and private, and that without the use of banking corporations, a just, equitable and efficient means of distribution direct to the people, at a tax not to exceed 2 percent per annum, to be provided as set forth by the sub-treasury plan of the Farmers' Alliance, or a better system; also by payments in discharge of its obligations for public improvements.

1. We demand free and unlimited coinage of silver and gold at the present legal ratio of 16 to 1.
2. We demand that the amount of circulating medium be speedily increased to not less than $50 per capita.
3. We demand a graduated income tax.
4. We believe that the money of the country should be kept as much as possi-

ble in the hands of the people, and hence we demand that all State and national revenues shall be limited to the necessary expenses of the government, economically and honestly administered.

5. We demand that postal savings banks be established by the government for the safe deposit of the earnings of the people and to facilitate exchange.

Transportation—Transportation being a means of exchange and a public necessity, the government should own and operate the railroads in the interest of the people. The telegraph and telephone, like the post office system, being a necessity for the transmission of news, should be owned and operated by the government in the interest of the people.

Land—The land, including all the natural sources of wealth, is the heritage of the people, and should not be monopolized for speculative purposes, and alien ownership of land should be prohibited. All land now held by railroads and other corporations in excess of their actual needs, and all lands now owned by aliens, should be reclaimed by the government and held for actual settlers only.

CHAPTER 5

Empire

In the final years of the nineteenth century, Americans suddenly awoke from their preoccupations with domestic life to find themselves with an empire on their hands. In 1895, while very few Americans paid any attention, inhabitants of Cuba, which was still a Spanish colony, staged an unsuccessful revolution—one more in a series of new world revolutions against European rule that had begun in 1776. But this one failed. The Spanish began a ruthless repression of guerrilla resistance, even herding men, women, and children into concentration camps. The American press took up the Cuban cause in shrill editorials and exaggerated reporting. Before anyone, even those in President McKinley's administration, quite knew what was happening, the American battleship *Maine*, calling at Havana, had been mysteriously sunk, perhaps sabotaged. McKinley asked Congress for a resolution permitting "forcible intervention" in Cuba. An American fleet that Secretary of the Navy Theodore Roosevelt had waiting in the Pacific steamed for Manila Bay in the Philippines to attack Spanish warships there. War was on.

The war lasted for only a few weeks, and when it was over, the United States "possessed" the Philippines, Cuba, and Puerto Rico, and was faced with the task of governing its new colonies for a time under military occupation. The British boasted that the sun never set on their empire. Americans could not yet make the same boast, but they could see from a quick look at the map that the sun never set for *long* on American possessions.

This simple story—of being drawn innocently into "a splendid little war," as John Hay called it, and waking up blinkingly to an unanticipated empire—probably is a fairly accurate summary of the way most Americans experienced the events of 1898 and 1899. But the story misses a lot.

It overlooks, to begin with, the fact that the history of the United States could be written as a history of expansion and conquest. Through exploration, purchase, treaty, and war, the United States had become, in the course of the nineteenth century, a vast nation. And all along there had been plans and dreams to expand even further, down into Mexico and the Caribbean. In this way, the Spanish-American War was a logical outcome to a long history.

The Cuban and Philippine occupations should also be seen as early examples of many similar interventions over the next two decades that together helped define the distinctly American version of empire. Carried out with the support of presidents known as reformers and progressives, these ventures added up to a major extension of American influence around the globe. Roosevelt's aid to Panamanian rebels in 1903 made possible American domination of the Canal Zone. Under William Taft, the United States asserted its right to intervene and to supervise the collection of customs receipts in Nicaragua, another nation with a potential canal route. Woodrow Wilson sent American forces into Haiti and the Dominican Republic, and in 1914, seeking to topple the Mexican government, he landed American troops and occupied the coastal city of Veracruz.

But this new expansion occurred in a new atmosphere. The 1890s was a decade of deep economic and social crisis. The depression of 1893 to 1897 was the worst in the nation's history and gave rise to the specter of collapse, as bands of tramps wandered the countryside in numbers large enough to be called "armies." Two of the most violent strikes in American history—one at Homestead, Pennsylvania, in 1892; the second at Pullman, Illinois, in 1894—intensified the sense that the country was at a desperate crossroads. For many, particularly for people like Theodore Roosevelt, the war and the chance to be an imperial power were a welcome relief from the brooding sense of decline and collapse that the decade had engendered.

In addition, whatever its origins, the new empire appeared to many Americans to be an opportunity, both for commercial and military development and for reform. The connection may seem odd in retrospect, but many Americans looked on the chance to govern Cuba or the Philippines as a chance to recover a sense of mission, to bring to "backward" nations government that was honest, efficient, enlightened, and democratic. In the process, such people hoped, the nation might begin to set its own house in order. Indeed, the experience of empire may have contributed as much as populism did to the emergence of the atmosphere of reform that was to give the first decades of the new century their characteristic flavor.

INTERPRETIVE ESSAY

Willard B. Gatewood, Jr.

Black Soldiers and the White Man's Burden

The quick and decisive defeat of the Spanish in the Philippines did not end conflict on the islands. Led by Emilio Aguinaldo, Filipino nationalists for several years resisted American domination using guerrilla tactics not unlike those employed against another American army by Vietnamese nationalists in the 1960s.

The following selection, by Willard B. Gatewood, Jr., touches on the character of this guerrilla war and the problems it posed for American soldiers. But Gatewood's primary interest is in the Philippines as a site of racial contact and interaction. He chronicles the experiences and feelings of black American combat units, led by white officers, engaging native populations of color and, ironically, taking up the "white man's burden"—and all of this at a time when, back home, whites were legalizing racial segregation and lynching about a hundred blacks each year.

What can be learned about race relations from the experience of these black soldiers in the Philippines? How did the racial contacts brought about by the conflict shape the beliefs of whites, blacks, and Filipinos? What stance did the black troops take toward their role in the imperial process, and how do you explain their outlook?

Black regulars were among the American troops whose service in the Philippines spanned the shift in insurgent strategy from conventional to guerrilla warfare. Arriving in Manila in July and August 1899, Negro soldiers of the Twenty-fourth and Twenty-fifth Infantry immediately took stations around the city from Calacoon to Balic Balic road. By mid-1900 the number of black regulars in the Philippines had increased to 2100 men. In January and February 1900, the Forty-eighth and Forty-ninth Infantry, the two Negro volunteer regiments recruited specifically for service in the islands, disembarked at Manila and remained in the field in Luzon until their enlistment terms expired a year and a half later. Eight troops of the Ninth Cavalry, originally destined for China to help put down the Boxer Rebellion, arrived in mid-September 1900. The Ninth first saw action in southern Luzon in the vicinity of Nueva Caceres and Legaspi, and later participated in operations in Samar and Panay. By December 1900, when the total strength of American forces stood at 70,000 men and officers,

Willard B. Gatewood, Jr., *Black Americans and the White Man's Burden, 1898 1903*, University of Illinois Press, Urbana, 1975, chapter 10. Copyright 1975 by the Board of Trustees of the University of Illinois. Used with permission of the University of Illinois Press.

there were over 6000 black regulars and volunteers stationed at dozens of small outposts scattered from northern Luzon to Samar.

During their first weeks in the Philippines the black soldiers became intimately acquainted both with the hazards of a tropical climate and with the deadly tactics of the insurgents. On August 21, 1899, eleven men of the Twenty-fourth Infantry who had started on a reconnaissance mission toward San Mateo drowned when their boat capsized in the Mariquina River, a swift stream swollen by several days of heavy rain. Early in September a party of the Twenty-fourth, on a scouting expedition in the mountains north of Manila, discovered in a valley "a body of Filipinos, drilling on extended order, such as used only in fighting." But upon descending to the site, the soldiers found only "peaceful citizens planting rice"—an occurrence that was to be repeated many times . . . as they pursued their elusive enemy.

Among the numerous engagements in which black regulars participated during the northern offensive, few attracted as much attention as the battle at O'Donnell. The Twenty-fifth, with headquarters at Bamban, learned that a large force of insurgents was encamped fifteen miles away at O'Donnell. Led by a Filipino guide, a detachment of four-hundred black soldiers under the command of Captain H. A. Leonhauser left Bamban on the night of November 17, 1899, headed for O'Donnell on a roundabout route through the foothills of the Zambales Mountains. Arriving at their destination just before sunrise, the troops staged a surprise attack on the insurgent stronghold. Once inside O'Donnell, the colored soldiers "showed a grim and great earnestness in their work of gathering in prisoners, rifles and bolos." One eyewitness reported: "Strong black arms caught fleeing insurgents upon the streets and hauled them from under beds and beneath houses. Native women screamed in alarm and on their knees offered money and food to the American troops." But the soldiers apparently refrained from acts of unnecessary brutality. In fact, a young white officer was deeply impressed by the "humanity and forebearance of the colored men of the 25th Infantry" in their taking of O'Donnell. "There might have been a hundred of these pitiful Filipino warriors killed," he wrote, "but the men apparently couldn't bring themselves to shoot them." Instead, the soldiers were satisfied to capture over one-hundred insurgents and a large supply of weapons, food, and ammunition. . . .

. . . By early 1900 resistance to American rule was almost wholly in the form of guerrilla warfare. Few engagements thereafter deserved to be called battles. But the hit-and-run tactics of Aguinaldo's widely dispersed forces and the marauding bands of robbers (ladrones) proved to be no less deadly to American troops who were constantly on patrol and scouting duty. Black volunteers of the Forty-eighth and Forty-ninth Infantry arrived in the Philippines early in 1900 anxious to confront the insurgents in conventional warfare; they were disappointed to discover that most of their efforts were devoted to "looking for rebel forces which are no where to be found." A Negro lieutenant probably expressed the sentiments of his comrades when on January 31, 1900, he wrote home: "While there is no enemy in sight, yet we are always on the lookout and we have slept in our shoes ever since we landed. The war may be over or it may have just commenced. No one can tell what these devils will do next." . . .

McKinley's victory in November was the signal for General MacArthur* to inaugurate a new policy designed to ensure the establishment of permanent control over the islands. This policy represented a shift from "benevolent pacification" to a more stringent approach, promising punishment for natives who continued to resist American authority and stressing the importance of isolating insurgents from their bases of supply in the villages. It also emphasized the need to protect villagers from intimidation and terror at the hands of insurgents. For the black soldiers, including the Tenth Cavalry, which arrived in May 1901, the new military policy meant not only garrison duty in towns and villages scattered over hundreds of miles across the archipelago, but also an endless succession of expeditions through rice paddies and dense forests and over treacherous mountains and swollen streams. . . .

From early 1901 until their departure from the Philippines more than a year later, the black troops who garrisoned numerous outposts on the islands did more than perform the usual scouting, patrol, and guard duties, and other activities involved in keeping the peace. They also assisted in laying "the foundations of civil government" and generally functioned as agents of the Americanization process. Their civil duties included the supervision of elections, the organization of educational and legal systems, and the maintenance of public health facilities. Lieutenant David J. Gilmer of the Forty-ninth Infantry, a former member of the Third North Carolina Volunteers, not only was popular with enlisted men but also won the affection of the people of Linao as commander of the post there. Gilmer later secured a commission in the Philippine Scouts, an army of natives organized and officered by Americans. Captain Frank R. Steward, also of the Forty-ninth, who was a graduate of the Harvard Law School, served as provost judge in San Pablo; there he organized and presided over the first American-type court. His father, Chaplain Theophilus Steward of the Twenty-fifth Infantry, supervised a series of schools taught by soldiers in the towns and villages north of Manila under the protection of his regiment. According to one observer, the chaplain's command of the Spanish language and capacity for hard work enabled him to achieve excellent results and to instill in Filipinos an appreciation for American values. Black soldiers often displayed considerable pride in their nonmilitary activities, which they described as significant contributions to the improvement of life among the natives. An enlisted man in the Twenty-fifth Infantry boasted in 1902 that "the colored American soldier has taught the Filipino thrift, economy and above all the customs of polite society." . . .

. . . No less than whites, blacks suffered from the boredom endemic to existence in remote outposts. Their diversions sometimes included activities considerably less wholesome than fishing, swimming, playing baseball, or participating in choral groups. Gambling and overindulgence in various alcoholic concoctions constituted the chief diversions of some soldiers, and drinking gamblers had a tendency to spawn fights. Black soldiers on leave in Manila sometimes became involved in disturbances in the tenderloin districts, especially in houses of prostitution that attempted to establish a color line.

*General Arthur MacArthur, military commander in the Philippines.

For many soldiers, black and white, female companionship offered the best respite from a monotonous existence. It was common practice for a Negro soldier to acquire a "squaw." Richard Johnson of the Forty-eighth Infantry claimed that the "first to acquire a querida' or lover (kept woman) was our captain and this set the pattern for all the men." Perhaps, as Archibald Cary Coolidge later wrote, "their pursuits of the native women provoked much anger among the [Filipino] men." But whether such activity gave "rise to fresh insurrection in districts which had been pacified," as Coolidge claimed, is open to question. Some black soldiers, especially those who planned to remain permanently in the Philippines at the termination of their military service, married Filipino women and settled in various parts of Luzon. For most soldiers, however, these relationships ended when they sailed for the United States in 1902. An enlisted man of the Twenty-fifth observed that in view of the number of deluded women who crowded the pier as soldiers shipped out for home, it was altogether appropriate for the band to play "The Girl I Left Behind."

Whatever the consequences of their relations with native women, black soldiers generally appear to have treated Filipinos with respect and compassion. Throughout the war, and especially after the army adopted a harsher policy toward insurgents, reports of atrocities circulated widely in the United States. Few prompted as much indignation as those regarding the use of the so-called water cure as "a persuader . . . to induce bad hombres to talk." Some Americans maintained that troops in the Philippines engaged in brutalities that surpassed anything committed by "Butcher" Weyler in Cuba. In May 1900, black newspapers in the United States published a letter from a Negro soldier who expressed horror at the looting, stealing, desecration of churches, and daily indignities against Filipinos committed by his white comrades. Even some high-ranking military officers protested against the severity of the war. The charges of unwarranted brutality achieved even greater credence late in 1901 when General Jacob Smith, in retaliation against the insurgents for their massacre of a contingent of American troops in Samar, ordered his army to turn the island into "a howling wilderness" and to kill every human being over the age of ten.

Although one writer asserted in 1904 that "the brutal conduct" of black soldiers "in the interior seriously jeopardized the hope of a peaceful solution" to the Philippine insurrection, the weight of testimony in regard to their treatment of natives contradicts this observation. Oswald Garrison Villard* maintained that "neither the officers nor the men of any colored regiment" figured in "the charges and counter-charges arising out of the use of the water torture, except one man who at the time of his offense was not with his regiment." There were, of course, other exceptions of which Villard was undoubtedly ignorant. For example, Lieutenant Samuel Lyons of the Twenty-fifth confided in a letter to his wife that he and his men had on occasion administered the water cure to recalcitrant insurgents. Nevertheless, it does appear that the black regiments used this particular form of torture far less frequently than some of the white outfits.

*the liberal, pacifist editor of the *New York Evening Post*.

The Ninth Cavalry developed its own method for extracting information from captured insurgents. In describing it one authority wrote: "A native . . . was taken into a semi-dark room and securely bound. Then a huge black, dressed only in a loin cloth and carrying a cavalry sabre, entered and danced around the victim making threatening gesticulations with the sabre. To an ignorant Filipino he undoubtedly looked like a devil incarnate." The method proved amazingly successful as a persuader; whatever its psychological consequences, it was obviously preferable to the physical torture inflicted by the water cure.

By the time the black troops departed from the Philippines, it was generally agreed that their relationships with natives were more cordial than those of white soldiers. When the Negro soldiers first arrived in the islands, Filipinos viewed them with awe and fear as an "American species of bête noir." A typical reaction was: "These are not Americans; they are Negritoes." But their fear quickly turned into friendliness and their awe into admiration. Filipinos came to accept black Americans as "very much like ourselves only larger" and gave them the affectionate appellation, "Negritos Americanos." Negro soldiers generally reciprocated the good will of peaceful natives and treated them with consideration and respect. In letters home they often referred to the contempt that white soldiers displayed toward all Filipinos and insisted that such an attitude underlay much of the natives' hostility to American rule. Military authorities, quick to recognize the rapport between black soldiers and natives, generally agreed that in towns and districts "garrisoned by colored troops the natives seem to harbor little or no enmity toward the soldiers and the soldiers themselves seem contented with their lot and are not perpetually pining for home." In 1902 Colonel [Andrew S.] Burt could "not recall of the many places where the 25th Infantry has been stationed on these Islands that the inhabitants were not genuinely sorry when they have been ordered to leave their towns." General Robert P. Hughes fully agreed, noting that black soldiers "mixed with the natives at once" and "whenever they came together, they became great friends." Hughes recalled that when he withdrew "a darkey company" from Santa Rita, the residents wept and begged him to allow the black soldiers to remain.

Not all white Americans in the Philippines were so favorably disposed toward black soldiers and their friendly relations with Filipinos. "While the white soldiers, unfortunately, got on badly with the natives," the correspondent Stephen Bonsal reported, "the black soldiers got on much too well." Some white officers came to suspect that Negro troops had more sympathy for the Filipinos' aspirations for independence than for American policy regarding the islands. Others complained that the racial identity that black soldiers established with the natives had resulted in a color line that discriminated against whites. Governor Taft* apparently shared some of these concerns. He felt that black troops "got along fairly well with the natives . . . too well with the native women"; the result was "a good deal of demoralization in the towns where they have been stationed." Taft was credited with engineering the withdrawal of Negro troops from the islands in 1902 "out of their regular turn."

*governor of the Philippines and future president William Taft.

Whatever the reaction of white soldiers to the rapport between their black comrades and the Filipinos, their overt expressions of racial prejudice toward both only strengthened that relationship. Writing about American forces in the Philippines early in 1900, Frederick Palmer maintained that color was a crucial factor and that if a man was nonwhite, "we include him in a general class called 'nigger,' a class beneath our notice, to which, so far as our white soldier is concerned, all Filipinos belonged." Another correspondent, Albert Gardiner Robinson, reported from Manila that "the spirit of our men is far too much one of contempt for the dark-skinned people of the tropics." White soldiers "almost without exception" referred to the natives as "niggers," and, as Major Cornelius Gardner of the Thirtieth Infantry observed, "the natives are beginning to understand what the word 'nigger' means." In 1899 both the *Manila Times* and the *Army and Navy Journal* became so concerned about the mischief done by the widespread use of the term in referring to black soldiers and Filipinos that they called upon Americans to banish it from their vocabulary. For quite a different reason white southerners in the islands also objected to calling Filipinos "niggers"—a term that they reserved for Negro Americans, soldiers as well as civilians. James H. Blount of Georgia, an officer in the Twenty-ninth Infantry who remained in the Philippines as a civil judge, claimed that southerners "instinctively resented any suggestion comparing Filipinos and negroes," because such comparison implied that their social intercourse with natives was "equivalent to eating, drinking, dancing and chumming with negroes"—things that no self-respecting white man would do.

Black soldiers were keenly aware of the racial attitudes of their white comrades toward all colored people, themselves as well as Filipinos. The men of the Twenty-fifth Infantry had scarcely landed in the islands in 1899 when, as they marched into Manila, a white spectator yelled: "What are you coons doing here?" The sentiment implicit in the question found expression in the establishment of "white only" restaurants, hotels, barber shops, and even brothels, and in tunes such as "I Don't Like a Nigger Nohow" sung by white soldiers. In mid-1900 a Negro regular observed that "already there is nowhere in Manila you can hardly [*sic*] get accommodated and you are welcomed nowhere." The color line being drawn against the black soldier in the Philippines was, in his opinion, "enough to make a colored man hate the flag of the United States." Patrick Mason of the Twenty-fourth Infantry wrote home not long before he was killed in combat: "The first thing in the morning is the 'Nigger' and the last thing at night is the 'Nigger.'" Such talk, according to Mason, was prompted by the assumption of white soldiers that no one except Caucasians had "any rights or privileges." Late in 1899 a black infantryman on duty near San Isidro wrote: "The whites have begun to establish their diabolical race hatred in all its home rancor . . . even endeavoring to propagate the phobia among the Spaniards and Filipinos so as to be sure of the foundation of their supremacy when the civil rule . . . is established." White officers often expressed admiration for the light-hearted, cheerful mood with which black soldiers undertook even the most difficult assignments, but few indicated an awareness of their deep resentment of the insults and discrimination to which they were regularly subjected.

A major source of black soldiers' grievances was the racial prejudice displayed by some of their white officers. While in the Philippines, the officer personnel of the four Negro regiments of the regular army changed frequently; according to black enlisted men and noncommissioned officers, the replacements too often included whites who, protected by their rank, gave full vent to their animosities against people of color. Though always generous in their praise of white officers whom they considered fair-minded, black soldiers complained bitterly about their treatment at the hands of those with a prejudice against Negroes. Specifically, they charged such officers with cursing and abusing enlisted men and with subjecting them to inhuman treatment for even minor infractions of military regulations. In a few instances the grievances found their way to the War Department; but as a member of the Twenty-fifth who filed a complaint correctly predicted, "an abnegation will confront this statement as has been the case heretofore."

The color prejudice manifested by white Americans in the Philippines substantially affected the black soldiers' view of the Filipino. The soldiers early classified the natives as colored people and looked upon themselves as part of an experiment pitting "Greek against Greek." Although some white Americans claimed that Filipinos deeply resented the presence of black troops because they regarded themselves "as belonging to a race superior to the African," such a view was contradicted by the testimony of black soldiers who almost without exception noted how the affinity of complexion between themselves and the natives provided the basis for mutual respect and good will. After a series of interviews with well-educated Filipinos, a black infantryman reported that although natives had been told of the "brutal natures" of black Americans and had at first feared for the safety of their senoritas, personal experience had demonstrated that Negro soldiers were "much more kindly and manly in dealing with us" than [were] whites.

Black soldiers might refer to Filipino insurgents as "gugus," a term used by white Americans usually to identify hostile natives, but they obviously did not join white soldiers in applying the more general term "nigger" to all Filipinos. Nor did they "kick and cuff" natives at will. According to one Filipino, the black soldier differed from his white comrade in one principal respect: he did not "connect race hatred with duty." Eugene R. Whitted of the Twenty-fifth Infantry agreed that the Negro soldier's lack of racial animosity toward colored people gave him an advantage over whites in dealing with the Filipinos. "Our men met treatment with like treatment," he declared, "and when they were in the field they were soldiers and when in town gentlemen." Despite breaches in the gentleman's code, Negro troops appear, as one Negro regular put it, to have gotten "along well with everybody but American [white] people."

Although color was important in determining the attitude of black soldiers toward Filipinos, it was not the only consideration. Some soldiers early detected a similarity between the predicament of the black man in the United States and the brown man in the Philippines: both were subjects of oppression. For such soldiers the struggle of colored Filipinos against their white oppressors had obvious ideological as well as racial implications. In view of the plight of colored citizens in the United States, it was not surprising that some black soldiers expressed doubts as to whether Filipinos under American rule would "be justly dealt by." Private William R. Fulbright of the Twenty-fifth described the war against the Filipinos as "a gigantic scheme of robbery and oppression." Writing from a military station on Luzon on Christmas Eve, 1900, a Tuskegee alumnus confided to Booker T. Washington that "these people are right and *we* are wrong and terribly wrong." The black soldier assured Washington that he would not re-enlist because no man "who has any humanity about him at all" would desire "to fight against such a cause as this." Another Negro infantryman who believed that the Filipinos had "a just grievance" maintained that the insurrection would never "have occurred if the army of occupation . . . [had] treated them as people." But the occupation forces, he declared, attempted to apply to the Filipinos the "home treatment for colored people," which they would not tolerate.

Few black soldiers were so forthright in expressing doubts about the wisdom and correctness of the American position in the Philippines. More typical was a statement by Sergeant M. W. Saddler: "Whether it is right to reduce these people to submission is not a question for the soldier to decide." Like others, Saddler preferred to emphasize the resolve with which Negro troops in the Philippines performed their duty in order to "add another star to the already brilliant crown of the Afro-American soldier." Captain W. H. Jackson of the Forty-ninth acknowledged that the soldiers of his regiment identified racially with the natives, but he insisted that, as members of the American army, black men took the position that "all enemies of the U.S. government look alike to us, hence we go along with the killing."

Despite such explanations, the correspondence of Negro soldiers revealed that they were continually plagued by misgivings about their role in the Philippines. For black regular William Simms of Muncie, Indiana, such misgivings were forcefully driven home by a Filipino boy who asked him: "Why does the American Negro come from America to fight us when we are much a friend to him and have not done anything to him [?] He is all the same as me and me all the same as you. Why don't you fight those people in America who burn Negroes, that make a beast of you . . . ?" For introspective and thoughtful soldiers like Simms, their racial and ideological sympathy for a colored people struggling to achieve freedom seemed always to be at war with their notions of duty as American citizens and their hope that the fulfillment of that duty would somehow ameliorate the plight of their people at home. As Sergeant John W. Galloway indicated, "the black men here are so much between the 'Devil and the deep sea' on the Philippine Question." But even those without such qualms who believed that the soldier's oath knew "neither race, color, nor nation" were troubled by the increasing hostility of black Americans at home toward the war in the Philippines. Negro soldiers, according to one infantryman, were "rather discouraged over the fact that the sacrifice of life and health has to be made for a cause so unpopular among our people."

Anti-imperialists in the United States were quick to detect the irony involved in the use of black troops to suppress the Filipino insurrection. A succession of poets, novelists, humorists, and journalists attacked the racist notions

implicit in the doctrine of the white man's burden and pointed up the disparities between the rhetoric and realities of "benevolent assimilation." George Ade
and Finley Peter Dunne called attention to the incongruities in the nation's use
of black troops to shoulder the "white man's burden" in the Philippines where
they, as representatives of an unassimilated segment of the American population, were supposed to bring about the "benevolent assimilation" of the Filipino. According to Dunne's Mr. Dooley, the government's policy in the Philippines was to "lake up th' white man's burden an' hand it to th' coons." Having
succeeded to the presidency in September 1901, upon McKinley's assassination,
Theodore Roosevelt admitted that Dunne's "delicious phrase about 'take up the
white man's burden and put it on the coons' exactly hit off the weak spot" in his
expansionist theory. But Roosevelt assured Dunne that he was not willing "to
give up the theory yet."

No less aware of the "weak spot" were the Filipino insurgents, who were
also thoroughly familiar with the plight of Negroes in the United States and of
the widespread anti-imperialist sentiment within the black community. Cog-
nizant of the ambivalent attitude of the black troops who found themselves
combatting an independence movement by another people of color, insurgent
propagandists directed special appeals "To the Colored American Soldier."
Here is one such proclamation signed by Aguinaldo and addressed to the
Twenty-fourth Infantry during its operations in 1899 in the vicinity of Mabala-
cat:

> It is without honor that you are spilling your costly blood. Your masters have
> thrown you into the most iniquitous fight with double purpose—to make you
> the instrument of their ambition and also your hard work will soon make the
> extinction of your race. Your friends, the Filipinos, give you this good warning.
> You must consider your situation and your history, and take charge that the
> blood . . . of Sam Hose proclaims vengeance.

Such appeals were sources of embarrassment for the vast majority of black soldiers, who protested that they were "just as loyal to the old flag as white Americans." Nevertheless, the insurgents' propaganda was not altogether barren of
results, and a few black soldiers actually joined the rebel ranks. . . .

Despite the publicity that a dozen or so Negro deserters attracted, the overwhelming majority of black soldiers in the Philippines ignored the blandish-
ments of the insurgents and hoped that their service would result in rewards
commensurate with their record. The Negro regular still believed that he was
entitled to "a commission from the ranks." During the congressional consideration of the Army Reorganization Bill, which passed in February, 1901, the black
press in the United States pleaded not only for an increase in the number of
Negro regiments in the regular army, but also for the appointment of black officers. Their efforts were unsuccessful in both respects. . . .

Despite such discrimination, black soldiers throughout their service in the
islands reported favorably on opportunities for enterprising black Americans.
They described the soil and climate as conducive to productive agriculture and
particularly emphasized the openings awaiting the Negro in business. F. H.

Crumbley of the Forty-ninth Infantry urged black Americans "of Christian education" who desired to labor "among an appreciative people" to migrate to the
Philippines at once. "They should not wait till the field is covered by others," he
advised, "but should come in the front ranks and assist in developing these people." Sharing Crumbley's enthusiasm, a black enlisted man of the Twenty-
fourth wrote home: "I shall say to all industrious and energetic colored Americans . . . that they cannot do anything more beneficial to themselves than to
come over here while the country is still in its infancy and help . . . reap the harvest which we shall soon begin to gather in. In this country will be many fortunes made." The soldiers believed that the friendly relations that they had established with the Filipinos would operate to the advantage of Negro
Americans who sought their fortunes in the islands.

On July 2, 1902. President Roosevelt issued a proclamation that, in effect,
announced the end of the Filipino Insurrection. Even before his announcement
American troops had begun to depart from the Philippines; beginning in May,
the first black troops had shipped out of Manila for San Francisco. By mid-au-
tumn all Negro soldiers, except those who chose to be mustered out in the
Philippines, had taken stations in the United States. Most of those taking up residence in the islands secured jobs in hotels and restaurants in Manila or appointments as clerks in the civil government. In addition, there were "several
school teachers, one lawyer and one doctor of medicine." One black American
to remain in Manila when his regiment left in 1902 was T. N. McKinney of Texas,
who first served on the city's police force and later as a minor civil servant. Ultimately McKinney acquired considerable wealth as the proprietor of the
Manila Commission House Company; he became the recognized leader of the
"colored colony in the capital city." Late in 1902 a black veteran of the Philippine
campaign stationed at Fort Assiniboine, Montana, made public his views on the
emigration of Negro Americans to the islands. Despite the fact that racial prejudice had "kept close in the wake of the flag" and was "keenly felt in that far-off
land of eternal sunshine and roses," he was nonetheless convinced that the islands offered "our people the best opportunities of the century."

SOURCES

William Connor

Combat: An Officer's Account

In the spring of 1899, Lt. William Connor wrote the following letter to Lt. Frederick Sladen, describing his experiences in a series of engagements that took place in and around Pasig, Malolos, and other locations within fifty miles of Manila on the island of Luzon. What attitude does Connor take toward the Filipino enemy? Toward combat? What can the account tell us about why Americans went to war in the Philippines and, more broadly, about why the nation became an imperial power?

[April 1, 1899]

. . . On Thursday reconnaissances were made in all directions to locate the enemy who had fled precipitately on Wednesday. This developed quite an engagement at Cainta when a Batallion of the 20th routed nearly 1000 natives behind entrenchments with a swamp in front. They then retired to Pasig, the natives burning the town before retiring. Every one who could walk had left Pasig during the bombardment and from the looks of several buildings I fancy they did so wisely. On one bell in the church belfry I counted fourteen bullet marks and four of them had passed through the metal. . . .

On Saturday night some of the Insurgents crept up and attacked a Company of the Washingtons and the outposts of the 22nd Infantry. We lost pretty heavily for a small engagement and the General was mad all through. We chased the Indians that night until 9, bivouacking for the night and all the next day followed them down the shore as far as San Pedro Tuason. (I hope you have a map of the country.) It was a running fight all the way, the Indian loss was heavy and they were going too rapidly to carry off their dead or wounded.

At the end of the week I simply had to come back to Manila and catch up in [*sic*] the office work (which needed it) so left the brigade and the last part of its operations.

I had burned my face to a blister and that, with a scrubby beard I looked more like a highway ruffian than a U.S. Officer.

I was in town just a week when I received a telegram from Gen. Wheaton asking if I could accompany him as A.D.C. [aide de camp] on the campaign to be made against Malolos. . . .

Oregon was meantime advancing toward Polo on the left and we could hear the rest of the Division firing on our right. As soon as line[s] could be formed the Indians opened fire and I took orders to General Egbert, 22nd Inft. to advance and take the trenches at the top of the hill. Those were the last orders the little

Lt. William Connor to Lt. Frederick Sladen, April 1, 1899, Personal Correspondence, Sladen Family Papers (Box 5), Archives, U.S. Military History Institute, Carlisle Barracks, Pennsylvania.

General ever got. I saw him 15 minutes later shot through and through. He died before he got to the dressing station. He recovered from a wound received in the Wilderness in the Civil war, was shot through the lungs in Cuba and recovered and then was caught by a bullet of one of the worthless niggers. The 22nd went right up and over one hill and up the next and the Indian was hunting other quarters at a splendid gait. . . .

The morning of the first advance was beautiful and to see those thousands of men (about 9000) leave the trenches just as day was breaking, to hear how the rifles commenced to crack and a distant boom of Hall's cannon, to see those lines march straight ahead all with their flags flying, to hear the shrill officers whistles and the trumpet calls and the faint [. . .] calls in the insurgent lines, then to see the dust fly up with more and more frequency when bullets struck, to get the Ping: Ping of the Mauser and the Ugh of the Remington and then to see men commence to drop and be carried off to the rear, were all things that now seem more and more like stories told by some one else than actual experience. . . .

There were lots of brave things done that day, many doubtless that will never be known to the world at large, but not done for the world at large, but for duty's sake.

It takes a few weeks of work like this to make one proud that he is an American. The average man here in the Army (Volunteer and Regular) is a type that the country can be proud of, daring fearless and generous. A Mighty poor "peace soldier" but a more than mighty good "war soldier."

William Connor

Edgar Rice Burroughs

The Search for the Primitive: Tarzan of the Apes

The soldiers who fought in the Philippines were real, flesh-and-blood participants in the new American empire. Most Americans experienced empire—and its complex racial and cultural currents—only vicariously and indirectly, through the newspapers and works of fiction. Among the most widely read of the novels about empire was Edgar Rice Burroughs's epic tale, Tarzan of the Apes *(1912). The story concerns an Englishman, Lord Greystoke (Tarzan), raised from infancy entirely by apes and mothered by the ape Kala, whose death—at the hands of a black man—Tarzan revenges.*

On the surface, Tarzan was no racist and no empire-builder. But he was a white man in black Africa. What are the novel's racial implications? What qualities does Tarzan have that make him such a force in the jungle? What does

Tarzan of the Apes *reveal about why Americans—or Europeans, for that matter—were so attracted to imperial adventures?*

Tarzan of the Apes lived on in his wild, jungle existence with little change for several years, only that he grew stronger and wiser, and learned from his books more and more of the strange worlds which lay somewhere outside his primeval forest.

To him life was never monotonous or stale. There was always Pisah, the fish, to be caught in the many streams and the little lakes, and Sabor, with her ferocious cousins to keep one ever on the alert and give zest to every instant that one spent upon the ground.

Often they hunted him, and more often he hunted them, but though they never quite reached him with those cruel, sharp claws of theirs, yet there were times when one could scarce have passed a thick leaf between their talons and his smooth hide.

Quick was Sabor, the lioness, and quick were Numa and Sheeta, but Tarzan of the Apes was lightning.

With Tantor, the elephant, he made friends. How? Ask not. But this is known to the denizens of the jungle, that on many moonlit nights Tarzan of the Apes and Tantor, the elephant, walked together, and where the way was clear Tarzan rode, perched high upon Tantor's mighty back.

Many days during these years he spent in the cabin of his father, where still lay, untouched, the bones of his parents and the skeleton of Kala's baby. At eighteen he read fluently and understood nearly all he read in the many and varied volumes on the shelves.

Also could he write, with printed letters, rapidly and plainly, but script he had not mastered, for though there were several copy books among his treasure, there was so little written English in the cabin that he saw no use for bothering with this other form of writing, though he could read it, laboriously.

Thus, at eighteen, we find him, an English lordling, who could speak no English, and yet who could read and write his native language. Never had he seen a human being other than himself, for the little area traversed by his tribe was watered by no greater river to bring down the savage natives of the interior.

High hills shut it off on three sides, the ocean on the fourth. It was alive with lions and leopards and poisonous snakes. Its untouched mazes of matted jungle had as yet invited no hardy pioneer from the human beasts beyond its frontier.

But as Tarzan of the Apes sat one day in the cabin of his father delving into the mysteries of a new book, the ancient security of his jungle was broken forever.

At the far eastern confine a strange cavalcade strung, in single file, over the brow of a low hill.

In advance were fifty black warriors armed with slender wooden spears with ends hard baked over slow fires, and long bows and poisoned arrows. On their backs were oval shields, in their noses huge rings, while from the kinky wool of their heads protruded tufts of gay feathers.

Across their foreheads were tattooed three parallel lines of color, and on each breast three concentric circles. Their yellow teeth were filed to sharp points, and their great protruding lips added still further to the low and bestial brutishness of their appearance.

Following them were several hundred women and children, the former bearing upon their heads great burdens of cooking pots, household utensils and ivory. In the rear were a hundred warriors, similar in all respects to the advance guard.

That they more greatly feared an attack from the rear than whatever unknown enemies lurked in their advance was evidenced by the formation of the column; and such was the fact, for they were fleeing from the white man's soldiers who had so harassed them for rubber and ivory that they had turned upon their conquerors one day and massacred a white officer and a small detachment of his black troops.

For many days they had gorged themselves on meat, but eventually a stronger body of troops had come and fallen upon their village by night to revenge the death of their comrades.

That night the black soldiers of the white man had had meat a-plenty, and this little remnant of a once powerful tribe had slunk off into the gloomy jungle toward the unknown, and freedom.

But that which meant freedom and the pursuit of happiness to these savage blacks meant consternation and death to many of the wild denizens of their new home.

For three days the little cavalcade marched slowly through the heart of this unknown and untracked forest, until finally, early in the fourth day, they came upon a little spot near the banks of a small river, which seemed less thickly overgrown than any ground they had yet encountered.

Here they set to work to build a new village, and in a month a great clearing had been made, huts and palisades erected, plantains, yams and maize planted, and they had taken up their old life in their new home. Here there were no white men, no soldiers, nor any rubber or ivory to be gathered for cruel and thankless taskmasters.

Several moons passed by ere the blacks ventured far into the territory surrounding their new village. Several had already fallen prey to old Sabor, and because the jungle was so infested with these fierce and bloodthirsty cats, and with lions and leopards, the ebony warriors hesitated to trust themselves far from the safety of their palisades.

But one day, Kulonga, a son of the old king, Mbonga, wandered far into the dense mazes to the west. Warily he stepped, his slender lance ever ready, his long oval shield firmly grasped in his left hand close to his sleek ebony body.

At his back his bow, and in the quiver upon his shield many slim, straight arrows, well smeared with the thick, dark, tarry substance that rendered deadly their tiniest needle prick.

Night found Kulonga far from the palisades of his father's village, but still headed westward, and climbing into the fork of a great tree he fashioned a rude platform and curled himself for sleep.

Three miles to the west slept the tribe of Kerchak.

Early the next morning the apes were astir, moving through the jungle in search of food. Tarzan, as was his custom, prosecuted his search in the direction of the cabin so that by leisurely hunting on the way his stomach was filled by the time he reached the beach.

The apes scattered by ones, and twos, and threes in all directions, but ever within sound of a signal of alarm.

Kala had moved slowly along an elephant track toward the east, and was busily engaged in turning over rotted limbs and logs in search of succulent bugs and fungi, when the faintest shadow of a strange noise brought her to startled attention.

For fifty yards before her the trail was straight, and down this leafy tunnel she saw the stealthy advancing figure of a strange and fearful creature.

It was Kulonga.

Kala did not wait to see more, but, turning, moved rapidly back along the trail. She did not run; but, after the manner of her kind when not aroused, sought rather to avoid than to escape.

Close after her came Kulonga. Here was meat. He could make a killing and feast well this day. On he hurried, his spear poised for the throw.

At a turning of the trail he came in sight of her again upon another straight stretch. His spear hand went far back the muscles rolled, lightning-like, beneath the sleek hide. Out shot the arm, and the spear sped toward Kala.

A poor cast. It but grazed her side.

With a cry of rage and pain the she-ape turned upon her tormentor. In an instant the trees were crashing beneath the weight of her hurrying fellows, swinging rapidly toward the scene of trouble in answer to Kala's scream.

As she charged, Kulonga unslung his bow and fitted an arrow with almost unthinkable quickness. Drawing the shaft far back he drove the poisoned missile straight into the heart of the great anthropoid.

With a horrid scream Kala plunged forward upon her face before the astonished members of her tribe.

Roaring and shrieking the apes dashed toward Kulonga, but that wary savage was fleeing down the trail like a frightened antelope.

He knew something of the ferocity of these wild, hairy men, and his one desire was to put as many miles between himself and them as he possibly could.

They followed him, racing through the trees, for a long distance, but finally one by one they abandoned the chase and returned to the scene of the tragedy.

None of them had ever seen a man before, other than Tarzan, and so they wondered vaguely what strange manner of creature it might be that had invaded their jungle.

On the far beach by the little cabin Tarzan heard the faint echoes of the conflict and knowing that something was seriously amiss among the tribe he hastened rapidly toward the direction of the sound.

When he arrived he found the entire tribe gathered jabbering about the dead body of his slain mother.

Tarzan's grief and anger were unbounded. He roared out his hideous challenge time and again. He beat upon his great chest with his clenched fists, and then he fell upon the body of Kala and sobbed out the pitiful sorrowing of his lonely heart.

To lose the only creature in all his world who ever had manifested love and affection of him was the greatest tragedy he had ever known.

What though Kala was a fierce and hideous ape! To Tarzan she had been kind, she had been beautiful.

Upon her he had lavished, unknown to himself, all the reverence and respect and love that a normal English boy feels for his own mother. He had never known another, and so to Kala was given, though mutely, all that would have belonged to the fair and lovely Lady Alice had she lived.

After the first outburst of grief Tarzan controlled himself, and questioning the members of the tribe who had witnessed the killing of Kala he learned all that their meager vocabulary could convey.

It was enough, however, for his needs. It told him of a strange, hairless, black ape with feathers growing upon its head, who launched death from a slender branch, and then ran, with the fleetness of Bara, the deer, toward the rising sun.

Tarzan waited no longer, but leaping into the branches of the trees sped rapidly through the forest. He knew the windings of the elephant trail along which Kala's murderer had flown, and so he cut straight through the jungle to intercept the black warrior who was evidently following the tortuous detours of the trail.

At his side was the hunting knife of his unknown sire, and across his shoulders the coils of his own long rope. In an hour he struck the trail again, and coming to earth examined the soil minutely.

In the soft mud on the bank of a tiny rivulet he found footprints such as he alone in all the jungle had ever made, but much larger than his. His heart beat fast. Could it be that he was trailing a MAN—one of his own race?

There were two sets of imprints pointing in opposite directions. So his quarry had already passed on his return along the trail. As he examined the newer spoor a tiny particle of earth toppled from the outer edge of one of the footprints to the bottom of its shallow depression—ah, the trail was very fresh, his prey must have but scarcely passed.

Tarzan swung himself to the trees once more, and with swift noiselessness sped along high above the trail.

He had covered barely a mile when he came upon the black warrior standing in a little open space. In his hand was his slender bow to which he had fitted one of his death dealing arrows.

Opposite him across the little clearing stood Horta, the boar, with lowered head and foam flecked tusks, ready to charge.

Tarzan looked with wonder upon the strange creature beneath him—so like him in form and yet so different in face and color. His books had portrayed the *Negro*, but how different had been the dull, dead print to this sleek thing of ebony, pulsing with life.

As the man stood there with taut drawn bow Tarzan recognized him not so much the *Negro* as the *Archer* of his picture book———

A stands for Archer

How wonderful! Tarzan almost betrayed his presence in the deep excitement of his discovery.

But things were commencing to happen below him. The sinewy black arm had drawn the shaft far back; Horta, the boar, was charging, and then the black released the little poisoned arrow, and Tarzan saw if fly with the quickness of thought and lodge in the bristling neck of the boar.

Scarcely had the shaft left his bow ere Kulonga had fitted another to it, but Horta, the boar, was upon him so quickly that he had no time to discharge it. With a bound the black leaped entirely over the rushing beast and turning with incredible swiftness planted a second arrow in Horta's back.

Then Kulonga sprang into a near-by tree.

Horta wheeled to charge his enemy once more; a dozen steps he took, then he staggered and fell upon his side. For a moment his muscles stiffened and relaxed convulsively, then he lay still.

Kulonga came down from his tree.

With a knife that hung at his side he cut several large pieces from the boar's body, and in the center of the trail he built a fire, cooking and eating as much as he wanted. The rest he left where it had fallen.

Tarzan was an interested spectator. His desire to kill burned fiercely in his wild breast, but his desire to learn was even greater. He would follow this savage creature for a while and know from whence he came. He could kill him at his leisure later, when the bow and deadly arrows were laid aside.

When Kulonga had finished his repast and disappeared beyond a near turning of the path, Tarzan dropped quietly to the ground. With his knife he severed many strips of meat from Horta's carcass, but he did not cook them.

He had seen fire, but only when Ara, the lightning, had destroyed some great tree. That any creature of the jungle could produce the red-and-yellow fangs which devoured wood and left nothing but fine dust surprised Tarzan greatly, and why the black warrior had ruined his delicious repast by plunging it into the blighting heat was quite beyond him. Possibly Ara was a friend with whom the Archer was sharing his food.

But, be that as it may, Tarzan would not ruin good meat in any such foolish manner, so he gobbled down a great quantity of the raw flesh, burying the balance of the carcass beside the trail where he could find it upon his return.

And then Lord Greystoke wiped his greasy fingers upon his naked thighs and took up the trail of Kulonga, the son of Mbonga, the king; while in far-off London another Lord Greystoke, the younger brother of the real Lord Greystoke's father, sent back his chops to the club's *chef* because they were underdone, and when he had finished his repast he dipped his finger-ends into a silver bowl of scented water and dried them upon a piece of snowy damask.

All day Tarzan followed Kulonga, hovering above him in the trees like some malign spirit. Twice more he saw him hurl his arrows of destruction—once at Dango, the hyena, and again at Manu, the monkey. In each instance the animal died almost instantly, for Kulonga's poison was very fresh and very deadly.

Tarzan thought much on this wondrous method of slaying as he swung slowly along at a safe distance behind his quarry. He knew that alone the tiny prick of the arrow could not so quickly dispatch these wild things of the jungle, who were often torn and scratched and gored in a frightful manner as they fought with their jungle neighbors, yet as often recovered as not.

No, there was something mysterious connected with these tiny slivers of wood which could bring death by a mere scratch. He must look into the matter.

That night Kulonga slept in the crotch of a mighty tree and far above him crouched Tarzan of the Apes.

When Kulonga awoke he found that his bow and arrows had disappeared. The black warrior was furious and frightened, but more frightened than furious. He searched the ground below the tree, and he searched the tree above the ground; but there was no sign of either bow or arrows or of the nocturnal marauder.

Kulonga was panic-stricken. His spear he had hurled at Kala and had not recovered; and, now that his bow and arrows were gone, he was defenseless except for a single knife. His only hope lay in reaching the village of Mbonga as quickly as his legs would carry him.

That he was not far from home he was certain, so he took the trail at a rapid trot.

From a great mass of impenetrable foliage a few yards away emerged Tarzan of the Apes to swing quietly in his wake.

Kulonga's bow and arrows were securely tied high in the top of a giant tree from which a patch of bark had been removed by a sharp knife near to the ground, and a branch half cut through and left hanging about fifty feet higher up. Thus Tarzan blazed the forest trails and marked his caches.

As Kulonga continued his journey Tarzan closed on him until he traveled almost over the black's head. His rope he now held coiled in his right hand; he was almost ready for the kill.

The moment was delayed only because Tarzan was anxious to ascertain the black warrior's destination, and presently he was rewarded, for they came suddenly in view of a great clearing, at one end of which lay many strange lairs.

Tarzan was directly over Kulonga, as he made the discovery. The forest ended abruptly and beyond lay two hundred yards of planted fields between the jungle and the village.

Tarzan must act quickly or his prey would be gone; but Tarzan's life training left so little space between decision and action when an emergency confronted him that there was not even room for the shadow of a thought between.

So it was that as Kulonga emerged from the shadow of the jungle a slender coil of rope sped sinuously above him from the lowest branch of a mighty tree directly upon the edge of the fields of Mbonga, and ere the king's son had taken a half dozen steps into the clearing a quick noose tightened about his neck.

So quickly did Tarzan of the Apes drag back his prey that Kulonga's cry of alarm was throttled in his windpipe. Hand over hand Tarzan drew the struggling black until he had him hanging by his neck in mid-air; then Tarzan climbed to a larger branch drawing the still threshing victim well up into the sheltering verdure of the tree.

Here he fastened the rope securely to a stout branch, and then, descending, plunged his hunting knife into Kulonga's heart. Kala was avenged.

Tarzan examined the black minutely, for he had never seen any other human being. The knife with its sheath and belt caught his eye; he appropriated them. A copper anklet also took his fancy, and this he transferred to his own leg.

He examined and admired the tattooing on the forehead and breast. He marveled at the sharp filed teeth. He investigated and appropriated the feathered headdress, and then he prepared to get down to business, for Tarzan of the Apes was hungry, and here was meat; meat of the kill, which jungle ethics permitted him to eat.

How may we judge him, by what standards, this ape-man with the heart and head and body of an English gentleman, and the training of a wild beast?

Tublat, whom he had hated and who had hated him, he had killed in a fair fight, and yet never had the thought of eating Tublat's flesh entered his head. It could have been as revolting to him as is cannibalism to us.

But who was Kulonga that he might not be eaten as fairly as Horta, the boar, or Bara, the deer? Was he not simply another of the countless wild things of the jungle who preyed upon one another to satisfy the cravings of hunger?

Suddenly, a strange doubt stayed his hand. Had not his books taught him that he was a man? And was not The Archer a man, also?

Did men eat men? Alas, he did not know. Why, then, this hesitancy! Once more he essayed the effort, but a qualm of nausea overwhelmed him. He did not understand.

All he knew was that he could not eat the flesh of this black man, and thus hereditary instinct, ages old, usurped the functions of his untaught mind and saved him from transgressing a worldwide law of whose very existence he was ignorant.

Quickly he lowered Kulonga's body to the ground, removed the noose, and took to the trees again.

The Cover of the September 10, 1912, Issue of *The All-Story* magazine, in which *Tarzan of the Apes* first appeared.

CHAPTER 6

Progressivism:
The Age of Reform

Historian Richard Hofstadter gave us the theme for this chapter in 1955 when he published his conclusions about populism and progressivism in a book titled *The Age of Reform*. Forty years later, it is not at all clear what this phenomenon called "progressivism" was, or whether its agents, the "progressives," were really very progressive. Hofstadter in fact argued that at the heart of progressivism was a vision of the past, an attempt to restore economic individualism and political democracy, values that had been buried under giant corporations, burgeoning unions, and currupt political bosses. With the exception of Theodore Roosevelt, who believed that most big business could not and should not be eliminated, progressives, according to Hofstadter, generally tried to disassemble existing institutions. The progressive movement, he wrote, was "the complaint of the unorganized against the consequences of organization."

Others have argued that progressivism was not nostalgic but aggressively future-oriented. According to this view, progressivism cannot be separated from the "organizational revolution" taking place at the turn of the century. Products of that revolution include trade associations, new government agencies, the organized professions, and an increased willingness to use federal rather than state and local agencies to achieve economic and social goals. But there are real problems even in placing specific movements within this organizational context. Did new government regulations represent the past or the future? Were they designed to bring change or to preserve the status quo?

The most recent effort to understand progressivism emphasizes the prominence of women in setting the progressive agenda and in the legislative process. This view foregrounds the creation of the U.S. Children's Bureau in 1912 (the first government agency run by women), the passage of mothers' pension laws in most states, and the Sheppard-Towner Act of 1921 (money for health-care clinics and to reduce infant mortality). At bottom, this women's perspective holds that the foundations of the American welfare state were poured not by male-dominated political parties but by women—most of them still without the right to vote—organized in a variety of voluntary associations.

The title of Hofstadter's study implies the ability to recognize a reform when we see one, and much of the history of the progressive period has been written from this assumption. But here, too, there are difficulties. When Theodore Roosevelt broke with the Republican party in 1912 and campaigned for the presidency under the banner of the Progressive party (not to be confused with the more general term "progressivism"), his Bull Moose platform was a classic summary of social reforms long identified with progressivism—minimum wages for women, prohibition of child labor, the eight-hour workday, and workmen's compensation. For years, however, Roosevelt had been involved with birth-control advocate Margaret Sanger and with Stanford University president David Starr Jordan and other luminaries in another "reform" effort, the eugenics movement, which many progressives found unappealing. In a letter written in 1914, Roosevelt described and explained his interest in eugenics:

> I wish very much that the wrong people could be prevented entirely from breeding; and when the evil nature of these people is sufficiently flagrant, this should be done. Criminals should be sterilized and feeble-minded persons forbidden to leave offspring behind them. But as yet there is no way possible to devise a system which could prevent all undesirable persons from breeding.

For Roosevelt, eugenics deserved the label "reform" every bit as much as the movement to abolish child labor. Others, including historians, have disagreed, and therein lies a central problem with the word "reform."

Nor is the difficulty resolved simply by focusing on what seem to be clearly benign reforms. One of the most popular progressive-period programs was state workmen's compensation legislation, under which injured workers were compensated according to predetermined schedules, rather than by virtue of what they could recover through legal action. By what standards is workmen's compensation "reform"? Is it an example of progressivism? Feminists of the 1970s and 1980s would raise similar, and worthwhile, questions about the many progressive-era laws that regulated hours and conditions for working women. In 1910 those laws seemed to be important measures of protection; today they seem to be obstacles to equality of the sexes. Were those laws, even in 1910, a clear example of social progress?

Still, certain features of progressivism stand out. One need only mention the major regulatory measures of the period to grasp the importance of regulation (a word, it should be emphasized, with no more real content than *reform*). Out of a financial panic in 1907 came the Federal Reserve System, created in 1913 to provide a more flexible currency. Several pieces of railroad legislation, including the Elkins Act (1903) and the Hepburn Act (1906), were designed to limit rebates (unfair price cutting by the carriers) and to give the Interstate Commerce Commission, then two decades old, the authority to fix maximum rates. Congress also provided for federal inspection of meat packers that shipped in interstate commerce and created the Federal Trade Commission (1914) to supervise the competitive relations of interstate businesses. State and local governments were also active in the regulatory movement and were the major agencies of change in such social-justice areas as hours of labor, child labor, mothers pensions, and tenement-house reform. The progressive period is also well known for a series of measures designed to change the terms of access to the political system: the direct election of United States senators, direct primaries for the nomination of elective officials, initiative, referendum, and recall.

Aside from the dramatic rise in the use of government as a social tool, the qualities that gave unity to progressivism were attitudinal and ideological. Progressives believed in data. They believed in the possibilities of "scientific" social welfare, supported by research; of market research in selling, and of measuring the abilities of employees through psychological testing. This faith in science was often accompanied by a fear of national moral collapse. It was this kind of thinking that led to the founding of the Boy Scouts of America in 1910 and to Roosevelt's enchantment with eugenics.

Finally, progressivism was not, at least on the surface, a matter of class interests, of one group seeking hegemony over another. For progressives, the political system was not a device by which conflicting interests compromised (or failed to compromise) their essential differences; it was a means through which the essential harmony of all interests might be expressed. Perhaps because of this emphasis on harmony, the declaration of war in April 1917 ushered in a brief period in which the progressive spirit of reform was reincarnated as a struggle against German autocracy. Led by Woodrow Wilson, Americans came to understand the war as a holy crusade, a great struggle, as Wilson put it, to "make the world safe for democracy."

INTERPRETIVE ESSAY

Mark H. Leff

Consensus for Reform:
The Mothers'-Pension Movement
in the Progressive Era

Between 1911 and 1920, forty states passed mothers' pension laws. These laws provided money to mothers for the support of children in cases where fathers were dead or absent. Except for military pensions for Civil War veterans and local efforts to relieve poverty, mothers' pensions were arguably the nation's first publicly funded benefits.

Mark Leff's account of the mothers'-pension movement offers a way into the complex social currents of the progressive era, as well as a means of evaluating the most recent interpretation of progressivism, with its emphasis on the role of women (see the introduction to this chapter). Who supported mothers' pensions laws? Who opposed them? And why? Taken as a whole, was the mothers'-pension movement socially progressive, or socially conservative, or both? If women were central to the movement, how could they have accomplished so much at a time when most women still lacked the franchise?

Just as important, the mothers'-pension movement of the progressive era can shed light on our own age. The mothers' pensions of the 1910s would become Aid to Families with Dependent Children (AFDC)—that is, "welfare"— a program that by the 1980s had become symbolic of the failure of the welfare state. Conservative critic George Gilder argued in 1981 that AFDC encouraged the poor to choose leisure over hard work while damaging the institutions of marriage and family. Were these concerns or similar ones apparent in the progressive era? Should the advocates of mothers' pensions have been more cautious? Was there a reasonable alternative to mothers' pensions?

Scoring its first statewide victory in Illinois in 1911, the mothers'-pension movement swept forty states in less than a decade. No plank of the social-justice platform, with the possible exception of workmen's compensation, mustered a better legislative record. Drawing upon historic American concerns with children, widows, and the home, mothers' pensions incorporated the major strains of progressivism. Moral reformers and economic-efficiency buffs, women's clubs and labor unions, middle-class do-gooders and relief recipients, New Freedom advocates and New Nationalism partisans, all jumped onto the bandwagon. Their clash with unconvinced charity workers and half-dormant conservatives was a mismatch.

Mark H. Leff, "Consensus for Reform: The Mothers'-Pension Movement in the Progressive Era," *Social Service Review*, vol. 47, September 1973, pp. 397–415. © 1973 The University of Chicago Press. Used with the permission of the University of Chicago Press.

The startlingly narrow scope of this consensus highlights the economic and social limitations of early twentieth-century reform. Mothers' pensions (also called widows' pensions or mothers' aid) were paltry long-term cash provisions for children without employable fathers, contingent upon their mothers' acceptance of middle-class behavioral norms. The program thus promised to be cheap and morally uplifting, while raising no specter of dissolute male misfits lining up for their monthly liquor money.

In 1935, the aid-to-dependent-children provisions of the Social Security Act tendered federal guidelines and financial support to state mothers'-aid agencies. This program has earned as great a consensus in its opposition as had formerly been secured in its favor. Yet popular principles regarding welfare have changed little; they still encompass reliance upon local administration, the rejection of a right to public aid, and the imposition of "suitable home" criteria. Today's "welfare mess" is, in no small part, a product of yesterday's welfare maxims.

THE DEVELOPMENT OF MOTHERS' PENSIONS

The case for mothers' pensions was airtight in terms of contemporary concerns. Seeing in children "infinite possibilities for good," progressives believed that "in the child and in our treatment of him rests the solution of the problems which confront the State and society today." But interest in children was not unique to progressivism. In the 1860s and 1870s, sympathy for war orphans, supplemented by a belief in the value of differential treatment of children and adults, had resulted in state campaigns to remove orphans and other children from almshouses and to place them in institutions. By the turn of the century, dissatisfaction with the "products" of orphanages, combined with objections to institutional regimentation, artificiality, and inability to dispense individual care, elicited substantial popular opposition. "Even a very poor home," it was said, "offers a better chance for [a child's] development than an excellent institution." By 1909, children's-home societies in twenty-eight states furthered the foster-home movement.

The widow, too, was an object of public sympathy. She could scarcely be held accountable for the death of her husband; yet the disintegration of the extended family in urban America often left her with pitifully little to fall back on. While it was expected that married women would not be gainfully employed (only 5–10 percent of them were), almost one-third of all widows found it necessary to hold jobs. It became a cliché to warn that "to be the breadwinner and the home-maker of the family is more than the average woman can bear." The results, it was said, were that "the home crumbles" and that "the physical and moral well-being of the mother and the children is impaired and seriously menaced." Aid to prevent this disintegration was distinguished from other relief because it buttressed traditional family roles: "Women and children ought to be supported, and there is no sense of degradation in receiving support."

The role of government in public relief aroused more controversy. Late in the nineteenth century, social workers and private charities challenged public outdoor-relief programs, and succeeded in abolishing or curtailing them in most major cities. Yet, by 1900, new state laws regulating private children's institutions reasserted the government position. Boards of public welfare were established in a number of midwestern cities, beginning in Kansas City in 1908 and reaching Chicago soon thereafter. Their proponents asserted that relief was a public responsibility rather than a private service, that relief needs had grown too large to be met by private resources, and that public agencies could apply the lessons of efficiency and scientific philanthropy as competently as private ones.

Many private agencies thus came to fear a pre-emption by government. Realizing that their failure to preserve the home was the chink in their armor, they established nurseries, along with job-placement services for widows. However, they still encouraged many widows to send some of their children to orphanages in order to provide adequate family support. A few charity institutions (particularly Jewish ones) disregarded the admonitions of scientific philanthropy that assured relief would be pauperizing, and began to give regular monetary aid to widows. Other organizations pointed out that regular private charity showed little commitment to meeting this need, and focused their efforts on widows' pensions alone.

Around the turn of the century, public aid for dependent children in their own homes had been proposed as an alternative to public outdoor relief and private charity. In 1898, the New York legislature passed a bill granting widowed mothers in New York City an allowance equal to the state expenditure for institutionalizing their children. However, the mayor of New York City, pressured by the interests of private charity, convinced the governor not to sign the bill. . . .

Probably the greatest spur to the subsequent passage of mothers'-pension laws was the 1909 Conference on the Care of Dependent Children. President Roosevelt opened the conference by discussing the plight of the widow unable to support her children. "Surely in such a case," he urged, "the goal toward which we should strive is to help that mother, so that she can keep her own home and keep the child in it; that is the best thing possible to be done for that child. How the relief shall come, public, private, or by a mixture of both, in what way, you are competent to say and I am not." In the debate that followed, several members called for public mothers' pensions. In rebuttal, a vocal minority desperately defended children's institutions. The fourteen conference resolutions, which reflected the most advanced ideas on child welfare of the time, laid the foundation for several future reforms. The creation of the Children's Bureau, for example, was one result of this conference. But the resolution relating to mothers' pensions attracted the most attention:

> Home life is the highest and finest product of civilization. It is the great molding force of mind and of character. Children should not be deprived of it except for urgent and compelling reasons. Children of parents of worthy character, suffering from temporary misfortune and children of reasonably efficient and deserving mothers who are without their parents, such aid being given as may be

necessary to maintain suitable homes for the rearing of the children. This aid should be given by such methods and from such sources as may be determined by the general relief policy of each community, preferably in the form of private charity, rather than of public relief. Except in unusual circumstances, the home should not be broken up for reasons of poverty, but only for considerations of inefficiency or immorality.

This resolution, though expressing a preference for privately funded mothers' pensions, catalyzed the drive for public legislation. Soon a stream of people declared their advocacy of pensions for mothers. With the passage of the first mothers'-pension laws, this stream became a flood.

The legislative breakthrough came with the passage of two mothers'-pension provisions in 1911. Missouri's statute, confined to Kansas City, was sponsored by Judge E. E. Porterfield of the Jackson County (Kansas City) juvenile court. The statewide law in Illinois benefited from lobbying efforts by the Chicago-based National Probation League (a recently formed organization primarily geared toward probation as an alternative to prison or reformatories for child and adult offenders); it also drew support from Judge Merritt Pinckney of the Cook County juvenile court, whose participation in the 1909 conference had reinforced his interest in mothers' pensions. As judges, both men had found it distasteful to separate children from their unsupported mothers on grounds of poverty, and they believed that many delinquent children became "bad" because their working mothers could not care for them.

Although 1912 was an off year for most state legislatures, momentum gathered in a Colorado referendum victory led by Denver juvenile court judge Ben Lindsey, and in several municipal and county ordinances adopting mothers' pensions. In 1913, the floodgates burst. Of the forty-two state legislatures in session, twenty-seven considered mothers'-pension legislation and seventeen passed it. Twenty states, sixteen of them in the west or midwest, had now enacted mothers'-pension laws. By 1915, the number had grown to twenty-nine; in 1919 it reached thirty-nine, plus Alaska and Hawaii. By this point, the mothers'-pension movement ceased to be a national concern. The next fifteen years were a mopping-up operation that gathered in the two remaining western and New England states, the District of Columbia, and five of the seven remaining southern states.

This "wildfire spread of widows' pensions," many commentators contended, exceeded that of any other social or humanitarian idea of their era. Mothers'-pension provisions usually carried by near-unanimous tallies; opposition successes depended on preventing the bills from coming to a vote. Referendums, too, proving no contest, won by majorities of more than two to one in both Colorado and Arizona.

The enactments resulting from this popular upsurge exhibited broad similarities. Funding and administration of the laws was locally based. Administrative duties usually fell to juvenile courts, a recent progressive attainment. Their existing bureaucracy and responsibility for dependent children, along with their dissociation from both outdoor relief and private charity, made them a natural choice for this function. Almost every statute established a maximum allowable monthly pension, which ranged from nine to fifteen dollars a month for the first child and four to ten dollars a month for additional children. To be eligible to receive this pension, a mother had to be "a proper person, physically, mentally and morally fit to bring up her children." Pensions could usually be granted only for children under the age of fourteen or sixteen. The state-residency requirement was one to three years; two states required the mother to be a United States citizen. Most states did not restrict eligible recipients to widows alone; pensions were occasionally authorized for women whose husbands had deserted them, were confined to mental hospitals or prisons, or were physically or mentally incapacitated. Only Michigan specifically included unmarried or divorced mothers, though several laws were general enough to include fathers. Rarely, however, were such opportunities exploited, since they were usually the result of legislative imprecision or fear that the law would otherwise be declared unconstitutional. All states required proof of extreme poverty, along with an agreement to cease or limit employment upon receipt of a pension.

But the rudimentary measures instituted between 1911 and 1919 had already forged one of the major contributions of the social-justice movement to the New Deal's formulation of the welfare state.

THE FORMATION OF THE CONSENSUS

The alignment of forces contesting mothers'-pension proposals was unique in the history of American reform. Even persistent conservative foes of social-justice legislation muted their criticism. In their stead, the vanguard of the social-justice movement itself rose in opposition to mothers' pensions. Swept aside by a movement that had advanced beyond their original reform intentions, a phalanx of prominent charity workers turned against many of their colleagues and most of their disciples.

Charity-worker opposition to widows'-pension legislation emanated from the perceived threat to the agencies that employed them and to their cult of scientific philanthropy. Only in the 1920s did mothers' pensions gain widespread social work support. By that time, as administrators, social workers had molded the program to suit their casework approach.

The social service profession polarized over what has been called "the well-nigh universal disagreement between settlements and organized charity on the question of widows' pension." Nowhere was this better illustrated than in New York City, where every major private charity in the state opposed the 1913 widows'-pension bill, while the Association of Neighborhood Workers, which represented the settlement houses of New York City, publicly favored it. Settlements had always been more prone than private charities to attribute individual problems to social ills and to seek government aid to make necessary economic and environmental changes. . . .

Most leading charity workers felt keenly threatened by the attack upon private philanthropy's hegemony. "Who are these sudden heroes of a brand new program of state subsidies to mothers?" asked Edward T. Devine, general secretary of the New York Charity Organization Society and the most vocal antagonist of mothers' pensions. "Who are these brash reformers who so cheerfully impugn the motives of old-fashioned givers, of the conscientious directors of charitable institutions, of pious founders of hospitals and all manner of benefactions?" Opposition to widows' pensions permeated almost every private charity agency and orphanage in the country. . . .

In their assault upon mothers' pensions, charity workers used two main lines of argument: a defense of orphanages and private charity and a restatement of the truths of scientific philanthropy. Especially in the debates on mothers' pensions in the 1909 conference, social workers such as Edward Devine and directors of children's institutions had acclaimed the benefits of institutional care for even nondelinquent children whose parents supported them but were not a "pure, moral influence." This argument had little currency in later mothers'-pension debates. But numerous social workers defended private charity throughout this period, contending that few children were separated from their parents on grounds of poverty alone ("inefficiency" of the mother, for example, might be the justification), and that private charity could finance wider private widows'-pension programs if they did not have to compete against government (one problem, though not stated explicitly, was that impoverished widows and children were good drawing cards for funds).

The philosophy of scientific philanthropy underpinned the case against public grants for dependent children. Opposition was particularly fierce in cities that had succumbed to intense private-charity pressure to dismantle their public outdoor-relief systems. The widow's plight had served as a justification for the maintenance of government relief; the re-emergence of this image thus presented a special threat. Defending their hard-won position, charity workers depicted mothers' pensions as "a step backward, a reversal of policy." Government was deemed incapable of learning the lessons of scientific philanthropy: it would be subject to corruption and political interference; it would fail to realize the importance of attracting competent trained administrators; and it would not provide adequate supervision. Combined with the subversive and fiercely assailed belief that certain forms of regular relief were a right, the result would be "pauperization," a "pathological parasitism" that would "inevitably create a new class of dependents." It was a scandalous mistake to give recipients cash rather than certain basic necessities; with pensions averaging twenty-three dollars a month for some families, "temptations come to spend money recklessly or foolishly." Moreover, mothers' pensions were "an insidious attack upon the family, inimical to the welfare of children and injurious to the character of parents." Not only did pensions encourage desertion in those few states that granted them to deserted families, but they failed to invoke the "great principle of family solidarity, calling upon the strong members of the family to support the weak." . . .

Unlike much social legislation, mothers'-pension programs were neither expensive nor disruptive to productive efficiency. They thus posed no threat to wealthy conservatives, who were disinclined anyway to exert their political muscle on the wrong side of motherhood. The infrequent public attacks trod fa-

miliar ground. Widows'-pension expenditures, it was predicted, would irre-
pressibly soar. Poor widows from other countries or other states would descend
upon states with new laws to make a quick pittance. The greatest danger, of
course, was socialism. It was warned that the guiding philosophy of mothers'
pensions was "not alms, but their right to share"—a principle that "represses
the desire for self-help, self-respect, and independence," and leads to old-age
pensions, free food for the unemployed, and state socialism. But such objections
seldom surfaced. Some conservative newspapers led campaigns against such
laws, but, except for the referendum fight in Colorado, these too seem to have
been rare. Even the large number of juvenile-court judges who opposed aid to
dependent children chose the strategy of nonenforcement in preference to public disputes with their reformist colleagues.

Support for mothers' pensions was neither so limited nor so reticent. Approval was widespread despite the polycentricity of the mothers'-pension
movement, which had no national coordinating committee or national leader.

Juvenile-court judges had initially spearheaded widows'-pension drives.
They had been pivotal in the passage of the first three state mothers'-pension
laws, and they were important advocates of later dependent-children provisions in New York, Wisconsin, and California. But the role of these judges in legislative campaigns waned as the growing strength of the movement was catalyzed by the first few state laws.

Progressive politicians played a less readily definable role. Many consider
the years from 1911 to 1915 to be the pinnacle or culmination of progressivism.
Especially in those western and midwestern states that proved the most fertile
ground for widows' pensions, this legislation was frequently accompanied by
statutes on child labor, working conditions and minimum wages for women
and children, or workmen's compensation, which drew more upon a concern
for women and children than is now generally realized. Mothers' pensions
dovetailed neatly with other reformist drives: they compensated certain families inadequately protected by accident-insurance laws, and they made child-
labor restriction and compulsory education less onerous to families of widowed
mothers.

Yet mothers' pensions were not a central political concern. The belief that
public aid and other social services were a local responsibility rendered them
a dead issue on the national level. Before the 1930s, the scattered mothers'-
pension bills proposed in Congress (starting in 1914) received little consideration, while aid-to-dependent-children planks emerged in the national platforms
of only two minor parties. Despite the widespread Progressive support for
mothers' pensions, which transcended party boundaries, this program rarely
even merited mention in the party platforms of states that enacted such laws.

Progressive newspapers and magazines participated . . . actively in the
mothers'-pension movement. Beginning in 1907 with the arrival of Theodore
Dreiser as its editor, the *Delineator*, a crusading mass-circulation women's fashion magazine, had championed foster homes as an alternative to institutional
care for dependent children. By 1912, the *Delineator* became a forceful advocate
for mothers' pensions and even sent a lecturer around the country to promote

this cause. Also active was Sophie Loeb, a thirty-seven-year-old staff reporter for the *New York Evening World*, a Democratic paper with strong ties to the Wilson administration. Loeb launched a personal crusade, through her columns and through lobbying efforts, to secure a New York child welfare law. To her belongs much of the credit for both the appointment of the previously mentioned New York mothers'-pension commission and the 1915 passage of the mothers'-pension law . . . [mothers'-pension] . . . legislation found acceptance throughout the spectrum of progressive magazines; it received endorsement from such journals as *Outlook, Nation,* and *Public.*

Labor also gave some encouragement to mothers'-pension laws. In the early 1900s, the concept of widows' pensions had been associated, rightly or wrongly, with labor interests. In 1911, the American Federation of Labor endorsed a federal mothers'-pension resolution. However, only in the middle 1920s, when it supported a mothers'-aid bill for the District of Columbia, did the AFL Executive Council play an active role in promoting mothers'-pension legislation.

Labor's slighting of mothers' pensions was more a matter of priority than of neutrality. Certain state federations of labor testified in favor of proposed mothers'-pension statutes, and a number of supporters of these laws (such as Secretary of Labor Wilson and the Socialist party) could be classified as sympathetic to labor. Other social-justice legislation, such as workmen's compensation and child labor, was of greater importance to labor, but mothers' pensions did not pass unnoticed.

Social-insurance advocates who were not charity workers were also likely to favor mothers' pensions. By asserting a public responsibility that entailed an enlarged government-welfare role, and by picturing private charity as an inadequate and improper repository for this function, the mothers'-pension movement borrowed and reinforced two of the main pillars of the case for social insurance. Thus, a number of social-insurance proponents, such as Ben Lindsey and Isaac Rubinow, held that these pensions would "prove at least a good entering wedge for those special and industrial-insurance laws that must come in time as the public is educated to their necessity." . . .

Women made up the principal component of the mothers'-pension movement. Around the turn of the century, women's organizations began to flourish under leadership that helped to direct the latent energies of middle-class women into reform channels. The politicization of the woman's role built upon society's concession of feminine expertise on child welfare matters; women were thus ritualistically appointed to mothers'-pension commissions, and occasional statutes even required their appointment as administrators.

Although the more militant wing of the suffrage movement feared that mothers' pensions might damage the cause of sexual equality by glorifying the woman's place at home, supporters of women's suffrage generally favored mothers' pensions. Moreover, the legislatures that most easily and quickly approved mother's pensions were usually those actively considering women's suffrage or chosen by a sexually unrestricted electorate. After women were enfranchised in Oregon in 1912 (a widow's-pension law was passed the next year), the *Portland Oregonian* pointed out that "neither Senators nor Representatives

are opposing any measures which will tend to be of assistance to the women."
In other states, too, the achievement of the franchise gave impetus to the enactment of new statutes on schools, public morality, women's working conditions,
and child welfare. The second decade of the twentieth century may have
marked the height of political influence for women. Legislators, apprehensive
of the female vote, did what they could to mollify suffrage advocates and to mitigate the threatened wrath of newly enfranchised women. But as they learned
in the 1920s that the only thing they had to fear was fear itself, the influence of
women's pressure groups declined accordingly.

The two main women's organizations, the General Federation of Women's
Clubs (whose membership may have exceeded 1 million) and the National Congress of Mothers and Parent-Teachers Associations (which had recently initiated
the PTA movement and later was subsumed under it), lent considerable support
to mothers'-pension drives. These organizations attracted principally middle-
aged, middle-class, poorly educated married women. These women sensed a
waning influence in an emerging industrial system that created a new social hierarchy, new social conditions, and altered values. Their reaction, spurred by increased leisure and Victorian role consciousness, was to impose upon that system the values of home, family, and moral purity that women had long been
charged with defending. The same group of resolutions that endorsed mothers'
pensions was also likely to condemn comic pages, cigarettes, intemperance, and
"the extravagant dress now in vogue among school girls," or to urge motion-
picture censorship, an alliance between the church and the schools, and tougher
divorce laws. . . .

Several other women's organizations also actively sought mothers'-pension
legislation. The National Consumers' League (a more militant group, whose
predominantly female membership tended to be younger, less likely to be married, better educated, and of a higher social station than other women's groups)
and its secretary, Florence Kelley, worked in favor of mothers'-pension laws and
other legislation oriented toward women and children. Members of the
Women's Suffrage League of Virginia were largely responsible for the passage
and later funding of a widows'-pension law in that state. In Tennessee, the
Women's Christian Temperance Union joined forces with women's clubs and
PTAs to push through the 1915 statute. Special "Mothers' Pensions Leagues,"
such as one formed by a "group of young women" in Allegheny County, Pennsylvania, cropped up in several states. Promotion of mothers' pensions was indeed women's work, and upon that work rested much of the success of this reform. . . .

Finally, the most intriguing supporter of this legislation was Henry Neil, the
self-styled and widely proclaimed "father of the mothers'-pension system."
Judge Neil, as he called himself (he was a former teacher and author who had
served as a justice of the peace), gained public exposure through the interviews
he arranged with various newspapers, which dutifully declared his paternity to
their readers. Available evidence fails to substantiate this reputation. Yet Neil, as
secretary of the National Probation League, organized mothers'-pension
leagues and apparently helped draft several state mothers'-pension provisions.

He also garnered support from a number of northern newspapers and legislators, and provided information to those interested in existing laws. . . .

. . . No individual or group of individuals was vital to the mothers'-pension movement. The consensus that it created depended largely on the ease with which it meshed with developing American attitudes. By adopting the name "widows' pensions," it even exploited the public support given to pensions for families of war veterans.

The most frequent argument of mothers'-pension advocates (especially women's groups and women's magazines), and the one that best demonstrates the moral base of this reform, was an indictment of orphanages and a corresponding sanctification of "a mother's love" and of the home. Spokesmen often bolstered their pleas for mothers' pensions with portrayals of juvenile-courtroom scenes, with "children clinging to a mother's skirts or sobbing in the mother's arms" as she unwillingly relinquished them to an orphanage in order to support them. Pension proponents depicted institutions as factories for "human machines" in which the "good innocent child" was "obliged to associate with undesirable children," and in which some children died or were mentally debilitated for lack of the "most sacred thing in human life—a mother's love." "Only in the home, and from his own mother," it was asserted, could a child "receive the love and personal care necessary to his complete development." In effect, the state was designated the promoter of the woman's hallowed position as rearer of her children. . . .

If any argument underlay the thrust of the mothers'-pension campaign, it was that private charity was neither an adequate nor an appropriate substitute for certain governmental welfare functions. Mothers'-pension crusaders avowed that "poverty is too big a problem for private philanthropy," or that 'private charity, in this particular matter of the widowed mother, is today a failure." . . .

Mothers'-pensions proponents also rebuked private philanthropy through their distinction between charity and the "right" to a mothers' pension. They insisted that the paternalism and opprobrium attached to charity must not be carried over to the pension. Some contended that, since society itself bore partial responsibility for the husband's death (either because he had been unable to earn sufficient wages or because his death was due to preventable disease or accident—a likely possibility for a man who was young enough to leave school-age children), society should alleviate the widow's poverty. Almost all their proponents depicted mother's pensions as payment for a service rather than as a dole. A mother caring for her children, they said, made a greater contribution to society than if she engaged in some other employment. The widows'-pension recipient, then, could be compared with a civil servant: "He is paid for his work; she for hers. And she should be paid by those for whom she does it—all the citizens of the state, not the subscribers to the charities." This view constituted a novel attitude toward American welfare recipients; a request for aid no longer constituted evidence of inefficiency or moral turpitude.

This assertion of a state responsibility involved a quantum jump in the line dividing the roles of public and private welfare agencies. As the restriction circumscribing governmental action came into question, so did the axiom of scientific philanthropy that private relief would necessarily be better administered than public relief. Private charity was never to recoup the premier position that it had held in the beginning of the twentieth century. . . .

As much as mothers'-pension proponents tried to differentiate their concept of supervision from that of private charity, their distinctions did not ring true. Their investigators, they asserted, would not be the "meddlesome," "policing," "I-am-responsible-for-your-general-development-as-a-human-being" type. Instead they would offer "only kindness, help, advice." They would be "family friends" who would "educate the mothers more and supervise them less." Perhaps, William Hard even suggested, this sort of compulsory "institution" might be good for all mothers. . . . [I]nvestigators were anything but unmeddlesome good friends. A number of jurisdictions (usually the ones that supplied either no grants or very meager ones) applied no supervision at all, but some mothers'-pension agencies vigorously injected themselves into the lives of their "pensioners." Use of tobacco and lack of church attendance were evidence of being an "unfit" mother. Families were forced to move from "neighborhoods whose morality was questionable." Investigators "visited" to enforce home cleanliness and rules against male boarders. The eviction of incapacitated husbands could be ordered if they were deemed "a menace to the physical and moral welfare of the mother or children." Mothers were obliged to prepare monthly budgets showing how they spent their pensions and met such requirements as "nourishment, no extras," or "warm clothes, not fancy." The Massachusetts Board of Charity was quite forthright in its statement of objectives: "The public authorities can make adequate relief a powerful lever to lift and keep mothers to a high standard of home care." More revealing, though less abrasive, is the observation of the chief probation officer of the Cook County Juvenile Court: "For the children of mothers with right motives and willingness to accept and follow kindly and intelligent advice, the system has been of great benefit."

Mothers'-pension advocates forecast a range of gains in social stability or morality. By protecting the home "against any theories of collectivism" and by showing government's concern with evident social needs, this legislation would serve as a bulwark against radicalism. Since "neglected children almost invariably become delinquent children," and since neglect was linked to the necessity for the mother to work and the "dangerously low standard of living" of the family, widows' pensions were touted as an anticrime measure. Pensions would also mitigate the poverty that drove dependent mothers and daughters to prostitution. Child labor would be reduced, for the mother would not need the earnings of her children to support the family. A similar argument applied to school attendance, especially since "the absence from home of wage-earning mothers contributes largely towards truancy."

Thus, widows' pensions were "a plain business proposition . . . to the end that [the children] become intelligent, industrious and respectable citizens and add to the industrial prosperity of the community." Implicit was an assumption that financial support would foster a value scheme that would transform poor children into upstanding men and women. But most mothers'-pension adherents were not averse to framing this expectation of family rehabilitation as a demand.

THE LEGACY OF THE
MOTHERS'-PENSION MOVEMENT

The legacy of the mothers'-pension movement meets neither past hopes nor present concerns. Especially in the early years of the law, most counties refused to enforce it, claiming that within their boundaries there were no cases to which it was applicable or that poor-relief authorities could do a better job. At no point before the enactment of the Social Security Act did more than half the counties in the United States provide mothers' pensions. There were also regional and urban-rural disparities. Per capita mothers'-pension expenditures in 1930 ranged from three cents in Louisiana to eighty-two cents in New York. Coverage was weighted heavily toward northern industrial states and against southern agrarian states (a pattern that survives today). Within states, cities made far greater per capital expenditures than rural areas.

Nothing receded like the mothers'-pension movement after its legislative success. Like most progressive reformers, mothers'-pension advocates proved more vigilant in promoting passage of the law than in monitoring its administration and assuring its adequate financial support. Pensions never reached a sufficient level for families to support themselves without resorting to supplementary public or private aid. Less than one-third of all eligible families, the Children's Bureau estimated in 1931, received any pension at all. Widows were favored over other categories of dependent mothers; they received over four-fifths of the aid. Blacks particularly faced discrimination; they received only 3 percent of the total pensions, with a number of counties and some southern states barring them totally from their programs. With the exception of this question of racial bias (which aroused little interest among supporters of aid to dependent children), these practices did not square with the rhetoric of the mothers'-pension campaign.

This rhetoric did, however, condone other shortcomings. Strictures against aiding families with unemployed but able-bodied fathers excluded some of the most impoverished families. Paradoxically, this restriction may also have caused some increase in desertion, thereby damaging the middle-class family structure that mothers'-pension advocates were intent on promoting. Mothers'-pension proponents were also sparing in employing their insight that home life suffered from the lack of an assured adequate income. Instead, they permitted, and sometimes encouraged, the imposition of the same behavioral demands that had characterized the private charity system that they maligned. These demands vitiated their concept of mothers' aid as a right, and stymied their attempt to remove stigma from the pension. Aid to dependent children became the government program most associated with official harassment and suspicion.

Yet the impact of mothers'-pension legislation had a large positive component. The past practice of juvenile court-martials, with poverty as the charge and family separation as the sentence, was abandoned. On the eve of the Social Security Act, the number of children aided by mothers' pensions rivaled the total in foster homes and orphanages combined. The widows'-pension program had burgeoned impressively, far faster than almost any other type of government expenditure. In 1931, the appropriation for mothers' pensions exceeded $33 million, distributed among more than 90,000 families with over 250,000 dependent children. Despite a budgetary crisis severe enough to cut back or to terminate a number of mothers'-pension programs during the Great Depression, mothers'-aid families were "the aristocrats of our relief population." For all their flaws, mothers'-pension programs made appreciable inroads into the poverty of a significant number of people.

The United States traveled a solitary road in its halting and hazardous trek to the welfare state. Although mothers'-pension adherents occasionally referred to European social-insurance schemes, they cited them more as precedents than as models. No other major industrial nation had such a special concern for its children and such a fear of providing assistance to indigent men. Thus, the United States was the world leader in mothers' pensions and a world laggard in social insurance.

The legacy of the mothers'-pension movement, though, went beyond the passage of one unique piece of child welfare legislation. It laid a foundation for later contentions that government had the responsibility to establish welfare as a right, independent of the compassion, altruism, and paternalism of the "better" members of society. It shattered the view of income support as a mere adjunct to more direct programs of social control. It undermined the prestige of private charities to such an extent that they never again so confidently asserted their prerogative to define the government-welfare role. The United States had reached a preliminary recognition of poverty as a public problem requiring governmental remedies.

SOURCES

Mothers' Day

Besides mothers' pensions, women championed many other progressive-era causes. Alice Hamilton, for example, tramped from one mine or factory to another, crusading for occupational health and safety; Florence Kelley headed the factory-inspection staff of the state of Illinois; Jane Addams and Lillian Wald spearheaded the settlement-house movement. Others lobbied for woman suffrage, which was granted just as the progressive era closed. In the midst of this remarkable activity, and just as the mothers'-pension movement was hitting its stride, another progressive, Woodrow Wilson, chose to honor a certain category of women—mothers. How does the Mothers' Day Proclamation fit with the aggressive politics of the era's women reformers? What link can you make between Mothers' Day and mothers' pensions?

Congress and the President
Legalize and Immortalize
Mothers' Day
Second Sunday in May

A PROCLAMATION

"Whereas, by a joint resolution, approved May 8, 1914, designating the second Sunday in May as Mothers' Day, and for other purposes, the President is authorized and requested to issue a proclamation calling upon the government officials to display the United States flag on all government buildings, and the people of the United States to display the flag at their homes, or other suitable places on the second Sunday in May, as a public expression of our love and reverence for the mothers of our country;

"And, Whereas, by the said joint resolution it is made the duty of the President to request the observance of the second Sunday in May as provided for in the said joint resolution;

"Now, therefore, I, Woodrow Wilson, President of the United States of America, by virtue of the authority vested in me by the said joint resolution, do hereby direct the government officials to display the United States flag on all government buildings, and do invite the people of the United States to display the flag at their homes, or other suitable places, on the second Sunday of May, as a public expression of our love and reverence for the mothers of our country. In witness whereof I have set my hand and caused the seal of the United States to be hereunto affixed.

"Done at the city of Washington this 9th day of May, in the year of our Lord, one thousand nine hundred and fourteen and of the Independence of the United States one hundred and thirty-eight.

"WOODROW WILSON.

"By the President,

"WILLIAM JENNINGS BRYAN,

"Secretary of State."

Woodrow Wilson
Proclaims Mothers' Day,
1914.

Education and Childhood

Progressive-period reformers were anxious to set education on a new and "scientific" footing. And they were just as concerned with the problem of "wayward" youth. All across the nation, there were studies of how children spent their time. And in institutions for "delinquent" children there was a similar determination to classify in scientific terms the kinds of vices that young people were prey to. Behind the science—and not far behind it, either—was an obvious moralism. The officials who made the studies that follow were sure that they knew what a good life was, and just as certain that knowledge was the key to solving the problem. The two photographs from the George Junior Republic speak more clearly than words about the kinds of ideological purposes that lay behind the statistics. What does the Cleveland play census reveal about the people who compiled it? What do you suppose the census takers meant when they recorded the children "doing nothing"? What kind of play did Cleveland reformers wish to see? What typically progressive traits are mirrored in the statistics on "delinquent" boys? For example, where were boys sent when discharged from the Maine State School for Boys? What characteristics of youth were found most offensive at the Indiana Boys' School, and why?

Recreation

A PLAY CENSUS OF CLEVELAND PUPILS

A play census, taken June 23, 1913, under the direction of the chief medical inspector and assistant superintendent in charge of physical education in Cleveland, seemed to show this same lack of relationship between the school and the out-of-school activities of children. The results of this study are shown in Table 6.1.

Conclusions Drawn from This Census

1. That just at the age (under 15) when play and activity are the fundamental requirements for proper growth and development 41 percent of the children seen were doing nothing. The boy without play is father to the man without a job.
2. Fifty-one percent of all the children seen were in the streets, in the midst of all the traffic, dirt, and heat, and in an environment conducive to just the wrong kind of play.
3. That only six percent of the children seen were on vacant lots despite the fact that in most of the districts vacant lots were available as play spaces. A place to play does not solve the problem: there must be a play leader.
4. That even though 36 playgrounds were open and 16 of them with appara-

Table 6.1   What 14,683 Cleveland Children Were Doing on June 23, 1913

		BOYS	GIRLS	TOTAL
Where they were seen	On streets	5,241	2,558	7,799
	In yards	1,583	1,998	3,581
	In vacant lots	686	197	883
	In playgrounds	997	872	1,869
	In alleys	413	138	551
What they were doing	Doing nothing	3,737	2,234	5,961
	Playing	4,601	2,757	7,358
	Working	719	635	1,354
What games they	Baseball	1,448	190	1,638
were playing	Kites	482	49	531
	Sand piles	241	230	471
	Tag	100	53	153
	Jackstones	68	257	325
	Dolls	89	193	282
	Sewing	14	130	144
	Housekeeping	53	191	244
	Horse and wagon	89	24	113
	Bicycle riding	79	13	92
	Minding baby	19	41	60
	Reading	17	35	52
	Roller-skating	18	29	47
	Gardening	13	14	27
	Caddy	6	0	6
	Marbles	2	0	2
	Playing in other ways mostly just fooling	1,863	1,308	3,171

From George E. Johnson, *Education Through Recreation*, The Survey Committee of the Cleveland Foundation, Cleveland, 1916, pp. 48–51. Reprinted with permission.

tus up, only 1869, or 11 percent, of the children seen within four blocks of a playground were playing on playgrounds. Last Friday 6488 children played on playgrounds.

5. That of the 7358 children reported to have been playing, 3171 were reported to have been playing by doing some of the following things: fighting, teasing, pitching pennies, shooting craps, stealing apples, "roughing a peddler," chasing chickens, tying can to dog, etc., but most of them were reported to have been "just fooling"—not playing anything in particular.

6. We need more and better playgrounds and a better trained leadership.

THE RECREATIONAL INTERESTS OF CLEVELAND PUPILS

That the play interests of children and youth answer to deep-seated needs and are essential for fullest development and education is now so universally admitted that only the mere statement is here necessary. It is also evident that these play interests are the prototypes of the great lines of human interest, endeavor, and achievement represented in adult life and in education work today.

Crime and Reformation

Table 6.2   Causes for Which Boys Were Committed to Louisville, Kentucky, Industrial School, 1906

	WHITE	BLACK	TOTAL
Incorrigibility	72	27	99
Delinquency	43	13	56
Larceny	4	3	7
Petit larceny	13	9	22
Grand larceny	8	1	9
Burglary	4	3	7
Burglary and larceny	19	3	22
Vagrancy and larceny	1	0	1
Vagrancy	8	2	10
Vagrancy and incorrigibility	3	0	3
Incorrigibility and immorality	1	0	1
Assault	2	1	3
Manslaughter in fourth degree	1	0	1
Felony	1	0	1
Attempted rape	0	1	1
Destruction of property	2	0	2
Obstructing railroad	1	0	1
Disturbing the peace	2	0	2

Table 6.3   State School for Boys, South Portland, Maine, 1906. Students Were Heavily Concentrated in the 10–15 Age Group

FACTS CONNECTED WITH THE MORAL CONDITION OF THE BOYS WHEN RECEIVED	
Whole number received	2615
Have intemperate parents	881
Lost father	816
Lost mother	654
Relatives in prison	335
Step parents	491
Idle	1658
Much neglected	907
Truants	1140
Sabbath breakers	992
Untruthful	2053
Profane	1908
DISPOSITION OF THOSE DISCHARGED SINCE OPENING OF THE SCHOOL	
Discharged on expiration of sentence	223
Discharged by trustees	731
Indentured to—	
Barber	1
Blacksmith	1
Boarding mistress	1
Boilermaker	1
Cabinetmaker	6
Carpenters	13
Cooper	1
Farmers	287
Harness makers	3
Laborers	9
Lumbermen	3
Machinists	5
Manufacturers	2
Mason	1
Miller	1
Sea captains	5
Shoemakers	14
Tailors	3
Tallow chandler	1
Allowed to leave on trial	1,026
Allowed to enlist	19
Illegally committed	19
Remanded	64
Pardoned	15
Finally escaped	81
Violated trust	49
Died	49
Delivered to courts	24
Returned to masters	4
NATIVITY OF ALL COMMITTED	
Foreigners	278
Born in United States	2,295
Nativity not known	41

Table 6.4   Demerit Offenses, Indiana Boys' School, Plainfield, 1906

Talk	10
Disobedience	10
Disorder	10
Laziness	10
Vandalism	10
Willful waste	20
Quarreling	50
Dormitory	50
Shielding	50
Profanity	50
Fighting	100
Tobacco or money	100
Falsehood	100
Theft	100
Obscenity	100
Disrespect and impudence	100
Vulgarity	200
Insubordination	200
Planning escape	500
Escape	1000
Secret vice	1000
Planning immoral association	1000
Immoral association	2000

From U.S. Congress, House Committee on the Judiciary, *Juvenile Crime and Reformation, Including Stigmata of Generation,* Being a Hearing on the Bill (H.R. 16733) to Establish a Laboratory for the Study of the Criminal, Pauper, and Defective Classes, by Arthur MacDonald, 60th Cong., Washington, D.C., 1908, pp. 115,107.

The George Junior Republic

The George Junior Republic was a progressive-era camp for destitute and delinquent youth. It had strong appeal for Theodore Roosevelt, economist John R. Commons, and General Robert Baden-Powell (British founder of the Boy Scouts, another progressive-era institution). According to these photos, what was the cause of delinquency among youth? What did the George Junior Republic choose to do about it?

The Court, c. 1905. A citizen judge presides.
Department of University Archives. Cornell University, Ithaca, N.Y.

The Republic Store, c. 1910. Citizens exchange Republic currency for groceries.
Department of Manuscripts and University Archives, Cornell University, Ithaca, N.Y.

The Photographer as Reformer:
Jacob Riis

Nothing is more embedded in our value structure than the notion that the photograph is objective, a precise rendering of reality ("pictures don't lie"). The photographs taken by Jacob Riis offer an opportunity to assess this belief, for Riis was a reformer as well as a photographer. A police reporter for two New York City newspapers, Riis wrote an important book about lower-class urban life, How the Other Half Lives *(1890), founded a settlement house (1901), and was active in the public-park and playground movements. What kind of world view did Riis bring to his work? What did he think of the people clustered at "Bandit's Roose"? Would Riis have argued that the subjects in this photograph were capable of changing their own lives? that their culture was a vital one?*

Bandit's Roost, 39½ Mulberry Street, New York City, c. 1888.
Photography by Jacob A. Riis. The Jacob A. Riis Collection; Museum of the City of New York.

CHAPTER 7

War, Normalcy, and Mass Consumption

The generation that came of age in the 1920s did so in the shadow of World War I. A nation led to expect that the struggle would be morally satisfying—that had boldly announced in song that "the Yanks are coming"—would be reduced to seeking meaning in an unidentifiable soldier, buried in Arlington, Virginia. That a war of such short duration—direct American involvement lasted little more than eighteen months—could have had such an impact may seem surprising. But part of an explanation may be found by examining how Americans experienced the conflict and what they were led to believe it would achieve.

Several groups experienced the war years as a time of increased opportunity. Blacks—migrating from the south into Chicago, Detroit, New York, and other industrial cities—and women—heretofore denied most jobs open to men—found themselves suddenly employable. The same circumstances allowed organized labor to double its membership in the four years after 1914. Farmers prospered because of rising European demand and, after 1917, because of government price guarantees. Soldiers, however, experienced the typical wartime "tax" on income, and many lost their positions on promotional ladders.

Continued deficit spending fueled the economy during demobilization. In 1919, activity in automobile production and building construction, two industries held back by the war, helped the nation avoid a prolonged postwar tailspin. But economic crisis could be postponed for only so long. By mid-1921, the economy was mired in a serious depression that cut industrial output by some 20 percent. It seems likely that a downturn in the postwar economy, deeply affecting a people who had no history of planning for such events, helped to dissolve the aura of economic progress and personal success that had been part of the war and to inaugurate a decade of conflict between young and old, employer and employee, country and city, religion and science, nation and locality. In the minds of many Americans, depression was inseparably linked to demobilization and the peace settlement.

Unlike World War II, World War I was not an especially popular conflict with Americans. It had to be sold, systematically and unabashedly, like any

141

other product. The government's advertising agency was the Committee on Public Information, headed by journalist George Creel. The Creel Committee employed an elaborate publicity apparatus to educate Americans to proper wartime values. In one advertisement, a smiling American soldier clenched a White Owl cigar between his teeth and said, "Did I bayonet my first hun? Sure! How did it feel? It *doesn't* feel! There *he* is. There *you* are. One of you has got to go. I preferred to stay."

Perhaps fighting a war—especially a war with which large numbers of the population disagreed—required a kind of artificially imposed unity. This would explain the Creel Committee propaganda. But when the fighting stopped—when the great crusade was over—a new crusade, called the Red Scare, took the place of wartime coercion of dissidents. When this latest hysteria subsided in the spring of 1920, hundreds of radicals of every persuasion—socialists, Communists, even ordinary union members—had been arrested, beaten, lynched, tried, or deported.

Just as wartime coercion had yielded to the Red Scare, so was the Red Scare reincarnated in the politics of Warren Harding. In May 1920, emphasizing that "too much has been said about bolshevism in America," Harding coined the word that would capture his appeal and win him the presidency, urging return to "not heroism, but healing, not nostrums, but normalcy." With "normalcy," Harding and the American people seemed to be rejecting the world that Woodrow Wilson had sought to create—the world in which words replaced concrete realities, in which dreams of world government (the League of Nations) transcended political facts. The Creel Committee had described the war as "a Crusade not merely to re-win the tomb of Christ, but to bring back to earth the rule of right, the peace, goodwill to men and gentleness he taught." When it proved much less than this, Americans beat an emotional retreat to the comfort of Harding's slogans.

By mid-decade, when prosperity had returned and "normalcy" was in full swing, it was clear that the economy was undergoing a gradual change of enormous importance: the old economy of "production" was yielding, decade by decade, to a new economy of "consumption." This change occurred partly because many of the problems of production appeared to have been solved; the moving assembly line and Frederick W. Taylor's scientific management had made possible a new level of productive efficiency. Now the roadblock to abundance seemed to be at the level of the consumer. One approach, decidedly unpopular with business and with the Republican presidents who held office in the decade, was to encourage consumption by using the tax system to distribute money to those who would spend rather than save it. Another approach was to teach (some would say condition) people to desire, and then to buy, the available products. This teaching or conditioning was the function of advertising, which grew by leaps and bounds during the 1920s. Many of the advertising agencies were staffed by people who had honed their skills at the Creel Committee. Indeed, the ad agencies of the twenties were simply applying what appeared to be the great lesson of wartime propaganda: that the "masses" could be manipulated—made to go to war, or to buy—using the techniques of modern psychology.

The 1920s had powerful currents of individualism, of course. In fact, the decade has been rightly famed for its affection for jazz, for its compulsion for mah-jongg and flagpole sitting, for the flapper, and for the iconoclast H. L. Mencken (for whom every group, even the New England town meeting, was a mob run by demagogues). Harding's "normalcy," however, seemed to center on a program of cultural conformity, and it was to infect the entire decade. The Ku Klux Klan, revived at a Georgia meeting in 1915, grew rapidly in the early 1920s through campaigns against blacks, Catholics, Jews, and immigrants. National prohibition, which required millions to give up deeply ingrained drinking habits or evade the law, was in effect throughout the decade. The first law establishing immigration quotas was passed in 1921; a second measure passed three years later was designed to reduce immigration from eastern and southern Europe—the later immigrants discussed in Chapter 3. If "normalcy" is broad enough to encompass these aspects of the 1920s, then perhaps wartime coercion, the Red Scare, the new economy of consumption, and "normalcy" were all variations on a theme—a theme perhaps placed in bold relief by the war, demobilization, and postwar economic crisis, but ultimately one set more deeply in the nation's character and its institutions than any of these events.

INTERPRETIVE ESSAY

Lizabeth Cohen

Encountering Mass Culture at the Grass Roots: The Experience of Chicago Workers in the 1920s

It is important to understand that scholars disagree on almost every aspect of the economy of production/economy of consumption thesis outlined in the introduction to this chapter. They disagree, first, on why the change took place. Some believe that the consumer economy was a natural and inevitable result of economic abundance; others contend that it was at least partly the result of efforts to make workers more conservative by refocusing their attention from the factory and workplace to the pleasures of leisure and consumerism. Second, scholars disagree about the extent to which workers were affected and shaped by the economy of consumption. One group argues that mass consumption was akin to the national origins laws of 1921 and 1924—a steamroller of assimilation and homogenization that crushed existing ethnic, racial, and class-based cultures. Another group argues that ordinary people were able to resist the homogenizing influences of mass consumption and mass culture and retain their distinctive values and ways of life.

Lizabeth Cohen's essay grounds this debate in history. It examines how ordinary people living in Chicago in the 1920s were affected by chain stores, the new movie palaces, the radio, and other aspects of mass consumption and mass culture. Where would you place Cohen in the debates described above? What kinds of evidence does she offer? How might one make a case different from hers?

In 1929, the publishers of *True Story Magazine* ran full-page advertisements in the nation's major newspapers celebrating what they called "the American Economic Evolution." Claiming to be the recipient of thousands of personal stories written by American workers for the magazine's primarily working-class readership, they felt well placed to report that since World War I, shorter working hours, higher pay, and easy credit had created an "economic millennium." Now that the nation's workers enjoyed an equal opportunity to consume, "a capital-labor war which has been going on now for upwards of three hundred years" had virtually ended. *True Story* claimed that twenty years earlier, Jim Smith, who worked ten to twelve hours a day in a factory and then returned home "to his hovel and his woman and his brats," was likely to resort to strikes and vio-

Lizabeth Cohen, "Encountering Mass Culture at the Grassroots: The Experience of Chicago Workers in the 1920s," *American Quarterly*, vol. 41, March 1989, pp. 6–33. Published by the American Studies Association. Copyright 1989.

lence when times got tough. Not so his modern-day counterpart. Today, the magazine asserted, Jim Smith drives home to the suburbs after a seven- or eight-hour day earning him three to seven times as much as before, which helps pay for the automobile, the house, and a myriad of other possessions. Now an up-standing member of the middle class, Jim has learned moderation. Mass con-sumption had tamed his militance. Advertising executives at the J. Walter Thompson Company shared *True Story Magazine*'s confidence in the homoge-nizing power of mass culture. In an issue of their own in-house newsletter de-voted to "the New National Market," they too claimed that due to standardized merchandise, automobiles, motion pictures and most recently the radio, the so-called lines of demarcation between social classes and between the city, the small town, and the farm had become less clear.

Sixty years later, historians are still making assumptions about the impact of mass culture that are similar to those of *True Story Magazine*'s editors and J. Walter Thompson Company's executives. With not much more data about con-sumer attitudes and behavior in the 1920s than their predecessors had, they too assume that mass culture succeeded in integrating American workers into a mainstream, middle-class culture. When workers bought a victrola, went to the picture show, or switched on the radio, in some crucial way, the usual argument goes, they ceased living in an ethnic or working-class world. This common ver-sion of the "embourgeoisement thesis" credits a hegemonic mass culture with blurring class lines. When labor organizing occurred in the 1930s and 1940s, the view holds, it stemmed not from industrial workers' class consciousness but from their efforts to satisfy middle-class appetites.

How can historians break free of the unproven assumptions of the era and reopen the question of how working-class audiences responded to the explo-sion of mass culture during the 1920s? Let me first acknowledge how difficult it is to know the extent to which workers participated in various forms of mass culture, and particularly the meanings they ascribed to their preferences. But I will suggest in this essay one strategy for discerning the impact of mass culture. Shifting the focus from the national scene, where data on audience reception is weak, to a particular locale rich in social history sources can yield new insights into the way that workers responded to mass culture. Chicago offers a particu-larly good case since it was the best-documented city in the United States dur-ing the 1920s and 1930s. In this period, Chicago was a laboratory for sociolo-gists, political scientists, and social workers—and a multitude of their students. Their numerous studies of urban life, along with ethnic newspapers, oral histo-ries, and other local sources, can serve social historians as revealing windows into working-class experience with mass culture. Chicago's industrial promi-nence, moreover, attracted a multiethnic and multiracial work force, which gives it all the more value as a case study.

In order to investigate how workers reacted to mass culture on the local level of Chicago, it is necessary to make concrete the abstraction "mass culture." This essay, therefore, will examine carefully how workers in Chicago responded to mass consumption, that is, the growth of chain stores peddling standard-brand goods; to motion picture shows in monumental movie palaces; and to the little box that seemed overnight to be winning a sacred spot at the family hearth, the radio.

While *True Story Magazine*'s Jim Smith may have bought his way into the middle class, in reality industrial workers did not enjoy nearly the prosperity that advertisers and sales promoters assumed they did. All Americans did not benefit equally from the mushrooming of national wealth taking place during the 1920s. After wartime, wages advanced modestly if at all in big manufacturing sectors, such as steel, meat-packing, and the clothing industry, particularly for the unskilled and semiskilled workers who predominated in this kind of work. And most disruptive of workers' ability to consume, unemployment remained high. Workers faced unemployment whenever the business cycle turned downward, and even more regularly, faced layoffs in slack seasons. So Chicago's average semiskilled worker did not have nearly as much money to spare for purchasing automobiles, washing machines, and victrolas as manufacturers and advertisers had hoped.

But people with commodities to sell worried little about workers' limited income. Instead, they trusted that an elaborate system of installment selling would allow all Americans to take part in the consumer revolution. "Buy now, pay later," first introduced in the automobile industry around 1915, suddenly exploded in the 1920s; by 1926, it was estimated that six billion dollars' worth of retail goods were sold annually by installment, about 15 percent of all sales. "Enjoy while you pay," invited the manufacturers of everything from vacuum cleaners to literally the kitchen sink.

But once again, popular beliefs of the time do not hold up to closer scrutiny: industrial workers were not engaging in installment buying in nearly the numbers that marketers assumed. Automobiles accounted for by far the greatest proportion of the nation's installment debt outstanding at any given time—over fifty percent. But while *True Story*'s Jim Smith may have driven home from the factory in his new automobile, industrial workers in Chicago were not likely to follow his example. One study of the standard of living of semiskilled workers in Chicago found that only three percent owned cars in 1924. Even at the end of the decade, in the less urbanized environment of nearby Joliet, only twenty four percent of lower income families owned an automobile, according to a *Chicago Tribune* survey. The few studies of consumer credit done at the time indicate that it was middle-income people—not workers—who made installment buying such a rage during the 1920s, particularly the salaried and well-off, who anticipated larger incomes in the future. Lower income people instead were saving at unprecedented rates, often to cushion themselves for the inevitable layoffs.

When workers did buy on credit, they were most likely to purchase small items like phonographs. The question remains, however, whether buying a phonograph—or a washing machine—changed workers' cultural orientation. Those who believed in the homogenizing power of mass consumption claimed that the act of purchasing such a standardized product drew the consumer into a world of mainstream tastes and values. Sociologist John Dollard argued at the

time, for example, that the victrola revolutionized a family's pattern of amusement because "what they listen to comes essentially from the outside, its character is cosmopolitan and national, and what the family does to create it as a
family is very small indeed." We get the impression of immigrant, wage-earning families sharing more in American, middle-class culture every time they
rolled up the rug and danced to the Paul Whiteman orchestra.

But how workers themselves described what it meant to purchase a phonograph reveals a different picture. Typically, industrial workers in Chicago in the
1920s were first- or second-generation ethnic, from eastern or southern Europe.
In story after story they related how buying a victrola helped keep Polish or Italian culture alive by allowing people to play foreign-language records, often at
ethnic social gatherings. Rather than the phonograph drawing the family away
from a more indigenous cultural world, as Dollard alleged, many people like
Rena Domke remembered how in Little Sicily during those years neighbors
"would sit in the evening and discuss all different things about Italy," and every
Saturday night they pulled out a victrola "and they'd play all these Italian
records and they would dance." In fact, consumers of all nationalities displayed
so much interest in purchasing foreign language records that in the 1920s
Chicago became the center of an enormous foreign record industry, selling repressed recordings from Europe and new records by American immigrant
artists. Even the small Mexican community in Chicago supported a shop that
made phonographic records of Mexican music and distributed them all over the
United States. And some American-born workers also used phonograph recordings in preserving their ties to regional culture. For example, southerners—
white and black—eased the trauma of moving north to cities like Chicago by
supporting a record industry of hillbilly and "race records" geared specifically
toward a northern urban market with southern roots. Thus, owning a phonograph might bring a worker closer to mainstream culture, but it did not have to.
A commodity could just as easily help a person reinforce ethnic or working-
class culture as lose it.

Of course, when the publishers of *True Story* spoke of a consumer revolution, they meant more than the wider distribution of luxury goods like the
phonograph. They were referring to how the chain store—like A & P or Walgreen Drugs—and the nationally advertised brands that they offered—like Lux
Soap and Del Monte canned goods—were standardizing even the most routine
purchasing. A distributor of packaged meat claimed, "Mass selling has become
almost the universal rule in this country, a discovery of this decade of hardly less
importance than the discovery of such forces as steam and electricity." Doomed,
everyone thought, were bulk or unmarked brands, and the small, inefficient
neighborhood grocery, dry goods, or drug store that sold them. Americans
wherever they lived, it was assumed, increasingly were entering stores that
looked exactly alike to purchase the same items from a standard stock.

Closer examination of the consumer behavior of workers in a city like
Chicago, however, suggests that workers were not patronizing chain stores.
Rather, the chain store that purportedly was revolutionizing consumer behav-

ior in the 1920s was mostly reaching the middle and upper classes. Two-thirds of the more than five hundred A & P and National Tea Stores in Chicago by 1928 were located in neighborhoods of above-average economic status. An analysis of the location of chain stores in Chicago's suburbs reveals the same imbalance. By 1926, chains ran 53 percent of the groceries in prosperous Oak Park, and 36 percent in equally well-off Evanston. In contrast, in working-class Gary and Joliet, only one percent of the groceries were owned by chains. As late as 1929, the workers of Cicero found chain management in only five percent of this industrial town's 819 retail stores. Chain store executives recognized that workers were too tied to local, often ethnic, merchants to abandon them, even for a small savings in price. A West Side Chicago grocer explained: "People go to a place where they can order in their own language, be understood without repetition, and then exchange a few words of gossip or news." Shopping at a particular neighborhood store was a matter of cultural loyalty. As one ethnic merchant put it, "The Polish business man is a part of your nation; he is your brother. Whether it is war, hunger, or trouble, he is always with you willing to help. . . . Therefore, buy from your people."

No less important, the chain store's prices may have been cheaper, but its "cash and carry" policy was too rigid for working people's limited budgets. Most workers depended on a system of credit at the store to make it from one payday to the next. In tough times, the loyal customer knew an understanding storekeeper would wait to be paid and still sell her food. So when an A & P opened not far from Little Sicily in Chicago, people ignored it. Instead, everyone continued to do business with the local grocer, who warned, "Go to A & P they ain't going to give you credit like I give you credit here." While middle-class consumers were carrying home more national brand, packaged goods in the 1920s, working-class people continued to buy in bulk—to fetch milk in their own containers, purchase hunks of soap, and scoop coffee, tea, sugar, and flour out of barrels. What standard brands working-class families did buy, furthermore, they encountered through a trusted grocer, not an anonymous clerk at the A & P.

When workers did buy mass-produced goods like ready-made clothing, they purchased them at stores such as Chicago's Goldblatt's Department Stores, which let customers consume on their own terms. Aware that their ethnic customers were accustomed to central marketplaces where individual vendors sold fish from one stall, shoes from another, the second-generation Goldblatt brothers, sons of a Jewish grocer, adapted this approach to their stores. Under one roof they sold everything from food to jewelry, piling merchandise high on tables so people could handle the bargains. The resulting atmosphere dismayed a University of Chicago undergraduate sociology student, more used to the elegance of Marshall Field's. To Betty Wright, Goldblatt's main floor was a mad "jumble of colors, sounds, and smells," Amidst the bedlam, she observed

> many women present with old shawls tied over their heads and bags or market
> baskets on their arms. They stopped at every counter that caught their eye,
> picked up the goods, handled it, enquired [sic] after the price, and then walked
> on without making any purchase. I have an idea that a good many of these

women had no intention whatsoever of buying anything. They probably found
Goldblatt's a pleasant place to spend an afternoon.

Most appalling to this student, "Customers seemed always ready to argue with
the clerk about the price of an article and to try to 'jew them down.'" Betty
Wright did not appreciate that behind Goldblatt's respectable exterior facade
thrived a European street market much treasured by ethnic Chicagoans.

Ethnic workers in a city like Chicago did not join what historian Daniel
Boorstin has labeled "national consumption communities" nearly as quickly as
many have thought. Even when they bought the inexpensive, mass-produced
goods becoming increasingly available during the 1920s, contrary to the hopes
of many contemporaries, a new suit of clothes did not change the man (or
woman). Rather, as market researchers would finally realize in the 1950s when
they developed the theory of "consumer reference groups," consumption involved the meeting of two worlds—the buyer's and the seller's—with pur-
chasers bringing their own values to every exchange. Gradually, over the 1920s,
workers came to share more in the new consumer goods, but in their own stores,
in their own neighborhoods, and in their own way.

In the realm of consumption, workers could depend on the small-scale enterprises in their communities to help them resist the homogenizing influences
of mass culture. But how did ethnic, working-class culture fare against forms of
mass culture—such as motion pictures and radio—which local communities
could not so easily control? Did the motion picture spectacle and a twist of the
radio dial draw workers into mainstream mass culture more successfully than
the A & P?

Workers showed much more enthusiasm for motion pictures than chain
stores. While movies had been around since early in the century, the number of
theater seats in Chicago reached its highest level ever by the end of the 1920s.
With an average of four performances daily at every theater, by 1929 Chicago
had enough movie theater seats for one-half the city's population to attend in
the course of a day; and workers made up their fair share—if not more—of that
audience. Despite the absence of exact attendance figures, there are consistent
clues that picture shows enjoyed enormous popularity among workers
throughout the twenties. As the decade began, a Bureau of Labor Statistics' survey of the cost-of-living of workingmen's families found Chicago workers
spending more than half their amusement budgets on movies. Even those fighting destitution made the motion picture a priority; in 1924, more than two-
thirds of the families receiving Mothers' Aid Assistance in Chicago attended
regularly.

But knowing that workers went to the movies is one thing, assessing how
they reacted to particular pictures is another. Some historians have taken the
tack of analyzing the content of motion pictures for evidence of their meaning
to audiences; the fact that workers made up a large part of those audiences con-
vinces these analysts that they took home particular messages decipherable
from the films. But my investigations into the variety of ways that consumers
encountered and perceived mass-produced goods suggests that people can
have very different reactions to the same experience. Just as the meaning of

mass consumption varied with the context in which people confronted it, so too the impact of the movies depended on where, with whom, and in what kind of environment workers went to the movies during the 1920s.

Chicago's workers regularly patronized neighborhood movie theaters near their homes in the 1920s, not "The Chicago," "The Uptown," "The Granada" and the other monumental picture palaces built during the period, where many historians have assumed they flocked. Neighborhood theaters had evolved from the storefront nickelodeons prevalent in immigrant, working-class communities before the war. Due to stricter city regulations, neighborhood movie houses now were fewer in number, larger, cleaner, better ventilated, and from five to twenty-cents more expensive than in nickelodeon days. But still they were much simpler than the ornate movie palaces that seated several thousand at a time. For example, local theaters in a working-class community like South Chicago (next to U.S. Steel's enormous South Works plant) ranged in size from "Pete's International," which sat only 250—more when Pete made the kids double up in each seat for Sunday matinees—to the "Gayety" holding 750 to the "New Calumet" with room for almost a thousand. Only rarely did workers pay at least twice as much admission, plus carfare, to see the picture palace show. Despite the fact that palaces often claimed to be "paradise for the common man," geographical plotting of Chicago's picture palaces reveals that most of them were nowhere near working-class neighborhoods: a few were downtown, the rest strategically placed in new shopping areas to attract the middle classes to the movies. Going to the pictures was something workers did more easily and cheaply close to home. As a U.S. Steel employee explained, it was "a long way"—in many respects—from the steeltowns of Southeast Chicago to the South Side's fancy Tivoli Theater.

For much of the decade, working-class patrons found the neighborhood theater not only more affordable but more welcoming, as the spirit of the community carried over into the local movie hall. Chicago workers may have savored the exotic on the screen, but they preferred encountering it in familiar company. The theater manager, who was often the owner and usually lived in the community, tailored his film selections to local tastes and changed them every few days to accommodate neighborhood people who attended frequently. Residents of Chicago's industrial neighborhoods rarely had to travel far to find pictures to their liking, which they viewed among the same neighbors and friends they had on the block.

When one entered a movie theater in a working-class neighborhood of Chicago, the ethnic character of the community quickly became evident. The language of the yelling and jeering that routinely gave sound to silent movies provided the first clue. "The old Italians used to go to these movies," recalled Ernest Dalle-Molle, "and when the good guys were chasing the bad guys in Italian—they'd say—Getem—catch them—out loud in the theater." Stage events accompanying the films told more. In Back of the Yards near the packinghouses, at Schumacher's or the Davis Square Theater, viewers often saw a Polish play along with the silent film. Everywhere, amateur nights offered "local talent" a moment in the limelight. At the Butler Theater in Little Sicily, which the com-

The 398-seat Pastime Theater on West Madison Street typified the small, neighborhood theaters that workers frequented during the 1920s. Admission was twenty-five cents in 1924, and most who attended were spared the additional cost of carfare as they lived within walking distance. Chicago Historical Society.

munity had rechristened the "Garlic Opera House," Italian music shared the stage with American films. In the neighborhood theater, Hollywood and ethnic Chicago coexisted.

Neighborhood theaters so respected local culture that they reflected community prejudices as well as strengths. The Commercial Theater in South Chicago typified many neighborhood theaters in requiring Mexicans and blacks to sit in the balcony, while reserving the main floor for white ethnics who dominated the community's population. One theater owner explained, "White people don't like to sit next to the colored or Mexicans. . . . We used to have trouble about the first four months, but not now. They go by themselves to their place." Sometimes blacks and Mexicans were not even allowed into neighborhood theaters. In contrast, the more cosmopolitan picture palaces, like those owned by the largest chain in Chicago, Balaban & Katz, were instructed to let in whoever could pay. Thus, the neighborhood theater reinforced the values of the community as powerfully as any on the screen. This is not to deny that working-class audiences were affected by the content of motion pictures, but to suggest that when people viewed movies in the familiar world of the neighborhood theater, identification with their local community was bolstered, and the subversive impact of the picture often constrained. . . .

The 4000-seat Tivoli Theater at Cottage Grove and 63rd Street on the South Side contrasted in almost every way with neighborhood theaters like the Pastime. This so-called picture palace was owned by Balaban & Katz, the largest theater chain in Chicago. Admission was a dollar in 1924; that price plus the carfare required from most working-class neighborhoods ensured that middle-class people, not workers, were the picture palace's primary patrons. Chicago Historical Society.

Neighborhood stores and theaters buffered the potential disorientation of mass culture by allowing their patrons to consume within the intimacy of the community. Rather than disrupting the existing peer culture, that peer culture accommodated the new products. Shopping and theatergoing were easily mediated by the community because they were collective activities. Radio, on the other hand, entered the privacy of the home. At least potentially, what went out across the airwaves could transport listeners, as individuals, into a different world.

As it turned out, though, radio listening did not require workers to forsake their cultural communities any more than shopping or moviegoing did. Radio listening was far from the passive, atomized experience we are familiar with today. It was more active; many working people became interested in early radio as a hobby, and built their own crystal and vacuum tube sets. Radio retailers recognized that workers were particularly apt to build their own radios. "If the store is located in a community most of the inhabitants of which are workmen," a study of the radio industry showed, "there will be a large proportion of parts," in contrast to the more expensive, preassembled models stocked by the radio stores of fashionable districts. That radio appealed to the artisanal interests of Chicago's workers was evident in their neighborhoods in another way. As early as 1922, a Chicago radio journalist noted that "crude homemade aerials are on one roof in ten along the miles of bleak streets in the city's industrial zones."

Even workers who bought increasingly affordable, ready-made radios spent evenings bent over their dial boards, working to get "the utmost possible DX" (distance), and then recording their triumphs in a radio log. Beginning in the fall of 1922, in fact, Chicago stations agreed not to broadcast at all after 7 P.M. on Monday evenings to allow the city's radio audience to tune in faraway stations otherwise blocked because they broadcasted on the same wavelengths as local stations. "Silent Nights" were religiously observed in other cities as well. In addition to distance, radio enthusiasts concerned themselves with technical challenges such as cutting down static, making "the short jumps," and operating receivers with one hand.

Not only was radio listening active, but it was also far from isolating. By 1930 in Chicago, there was one radio for every two or three households in workers' neighborhoods, and people sat around in local shops or neighbors' parlors listening together. Surveys showed that on average, four or five people listened to one set at any particular time; in 85 percent of homes, the entire family listened together. Communal radio listening mediated between local and mass culture much like the neighborhood store or theater.

Even Chicago's working-class youth, whose parents feared they were abandoning the ethnic fold for more commercialized mass culture, were listening to the radio in the company of other second-generation ethnic peers at neighborhood clubs when not at home with their families. Known as "basement clubs," "social clubs," or "athletic clubs," these associations guided the cultural experimentation of young people from their mid-teens to mid-twenties. Here, in rented quarters away from parental eyes and ears, club members socialized to the constant blaring of the radio—the "prime requisite" of every club, according to one observer. The fact that young people were encountering mass culture like the radio within ethnic, neighborhood circles helped to minimize the disruption.

But even more important to an investigation of the impact of the radio on workers' consciousness, early radio broadcasting had a distinctly grass-roots orientation. To begin with, the technological limitations of early broadcasting ensured that small, nearby stations with low power dominated the ether waves. Furthermore, with no clear way of financing independent radio stations, it fell to existing institutions to subsidize radio operations. From the start, nonprofit ethnic, religious, and labor groups put radio to their service. In 1925, 28 percent of the 571 radio stations nationwide were owned by educational institutions and churches, less than 4 percent by commercial broadcasting companies. In Chicago, ethnic groups saw radio as a way of keeping their countrymen and women in touch with native culture. By 1926, several radio stations explicitly devoted to ethnic programming broadcasted in Chicago—WGES, WSBC, WEDC, and WCRW—while other stations carried "nationality hours." Through the radio, Chicago's huge foreign language-speaking population heard news from home, native music, and special broadcasts like Benito Mussolini's messages to Italians living in America. One of the stations that sponsored a "Polish Hour" and an "Irish Hour" is also noteworthy for bringing another aspect of local, working-class culture to the radio. The Chicago Federation of Labor organized WCFL, "the Voice of Labor," to, in its own words, "help awaken the slumbering giant of labor." Having suffered a variety of defeats after World War I, most notably the failure to organize Chicago's steel mills and packing plants, the federation seized radio in the 1920s as a new strategy for reaching the city's workers. "Labor News Flashes," "Chicago Federation of Labor Hour," and "Labor Talks with the International Ladies Garment Workers' Union" alternated with entertainment like "Earl Hoffman's Chez Pierre Orchestra" and "Musical Potpourri."

Radio, therefore, brought familiar distractions into the homes of workers: talk, ethnic nationality hours, labor news, church services, and vaudeville-type musical entertainment with hometown—often ethnic—performers. More innovative forms of radio programming, such as situation comedy shows, dramatic series, and soap operas, only developed later. And a survey commissioned by NBC in 1928 found the 80 percent of the radio audience regularly listened to these local, not to distant, stations. Sometimes listeners even knew a singer or musician personally, since many stations' shoestring budgets forced them to rely on amateurs; whoever dropped in at the station had a chance to be heard. Well-known entertainers, moreover, shied away from radio at first, dissatisfied with the low pay but also uncomfortable performing without an audience and fearful of undercutting their box office attractiveness with free, on-air concerts. While tuning in a radio may have been a new experience, few surprises came "out of the ether."

As a result, early radio in Chicago promoted ethnic, religious, and working-class affiliations rather than undermining them, as many advocates of mass culture had predicted. No doubt radio did expose some people to new cultural experiences—to different ethnic and religious traditions or new kinds of music. But most important, workers discovered that participating in radio, as in mass consumption and the movies, did not require repudiation of established social identities. . . .

By letting community institutions—ethnic stores, neighborhood theaters, and local radio stations—mediate in the delivery of mass culture, workers avoided the kind of cultural reorientation that Madison Avenue had expected. Working-class families could buy phonographs or ready-made clothing, go regularly to the picture show, and be avid radio fans without feeling pressured to abandon their existing social affiliations.

While this pattern captures the experience of white ethnic workers in Chicago's factories, it does not characterize their black coworkers, who came north in huge numbers during and after World War I to work in mass production plants. Blacks developed a different, and complex, relationship to mass culture. Black much more than ethnic workers satisfied those who hoped a mass market would emerge during the twenties. Unlike ethnic workers, blacks did not reject chain stores and standard brands, nor try to harness radio to traditional goals. But blacks disappointed those who assumed an integrated, American culture would accompany uniformity in tastes. For ironically, by participating in mainstream commercial life—which black Chicagoans did more than their ethnic coworkers—blacks came to feel more independent and influential as a race, not more integrated into white middle-class society. Mass culture—chain stores, brand goods, popular music—offered blacks the ingredients from which to construct a new, urban black culture.

Blacks' receptivity to mass culture grew out of a surprising source, a faith in black commercial endeavor not so very different from ethnic people's loyalty to ethnic businesses. During the 1920s, a consensus developed in northern black communities that a separate "black economy" could provide the necessary glue to hold what was a new and fragile world together. If blacks could direct their producer, consumer, and investment power toward a black marketplace by supporting "race businesses," the whole community would benefit. Less economic exploitation and more opportunity would come blacks' way. This was not a new idea. "Black capitalism" had been fundamental to Booker T. Washington's accommodationist, self-help philosophy at the turn of the century. What changed in the 1920s was that now blacks of all political persuasions—including the Garveyite nationalists and even the socialist-leaning "New Negro" crowd—shared a commitment to a separate black economy. In the face of racial segregation and discrimination, the black community would forge an alternative "Black Metropolis" that rejected white economic control without rejecting capitalism.

At the center of the separate black economy stood "race businesses." Black consumers were told that when they patronized these enterprises, they bought black jobs, black entrepreneurship, and black independence along with goods and services, and bid farewell to white employment prejudice, insults, and overcharging. "You don't know race respect if you don't buy from Negroes," sermonized one pastor. Central to the nationalist program of Marcus Garvey's United Negro Improvement Association, not surprisingly, were commercial enterprises—a steamship line, hotel, printing plant, black doll factory, and chains of groceries, restaurants, and laundries.

But the "black economy" strategy was only moderately successful. Those black businesses that did best were geared solely to black needs, where there was a large Negro market with little white competition. For example, undertakers, barbers, and beauticians faced few white contenders; black cosmetic companies even succeeded in selling hair products like Madame C. J. Walker's hair growth and straightening creams through nationwide chains. And black-owned insurance companies whose salesmen knocked on doors up and down blocks of the Black Belt proved the greatest business triumph of all. But insurmountable economic barriers kept other Negro entrepreneurs from competing viably. Black merchants and businessmen suffered from lack of experience, lack of capital (there were only two black banks in the city to provide loans, and these had limited resources), and an inability to offer customers the credit that ethnic storekeepers gave their own countrymen or Jewish businessmen in black areas gave black customers. The short supply of cash in black stores, moreover, kept wholesale orders small, retail prices high, and shelf stock low, all of which forced black customers to shop elsewhere.

The poor showing of black business made black customers, even those deeply committed to a black economy, dependent on white business. But concern with black economic independence nonetheless left its mark. Within the white commercial world, blacks developed two preferences, which they pursued when financially able: standard brand goods and chain stores. Blacks shopping in nonblack stores felt that packaged goods protected them against unscrupulous storekeepers or clerks. Not sharing the ethnic worker's confidence in his compatriot grocer, the black consumer distrusted bulk goods. This reliance on brand names only grew, moreover, when black customers who could survive without credit increasingly chose to patronize chain stores, attracted to their claims of standardized products and prices.

No less important, the chain store could be pressured to hire black clerks, while the Jewish, Greek, or Italian store in a black neighborhood was usually family-run. If blacks could not own successful businesses, at least they should be able to work in them. By the mid- to late 1920s, consumer boycotts to force chains to hire blacks flourished in black neighborhoods. "Don't Spend Your Money Where You Can't Work" crusades sought black economic independence through employment rather than entrepreneurship. By 1930, consumers in Chicago's enormous South Side Black Belt had pressured local branches of The South Center Department Store, Sears Roebuck, A & P, Consumers' Market, Neisner's 5 Cents to a Dollar, Woolworth's, and Walgreen's Drugs to employ blacks, some almost exclusively.

With strict limitations on where blacks could live and work in Chicago, consumption—both through race businesses and more mainline chains—became a major avenue through which blacks could assert their independence. But chain stores were not the only aspect of mass culture to contribute to the making of an urban, black identity. Blacks also played a role in shaping another major feature of mass culture in the twenties—jazz. In contrast to black commercial schemes that mimicked white examples or black consumption, which contented itself largely with white products, here the trendsetting went the other way. Black folk culture, black inventiveness, black talent gave the twenties its distinctive image as the "Jazz Age" and dictated the character of mainstream American popular music for many years to come.

Chicago was the jazz capital of the nation during the 1920s. Here, in the middle of the Black Belt, mixed audiences in "Black and Tan" cabarets tapped to the beat of King Oliver, Louis Armstrong, Lil Hardin, "Fats" Waller, Freddy Keppard, Jelly Roll Morton, and others. In segregated company, blacks relished Chicago's "hot jazz" at their own more modest clubs, black movie theaters, and semi-private house parties; whites, meanwhile, danced black dances like the Charleston to black bands playing in palatial ballrooms that prohibited Negro patronage.

The Chicago jazzmen's music reached far beyond the city's night clubs. Blacks—and some whites—all over the country bought millions of blues and jazz phonograph recordings, known as "race records."At record stores on Chicago's South Side, one store owner remembered, "Colored people would form a line twice around the block when the latest record of Bessie or Ma or Clara or Mamie come in." With the exception of Negro-owned Black Swan Records, white recording companies like Paramount, Columbia, Okey, and Victor were the ones to produce special lines for the Negro market. But because white companies depended on the profitable sales of race recordings as the phonograph business bottomed out with the rise of radio, they had little interest in interfering with the purest black sound. . . . Here again, then, mass culture in the form of commercial record companies and radio helped blacks develop and promote a unique, and increasingly national, black sound. . . . Black jazz recordings, or black employment in chain stores, became a vehicle for making a claim on mainstream society that racism had otherwise denied. When blacks patronized chain stores, they were asserting independence from local white society, not enslavement to cultural norms. No doubt their consumption of mass cultural products did give them interests in common with mainstream American society, and subjected them to the vagaries of the capitalist market. But with mass culture as raw material, blacks fashioned their own culture during the 1920s that made them feel no less black.

So it would seem that despite the expectations of mass culture promoters, chain stores, standard brands, motion pictures, and the radio did not absorb workers—white or black—into a middle-class, American culture. To some extent, people resisted aspects of mass culture, as ethnic workers did chain stores. But even when they indulged in Maxwell House Coffee, Rudolph Valentino, and radio entertainment, these experiences did not uproot them since they were encountered under local, often ethnic, sponsorship. When a politically conscious Communist worker asserted that "I had bought a jalopy in 1924, and it didn't change me. It just made it easier for me to function," he spoke for other workers who may not have been as self-conscious, but who like him were not made culturally middle class by the new products they consumed.

Beginning in the late 1920s and increasingly in the 1930s, local groups lost their ability to control the dissemination of mass culture. Sure of their hold over the middle-class market, chain stores more aggressively pursued ethnic, working-class markets, making it much harder for small merchants to survive. The elaboration of the Hollywood studio system and the costs of installing sound helped standardize moviegoing as well. Not only were neighborhood theaters increasingly taken over by chains, but the "talkies" themselves hushed the audience's interjections and replaced the ethnic troupes and amateur talent shows with taped shorts distributed nationally. Similarly, by the late 1920s, the local nonprofit radio era also had ended. In the aftermath of the passage of the Federal Radio Act of 1927, national, commercial, network radio imposed order on what admittedly had been a chaotic scene, but at the expense of small, local stations. When Chicago's workers switched on the radio by 1930, they were likely to hear the A & P Gypsies and the Eveready Hour on stations that had almost all affiliated with either NBC or CBS, or had negotiated—like even Chicago's WCFL, "the Voice of Labor"—to carry some network shows. The great depression only reinforced this national commercial trend by undermining small distributors of all kinds.

Thus, grass-roots control over mass culture did diminish during the thirties. But the extent to which this more national mass culture in the end succeeded in assimilating workers to middle-class values remains an open question. It is very likely that even though the structure of distributing mass culture did change by the 1930s, workers still did not fulfill the expectations of *True Story Magazine* editors and J. Walter Thompson Company executives. It is possible that workers maintained a distinctive sense of group identity even while participating, much the way blacks in the twenties did. Historical circumstances may have changed in such a way that workers continued to put mass culture to their own uses and remain a class apart. And increasingly over time, mass culture promoters—moviemakers, radio programmers, chain store operators, and advertisers—would recognize this possibility, and gear products to particular audiences; the 1930s mark the emergence of the concept of a segmented mass market, which gradually displaced expectations of one homogenous audience so prevalent in the 1920s.

Relatedly, we should not assume—as advocates of the embourgeoisement school do—that as workers shared more in a national commercial culture, they were necessarily depoliticized. In fact, there is much evidence to suggest that a more national mass culture helped unify workers previously divided along ethnic, racial, and geographical lines, facilitating the national organizing drive of the CIO. A working population that shared a common cultural life offered new opportunities for unified political action; sit-down strikers who charted baseball scores and danced to popular music together and union newspapers that kept their readers informed about network radio programs testified to the intriguing connections between cultural and political unity. Extension of this study into the 1930s and beyond might reveal that, ironically, mass culture did more to create an integrated working-class culture than a classless American one. In taking this study beyond the 1920s, thus, it is imperative that investigators continue to pay careful attention to the context in which people encountered mass culture, in order not to let the mythical assumptions about mass culture's homogenizing powers prevail as they did in our popular images of the twenties.

SOURCES

Bruce Barton

The Man Nobody Knows

"The business of America," remarked President Calvin Coolidge in 1925, "is business." Coolidge was right. Relieved of the burden of the Great War and victorious over the forces of alien radicalism, Americans gave themselves up to the world of business with an abandon not matched until the 1980s.

In this climate of materialism, religion, too, made accommodations and concessions. Advertising executive (and son of a Congregational minister) Bruce Barton captured the tone of the age in The Man Nobody Knows, *a 1925 best-seller that dramatically recast the image of Jesus Christ. Another Barton creation was Betty Crocker.*

What sort of a portrait of Jesus does Barton draw? Do you see any relationship between the Jesus presented here and the new consumer economy? Why might Americans have been receptive to Barton's account?

HOW IT CAME TO BE WRITTEN

The little boy sat bolt upright and still in the rough wooden chair, but his mind was very busy.

This was his weekly hour of revolt.

The kindly lady who could never seem to find her glasses would have been terribly shocked if she had known what was going on inside the little boy's mind.

"You must love Jesus," she said every Sunday, "and God."

The little boy did not say anything. He was afraid to say anything; he was almost afraid that something would happen to him because of the things he thought.

Love God! Who was always picking on people for having a good time and sending little boys to hell because they couldn't do better in a world which He had made so hard! Why didn't God pick on someone His own size?

Love Jesus! The little boy looked up at the picture which hung on the Sunday-school wall. It showed a pale young man with no muscle and a sad expression. The young man had red whiskers.

Then the little boy looked across to the other wall. There was Daniel, good old Daniel, standing off the lions. The little boy liked Daniel. He liked David, too, with the trusty sling that landed a stone square on the forehead of Goliath. And Moses, with his rod and his big brass snake. They were fighters—those three. He wondered if David could whip the champ. Samson could! That would have been a fight!

But Jesus! Jesus was the "Lamb of God." The little boy did not know what that meant, but it sounded like Mary's little lamb, something for girls—sissified. Jesus was also "meek and lowly," a "man of sorrows and acquainted with grief." He went around for three years telling people not to do things.

Sunday was Jesus' day; it was wrong to feel comfortable or laugh on Sunday.

The little boy was glad when the superintendent rang the bell and announced, "We will now sing the closing hymn." One more bad hour was over. For one more week the little boy had left Jesus behind.

Years went by and the boy grew up.

He began to wonder about Jesus.

He said to himself: "Only strong men inspire greatly and build greatly. Yet Jesus has inspired millions; what he founded changed the world. It is extraordinary."

The more sermons the man heard and the more books he read the more mystified he became.

One day he decided to wipe his mind clean of books and sermons.

He said, "I will read what the men who knew Jesus personally said about Him. I will read about Him as though He were a character in history, new to me, about whom I had never heard anything at all."

The man was amazed.

A physical weakling! Where did they get that idea? Jesus pushed a plane and swung an adz; He was a good carpenter. He slept outdoors and spent His days walking around His favorite lake. His muscles were so strong that when He drove the moneychangers out, nobody dared to oppose Him!

A kill-joy! He was the most popular dinner guest in Jerusalem! The criticism which proper people made was that He spent too much time with publicans and sinners (very good fellows, on the whole, the man thought) and enjoyed society too much. They called Him a "wine bibber and a gluttonous man."

A failure! He picked up twelve humble men and created an organization that won the world.

When the man had finished his reading, he exclaimed, "This is a man nobody knows!

"Someday," said he, "someone will write a book about Jesus. He will describe the same discovery I have made about Him, that many other people are waiting to make." For, as the man's little-boy notions and prejudices vanished, he saw the day-to-day life of Him who lived the greatest life and was alive and knowable beyond the mists of tradition.

So the man waited for someone to write the book, but no one did. Instead, more books were published that showed the vital Christ as one who was weak and unhappy, passive and resigned.

The man became impatient. One day he said, "I believe I will try to write that book myself."

And he did.

THE SOCIABLE MAN

A wicked falsehood has come down through the ages.

It reappears every once in a while, usually in works by reputable and well-meaning writers, and usually in some such form as this: The author will, in his reading and research, have come onto the supposed description of Jesus by the Roman Lentulus, who succeeded Pilate as governor of Jerusalem. Lentulus's description was detailed, and it concluded with the unfortunate statement: "Nobody has ever seen him laugh."

We want to be reverent. But to worship a Lord who never laughed—it is a strain.

The quotation from Lentulus is a forgery, penned by an unknown impostor in a later century; yet how persistently it has lived, and with what tragic thoroughness it has done its work. How many millions of happy-minded folk, when they have thought of Jesus at all, have had a feeling of uneasiness! "Suppose," they have said, "He were to enter the room and find us laughing and enjoying ourselves! When there is so much suffering and sin in the world, is it right to be happy? What would Jesus say?" . . .

All of the four Gospels contain very full accounts of the weeping which attended the crucifixion—the final miracle; John alone remembered the laughter amid which the first one was performed. It was in the little town of Cana, not far from Nazareth. Jesus and His mother had been invited to a wedding feast. Often such a celebration continued for several days. Everybody was expected to enjoy himself to the utmost as long as the food and drink lasted—and it was a point of pride with the bride's mother that both food and drink should last a long time.

Enthusiasm was at a high pitch on this occasion when a servant entered nervously and whispered a distressing message to the hostess. The wine had given out. Picture if you will the poor woman's chagrin! This was her daughter's wedding—the one social event in the life of the family. For it they had made every sort of sacrifice, cutting a little from their living expenses, going without a new garment, neglecting a needed repair in the house. After it was over they could count the cost and find some way to even up; but until the last guest had gone, no effort should be spared to uphold the family's dignity in the neighborhood. To this end the poor woman had planned it all in her proud sensitive fashion, and now, at the very height of success, the whole structure of her dreams came tumbling down. The wine had given out.

Most of the guests were too busy to note the entrance of the servant or the quick flush that mounted to the hostess's cheek. But one woman's sight and sympathy were keener. The mother of Jesus saw every move in the little tragedy, and with that instinct which is quicker than reason she understood its meaning.

She leaned over to her son and confided the message which her friendly eyes had read. "Son, the wine is gone."

Well, what of it? He was only one of a score of guests, perhaps a hundred. There had been wine enough as it was; the party was noisy and none too restrained. Let them quiet themselves, say good-by to their hostess and get off to bed. They would feel much better for it in the morning. . . . Or, if they persisted in carrying on, let the relatives of the hostess make up the deficiency. He was only a guest from another town. Doubtless the woman's brothers were present, or, if not, then some of her neighbors. They could easily slip out and bring back wine from their own stores before the shortage was commented on. . . . Why should He be worried with what was none of His affair?

Besides, there was a precedent in the matter. Only a few weeks before when He was tortured by hunger in the wilderness, He had refused to use His miraculous power to transform stones into bread. If the recruiting of His own strength was beneath the dignity of a miracle, surely He could hardly be expected to intervene to prolong a party like this. . . . "My friends, we have had a very pleasant evening and I am surely indebted to our hostess for it. I think we have trespassed as far as we should upon her generosity. I suggest that we wish the happy couple a long and prosperous life, and take our way home." Surely this is the solemn fashion in which a teacher ought to talk.

Did any such thoughts cross His mind? If they did, we have no record of it. He glanced across at the wistful face of the hostess—already tears sparkled under her lids—He remembered that the event was the one social triumph of her self-sacrificing life, and instantly His decision was formed. He sent for six pots and ordered them filled with water. When the contents of the first one was drawn, the ruler of the feast lifted his glass to the bridegroom and the bewildered but happy hostess: "Every man setteth on first the good wine," he cried, "and when men have drunk freely, then that which is worse; but thou hast kept the good wine until now."

The mother of Jesus looked on in wonder. She had never fully understood her son; she did not ask to understand. He had somehow saved the situation; she did not question how. And what was sufficient for her is sufficient for us. The whole problem of His "miracles" is beyond our arguments at this distance. We either accept them or reject them according to the makeup of our minds. But if they are to be accepted at all, then surely this first one ought not to be omitted. It often is omitted from the comments on His life or at least passed over hastily. But to us who think first of His friendliness, it seems gloriously characteristic, setting the pattern for all the three years that were to follow. "I came that ye might have life," He exclaimed, "and have it more abundantly." So, at the very outset, He makes use of His mighty power, not to point a solemn moral, not to relieve a sufferer's pain, but to keep a happy party from breaking up too soon, to save a hostess from embarrassment. . . . See, the ruler of the feast rises to propose a toast . . . hark to the discordant strains of the neighborhood orchestra. Look, a tall broad-shouldered man towers above the crowd . . . listen, hear His laugh! . . .

He loved to be in the crowd. Apparently He attended all the feasts at Jerusalem not merely as religious festivals but because all the folks were there and He had an all-embracing fondness for folks. We err if we think of Him as a social outsider. To be sure it was the "poor" who "heard him gladly," and most of His close disciples were men and women of the lower classes. But there was a time when He was quite the favorite in Jerusalem. The story of His days is dotted with these phrases: "A certain ruler desired him that he should eat with him." . . . "They desired him greatly to remain and he abode two days." Even after He had denounced the Pharisees as "hypocrites" and "children of the devil," even when the clouds of disapproval were gathering for the final storm, they still could not resist the charm of His presence, nor the stimulation of His talk. Close up to the end of the story we read that a "certain chief of the Pharisees desired him that he would dine at his house." . . .

. . . Indeed, we must often wonder how much of His humor had been lost to us by the literal-mindedness of His chroniclers. How about that incident, for example, at the pool of Bethesda? The pool was in Jerusalem near the sheep market and was supposed to have magic properties. Hundreds of sick people were left along the edges to wait for the moment when the waters would be stirred by the visit of an angel from Heaven; whoever managed to get into the water first, after the stirring, was healed. Passing by it one afternoon, Jesus heard the whining voice of an old fellow who had been lying there for thirty-eight years. Every time the pool stirred, he made a half-hearted effort to jump in; but there was always someone with more determination or more helpful friends. So the old chap would drop back onto his couch and bemoan his hard luck. He was bemoaning it on this day when Jesus stopped and looked at him with a whimsical smile.

"Wilt thou be made whole?" Jesus demanded.

The old man was instantly resentful. What an absurd question! Of course he wanted to be made whole! Hadn't he been trying for thirty-eight years? Why annoy him with such an impertinence?

The smile on the face of Jesus broadened. He knew better. Enjoying poor health was the old fellow's profession. He was a marked man in those parts; in the daily grumblings when the sufferers aired their complaints he was the principal speaker. Nobody had so many pains as he; no other symptoms were so distressing. Let these newcomers take a back seat. His was the only original hard-luck story. He had been there for thirty-eight years.

The keen eyes of Jesus saw deep into the souls of men. There was a twinkle in them now.

"Get up," He said briskly, "and walk."

The old chap spluttered and grumbled, but there was no resisting the command of that presence. He rose, discovered to his own amazement that he could stand, rolled up his bed, and walked off. A reverent hush fell on the assembled crowd, but before they could find their voices Jesus, too, was gone. The disciples were too deeply impressed for comment; they dropped back a respectful distance and Jesus walked on alone. Suppose they had followed closer? Wouldn't their ears have been startled by something suspiciously like a chuckle? It was a good joke on the old chap. He imagined that he'd had hard luck, but his real hard luck was just beginning. . . . No more of the pleasure of self-pity for him. . . . What would his folks say that night when he came walking in? What a shock to him in the morning when they told him that he'd have to go to work! . . .

That was the message of Jesus—that God is supremely better than anybody had ever dared to believe. Not a petulant Creator, who had lost control of His creation and, in wrath, was determined to destroy it all. Not a stern Judge dispensing impersonal justice. Not a vain King who must be flattered and bribed into concessions of mercy. Not a rigid Accountant, checking up the sins against the penances and striking a cold hard balance. Not any of these . . . nothing like these; but a great Companion, a wonderful Friend, a kindly indulgent, joy-loving Father. . . .

For three years Jesus walked up and down the shores of His lake and through the streets of towns and cities, trying to make them understand. Then came the end and, almost before His fine firm flesh was cold, the distortion began. He who cared nothing for ceremonies and forms was made the idol of formalism. Men hid themselves in monasteries; they lashed themselves with whips; they tortured their skins with harsh garments and cried out that they were followers of Him—of Him who loved the crowd, who gathered children about Him wherever He went, who celebrated the calling of a new disciple with a feast in which all the neighborhood joined! "Hold your heads high," He had exclaimed; "you are lords of the universe . . . only a little lower than the angels . . . children of God." But the hymn writers knew better. They wrote:

"Oh to be *nothing, nothing*"
and
"For such a *worm* as I."

His last supper with His disciples was an hour of solemn memories. Their minds were heavy with foreboding. He talked earnestly, but the whole purpose of His talk was to lift up their hearts, to make them think nobly of themselves, to fill their spirits with a conquering faith.

"My joy I leave with you," He exclaimed.

"Be of good cheer," He exclaimed.

Joy, cheer—these are the words by which He wished to be remembered. But down through the ages has come the wicked falsehood that He never laughed.

The New Woman: A Photo Essay

By the 1920s, the image of the Victorian woman, with her corsets, floor-length gowns, full figure, and long hair, had passed into the realm of nostalgia. The "modern" woman of the 1920s was strikingly different. The "flapper" look featured knee-length (or shorter) skirts, a thin, boyish figure, and short, bobbed hair.

It is easier to describe the New Woman than to decide what this image means. From the photographs on the following pages, all from the 1920s, what can one say about the New Woman? What relationship might one postulate between the New Woman and the nineteenth Amendment (1920), which provided for woman suffrage? Between the New Woman and the Great War? Between the New Woman and the mass consumption economy?

Miss Suzette Dewey, daughter of Assistant Secretary of the Treasury and Mrs. Chas. Dewey beside her roadster, 1927.
Library of Congress.

Margaret Gorman, Miss America, 1921.
Library of Congress.

Tyhee Beach No. 6, Savannah, Georgia.
Library of Congress.

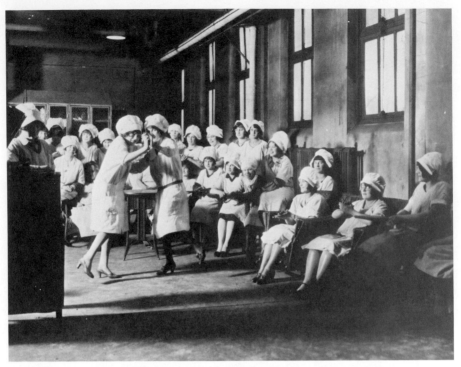

Girls Dancing During Noon Hour at Armour & Company Plant, 1927.
National Archives.

CHAPTER 8

The Great Depression and the New Deal

The economic decline that followed the stock market crash of October 1929 was unparalleled in the nation's history. Over 4 million people were unemployed in 1930, 8 million in 1931, and almost 13 million, or close to one-quarter of the total civilian labor force, in 1933. Detroit, a city symbolic of the high-flying consumer economy of the 1920s, suffered in proportion to its earlier prosperity. Of the city's 690,000 gainful workers in October 1930, 223,000 were without jobs in March 1931. Because millions of small farmers reacted to falling prices by continuing to produce full crops, agricultural production fell little; farm income, however, was halved in the four years after 1929.

Work for wages was the heart of the economy of the early 1930s, and when it faltered, the effects rippled through every area of American life. In one sixty-day period in Detroit, for example, some 50,000 homeowners lost the equity in their property—the banks foreclosed on their mortgages and took their homes. Black children went to school without food. Throughout that city, people of all races rummaged through garbage cans in the city's alleys, stole dog biscuits from the pound, and even tried to dig homes in the ground.

Herbert Hoover was not a do-nothing president. His attempts to persuade business to maintain wage rates were moderately successful for more than two years. Through the Agricultural Marketing Act, passed four months prior to the crash, the national government sought to maintain agricultural prices. National expenditures on public works increased. The Reconstruction Finance Corporation lent funds to banks, railroads, building and loan associations, and insurance companies. It saved a number from bankruptcy.

Perhaps Hoover's greatest failure was his firm opposition to national expenditures for relief. Private charity and city government, the primary agencies of relief, soon provided inadequate. Even in Philadelphia, where philanthropic traditions ran deep, the city's Community Council described its situation in July 1932 as one of "slow starvation and progressive deterioration of family life." Detroit, with its highly developed *public* welfare system, in 1931 debated whether

169

to cut its welfare rolls in half or reduce payments by 50 percent—whether to "feed half the people or half-feed the people."

As people gradually became aware just how deep the crisis went, and as the government under Hoover failed to deal with it, it became obvious that fundamental change of one kind or another might be the only solution. One possible direction of change was dictatorship. The great depression was not a domestic crisis only. European nations were hit just as severely as the United States. And there, turning to an authoritarian figure—a Hitler in Germany or a Mussolini in Italy—at least promised to restore order and a sense of purpose. Europe's dictators frightened many Americans. But they also led many to think of strong leadership as a necessary phenomenon of the age, a prerequisite to the restoration of international order and domestic prosperity.

Another possible direction—a threat or a promise, depending on where one stood politically—was revolution. To many, some sort of socialist or communist transformation of the economic and political order seemed the only answer. Early in the decade, the Communist party did make some gains. The party tried to organize unemployed urban workers into "councils," built around neighborhoods, blocks, or even apartment houses. In 1930, these Unemployed Councils managed a series of demonstrations in major cities, drawing crowds ranging from 5000 to 35,000. Later, after they deemphasized their talk of immediate revolution, the Communists had some substantial successes within the Congress of Industrial Organizations (CIO), a new and powerful labor union. Large numbers of intellectuals—writers, scientists, teachers, and bureaucrats—also joined the party. The Socialist party, too, began a vigorous program of recruitment and political campaigning, with the very popular Norman Thomas as its presidential candidate.

Into this atmosphere of uncertainty came Franklin Delano Roosevelt. A master at capturing the national mood in his speeches, Roosevelt talked of action, of advance, of what he called a New Deal for the American people.

It was not all talk, of course. Within three months of his inauguration in March 1933—the so-called Hundred Days—Roosevelt had signed into law a bewildering variety of legislation, much of it designed either to restructure the economy or to bring recovery. In the Emergency Banking Act, Congress gave the president broad discretionary powers over financial transactions. The Government Economy Act cut government employees' salaries and veterans' pensions in an attempt to balance the federal budget. The Agricultural Adjustment Act (AAA) granted subsidies to farmers who voluntarily reduced acreage or crops. In an act of boldness not to be repeated, development of the Tennessee River Valley was turned over to a public corporation.

Akin to the policy toward agriculture but more comprehensive, the National Industrial Recovery Act (NIRA) attempted to promote recovery by granting businesses the right to cooperate. Each industry wrote its own code of fair competition—setting minimum wages and maximum workweeks, limiting construction of new capacity, even fixing prices by prohibiting sales below cost. In addition, section 7(a) of the NIRA appeared to give workers the right to bargain collectively with employers. (The NIRA is perhaps the best evidence that the New Deal sought to strengthen capitalism rather than replace it with social-ism.)

Relief efforts went well beyond those of the Hoover administration. To ab-sorb the unemployed, Congress created the Civilian Conservation Corps (CCC) and set up the Public Works Administration to promote construction in the pub-lic interest. In 1935, the Works Progress Administration (WPA) was established to coordinate public works. The Emergency Relief Act directed Hoover's Re-construction Finance Corporation to make relief funds available to the states and signaled the shift away from Hoover's opposition to using federal money for relief. The Social Security Act of 1935 brought the national government into old-age assistance and insurance and unemployment compensation.

For all its accomplishments, the New Deal made no commitment to reme-dying even the worst aspects of race relations: racial segregation, racial dis-crimination, denial of the suffrage in the south, the lynching of black Americans. Fearful that a strong stand on racial issues would alienate the southern wing of his Democratic party and bring an end to the New Deal, Roosevelt refused to use the fourteenth Amendment to help blacks, and although sympathetic to the cause, he failed to support the growing movement for a federal antilynching statute. Because they were poor (rather than because they were black), many black Americans benefited from New Deal relief programs. For example, al-though blacks made up 10 percent of the population, they filled 18 percent of the WPA rolls. Yet some New Deal programs actually made life worse for blacks. When, for example, southern farmers took land out of production under the AAA, some 200,000 rural black farm workers were left jobless. Moreover, nu-merous New Deal programs gave blacks less than they should have received. Many NIRA wage codes allowed businesses to pay lower wages to black than to white workers. Federal public housing programs often amounted to "Negro clearance." And the showy New Deal model communities, like Greenbelt, Maryland, had no black residents.

Historians have long debated whether the New Deal had any significant ef-fect on the depression, and there is no more agreement on the New Deal's legacy for black Americans. But of one thing there can be little doubt. Roosevelt did manage to steal the rhetorical thunder from *both* the advocates of dictatorship and the proponents of revolution and to convince most blacks that the New Deal was worthy of their support. When he presented his legislative program to Congress, he could sound as though he meant to do everything that any Euro-pean leader could, asking for "broad executive power to wage a war against the emergency, as great as the power that would be given to me if we were in fact invaded by a foreign foe." And he could now and then sound like a bit of a so-cialist, lambasting the "economic royalists" who controlled the nation's wealth. Most of the Rooseveltian rhetoric designed to appeal to blacks came from the lips of Eleanor rather than Franklin, but significantly, in 1936, to his famous phrase "forgotten man" he added "forgotten races."

Historians have also argued about whether Roosevelt's New Deal "saved" American capitalism or fundamentally altered it. What he was probably most anxious to save, however, was not the economic system, or even the political structure, but the faith of his constituents *in* the system. The nation did not respond to calls for revolution. The actual power of the Communist party probably declined after Roosevelt's election. Blacks affirmed their commitment to a political party—the Democratic party—with an influential southern, racist component. The "deal" Roosevelt offered the people may not have been as "new" as he made it sound, but he did convince most Americans—and most black Americans—that he was in charge of the only game in town.

INTERPRETIVE ESSAY

Cheryl Lynn Greenberg

Mean Streets: Black Harlem in the Great Depression

On the eve of the great depression, the area of upper Manhattan known as Harlem was two very different places. For white, middle- and upper-class Americans, who did not live there, it was a symbol of the "jazz age," the antithesis of Main Street, a place where "expressive," "primitive," and "exotic" Negroes sang and danced and laughed and otherwise rebelled against the materialism and monotony of American life. For many of its black residents, Harlem was a slum, albeit a newly created one. As late as 1910, Harlem was a racially and ethnically diverse and reasonably prosperous community. During the 1910s and 1920s, massive in-migration of blacks from the rural south and from the West Indies, along with the out-migration of Italians, Jews, and other whites, created a community that was mostly black and very poor—in some respects, today's Harlem. Thus even before the stock market crash of October 1929 triggered economic decline, life in Harlem was difficult. Blacks paid high rents, did the menial and unskilled tasks regarded as "Negro jobs," and suffered from the highest rates of infant mortality and tuberculosis of any New York City neighborhood.

Cheryl Lynn Greenberg's essay can help us understand some of the ways in which the black people of Harlem understood and dealt with their basic poverty and with the additional burdens imposed by the great depression. It is a complex story, involving federal, state, and local governments, private agencies, and community organizations, as well as some creative family management. Having read Greenberg's account, do you think Harlem blacks survived the great depression with dignity, or were they demeaned by the crisis? What evidence is there that black economic problems were significantly exacerbated by race? And how might Greenberg's essay lead one to be more critical of the inactivity of the New Deal on racial issues (chronicled in the introduction to this chapter)?

Whether on relief or employed in private industry (and most black families experienced both at some point in the depression), few managed to make ends meet without some sort of extra income. People with little helped those with less; ties of family and community proved strong and durable. Men and women picked up temporary work whenever possible. Families took in lodgers or boarders or moved into the homes of relatives. Many borrowed money from friends or kin or bought groceries on credit from local merchants. Some engaged in illegal activities. A large proportion of Harlem arrests during the depression were for possession of policy slips, prostitution, and illegal distilling, all income-producing rather than violent crimes. These activities were certainly not new to the 1930s; blacks had been poor before this. But more families resorted to them in the years of the depression.

One woman's experiences illustrate the available choices—and their limitations. Thirza Johnson was twenty-one years old with three young children. Her husband had worked for the WPA for eighteen months. Despite that income the family could not pay its bills, and Mr. Johnson "tampered with the gas meter." For this he received sixty days in jail. The family had been receiving $5.40 every two weeks to supplement Mr. Johnson's paycheck, but without the WPA income that amount was completely inadequate. The utility companies cut off the gas and the electricity and Mrs. Johnson fell a month behind in paying the rent. When all three children fell ill, she asked her mother to come in from New Jersey to help. Her mother told her employer she needed a few days off to tend to her grandchildren. He fired her. This brought the number in the house to five, but the relief agency refused to increase the family's relief allotment because Mrs. Johnson's mother was not a New York resident. The grocery store gave her no more credit. Completely desperate, Mrs. Johnson turned to the Universal Negro Improvement Association (UNIA) for aid, and the Home Relief Bureau at last agreed to help.

Families like the Johnsons were so poor they were often forced to choose among necessities. Consumption patterns of Harlem families reveal both their real poverty and the constraints of living in a segregated community. Because of low incomes, African-Americans lived in poor, overcrowded housing, with high disease and death rates and high crime. Yet, . . . the New Deal programs had brought some progress to Harlem as well: health care, for example, improved in the depression decade, and for a few, new public housing became available.

Certainly black Harlem was not one homogeneous neighborhood. Within it lived population clusters divided by income and nativity. On some blocks only a few families received relief; on others, a majority did. Particular streets hosted the grocery stores, benefit societies, or restaurants of different national groups. As Vernal Williams, lawyer for the Consolidated Tenants League, explained:

> Why, every one of us have our own standards of living. We don't all live together. Just as you have Riverside, West End and Park Avenues, we have the same standard among our people, and you won't find that doctors [are] willing to go to the cheaper quarters along where the longshoremen live. . . . [To live in the Dunbar apartments, for example] you had to be a doctor or a wealthy business man or work in the Post Office.

Nevertheless, virtually no family was immune from the depression's ravages, and all shared both the burdens of life in a discriminatory society and the strengths found in networks of support within the black community.

MAKING ENDS MEET

The most important first step for impoverished Harlem families was to supplement their earnings. Many families in the New Deal era turned to the long-standing practice in black communities of taking in lodgers. Perhaps because everyone was poor, the number of lodgers in black families in this period did not appear to bear a relation to any economic consideration. In the Harlem sample of the 1935 Bureau of Labor Statistics study, neither the family's earnings nor its expenditures provided a reliable predictor of whether or not that family would take in lodgers. The decision did depend on family size to some extent; families with many children seldom had lodgers. . . .

Black families in Harlem as elsewhere also turned to nonfinancial solutions, such as swapping and borrowing, and relied on the generosity of those temporarily better off. Evidence of these sorts of alternative economic strategies comes from many sources. Relief agencies, for example, demanded from applicants an accounting of expenses and income for the previous twelve months. Other agencies, such as the Bureau of Labor Statistics, investigated current earnings of nonrelief families. Private organizations conducted their own studies. Of the eighty-one Harlem families in the BLS sample, sixteen reported receiving gifts, and one a loan, from friends or relatives. Three others had picked up odd jobs and thirteen received "other income" from interest, "pool game," or sickness benefits from a lodge. If the number of families receiving money from gifts, loans, insurance, winnings, odd jobs, and lodgers are added together, over half the BLS survey families supplemented their earnings over the year, with an average of $153 per family with such added income. Families turning to the Unemployed Unit of the UNIA for help in obtaining relief also reported a heavy reliance on such means of supplementing their incomes.

Several families told of moving in with friends or relatives or receiving economic help from them. Both Nathan Campbell and Sarah Johnson told the UNIA that their family received money from friends. Minnie Jones complained she had to borrow money from her employer for food. In every income category, almost twice as many blacks as whites in New York City reported contributing to the support of relatives in 1935. Many men and women worked in exchange for free rent. Madeline Bright served as superintendent of an apartment building in return for lodgings. This, too, was common practice; one-fifth of single black women not living with families surveyed in Philadelphia, and two-fifths of such women in Chicago, engaged in this sort of exchange as well.

The proportion of all black families relying on these practices cannot be precisely documented. But impressionistic evidence suggests such interactions were commonplace. Francie, the protagonist of Louise Meriwether's Harlem-based novel, *Daddy Was a Number Runner*, borrows from her neighbor:

> [Mother] gave me a weak cup of tea.
> "We got any sugar?"
> "Borrow some from Mrs. Caldwell."
> I got a chipped cup from the cupboard and going to the dining-room window, I knocked at our neighbor's window-pane. The Caldwells lived in the apartment next door and our dining rooms faced each other. . . . Maude came to the window.
> "Can I borrow a half cup of sugar?" I asked.
> She took the cup and disappeared, returning in a few minutes with it al-

most full. "Y'all got any bread?" she asked. "I need one more piece to make a sandwich."

"Maude wants to borrow a piece of bread," I told Mother.

"Give her two slices," Mother said.

Loften Mitchell remembered: "In this climate [Harlem] the cooking of chitterlings brought a curious neighbor to the door. Mrs. Mitchell, you cooking chitterlings? I thought you might need a little cornbread to go with em.' A moment later a West Indian neighbor appeared with rice and beans. Another neighbor followed with some beer to wash down the meal. What started as a family supper developed into a building party." As another contemporary wrote, "The people [of Harlem] are the kindest and most sympathetic people that can be found. They will take one into the home and share everything there except the mate or sweetheart."

Some turned to illegal activities such as bootlegging and numbers running. Between 1931 and 1935, over half of all black arrests in Harlem were for "possession of policy slips," and police charged three-quarters of all black females arrested with vagrancy and prostitution. One woman included in a Welfare Council study explained that she earned money from "rent parties and home brew sales" and rented out rooms in her apartment for "immoral" purposes. The investigator suspected another family of earning money in this fashion as well, but that family did not admit it. Several people reported altering gas pipes and electrical wiring to avoid paying utilities; arrests for "tampering with gas meter" or similar offenses dotted the Harlem precinct records.

> Our electricity had been cut off for months for nonpayment . . . [explained Francie] so Daddy had made the jumper. . . . I took the metal wire from behind the box where we hid it, and opening the box, I inserted the two prongs behind the fuse the way Daddy had showed me. . . . Daddy said almost everybody in Harlem used a jumper.

Lillian Holmes, to document her need for relief, told the UNIA how she earned money in the past. For several years, she reported, she had been "engaged in the illegitimate business of *manufacturing liquor*" (UNIA's emphasis): six gallons of 100-proof alcohol a week. Her living costs, including manufacturing, came to $199.90 a month, while she earned approximately $208. In April 1937, however, there was a *"RAID"* (UNIA emphasis), at which time she applied for relief but was rejected. Paroled, the UNIA record concludes, she "return[ed] to making 'hot stuff.'" The record does not reveal whether the UNIA persuaded the relief agency in question to accept Ms. Holmes or whether she continued her life of crime.

Income-producing strategies did not add enough income for most families to live comfortably. They had to budget carefully and often deprive themselves of one necessity to afford another. The widespread poverty of Harlem and its character as a segregated community were reflected in consumption decisions made by black families. High rents required large portions of family earnings, and family size determined the amount spent on food and other household goods.

The amount families set aside for such items as recreation and personal care, by contrast, varied according to personal decision. Consumption decisions therefore depended on many factors, some beyond the control of the family. How Harlemites chose to spend their money reflected all these considerations and demonstrates the extreme poverty of the area.

The average family in the Harlem sample of the Bureau of Labor Statistics study spent $548 per person for the year. Both income and the size of the family, of course, affected this figure. Not unexpectedly, the poorer the family, the more per-person expenditures depended on the number of members; as more people sit down to eat a small pie, each slice becomes smaller. At higher income levels, families spent with fewer constraints; a larger family could spend as much per person as a smaller family and simply save less.

The typical blue-collar and clerical nonrelief black family earned $1446 and spent $1459, compared with white earnings of $1745 and expenditures of $1839. On average, black families spent just under a third of their total expenditures, $450, on food and almost as much, $417, on rent. White families, by contrast, spent approximately 40 percent of their budget on food and 20 percent on rent. Controlling for income yields similar results. Black families at each economic and occupational level spent a lower proportion of their total income on food, and a higher proportion on rent, than did comparable whites. Blacks at each level spent more than whites on other housing costs, personal care, and clothing, but less on medical care. . . .

Blacks spent less of their total income on food than whites at the same economic level, in part because their families were smaller and in part because so much of their income was used for rent. But food was costly; food prices did rise during the depression, and they were higher in Harlem. Between 1934 and 1935, for example, food prices rose 11 percent. In the later year, a dozen eggs cost approximately 40 cents in most city neighborhoods, and 42 cents in Harlem. Flour cost 6 cents a pound; cornmeal 7 cents; again slightly higher in Harlem. Milk cost 13 cents a quart, potatoes 2 cents a pound, and carrots 6 cents a bunch. Meat was more expensive. Bacon cost 37 cents a pound; ham 29 cents citywide, and more in Harlem. *Amsterdam News* columnist Roi Ottley noted that food prices in Harlem were "considerably higher" than elsewhere in the city during the depression. "For every dollar spent on food the Negro housewife has to spend at least six cents in excess of what the housewife in any other comparable section is required to pay." Adam Clayton Powell, Jr., claimed "foodstuffs were 17 percent above the general level." The Reverend Mr. Garner of Grace Church complained: "Our food in Harlem is higher than the food we can get elsewhere. Food on the east side is much cheaper than food in the immediate neighborhood." The Department of Markets received more complaints from Harlem than from anywhere else about unfair costs and "shortweight practices."

Black families spent slightly more on clothing, household furnishings, and personal care than comparably impoverished whites possibly because, poor for a longer time, they could not continue to defer those needs. For medical care, white spending exceeded black in both amount and percentage of income. For both races, families with lower incomes were less likely to have annual medical exams or to go to a private doctor rather than a free clinic. Many poor families deferred dental visits.

The poorest spent less on every item in the budget than the general pool of blacks did. In fact, in the Harlem sample the poorest blacks had so little disposable income that the amount allotted for food did not change, regardless of family size. With more members a family might vary the quality of food it bought (less meat, for example, and more vegetables), but it could not afford to increase its overall food budget.

A British West Indian family of six in the BLS survey typifies this frugality. The mother worked intermittently as a general helper in a laundry for $3 a day. The father, a painter's helper, worked all fifty-two weeks that year but earned $22 per week for six months, and only $19 a week during the next six months. The two adult sons living at home worked only sporadically, one as a porter in a tailor shop and the other as a helper in the meat market. Two other sons attended high school. This family reported monthly expenditures of $40 for rent, $10.87 for "household operation," $14.72 for clothing, and $54.08 for food. They held their other expenses to a minimum: less than $15 for "furnishings and equipment" for the entire year, $39 for recreation, and the same amount for "personal care." Six dollars that year went for medical care, $4 for education, and $4 for "community welfare"—even in poverty, the family helped others in need. Despite their best efforts and a $15 gift or loan, the family reported debts of $55 at the end of the year.

This family was by no means unique. Most of the Harlem families in the survey did not break even; fully three-quarters of them ended the year with some small deficit. Interestingly, the percentage of families with deficits did not decline as income rose. Rather, most families appeared to live at a level slightly above their actual income. Presumably, these families had all suffered a decline in their usual earnings and had not yet adjusted completely.

Still, for each income level, the average deficit of white families far exceeded that of black. Ninety-five percent of all Harlem black families in the survey either overspent by less than 5 percent of their total income or actually saved money. Only two families exceeded their income by more than 10 percent. The average debt for whites who had debts was $265, or 15 percent of their total expenditures, according to the BLS citywide study of wage earners; while for blacks it was $115, or 8 percent. . . .

Poverty alone could not account for indebtedness, since, according to the Harlem sample, black families at all income levels were equally likely to fall into debt. Nor could family size: among nonrelief families, those with deficits were no larger than those without. In other words, families of all types used debt as one way to stretch tight budgets. This did not imply extravagance, however, since those families with surpluses and those with debts spent approximately the same amount for food, rent, and all other items. In practical terms, then, any wage-earning family could find itself in the red. An emergency need would probably force a family into debt since virtually all lived close to the edge of their income level. As Myrtle Pollard explained, impoverished Harlemites got along by buying one thing at a time. If someone needed a new coat, the rent would have to go unpaid that month. When this strategy failed, a family could find itself forced to turn to relief.

The Bennett family illustrates the preceding discussion: the all-too-common pattern of economic decline, a cut in consumption, debt, and finally application for relief. David Bennett, a thirty-three-year-old laborer, and his wife and two children lived on his WPA wages until January 1937, when he received his last $14.46 check. He had found work as a longshoreman and earned $88 that month. He also supplemented this with $32 in tips he received as a "helper" at the Washington Market. That month, despite $15 in medical bills, the family met all its obligations, paying $24 in rent, $37 on food, and an $8 insurance premium. After these costs, plus clothing, utilities, and carfare, there was still something left over for cigarettes and "entertainment." The following month David earned only $66 at the docks and $14 at the market, but the family still managed by cutting food purchases down to $30, paying only half the insurance, and foregoing clothing and "entertainment." The family struggled on this way for a while; David earning between $80 and $110 a month, and everyone spending less.

The third week in August, however, David lost his longshoreman's job, and his wife hired herself out as a domestic worker to two families. One paid her $7 a week, the other $4. By skimping on food they managed again, but September was much worse. With only Mrs. Bennett's wages of $44 and the $12 David earned shining shoes, they eliminated all spending but rent and food (which they had cut again). In October they decided to take in a lodger who paid $3.50 a week. They broke even only by pawning a watch and eight pairs of shoes.

In November, David's wife lost her previous jobs and hired on with two new families. She now earned $4 from one, and $3 from the other. That month the Bennetts went into debt. Food, rent, and utilities cost $65, while David's $12 from shoeshining, his wife's $28, and the lodger's $14 came to only $54. They withdrew money from their Christmas fund in December, but still could pay only half their rent that month. By the new year, they had to accept a loan of $10 and a gift of $3.50 from friends because Mrs. Bennett had again lost her jobs. Now able to afford only $22 for food, and paying no rent or utilities, they applied for public relief. Rejected with no explanation, they took another loan of $15, and turned to the UNIA for help. The file ended with the notation "no food."

CONSEQUENCES

The constant choosing between necessities or going without, the struggle to maintain a livable income, and the weight of discrimination and segregation resulted in poor housing and health, high crime, and inadequate public facilities in Harlem.

Neither the depression nor the New Deal lessened the segregation that trapped black families in substandard housing. Rental costs for Harlem residents remained high in the depression, although absolute costs fell slightly. In

1933, the City Affairs Committee reported Harlem to have "the worst housing conditions in the city. . . . Negro tenants pay from one percent to twenty percent more of their income for rent than any other group, despite the fact that the income of the Negro family is about 17 percent lower than that of the typical family in any other section of the city." This committee in fact understated the problem. The Neighborhood Health Committee surveyed rental costs in Manhattan in the depression's early years. It found that while the average Manhattan apartment rented for $44 a month, most in poor areas paid significantly less. In East Harlem, for example, where poor Italians and Puerto Ricans lived, rents averaged $30. In Central Harlem, however, rents never fell below $31 a month, and often ran as high as $70. The average resident of Central Harlem paid $52. The League of Mothers' Clubs found tenement-house blacks paid almost $1 more per room, per month, than comparably poor whites. Thus, for most Harlem residents, rents had not declined much; they were in some cases even higher than pre-depression rates. Even the Brotherhood of Sleeping Car Porters was forced to resort to rent parties to pay for its offices.

The policies of relief agencies aggravated housing problems. The enormous demand on their limited funds led several to provide no rent payments until eviction was threatened. Landlords learned that the sooner they made such threats the sooner they received overdue rent. Families who did not qualify for aid therefore faced eviction earlier than they otherwise might have. The Communist party, which fought eviction notices in the courts and carried the furniture of evicted families back into their apartments in an effort to stop the process, reported that hundreds of successful evictions occurred each week. . . .

Some black families economized by moving to smaller apartments of lesser quality or by moving in with relatives. The biggest problem in Harlem, the Welfare Council reported, was "the changes . . . in living conditions. . . . 'Doubling up' of families was common." Previously independent children returned to their parents' homes. The Charity Organization Society reported that, of families receiving care, twice as many families lived with relatives in 1931 as two years earlier; three times as many took in lodgers. A study of city slums found the average number of persons per room had risen in Harlem since the beginning of the depression because of such changes in household composition.

All this was due not only to poverty but also to segregation. As the New York State Temporary Commission on the Condition of the Urban Colored Population pointed out, blacks gained access to apartments only when conditions there deteriorated and white tenants could not be found. In other words, blacks inherited bad conditions that simply got worse. Landlords neglected these apartments, but charged high rents because blacks could not find housing elsewhere. Mrs. S. Jecter of 16 West 136th Street, who supported her three children on her part-time earnings, complained that her landlord refused to make any repairs. She reminded him often of the fact that her gas stove was broken and she had no doorknobs, making the apartment impossible to lock. She paid her rent every month, nonetheless. She came home one day to find an eviction notice. Her landlord had grown tired of her complaints, and she was left without recourse. . . .

The cost of the housing did not reflect its quality. Of the thirty-one inhabited buildings on two blocks studied by the Housing Commission, nine had been officially condemned. The Housing Authority concluded after a survey of Harlem that "due to circumstances over which they have no control, many families are compelled to accept the old law tenement accommodations [buildings erected before 1901 and therefore not subject to the health and safety codes passed that year]. These houses are usually without heat, hot water and bathrooms together with improper plumbing, inadequate light and air, and have hall party lavatories." The Citywide Citizens' Committee on Harlem found that of 2191 occupied Class B buildings they examined in West Harlem in 1941, 1979 had major violations. Over 29,000 people lived in them. (Housing was classified by the type and number of facilities—heat, hot water, toilet, bath—provided, with A as the best and F as the worst.) The Mayor's Commission estimated that 10,000 blacks lived in cellars and basements with no toilets or running water. A former manager of Harlem apartments, an "agent for one of Harlem's largest real estate concerns," the New York Life Insurance Company, informed the Mayor's Commission:

> Do you know that apartments in my houses reeked with filth through no fault of the tenant? Bad plumbing—rats—mice—bugs—no dumbwaiters—no paint—heat—water and would you believe it I have been in apartments where young children lived and the toilet of the floor above flushed upon them. In fact things were so bad that I even appropriated money from the rents to help make the dumps livable much to the chagrin of my superiors.

Because Harlem had been built more recently than many areas in Manhattan, some of the housing there did provide modern conveniences. A higher proportion of Harlem apartments had private bathrooms, hot water, and heat than did apartments elsewhere in Manhattan, one study found, although these amenities did not always work. It listed approximately the same proportion of Harlem as non-Harlem Manhattan apartments in "good," "fair," and "poor" condition. That these newer apartments did not receive a "good" rating more often than the rest of the borough supports the conclusion that landlords in Harlem did less to maintain properties than they did elsewhere. . . .

The Harlem River houses on Seventh Avenue between 151st and 155th streets, built by the Public Works Administration (PWA) in 1937, offered modern, clean, spacious apartments at rents of $19 to $31 a month. The Houses also provided playgrounds, a nursery school, a health clinic, and laundry facilities. The United Tenants' League of Greater New York chose it as "the cleanest and most beautifully kept project in the city." But 20,000 families applied for the 574 spots.

As a result, more people lived in a smaller area in Harlem than anywhere else in the city. As Langdon Post, commissioner of housing, testified:

> A recent survey of . . . Harlem . . . [revealed] the average family income is $17.14. Forty percent of that went for rent. . . . In other parts of the city it is 20 to 25 percent for rent. . . . There are of course violations . . . but the problem of Harlem is

not so much the bad housing, although there are plenty of them, it is the congestion to which they are forced through high rents.

On the block of 133d and 134th streets between Seventh and Lenox avenues, 671 people per acre crowded together, the highest density in the city. The block of 138th and 139th streets between the same avenues held 620 per acre. The Mayor's Commission on City Planning found 3871 people living between Lenox and Seventh avenues on 142d and 143d streets in 1935: "the city's most crowded tenement block." As the *Herald Tribune* reported, this block

> is tenanted exclusively by Negroes. On its four sides the area presents a front of gray and red brick fire escapes broken only by dingy areaway entrances to the littered backyard about which the rectangle of tenements had been built. . . . Half of all the tenants are on relief and pass their days and nights lolling in the dreary entrances of the 40 apartments which house them or sitting in the ten by fifteen foot rooms which many of them share with a luckless friend or two. Unless they are fortunate their single windows face on narrow courts or into a neighbor's kitchen and the smell of cooking and the jangle of a dozen radios is always in the air. . . .

Black nationalists and the Communist and Socialist parties all tried to mobilize tenants to protest these inexcusable conditions, and occasionally took landlords to court. While they won some victories, segregation proved stronger than activism in Harlem. At the Harlem River Houses, for example, the long waiting list proved too great an intimidation to those lucky enough to have an apartment there. There was nowhere else to move. In any building, tenants who made trouble could be evicted, but in Harlem there were low vacancy rates, and outside Harlem, few would rent to blacks. Thus, blacks expelled from their apartments faced homelessness as their most likely fate. Segregation, then, inhibited the emergence of black activism on housing, despite efforts of the Consolidated Tenants League and others.

Every housing report of the period linked Harlem's poor housing to other social ills, especially poor health. The existing situation, argued the Housing Authority, "spells many evils the most salient of which are disease, immorality, crime and high mortality. But the vast amount of unemployment is the greatest of all evils for that and that alone is the propelling force which drives the populace to seek cheaper rentals and into dilapidated homes." Harlem housing conditions constituted a "serious menace . . . not only to the health of the residents but to the welfare of the whole city," argued the Mayor's Committee on City Planning. It concluded that "large areas are so deteriorated and so unsuited to present needs that there is no adequate solution but demolition."

Certainly health statistics in Harlem did not compare favorably with those in the rest of the city, because of both substandard housing and inadequate incomes. In 1934 in Central Harlem, fourteen people died per thousand, compared with ten per thousand in the city as a whole. The area's tuberculosis rate was over four times higher. Of every one thousand live births, ninety-four Central Harlem babies died, almost double the city's rate. Black women died in childbirth twice as often as whites; in part because over one-third of the black deaths compared with one-seventh of the white came as a result of an illegal abortion. For every cause of death, and virtually all health problems, Central Harlem had the highest rate of all Manhattan Health Districts. Of 1921 students registered in P.S. 157 at 327 St. Nicholas Avenue, only 248 had no "observable" health defects in 1934. With the exception of bad teeth (942 with dental problems), the largest problem was "nutrition," with 641 students suffering from inadequate diets. While citywide rates of malnutrition among school children ranged between 17 and 20 percent in the years after 1929, a 1936 study claimed that fully 63 percent of Harlem school children "suffer[ed] from malnutrition."

On the other hand, these mortality and morbidity rates, though worse than those for the rest of the city, had declined since the 1920s and the pre-New Deal years. A comparison of health statistics for these earlier periods suggests that both races had seen dramatic improvement in the quality of health care. While medical advances contributed to the mortality decline, of course, the improvement also resulted from the increased availability of free health clinics. Clinic use had risen, especially for blacks. The number of prenatal care clinics operated by the Department of Health rose from seventeen in 1928 to twenty-three in 1935. The number of tuberculosis patients in Central Harlem using clinics rose from one percent of the total in 1930 to 22 percent in 1940, while the overall Manhattan rate rose from 6 to 23 percent. In 1937, a large new facility at Fifth Avenue between 136th and 137th streets became the Central Harlem Health Center. In New York City as a whole, a fifth of all native-born blacks and almost a tenth of all native-born whites in 1935–1936 reported receiving some free medical care. At all income levels but one, black reliance on free clinics exceeded white. (For both races these rates were comparable to those of other cities.) In many cases this meant a lessening of the gap between black and white because of a substantial improvement in black access to health care and a slowing of improvements in white health as depression conditions worsened.

Mortality statistics continued to drop during the rest of the decade. In 1940, the general death rate in Central Harlem had dropped to 12.4 per thousand, the Manhattan rate to 11.5, and, for the first time, the mortality rate in another health district surpassed Harlem's. Harlem's tuberculosis deaths and infant mortality rates declined. Because the black community had been so destitute before the depression, in some ways conditions for them had improved with the advent of New Deal programs.

Relief programs correlated with some health improvements as well. While those on relief—the poorest—had a higher overall death rate, according to E. Franklin Frazier, they had lower rates of infant mortality. Probably relief babies were healthier because caseworkers advised their parents about prenatal and child care, and because of the medical care available to them. Pregnant women also received higher home relief food allotments. Thus, in terms of public services, the depression worsened conditions in Harlem while the New Deal improved them.

Poverty, poor housing, and poor health intensified other problems in Harlem. The Citywide Citizens' Committee on Harlem argued that "the poverty, the dif-

ficulties of home life and overcrowding, and the suffering of the adult population as a result of the unemployment in [Harlem] have . . . made educational
needs greater than that of the average neighborhood of the city." Yet old buildings, scarce playgrounds, and overcrowded schools worsened the educational
situation, demoralizing both teachers and students. The Mayor's Commission
heard testimony from the executive secretary of the Central Committee of the
Harlem Parents' Associations expressing her "great distress" about overcrowding and the poor facilities in Harlem. She politely "beg[ged] and petition[ed]"
the commission to "do something about this because we, the parents of the children, are suffering because our children are involved." Mrs. William Burroughs
of the Harlem Teachers' and Students' Association echoed these remarks, demanding that the city

> remedy overcrowding . . . safeguard life and health of pupils—immediate
> abandonment of old unsanitary firetraps, four in . . . Harlem . . . clinics in
> schools. . . . Retardation . . . is a vital problem in Harlem. . . . Many pupils come
> from an area with small educational facilities. In addition to this, the scandalous
> conditions here, inadequate staff, crowded classes, outmoded buildings,
> skimpy supplies, frequent lack of sympathy, lifeless curriculum, do not help;
> but hinder a slow pupil.

Ira Kemp forthrightly tied these conditions to racial discrimination and advocated the nationalist position he had articulated in the "Don't Buy" campaign.

> . . . We believe that the various school institutions in Harlem are overpopulated
> with teachers who aren't our people. . . . We feel a considerable percentage of
> teachers [in Harlem] should be colored.
>
> Q. Do you mean to insinuate that there is discrimination?
>
> A. I do. . . .
>
> Q. The specific question is whether you know of any instances where there is a
> violation of the law. Do you know of any girl [teacher] that has been discrimi-
> nated against?
>
> A. My answer is that the system of keeping colored girls off the rolls who are on
> the eligible lists is so systematic that you can't get at it.
>
> Q. We are asking for proof. . . .
>
> A. I explained before that it is impossible to get facts from the authorities. We
> have had many complaints.

Ultimately, the Mayor's Commission on Conditions in Harlem concluded:

> The school plant as a whole is old, shabby . . . in many instances not even sani-
> tary or well-kept and the fire hazards . . . are great. The lack of playgrounds and
> recreational centers . . . is all the more serious when it is considered that some
> of the schools are surrounded by . . . corrupt and immoral resorts of which the
> police seem blissfully unaware. Four of the schools lack auditoriums; one
> endeavors to serve luncheons to 1,000 children when there are seats for only

175. Most of all, no elementary school has been constructed in Harlem in 10 years. . . .

Prejudical discrimination appears from the fact that the Board of Education, asking funds from the federal grovernment for 168 school buildings, asked for but one annex for Harlem. . . .

The Teachers Union, Local 5 of the American Federation of Teachers, endorsed the Mayor's Commission's findings of poor school facilities in Harlem and cited "overcrowded classes, dangerous lack of adequate recreational facilities, antiquated and unsanitary school plant, 'horrifying' moral conditions, inadequate handling of the over-age child, and shortage of teaching staff." It concluded: "The conditions described . . . make proper teaching and proper receptivity to the teaching process impossible." The union's proposals—reducing class size, funding new school buildings, modernizing the old, hiring unemployed teachers to take children to nearby parks for recreation, staffing school playgrounds until six o'clock, and providing free lunches and winter clothing to the children of the unemployed—were endorsed by, among others, the Mayor's Committee on Harlem Schools, Father Divine's Peace Mission, the Joint Conference Against Discriminatory Practices, the Adam Clayton Powells, William Lloyd Imes and other ministers, YWCA and YMCA representatives, and Countee Cullen. To spur government action, the union reminded the mayor of the link between these problems and the 1935 riot: "The unhealthful and inadequate school buildings in Harlem had much to do with the unrest which led to the disorders of March 19."

Harlem residents added their voices, circulating petitions to the Board of Education:

Public education in Harlem has been . . . long and grossly neglected. The facts are notorious.

Dirt and filth and slovenliness have no more educational value for our children than for yours. . . . New school-houses with ample grounds and appropriate modern facilities are urgently needed to supplement or replace overcrowded and outmoded structures, to provide for the large increase in our population during the past decade or more. . . .

Teachers, principals and superintendents are needed who have abiding faith in our children and genuine respect for the loins and traditions from which they have sprung. . . .

So far as public education is concerned, we beg you to dispel by concrete action the widespread conviction that this region is neglected because its people are comparatively poor in this world's goods and in social and political influence, because many of them are of African descent.

In March 1936, Harlem organizations, including the Communist party and several black churches, created a Permanent Committee for Better Schools in Harlem, meeting in the New York Urban League building "with 400 delegates representing every phase of social, political, religious, cultural and civic activity in Harlem." These efforts, the commission report, and the memory of the Harlem riot brought some improvements within the year: the city budget included appropriations for four new school buildings, some repairs were made at most Harlem schools, and "many individual cases of discriminatory zoning have been satisfactorily settled." That year for the first time students could take a course in black history.

Of course Harlem's educational problems were by no means solved. In 1941, the Citizens' Committee reported that overcrowding forced many Harlem schools to run on a three-shift school day. From West 114th Street to West 191st, there was not a single public vocational or secondary school. One junior high school served the entire area from 125th Street to 155th, between the Harlem River and St. Nicholas Avenue. In one elementary school, ten classes lacked classrooms; in another, six did.

Still, educational levels among blacks did rise in the 1930s. Whether because Harlem's schools provided a better education than those of the south, because jobs were scarce in the depression, or because relief eased families' desperation, black children from both relief and nonrelief families attended school for longer during the depression than they had before. The proportion of black children aged fourteen to twenty-four remaining in school rose through the 1930s until it approached the figures for whites.

Education problems, aggravated by low incomes and high living costs, led to continued high juvenile delinquency rates in Harlem in the 1930s. Miss Hill, assistant housing director at the YWCA, told a *Herald Tribune* reproter: "It's a vicious circle in a city of such color segregation. . . . The Negroes can't pay these rents without help so they jam the houses. Juvenile delinquency is terrible under such conditions. Many mothers . . . have to go out to work and the children come to school with the keys of their houses around their necks. There is no one there when they go home and so they simply play around in the alleys." . . .

Despite the high numbers of black children adjudged delinquent in the depression, the type of criminal behavior did not change from earlier years. In fact, numbers of delinquents (or at least, arrests for delinquency) actually declined slightly over the decade for both blacks and whites. While theft (including burglary, larceny, holdups, and pickpocketing) remained boys' most frequent crime, hitching rides on various forms of public transportation, and peddling without a license followed directly after. As noted earlier, these crimes primarily indicated the depth of economic need in the community.

As in previous years, the problem of high rates of conviction for delinquency did not necessarily lie in an overtly racist court system, although doubtless racist judgments were given. The story was more complex; the courts were able to act only to ameliorate existing difficulties and provide a sort of bandage. When Benedict Lucy, twelve, came before the Children's Court, it was his third appearance. A year earlier he had received six months' probation for deserting home. The next time, he was charged with stealing his mother's purse. The judge again placed him on probation. Finally his mother asked that, since he kept running away, he be sent to Warwick. The court-appointed psychologist concurred, hoping the institution would help him "[stop his] bedwetting [and provide] regular schooling, church attendance, trade training. . . ." Obviously

Benedict's thefts and desertions reflected far deeper problems, which city services had not or could not address. And so he ended up in court and in juvenile detention, the court having few other alternatives, even though his difficulties cried out for other solutions. As Agnes Sullivan of the Welfare Council commented about several such cases, it "indicates that it was handled on the basis of the offense rather than in terms of his needs."

Gene Wooley stole letters from a mailbox at age nine, "ladies hose valued at $14.41" at eleven and a half, and a "box of ladies vests values at $9" a year later. For this the judge remanded him to Warwick. Yet, while punishment may have been the court's only option for Gene as well as for Benedict, the real problem lay elsewhere. "From his early childhood there has been economic stress in the home due to Mr. Wooley's irregular employment. In 1926, when Gene was five years old, the economic situation became acute when his father was committed to a State Hospital with a diagnosis of dementia praecox." The economic instability of many Harlem families bred emotional upheaval as well as pecuniary need, perhaps felt most acutely by youths. Thus black children were more often found delinquent. But incarceration did not address the problems these children faced.

Unlike delinquency, adult crimes rose. While most death rates declined in Harlem during the depression, homicides rose from nineteen per 100,000 in 1925 to twenty-four in 1937, while city rates fell. A 1931 investigation of the relationship between housing and crime found, not unexpectedly, that Manhattan's slum areas had higher rates of arrests of all types and a higher rate of convictions than the borough's average. The top two areas were both in Central Harlem. The same held for later years. Still, like delinquency, by and large, Harlem crimes by adults were more often income-producing than violent. As already noted, arrests for prostitution, operating illegal stills, and playing the numbers rose. Of a random sample of Harlem arrests in the first six months of 1935, all types of theft, from shoplifting to grand larceny, constituted only an eighth of the total, despite the fact that the period surveyed included the riot, with its many burglary arrests. Possession of policy slips, by contrast, accounted for about a third of all Harlem arrests. Except for the rise of arrests for policy slips and the decline for other gambling offenses since the early years of the depression, the rates for the different sorts of crimes remained fairly constant.

Of those arrested statewide, a smaller proportion of blacks than whites were charged with homicide or with theft of any sort, which suggests that whites were less often arrested for minor crimes than blacks were. The black rate for these more serious crimes proportional to their population, however, was greater than the white. Statewide, the ratio of whites arrested to their total population was 140 to 100,000, compared with 853 for blacks.

As we have seen, crime statistics are not foolproof indicators of community behavior. As with delinquency, discrimination or racism may have led to selective arrest, prosecution, and conviction. Perhaps police cared less about black crime and therefore acted less vigorously on Harlem cases. This would mean that arrest rates were lower than actual criminal behavior. Similarly, the rise in

Harlem homicide deaths may have been due to a new vigilance by police rather than a real rise in the number of murders. An alternative possibility is that racism provoked officers to arrest blacks more readily than whites. The greater poverty of blacks might further skew their arrest rates, since the rich are generally more able to avoid arrest for minor crimes such as disturbing the peace than the poor are. Racist juries and judges might be similarly disposed to distrust blacks. Thus high black arrest and conviction rates may reflect factors other than strictly higher rates of criminality. Nevertheless, whatever the actual rates, criminal behavior in Harlem offers hints of the problems faced by a poor black community. Criminality reflected not only black behavior, but white as well.

Police corruption led to selective and discriminatory enforcement of the laws in Harlem. An NAACP memorandum argued that Harlem's high rate of arrests for prostitution and illegal sale of alcohol was attributable to police corruption: "We are made to look more immoral, less decent than anyone else and the environment of prostitution is being fostered [sic] on our women and young girls by the Harlem police officials in their scheme and business of tribute." A second memorandum estimated "perhaps forty to fifty percent of [prostitutes] ... (colored) are forced or semi-forced and the rest act voluntarily." This memorandum cited the Cotton Club and several Italian-owned saloons as central "clearing house[s]" for these women. While the memo noted that the NAACP did not advocate illegal activity, it pointed out that it hardly seemed fair that black women were arrested for prostitution more often than white. The NAACP was convinced police arrested black women more often because they feared public outcry if they arrested too many whites. . . .

The police were known in Harlem not only for their corruption, but for their readiness to harass local residents. A draft of the Mayor's Commission's report on the Harlem riot noted: "The police themselves admit that they entered the homes of Negro citizens WITHOUT A WARRANT AND SEARCHED THEM AT WILL . . . [they admit to] interference in the association of white and colored people; searching of homes without a warrant, detention of innocent men in jail, and even the MUTILATION AND KILLING of persons upon slight provocation!!! . . . [but Commissioner Valentine] maintained that there was NO REASON FOR DISCIPLINARY ACTION" [emphasis theirs]. William Patterson, a black man, was falsely accused of a crime and subsequently released. When he complained about his arrest, the Mayor's Commission on Conditions in Harlem discovered, "detectives threatened Patterson if he did not withdraw his complaint. . . . There were other cases similar to this case in which Negro citizens' homes were entered and searched by officers of the law without warrants to take such action." The commission's investigations not only provided information, but moved some of the victims to action: the commission reported that as a result of its findings, "Patterson instituted Civil action against the officers responsible for his arrest."

Many different black organizations reported incidents of police brutality involving black citizens. Walter White of the NAACP sent a telegram to Mayor LaGuardia and Police Commissioner Lewis Valentine in 1939:

> Rookie policeman beating up negro in new york city without cause . . . 40th and broadway . . . When policeman, shield #8589 beat unmercifully negro bootblack he stopped only because crowd intervened. Boy was later released but had been

beaten so badly he required medical treatment. We ask immediate suspension of offending officer pending investigation and issuance of drastic order by you and commissioner valentine . . . with respect to such violence.

Valentine reported to the mayor: "Investigation disclosed that only sufficient force necessary to effect arrest was used . . . and that there is no cause for disci plinary action. Complainant interviewed and now requests matter be dropped."

Adam Clayton Powell, Jr., reported another incident. Tommie Aiken, stand- ing on the bread line at 142nd Street and Lenox Avenue since morning, was pushed out of line. A policeman (Officer #9761) told him to move to the end of the line. When he explained that he was simply trying to get back to his original place, the officer hit him in the face. He "beat him over the head with a black- jack and after he was knocked down unconscious [the officer] struck him in the face and especially in the eyes. . . . [Aiken was] rushed to Harlem hospital . . . [and] operated on in an attempt to save his sight. The operation was unsuccess- ful."

According to the police report, Aiken was arrested for "wilfully and wrongly striking [an] officer . . . with clenched fist while officer was attempting to arrest him for causing a disturbance, using loud and boisterous language, tending to excite several hundred men . . . possibly thereby tending to cause a riot." Commissioner Valentine supported the officer's report. Aiken told a dif- ferent story.

> I was arrested for felonious assault. I was in 142nd Street Armory [where it was] said there were free meals. . . . The officer tried to shift me out of line. I told him I was there a long time so he pushed me and hit me with a night stick in the eye and knocked me out. I was unconscious and I was taken to Harlem Hospital. I woke up, I think, 45 minutes later.

A witness supported Aiken's story. "The officer came through one door and two white fellows got in back of Aiken. The officer thought Aiken was with those two fellows. He said get in the back of the line. Aiken said, 'This is my original place and I am here since early this morning' . . . Officer Redcliff said to him. 'You black son of a bitch' and struck him over the head. Aiken fell to the floor, another officer ran from the front side with a blackjack and Redcliff kicked him."

At Harlem Hospital, Dr. Epstein reported Aiken was suffering "from possi- ble fracture sustained when officer struck prisoner with baton." According to the doctor, this caused a "rupture of [his] left eyeball." After Aiken gave his statement the doctor reported him "clear and orientated. Well behaved and quiet. . . ."

Harlem crime rates documented police bigotry and corruption as much as they revealed Harlem's poverty and unsatisfactory conditions.

COMMUNITY

Yet while blacks in Harlem recognized the harsh conditions they lived under and the pernicious effects of their poverty, few believed the solution was wholesale abandonment of the area. Living together offered resources and strengths unavailable to dispersed individuals. Rather, African-Americans demanded better services where they lived, recognizing the positive power of community. The Reverend Mr. Garner, minister of the Grace Congregational Church, testified before the Mayor's Commission: "We find that our rents are higher than anywhere else in the city in proportion to what we get. Our food in Harlem is higher." But he refused to consider the suggestion that blacks move elsewhere to find less expensive housing:

> Our industrial life and social and economic and religious lives are centered in Harlem at the present time. We object to the beating up of our community on those grounds. . . . To break up the community in small segregated groups gives no opportunity for the friends to develop themselves on and among themselves [sic].

Street surveys of the Mayor's Commission and the "Negroes in New York" study of the Federal Writers' Project documented the large numbers of storefront churches, billiard halls, social clubs, dance halls, and mutual welfare lodges that provided social space throughout the depression decade. Over two thousand social, political, and mutual aid societies flourished in Harlem, including the United Aid for Peoples of African Descent, the Tuskeegee Alumni Association, Iota Phi Lambda (a sorority for business women), the King of Clubs (half of whose members were black police officers), the Hampton Alumni Club, the Bermuda Benevolent Organization, the Southern Aristocrats, the Trinidad Benevolent Association, the Anguilla Benevolent Society, the St. Lucia United Association, California #1, the New Englanders, the Hyacinths Social Club, the Montserrat Progressive Society, St. Helena's League and Benefit Club, and hundreds of others.

Both poverty and community, then, shaped Harlem family and social life. As Loften Mitchell recalled,

> [T]he child of Harlem had the will to survive, to "make it." . . . This Harlem child learned to laugh in the face of adversity, to cry in the midst of plentifulness, to fight quickly and reconcile easily. He became a "backcapping" signifying slicker and a suave, sentimental gentleman. From his African, Southern Negro and West Indian heritage, he knew the value of gregariousness and he held group consultations on street corners to review problems of race economics, of politics.
>
> He was poor but proud. He hid his impoverishment with clothes, pseudo-good living, or sheer laughter.
>
> . . . In the nineteen thirties we had our own language, sung openly, defiantly. . . .
>
> We celebrated, too—our biggest celebrations were on nights when Joe Louis fought. . . . When he won a fight I went into the streets with other Negroes and I hollered until I was hoarse. . . . We had culture too. The Schomburg collection, a mighty fortress . . . three theaters, Louis Armstrong, Cab Calloway . . . Bill "Bojangles" Robinson . . . Bessie Smith . . . Langston Hughes . . . Romare Bearden . . . Augusta Savage. . . .

Richard Wright explained the energy and joy in black culture as rooted in poverty and anger:

> Our music makes the whole world dance. . . . But only a few of those who dance and sing with us suspect the rawness of life out of which our laughing-crying tunes and quick dance steps come; they do not know that our songs and dances are our banner of hope flung desperately up in the face of a world that has pushed us to the wall.

Others offered even less sanguine pictures. Alfred Smith of the FERA [Federal Emergency Relief Administration], a black man, discussed the African-American family in terms that today might be viewed as racist, but that nonetheless raised important questions about the impact of dire poverty on family life:

> The comparatively unstable family life of the Negro in urban areas may be ascribed to poor living conditions. Illegitimacy, illiteracy and a lack of a sense of responsibility or obligation all have their roots in the Negroes' unfortunate past, but are nurtured and fostered in city slums. Negroes are required to pay a larger proportion of their income for rent than any other group and they get less for their expenditure. The landlord who rents to the Negro mass in urban aras has no sense of responsibility to his renters. Negroes are forced to live in proscribed areas of the city, and in quarters where their health and morals suffer. They get little attention, little notice (other than being occasionally photographed in his slums as examples of need for "better housing") and much sympathy.

One part of his equation, "unstable family life," deserves some attention. Black and white leaders lamented the frequency of female-headed households. Clayton Cook of the Children's Aid Society reported 20 percent of Harlem black children "come from 'broken homes'—that is—families that have only a woman at the head. At one school in 699 families out of 1,600 . . . the father was either dead or had deserted." Certainly the high number of widows attests to the evil effects of poverty on adult (particularly male) longevity. Some social problems such as juvenile delinquency occurred more often in families without fathers according to contemporary studies (although, interestingly, the effects were more pronounced for girls than for boys). Yet other measures of "social disorganization," such as reliance on relief, seemed to bear no relationship to whether or not a man was present at home.

Many feared an absent male would ensure that these families would live in poverty, since black women had even lower earning potential that black men did. In fact, ironically, these economic liabilities were mitigated by the depression. While black working women did earn less, on average, then working men, female-headed families more often had additional earners. Thus, in the BLS sample, for example, families without a husband present earned no less per person than those with both husband and wife. Nor were black families with women at the head more likely than others to be on relief: the figure for black female-headed families on relief, 20 percent in New York City, was no higher than the proportion of female-headed families in the black population. A study of 675 Harlem families done by the Mayor's Commission found families on different blocks had very different average incomes. But in both high-income and low-income blocks, the proportion of female-headed families was identical.

Thus, while the likelihood of some social problems (such as juvenile delinquency) seemed correlated with the presence or absence of a father, other measures of "social disorganization" (such as reliance on relief) seemed to bear no relationship to that question. It may be that the depression threw so many men out of work that their absence made little economic difference to the family. When employment opportunities improved in the next decade, two-headed families would fare better than single-parent households, on the whole. But in an era of high unemployment and highly fluid household structures in which a family's income came from a variety of contributors, the presence of a male mattered less economically than one might expect.

Making ends meet was a difficult business in depression Harlem, and families used a variety of financial and nonfinancial, legal and illegal methods to do so. No one starved, but few in Harlem prospered, and the consequences of such grinding poverty reached into all areas of life. Housing and health were poor, mortality and crime rates high. Strong kin and community networks prevented much of the worst from occurring, and New Deal programs provided some help. Harlem itself, though, remained a ghetto and a slum and its people trapped in the conditions brought on by poverty and discrimination. As the New York State Temporary Commission on the Condition of the Urban Colored Population concluded in 1939:

> While the Commission has no desire to indulge in dramatic over-statement it does earnestly wish to impress upon your honorable bodies the extreme seriousness of the conditions which it has studied. The conditions often seem almost incredible in so advanced a commonwealth as the State of New York, and they cannot remain uncorrected without general danger to the public welfare of the State as a whole.

SOURCES

Images from the 1930s:
A Visual Essay

The works of art reproduced on the following pages were among hundreds of paintings and frescoes produced under the Federal Art Project of the Works Progress Administration and other, similar programs. The New Deal found itself in the art business partly because subsidies to artists did not bring the government into competition with private enterprise; and partly because government officials understood that post office murals might have a certain public relations value.

The artists who produced these works had to pay attention to the needs of their patron, the national government; to the desires of the local community in which the finished work would reside; and to the voices of the "people" in an era of depression. While these multiple demands on the artists make it impossible to isolate any single source for a work of art, the same multiplicity ensures that the artworks have some broad, social meaning.

What do you see in the following works of art? What do they tell us about how Americans understood and coped with the great depression? What ideas of gender do they present? Do they suggest that Americans feared technology or welcomed it? What balance is struck between urban and rural values? What would Harlem blacks think of any one of these murals if they encountered it at their local post office?

Allan Thomas, *Extending the Frontier in Northwest Territory,* **Crystal Falls, Minnesota.**
National Archives and Records Administration.

Xavier Gonzalez, *Pioneer Saga,* **Kilgore, Texas.**
National Archives and Records Administration.

Paul Meltsner, *Ohio,* **Bellevue, Ohio.**
National Archives and Records Administration.

Caroline S. Rohland, *Spring,* **sketch, Sylvania, Georgia.**
National Archives and Records Administration.

Howard Cook, *Steel Industry,* **Pittsburgh, Pennsylvania.**
National Archives and Records Administration.

These illustrations appear in Barbara Melosh, *Engendering Culture: Manhood and Womanhood in New Deal Public Art and Theater,* Smithsonian Institution Press, Washington, D.C., 1991. I am grateful to Professor Melosh for making the prints available for use in *The American Record.*

Migrant Mother

*Between 1935 and 1942, photographers for the New Deal's Farm Security Ad-
ministration Photographic Project took some 80,000 photographs of depres-
sion-era America. Together, they constitute a remarkable record of rural and
small-town life—truly one of the great achievements of "documentary" photography. Dorothea Lange's* Migrant Mother *is the best known of all the FSA
photographs and one of the most famous photographs of the twentieth century.*

*But what does it "document"? According to historian James Curtis's ac-
count of the evolution of this photograph,* Migrant Mother *was the sixth and
last of a series. The early photos in the series were from a distance and encompassed migrant mother's tent and four children, including a teenage daughter.
The third was of the mother alone, breastfeeding her baby. Photos four and five
brought one young child back into the frame, looking over the mother's shoulder toward the camera. To achieve the undeniable power of* Migrant Mother,
*Lange asked the two young children to turn away from the camera, and she told
the mother to bring her hand to her face. The whole process took only minutes.*

*Does Lange's manipulation of the mother, her children, and the scene
change your mind about the photograph? Does it mean that the photograph is
somehow less truthful, less a "document"?*

Dorothea Lange, *Migrant Mother* **(no. 6), Nipomo, California, March 1936 (FSA).**
Library of Congress.

CHAPTER 9

The Age of Anxiety

When older Americans reflect on the 1940s, they recall the decade in halves: the first half, dominated by World War II, a difficult time when men and women fought for democracy against the forces of tyranny; and the second half, remembered as the beginning of a long period of prosperity and opportunity that would reach into the 1960s. There is much to be said for this view of the decade. Although Americans had been reluctant to go to war (the United States remained formally neutral when France was invaded by Germany in 1940), the Japanese attack on Pearl Harbor in December 1941 brought a flush of patriotism that temporarily buried most remaining doubts. A Virginia politician announced that "we needed a Pearl Harbor—a Golgotha—to arouse us from our self-sufficient complacency, to make us rise above greed and hate." Vice President Henry Wallace was one of many who revived Wilsonian idealism. "This is a fight," he wrote in 1943, "between a slave world and a free world. Just as the United States in 1862 could not remain half slave and half free, so in 1942 the world must make its decision for a complete victory one way or another." When the United States ended the war in the Pacific by exploding atomic bombs over Hiroshima and Nagasaki, many Americans considered the act appropriate retribution for the attack at Pearl Harbor by a devious and immoral enemy.

In many ways, the war justified idealism, for it accomplished what the New Deal had not. Organized labor prospered. The name "Rosie the Riveter" described the new American woman who found war-related opportunities in the factories and shipyards. Black people—segregated by New Deal housing programs, injured as tenant farmers by New Deal farm policies, and never singled out as a group worthy of special aid—found skilled jobs in the wartime economy. They also received presidential assistance—in the form of the Fair Employment Practices Committee—in their struggle to end racially discriminatory hiring practices. A growing military budget in 1941 produced the nation's first genuinely progressive income tax legislation. Despite a serious and disruptive wave of postwar strikes that was triggered by high unemployment, for the most part the prosperity and economic growth generated by the war carried over into the late 1940s and 1950s.

Yet this *good war/good peace* view of the 1940s leaves too much unexplained and unaccounted for. It does not explain that the very patriotism that made Americans revel in war time unity also had negative consequences. For example, on the Pacific Coast, more than 100,000 Japanese-Americans, including many American citizens, were taken from their homes and removed to distant relocation centers, where they remained for the "duration." *Good war/good peace* does not explain that the effects of combat lasted long beyond the formal end of conflict, as the Mickey Spillane excerpt in this chapter demonstrates. Nor does it reveal how thoroughly the war disrupted existing gender and race relations, setting the stage for the silly and absurd things postwar Americans did to restore the prewar status quo. And *good war/good peace* does not explain the popularity between 1942 and 1958 of *film noir*, a gloomy black-and-white film genre that pictured a world in which ordinary, decent people were regularly victimized by bad luck.

Beneath the surface of 1940s America was a pervasive anxiety. Some of this anxiety was economic; those who had experienced the great depression could never quite believe that another one wasn't around the corner. But far more important were anxieties linked to the use of the atomic bomb on the Japanese, the killing of 6 million Jews by the Nazis, the war-related deaths of 60 million people worldwide and the increasing seriousness of the cold war. These extraordinary facts and events created the most elemental form of insecurity: the knowledge that any human life could end senselessly and without warning. And many thoughtful Americans began to question—in a way they had not even during the great depression—whether history was still the story of civilization and progress, or a sad tale of moral decline. The concepts *good war* and *good peace* remained vital to Americans' understanding of their world, but they could not encompass the haunting feeling, so much a part of the late 1940s, that something very important had gone wrong.

INTERPRETIVE ESSAY

Allan Bérubé

Coming Out under Fire

There is a school of thought that holds that almost every significant social change in the late twentieth century can be traced to World War II. In this view, the civil rights activism of the late 1950s and early 1960s was set in motion by changes in the wartime economy; the feminist movement of the late 1960s was spearheaded by the daughters of women who had experienced the war as a field of opportunity; and the campus protests of the Vietnam War era were led by young people raised in the shadow of the atomic bomb or (in a claim that appeals to conservatives) by spoiled brats brought up under the permissive, democratic child-rearing regimen popularized by Dr. Benjamin Spock in his 1946 The Common Sense Book of Baby and Child Care, *itself a product of the war.*

Allan Bérubé's account of how the nation's gay community was affected by, and responded to, government policies during and after the war fits that model in some respects. Like the stories of blacks and feminists, it is the story of an emerging community (or communities), and it is a story anchored, like the others, in wartime events and experiences. In this case, what was it about the war—and about the status and claims of the veteran—that contributed to social change? It is also a story about repression, and the intensity and character of that repression needs to be described and understood. Was the military, and later the Senate and President Dwight Eisenhower, really concerned about homosexuals? Or was the attack on the gay community a way to achieve some other purpose? Why were Americans—or their public officials—so anxious about questions of sexuality?

The massive mobilization for World War II propelled gay men and lesbians into the mainstream of American life. Ironically the screening and discharge policies, together with the drafting of millions of men, weakened the barriers that had kept gay people trapped and hidden at the margins of society. Discovering that they shared a common cause, they were more willing and able to defend themselves, as their ability to work, congregate, and lead sexual lives came under escalating attack in the postwar decade.

Long before the war a chain of social constraints immobilized many gay men and women by keeping them invisible, isolated, silent, ignorant, and trivialized. As young people they learned to hide their homosexual feelings in fear and in shame, helping to perpetuate the myth that people like them didn't exist. Locked in a closet of lies and deceptions, many people with homosexual desires mistakenly believed that they were the only ones in the world, often not even knowing what to call themselves. Isolated from each other and kept ignorant by a "conspiracy of silence" in the media, they lacked the language and ideas that could help them define themselves and understand their often vague feelings and desires. When publicly acknowledged at all, they were caricatured as "fairies" and "mannish" women, freaks whose lives were trivialized as silly and unimportant, so that many lesbians and gay men learned not to take themselves or each other seriously. Such insidious forms of social control worked quietly below the surface of everyday life through unspoken fears and paralyzing shame, coming into view only in sporadic acts of violence, arrests, school expulsions, firings, or religious condemnations.

Ironically the mobilization for World War II helped to loosen the constraints that locked so many gay people in silence, isolation, and self-contempt. Selective Service acknowledged the importance of gay men when it drafted hundreds of thousands to serve their country and broke the silence when examiners asked millions of selectees about their homosexual tendencies. The draft, together with lax recruitment policies that allowed lesbians to enter the military, placed a whole generation of gay men and women in gender-segregated bases where they could find each other, form cliques, and discover the gay life in the cities. Classification officers assigned even the most "mannish" women and effeminate men to stereotyped duties, recognizing that these previously marginal people were useful and even indispensable to the war effort. Officers confirmed the competence, value, and courage of gay soldiers when they sent many into combat, some to die, even after they had declared their homosexuality.

Changes in policy brought about similarly dramatic effects. Military officials intensified the significance of homosexuality by building a special bureaucratic apparatus to manage homosexual personnel. In the process, they inadvertently gave gay inductees and soldiers the option to avoid compulsory military service by coming out. Psychiatrists, as the military's pioneer experts on homosexuality, gave soldiers as well as military officials a biased but useful new language and set of concepts—such as the word *homosexual* and the idea of a "personality type"—that some did use to categorize homosexuals, understand homosexuality, and even define themselves. During purges interrogators terrorized suspects into breaking their protective silence, forcing them to describe their homosexual lives, to make confessions, and to name their friends and sexual partners. Officers who aggressively rooted out homosexuals and exposed them to their draft boards, company mates, and families further destroyed their ability to hide in the closet, forcing them to lead new lives as known homosexuals. As these soldiers were thrown together into psych wards and queer stockades, they endured the same hardships together in small groups, better able to perceive themselves as compatriots who were victims of the same persecution. When they were discharged as undesirables without benefits and without having been charged with any crime, gay men and women gained a cause, a target to attack, and new avenues of appeal to defend their rights as gay GIs and veterans.

Disrupted and exposed by the war, gay life in the postwar years seemed to be growing at an unprecedented rate. Gay men and lesbians often saw this growth as a sign of hope, while government officials and the press saw it as a dangerous threat. The proliferation of gay bars, the broadening of public discussion of homosexuality, the formulation of the idea that homosexuals constituted a minority, the widespread acceptance of the psychiatric model of homosexuals as sexual psychopaths, the emergence and growth of federal antihomosexual policies and bureaucracies, and the opening of new avenues through which gay citizens could appeal government injustices against them were some of the many legacies of World War II. These changes had a powerful impact on how a nation and its people would respond to homosexuality long after the war.

The veterans of World War II were the first generation of gay men and women to experience such rapid, dramatic, and widespread changes in their lives as homosexuals. Their common experience and shared memories as a generation helped determine how they would fit into this new world. Having grown up during the depression under New Deal reforms, many had learned to view the government as a provider of social welfare programs, a tradition that continued with the 1944 Servicemen's Readjustment Act. These men and women had matured at a time when the government was waging a war against fascism and when President Roosevelt's "Four Freedoms" had come to embody the principles for which the United States and its allies were fighting. In many ways their attitudes resembled those of second-generation immigrants who were passionately pro-American and who gained legitimacy as Americans by serving in the armed forces. Despite their griping in the military, gay veterans were patriotic and proud of their service to their country. They took advantage of the GI Bill and the postwar prosperity to try to settle down as civilians into stable, secure lives and to fit into American society whenever and wherever they could.

But beneath their desire to assimilate loomed an uneasiness, a sense of possibility mixed with fear. They saw the gay life begin to grow while the military, the federal government, and the press increasingly focused public attention on them. Like the Nisei generation of Japanese-Americans, who had been interned by the government that questioned their loyalty but from which they sought approval, this generation of gay Americans felt deep conflicts during and after the war. Often blaming themselves for being arrested or losing their jobs, they retained a strong faith in their government and a desire to fit in. Yet they felt a growing sense that as veterans they were being treated unfairly when singled out for persecution and should instead be able to live their lives in peace so long as they did their jobs and didn't hurt anybody else.

By the late 1940s, however, the ability of gay men and lesbians to blend into normal life became increasingly difficult as the attention of the nation's media, government officials, and church leaders turned toward issues of conformity and deviance. As families were reunited and struggled to put their lives back together after the war, articles, books, advertisements, and the media promoted idealized versions of the nuclear family, heterosexuality, and traditional gender roles in the home and in the workplace. Accompanying this preoccupation with conformity was a fearful scapegoating of those who deviated from a narrowing ideal of the nuclear family and the American way of life. Lesbians and gay men, many of them unable or unwilling to conform to such a narrow family idea, stood out more than they had during the war as "queers" and "sex deviates."

The media and government propaganda associated homosexuals and other "sex psychopaths" with Communists as the most dangerous nonconformists— invisible enemies who could live next door and who threatened the security and safety of children, women, the family, and the nation. From 1947 to 1955 twenty-one states and the District of Columbia, following local panics over child murderers and rapists, enacted sex psychopath laws. Supported by psychiatrists interested in extending the authority of their profession further into the criminal justice system, these laws targeted personality types, including homosexuals, more than their crimes, allowed their indefinite incarceration in institutions for the mentally ill until they were cured, and often required their registration as sex offenders with police departments wherever they lived.

During the nationwide campaigns against sexual psychopaths, the terms *child molester, homosexual, sex offender, sex psychopath, sex degenerate, sex deviate,* and sometimes even *Communist* became interchangeable in the minds of the public, legislators, and local police. In such a hostile climate, gay blue-discharge veterans could feel especially threatened because the military had diagnosed them on their military records as sexual psychopaths. The local panics that followed violent sex crimes, especially those against children, sometimes ended in rounding up gay men as potential suspects. "I suppose you read about the kidnapping and killing of the little girl in Chicago," wrote Marty Klausner in a letter to a gay friend in January 1946. "I noticed tonight that they 'thought' (in their damn self-righteous way) that perhaps a pervert had done it and they rounded up all the females [gay men]—they blame us for everything."

The press added to the national hysteria by portraying gay men as molesters of children, corrupters of youths, and even perpetrators of violent sexual crimes; lesbians were sometimes portrayed as malevolent seducers of women and girls. Some pulp magazines ran antigay articles in nearly every issue with titles such as "Homosexuals Are Dangerous" and "Lesbians Prey on Weak Women." Such an image of the homosexual as a dangerous sex pervert suited the paranoid political climate in the 1950s in which the national enemy was seen as lurking within. When America had needed its men and women to fight powerful enemies overseas during World War II, the military organization had found it more useful to project the image of the homosexual man as an effeminate weakling who was incapable of fighting or killing and of the aggressive, masculine woman as a patriot.

The enforcement of sex psychopath laws had the greatest impact on gay men and lesbians who led sexual or social lives outside their homes. While arrests for violent sexual crimes did not increase significantly in the postwar years, arrests did increase for gay men who were charged with nonviolent offenses such as consensual sodomy, sexual perversion, and public indecency, as well as for both men and women charged with patronizing a gay bar, touching in public, or wearing the clothing of the other gender. Some of these people, under the new laws, were sent to prison or committed to mental hospitals, then, upon their release, forced to register as sex offenders with their local police departments. . . .

While the sex psychopath panic was under way, military officials set out to consolidate the experimental antihomosexual policies they had developed during the war, but now working unconstrained by the wartime pressure to utilize all available personnel. The Navy Department led the other branches in centralizing and refining its homosexual procedures. In September 1947, Secretary of the Navy John L. Sullivan initiated the Navy's first postwar study of the way it managed homosexual personnel, hoping that the Navy would "take the leadership in a medical attack on a problem which appears to be growing." The secretary established a special "Committee for the Review of the Procedures for the Disposition of Naval Personnel Involved in Homosexual Offenses," which proposed several reforms, most of which in July 1949 were incorporated into a directive that superseded all the homosexual policy directives that the Navy had issued during the war.

This more comprehensive directive affirmed most aspects of existing policy while extending the Navy's power over its homosexual personnel. It directed officers to consider both the active and passive partners, whether two men or two women, as equally homosexual and equally responsible for their acts. It attempted to protect heterosexuals from "malicious charges" of homosexuality by requiring a more complete system of investigation and record keeping on each case. And it tried to protect the Navy from gay dischargees' charges of unjust discrimination by requiring homosexuals to sign the following statement of consent before being discharged: "I understand that I may be deprived of virtually all rights as a veteran under both Federal and State legislation; and that I may expect to encounter substantial prejudice in civilian life." A refusal to sign this statement of consent meant that the suspect would instead be tried by court-martial on criminal charges. . . .

The Defense Department adopted the committee's recommendations, extending the reach of the military's antihomosexual net even farther. These included adopting a clear policy statement that "homosexual personnel, irrespective of sex, should not be permitted to serve in any branch of the Armed Forces in any capacity, and prompt separation of known homosexuals from the Armed Forces is mandatory." This was broader than wartime policies that had required the rehabilitation of some gay male and lesbian personnel. The committee also recommended that each branch of the armed forces give indoctrination lectures on homosexuality modeled on existing venereal disease lectures. They proposed dividing all homosexual cases into three classes—those who used force, those who were consenting adults, and those with tendencies who had committed no provable acts in the service. . . .

At the same time Congress was taking steps to increase civilian control over military disciplinary procedures. In 1950 it enacted the Uniform Code of Military Justice (UCMJ), which was designed to protect the due process rights of individual military personnel and went into effect on May 21, 1951. Congress also established an all-civilian Court of Military Appeals to review court-martial decisions. By 1951 the Uniform Code, together with the Defense Department's uniform guidelines, established the basic policies, discharge procedures, and appeal channels for the disposition of homosexual personnel that remained in effect, with periodic modifications, in all branches of the armed forces for the next four decades.

While these changes were taking place at the policy level, the military's grip on homosexual personnel was tightening in practice as well. . . . During the peacetime years from 1947 to early 1950, the rate of discharge for homosexuals more than tripled the wartime rate. Except for a sharp drop in the Navy during the Korean War—suggesting that once again the military found it expedient to utilize homosexual personnel during a time of war—the discharge rate remained at postwar levels throughout the 1950s.

Nowhere was this tightening grip after the war more dramatic than in the military's about-face treatment of lesbians. During World War II the personnel shortages had allowed large numbers of American women to enlist in the armed forces. After the war when women were encouraged to return to civilian life and reassume traditional gender roles, those unmarried women who chose to remain in the military or who enlisted during peacetime increasingly stood out as members of a deviant group that was easily stereotyped as lesbian. As the wartime constraints against antilesbian witch hunts were lifted, purges of lesbians increased. Pat Bond, a WAC stationed in Tokyo, and Sarah Davis, a WAVE stationed in Florida, were both interrogated during extensive antilesbian witch hunts in the late 1940s, and each narrowly escaped being discharged as an undesirable, Bond because she had wed a gay man in a marriage of convenience and so passed as heterosexual, Davis because she successfully denied knowing her friends. During the Tokyo purge one woman committed suicide. By the mid-1950s, Navy officials secretly acknowledged that the homosexual discharge rate had become "much higher for the female than the male."

Another dramatic shift in postwar policy and practice was the introduction of programs to give all recruits lectures on homosexuality. This was a reversal of wartime policies to protect recruits from any discussion of homosexuality, especially in the women's branches, that might arouse their curiosity. The postwar introduction of lectures expanded the military's antihomosexual apparatus by adding a system of indoctrination to the prewar criminal justice system and the wartime systems for screening, discharge, and appeal.

These lectures reflected the growing preoccupation during the 1950s with stigmatizing not only homosexuals but also any women or men who deviated from a narrow gender norm. Retreating from the psychiatric advances of the war, Navy lecturers in 1952 were instructed that homosexuality "is not to be condoned on the grounds of 'mental illness' any more than other crime such as theft, homicide or criminal assault." Postwar lectures to WAVES recruits specifically rejected the guidance, counseling, and reassignment that had been recommended to WAC officers during the war. They told WAVES recruits that first-timers were as guilty as "confirmed" lesbians, encouraged them to inform on one another and warned that homosexuality threatened their ability to assume their proper roles in life as feminine women, wives, and mothers. While the wartime lectures had minimized the differences between lesbians and other women, the postwar lectures portrayed lesbians as exotic and dangerous perverts ready to seduce any woman who was young and naive. . . .

With these and other lectures, the military began to teach millions of young men and women to accept a uniform image of homosexuals, to fear them and report them, and to police their own feelings, friendships, and environment for signs of homosexual attractions. In a word, military officials began systematically to indoctrinate in its young recruits a response that psychiatrists and the gay rights movement later identified as homophobia: the irrational fear of homosexuality and of homosexual people. This fear reinforced a set of cold war political beliefs regarding homosexuals: To ensure public safety it was necessary to discuss the "homosexual menace" openly and to increase public awareness that unidentified homosexuals could be lurking anywhere; the government had a duty to root out and eliminate them; and all citizens needed to be ever vigilant in order to identify hidden sex perverts and report them to authorities. In this context Kinsey's findings on the high incidence of homosexual behavior among American males were used to indicate the magnitude of the homosexual threat. . . .

One of the thorniest administrative problems that military officials confronted as their antihomosexual project expanded after the war was what to do with the growing lists of names that were being generated as by-products of the discharge system. Some officials proposed releasing these names to the FBI and other government agencies to protect the general public by keeping known or suspected homosexuals under government surveillance. In January 1946, during the brief period of tolerance and gratitude following the war, such a proposal from the twelfth Naval District in San Francisco was stopped by the strong objections of Navy Surgeon General Ross McIntire. He argued that turning these files over to the FBI and local police would betray "the confidence of the individuals concerned" and "would be a prostitution of the art of medicine and contrary to the ethics of the medical profession." He also argued that it would jeopardize the chances of discharged homosexual men to re-establish themselves as "useful and self-supporting citizens in civil life" and questioned whether these men "constitute any particular danger to the security of the social order as a whole." . . .

But as the names continued to accumulate, and the social and political climate became increasingly hostile to homosexuals, pressure to release the lists mounted, especially from the offices of Army and Navy intelligence. These had been largely responsible for compiling the lists of names from the confessions, seized letters, and address books of the gay men and lesbians their personnel had interrogated. As a result intelligence officers earned a reputation as being among the most antihomosexual in the armed forces. They eventually found sympathetic ears not among top military administrators but rather among senators who began their own crusade against the employment of homosexuals in the federal government.

The military organization has often served as a testing ground for social policies and programs that later have been adopted by civilian bureaucracies.

The military's expansion of its antihomosexual policies during and after the war served as such a model for senators who in 1950 launched the most aggressive attack on homosexual employees that had ever taken place in the federal government. Their crusade was in sharp contrast to the sympathetic concern congressmen had expressed in 1946 for the plight of the blue-discharge veterans.

The 1950 antihomosexual hearings in the Senate began as a by-product of the cold war anticommunist scare. On February 28 Under Secretary of State John Peurifoy, testifying before a Senate Committee investigating the loyalty of government employees, admitted that most of the ninety-one State Department employees who had been dismissed as security risks were homosexual. Republicans seized the opportunity to attack the Truman administration and turned Peurifoy's revelation into a partisan issue that each month increased in intensity and even gained the support of several Democrats. For the rest of the year, new antihomosexual revelations or actions took place in Washington almost weekly. Republican Senator Kenneth Wherry of Nebraska and Democratic Senator Lister Hill of Alabama immediately formed a subcommittee to make preliminary investigations into the "Infiltration of Subversives and Moral Perverts into the Executive Branch of the United States Government." In June the full Senate authorized the formation of a subcommittee, headed by Senator Clyde Hoey of North Carolina, to investigate the "Employment of Homosexuals and Other Sex Perverts in Government." The subcommittee submitted its report to the Senate on December 16, describing its "government-wide" investigation into homosexuality as "unprecedented."

It was through the vehicle of these hearings by Senators Wherry, Hill, and Hoey that the military's policies and procedures for discharging homosexual personnel were extended to every employee of the federal government. Until these hearings, the Hoey committee reported, government administrators had never considered homosexuality to be a "personnel problem" and were grossly negligent in employing homosexuals. Some administrators actually "condoned the employment of homosexuals" based on the "false premise that what a Government employee did outside of the office on his own time . . . was his own business." Others took a "head-in-the-sand attitude toward the problem of sexual perversion," hoping to avoid dealing with an unpleasant issue by ignoring it. Civil Service Commission regulations had not explicitly mentioned homosexuals or "perverts" as candidates for removal from the federal service, making it easier for personnel officers to retain them as employees.

The result of this negligence, the Hoey committee noted, was that few homosexuals had been fired from government jobs. Instructing federal agencies to submit statistics regarding homosexual dismissals, the committee discovered that from January 1, 1947, to the end of 1950, the government had handled 4954 homosexual cases, the vast majority (4380) of which were in the military. Two-thirds of the few civilian cases during this four-year period occurred in 1950, mostly after the antihomosexual campaign had received wide publicity in March. The armed services clearly had a head start on other government agencies because they had discharged the most homosexuals and because, a decade earlier, they had been the first branch of the government to define homosexuality as a personnel problem. The committee concluded that the military's policy and procedures should be used as the model for other government agencies.

To strengthen their arguments, members of the Hoey committee invited intelligence officers—whose job it was to interrogate suspected homosexuals—to present the military's rationale for eliminating such people. They testified that male homosexual personnel were dangerous because they preyed on young boys in the service, they were high-strung and neurotic from leading double lives, and they were security risks. "This reasoning by authorities in the Armed Forces," concluded Senator Wherry, "based on years of observation and experience applies with equal force to other departments and agencies of the Government." In the areas of explicit policies, standardized procedures, uniform enforcement, constant vigilance, and coordination with law enforcement agencies regarding homosexuals, the committee regarded the armed services as the standard against which all other government agencies were compared and found lacking.

The major purpose and achievement of both the Hoey and Wherry-Hill committees, however, was to construct and promote the belief that homosexuals in the military and the government constituted security risks who, as individuals or working in conspiracy with members of the Communist party, threatened the safety of the nation. They wanted to apply this reasoning to military as well as federal personnel policies. But the military had its own rationale for excluding homosexual personnel based on the belief that they were unfit for military service and that they disrupted morale and discipline. The Navy Surgeon General's Office in 1941 and the Defense Department's 1949 Project M-46 report had both raised the security risk issue but considered it unimportant; the 1948 Navy lectures, although vehemently antihomosexual, had not mentioned the security risk issue at all. The military establishment had won the greatest war in its history without anyone in its ranks having threatened national security because of [his or her] homosexuality. Even under pressure from senators and their own intelligence officers, the initial response of military authorities was to give the security risk argument little credence except as a political issue outside the military domain.

To build their case that homosexuals were security risks, the Senate committees solicited testimony from intelligence officers working in police departments, the FBI, the CIA, and the armed forces. The senators interpreted the opinions of military intelligence officers as representing those of the armed forces and concluded, without releasing the testimony, that "all of these agencies are in complete agreement that sex perverts in Government constitute security risks." The evidence that these witnesses provided, however, was flimsy at best, consisting of one anecdote about an Austrian intelligence officer, Colonel Alfred Redl, who was blackmailed in 1912. Witnesses also referred to unspecified cases in which "Nazi and Communist agents have attempted to obtain information from employees of our Government by threatening to expose their abnormal sex activities," and reported unsubstantiated rumors that during the war Adolf Hitler had "amassed the names of homosexuals around the world" and that this list had been "acquired by Russia" after Germany's defeat.

Ironically the strongest argument for portraying homosexuals as susceptible to blackmail by Communists was the military's own success in emotionally
breaking down gay men and lesbians during and after the war. Intelligence officers testified that, in their own experience, "perverts are vulnerable to interro-
gation by a skilled questioner and they seldom refuse to talk about themselves."
Despite the fact that in all these cases the interrogators and blackmailers were
officers of the United States military, not agents of enemy governments, the
Hoey report concluded that homosexuals did constitute security risks. They recommended that government officials should "get sex perverts out of Government and keep them out," and that all government agencies should pool their
information on homosexuals through the FBI to make this process more efficient.

The immediate impact of the 1950 antihomosexual scare in Congress on the
careers of civilian government workers was dramatic. Before the investigations,
from 1947 through April 1950, the government had dismissed an average of five
homosexuals each month. During the second half of 1950, this rate had grown
to more than sixty per month. In July Max Lerner, in a *New York Post* column entitled "Panic on the Potomac," compared these cold war "witch hunts" to the
military's wartime actions against homosexuals. "In the Army it used to be
called 'blue discharge,'" Lerner wrote. "The Senators call it the 'purge of the pervert.'"

While the panic generated by the Senate hearings led to an immediate increase in firings, members of Congress, as well as government and military officials, began to translate the Hoey committee's recommendations into new
laws and policies. . . . But the strongest action was taken by President Dwight
Eisenhower shortly after he took office. In April 1953 he signed Executive Order
10450, which tightened loyalty and security regulations and, for the first time in
civil service law, explicitly stated that "sexual perversion" was necessary
grounds for not hiring and for firing federal workers.

With Eisenhower's executive order the government's antihomosexual policies and procedures, which had originated in the wartime military, expanded to
include every agency and department of the federal government and every private company or corporation with a government contract, such as railroad companies and aircraft plants. This affected the job security of more than six million
government workers and armed forces personnel. By the mid-1950s, similar
policies also had gone into effect in state and local governments, extending the
prohibitions on the employment of homosexuals to over twelve million workers, more than 20 percent of the United States labor force, who now had to sign
oaths attesting to their moral purity in order to get or keep their jobs. Similar
policies were adopted independently by private companies and even by private
organizations such as the American Red Cross, which "summarily dismissed"
employees involved in homosexual conduct, whether they were "habituals,
one-time offenders, or mere tendency cases." Within only a few years antihomosexual policies had spread from the military to nearly all levels of employment in the United States.

The prominent coverage given to this federal antihomosexual campaign, combined with state crusades against sexual psychopaths, contributed to a climate that fostered local panics and crackdowns. The gay and lesbian bars that had proliferated after the war became particular targets. As they emerged in more cities and multiplied in others, the legislatures of California, Michigan, and other states, which were charged with the duty of licensing and regulating liquor establishments, took steps in conjunction with local police to regulate or ban those they identified as "homo hangouts" or "resorts for sexual perverts." Highly publicized antigay crusades swept through Miami, Wichita, Boise, Portland (Oregon), Tacoma, San Francisco, and many other cities, especially where gay bars were expanding or where politicians exploited the antihomosexual climate to further their careers, leading to street sweeps and mass arrests of hundreds of people at a time. As refugees from these local crackdowns and from federal and military purges looked for safer harbors, city after city imagined that an "invasion of homosexuals" was turning it into the homosexual capital of America. In the words of one newspaper's headline, the 1950s had turned into a "war on homosexuals," one that was more widespread and publicized than any antihomosexual campaigns that had occurred during World War II.

Under heavy attack during the postwar decade, most gay male and lesbian citizens refrained from publicly standing up for themselves, fighting for their rights, or even talking about their lives. In 1951, Donald Webster Cory, protected by his pseudonym, tried to explain why he and other gay people didn't fight back. The "worst effect of discrimination," he wrote, "has been to make the homosexuals doubt themselves and share in the general contempt for sexual inverts." When an injustice was done against them, the fear of exposure led many to accept what had happened and then "make an effort to hide their homosexuality even more carefully." When arrested in gay bar raids, most people pleaded guilty, fearful of publicly exposing their homosexuality during a trial that might prove they were innocent of any crime. Legally barred from many forms of private and government employment, from serving their country, from expressing their opinions in newspapers and magazines, from gathering in bars and other public places as homosexuals, and from leading sexual lives, gay men and women were denied the civil liberties and even the channels of protest that were open to many other minorities. To make matters worse, no civil liberties organizations were willing to speak up in their behalf. Caught in what Cory called a "vicious circle," those who were honest about their lives became outcasts and martyrs, while those who lived a lie faced the shame of their own debasement, wondering if the contempt so many people felt toward them was justified. Such conditions led to stifled anger, fear, isolation, and helplessness, not collective protest or political action.

But the postwar years were also a period of new possibilities that helped to strengthen and develop gay culture. Despite and sometimes because of the mounting political war against them, the generation of World War II gay veterans did find ways to break through their isolation. They responded to a hostile environment by expanding their "closet," making it a roomier place to live. Previous generations had invented the closet—a system of lies, denials, disguises, and double entendres—that had enabled them to express some of their homo-sexuality by pretending it didn't exist and hiding it from view. A later genera-tion would "come out of the closet," learning to live as proud and openly gay men and women and demanding public recognition. But the World War II gen-eration slowly stretched their closet to its limits, not proclaiming or parading their homosexuality in public but not willing to live lonely, isolated lives.

In increasing numbers these men and women went to gay and lesbian bars that proliferated despite new state laws designed to put them out of business. In the late 1940s gay bars opened for the first time in such medium-size cities as Kansas City, Missouri; Richmond, Virginia; Worcester, Massachusetts; and San Jose, California. These meeting places evolved into the primary gay social insti-tution in cities after the war. By providing patrons with public spaces in which to gather, bars helped shape a sense of gay identity that went beyond the indi-vidual to the group. When patrons were caught in raids, they knew they were being arrested and harassed for gathering in public as homosexuals. Through-out the 1950s and 1960s, gay and lesbian bars became a major battleground in the fight to create public gathering places for homosexuals that were legal and free from harassment. In June 1969 gay riots in response to a routine police raid of the Stonewall Inn, a gay bar in New York's Greenwich Village, sparked the beginning of the gay liberation movement. Another gay institution, the bath-house, also proliferated after the war, creating a relatively safe, semipublic space that affirmed gay male eroticism and provided any man an anonymous outlet for his homosexual desires.

Their widespread use of pseudonyms enabled this generation to expand the closet while minimizing the risk of being exposed. Under pen names they wrote honestly about their lives and their sexuality in books, paperbacks, magazines, and pornography. Gay men published male physique magazines, creating a market that evolved into a flourishing gay erotica industry. Lesbians wrote and devoured hundreds of lesbian romance paperbacks, which became so popular that they were sold in five-and-dimes and drugstores across the country, reach-ing even the loneliest, most isolated lesbian or gay man in Kansas or North Dakota.

It was in this social climate—when antihomosexual campaigns terrorized gay Americans while the expansion of gay culture and the public discussion of homosexuality opened up new possibilities—that the first signs of a continuous gay political movement and press emerged in the United States. In 1950 the Mat-tachine Society was organized in Los Angeles in response to the antihomosex-ual campaigns in Washington, police arrests in Los Angeles, the state sexual psychopath panics, the treatment of homosexuals by the military, and the crack-downs on gay and lesbian bars. In 1955 women in San Francisco started the Daughters of Bilitis, the first lesbian rights organization in the United States. The esoteric names of both of these groups hid that they were homosexual, help-ing to protect them from harassment. Most of their officers used personal pseu-donyms as well.

Charles Rowland recalled that he and most of the other founders of the Mat-tachine Society had been veterans. Rowland's own interest in starting a gay organization grew indirectly out of his military experience. World War II was a war against fascism, he explained. After his discharge he continued his wartime "save the world" idealism first by organizing other veterans in the Midwest as a field representative of the liberal American Veterans Committee, then by joining the Communist party. When he fled the Midwest to Los Angeles during the anticommunist scare, it was this same idealism that led him to join original founder Harry Hay and others in starting a homosexual rights organization.

From the start the gay male and lesbian organizations published and distributed their own little magazines, which actively took on the cause of homosexual soldiers and veterans. Beginning in 1953 issues of the predominantly gay male magazines *ONE* and *Mattachine Review* and the lesbian magazine the *Ladder*, published by the Daughters of Bilitis, included pieces on the status of lesbians and gay men in the military. They reprinted congressional testimony and newspaper clippings concerning veterans with undesirable discharges and printed anonymous interviews with lesbian and gay male veterans as well as their poems, letters, stories, and personal statements. They published editorials and advice columns, as well as news of witch hunts, changes in military policy, and accounts of individuals who appealed their bad discharges. They ran special features, including cover stories, with such titles as "Homosexuals in Uniform," "Homosexual Servicemen" and "Undesirable Discharges."

In 1954 *Mattachine Review* published an open letter to Senator Everett Dirksen, who had made an offhand complaint that it had been "no picnic" to purge homosexuals from the government. The letter's anonymous author, writing in memory of the gay soldiers who had died in World War II, captured many veterans' sense of quiet outrage at being persecuted by the government they had fought for. "Thousands of graves in France," the letter read, "many many thousand more graves on South Pacific Islands and beneath the seas, contain the sad remains of men who were brave soldiers, airmen, sailors, and marines *first* and homosexuals second. They were no less brave, they did no less to win the war for democracy, than did their heterosexual compatriots. But the democracy for which they did fight and die, and still fight and still die, and will yet fight and yet die, denies them and us our rights."

The issue of military discrimination remained of vital concern to the growing gay rights movement. In 1966 the first nationwide protest by gay male and lesbian organizations in the United States was one that opposed the military's discrimination against gay personnel and veterans. But by this time such a position appeared old-fashioned to a baby-boom generation of gay activists who, as the Vietnam War heated up, began to question why homosexuals wanted to join the military at all. . . .

The military's policy remains staunchly antihomosexual while many other bureaucracies, from federal agencies to private corporations, have abandoned similar stands and have even adopted policies of nondiscrimination. It defines homosexuality as a threat to the very essence of the military organization, and the bureaucracy that puts this ideology into practice both legalizes and reinforces the social hostility toward homosexuals that helps to keep it in place. By taking such an extreme position, policymakers make it difficult for themselves to stop excluding gay personnel without losing face and credibility, and without appearing to condone homosexuality and embrace homosexuals.

Despite the strictness of their policies, military officials can never eliminate homosexuals or homosexuality from the armed forces. During World War II military psychiatrists and other administrators began to identify some of the most common personnel problems regarding homosexuality: Gender-segregated living conditions intensify homosexual fears and tensions; the hostility that some soldiers express toward homosexuals can threaten morale and affect job performance; and sexual relations between officers and enlisted personnel, whether homosexual or heterosexual, can threaten discipline. But the solution that was developed during the war—the punitive elimination of homosexuals—only magnified the military's "homosexual problem." The discharge policy increased fear, reinforced hostility and prejudice, encouraged scapegoating and witch hunting, and helped to solidify gay men and women into a political movement against the military's exclusion of homosexuals. The discharge policy continues to intensify the importance of homosexuality as a military problem rather than make it go away.

Since the antigay policies were introduced during World War II, military officials have spent much time and resources denying that the armed forces have any significant problem with homosexuality. They have done this by erasing the history of the policies, refusing to discuss them in public, and suppressing even the friendliest internal criticism. In the process, military officials have successfully perpetuated three myths: that the armed forces always had an antigay discharge policy, that known homosexuals cannot fit into the military organization and are routinely discharged, and that organized opposition to the policy comes only from outside and not from within. A policy that appears to have existed for all time, to be unanimously supported within the military, and to allow for no exceptions is not easily abandoned.

But the military's hidden history shows that the discharge policy itself was the product of liberal reform, having been put in place in 1943 by officers who in part wanted to improve the lot of the homosexual soldier out of a sense of fairness and justice. It has always been used flexibly, being modified or completely ignored—although usually in secret—to meet the demands of fluctuating personnel needs particularly during times of war. And since its inception the discharge policy has been surrounded by internal debate.

The long tradition of dissent within the military, as old as the discharge policy itself, has continually offered alternatives to the blanket elimination of homosexuals from the military, identifying antihomosexual prejudice rather than homosexuals as the problem. In 1945 Lewis Loeser, Clements Fry, and Edna Rostow all recommended that homosexuals not be treated as a class but be accepted and integrated into the military, assigned to duty based on individual skills and talents, and discharged only if their homosexuality prevented them from doing their jobs. In 1952 a Defense Department committee appointed to review homosexual policy could not reach agreement and issued two reports, with only the dissenting minority maintaining that homosexuals constituted security risks and that no homosexuals should be retained in the service. In 1957 the Navy's Crittenden Board concluded that there was no evidence to support the idea that homosexuals as a class "cannot acceptably serve in the military" or that they were security risks. The board even suggested that homosexuals might be more reliable in espionage and other top-secret jobs than some heterosexuals.

This long tradition of dissent, however, has been accompanied by a long record of suppression. The reports of Fry and Rostow, the Crittenden Board, and virtually every other team of military researchers have been kept secret or destroyed. In September 1977, after thirty-five years of studying homosexuals and their own antihomosexual policies, Army officials stated that their files revealed "no evidence of special studies pertaining to homosexuals" and Navy officials maintained that they could not locate any of their own studies on homosexuality. It was only under orders from a federal judge in 1977 that the Crittenden Report and other Navy studies were released.

Today the same pattern of dissent and suppression continues, although it has become more public. In October 1989 members of Congress released to the press a report by researchers at the Defense Department's Personnel Security Research and Education Center (PERSEREC) in Monterey, California. The report concluded that homosexuals were no more of a security risk and no more susceptible to blackmail than heterosexuals, and that the military should consider accepting homosexuals. It recommended that the military begin research to test the hypothesis that gay men and women "can function appropriately in military units," as the military had done before it integrated blacks into the military immediately after World War II. Members of Congress released another report from the same research center that concluded that personnel discharged as homosexuals were better qualified and had fewer personal problems than the average heterosexual in the service. Defense Department officials rejected and condemned both these reports. They charged that the research was biased and technically flawed and that the researchers had exceeded their authority by criticizing policy. Refusing to participate in a public debate, the Pentagon stated that "we cannot comment on matters that remain unresolved before the court."

In 1957, the secret Crittenden Report had made nearly the same conclusions as the 1989 PERSEREC Reports. The Crittenden Report, however, recommended no change in policy because the military "should not move ahead of civilian society" in accepting homosexuals, although it advised the Navy to "keep abreast of any widely accepted changes in the attitude of society." In the three decades that followed the Crittenden Report, dramatic changes significantly altered social attitudes, leading to the rise of movements for women's rights and gay rights, the repeal of sodomy laws, and the adoption of corporate and government nondiscrimination policies. The PERSEREC Report, addressing the issue of leadership raised by the Crittenden Report, suggested that the military had fallen behind civilian society and the time had come for it to stop excluding homosexuals. Summarizing the broad changes that had taken place during the twentieth century, the report concluded that the earlier categorizations of homosexuality as "sin, crime, and sickness" were obsolete and that the military should begin to accept homosexuals as members of a "minority group."

With this recommendation, the process by which the military's expanding anti-gay policy had pressured gay men and women to identify themselves as members of a persecuted minority had come full circle: Military researchers were now using the idea that homosexuals constituted a minority group to call for an end to the antigay policy.

The generation of gay men and women who served in World War II grew into adulthood fighting one war for their country and another to protect themselves from their government's escalating mobilization against them. When they returned to civilian life, some fought for their right to be treated fairly as patients, veterans, and citizens. For others a quiet sense of belonging was victory enough, to have the chance to fit into the country they fought for, leading ordinary but unapologetic lives. As they grow into old age and once again face their own and each other's deaths, most still blend into the world around them, while some have come out either under fire or on their own. Today they witness an expanding public debate over the military's exclusion of homosexuals. If that debate is to be at all serious, it must include a sense of history—not only of how the military established its antigay policy during World War II and then suppressed all internal dissent, but also of how the men and women who were the policy's first targets fought and died for their country with the rest of their generation.

SOURCES

Sex Crime Panic

The items on this page are typical of the kinds of images that circulated during the nationwide panic over sexual psychopaths in the late 1940s. The first appeared as an illustration to FBI Director J. Edgar Hoover's article, "How Safe Is Your Daughter?" (1947). The second is from a brochure for school children distributed by the City of Detroit. What messages do they contain? If the photo of the three girls were made into a film, what genre would it be?

"The nation's women and children will never be secure . . . so long as degenerates run wild"

big hand reaching out for little girls

NEVER go
with strangers
when they ask
for directions.

NEVER go
with strangers
who offer you
a job with pay.

brochure, "never go with strangers"

Truman on Hiroshima (August 6, 1945)

On the day the Enola Gay *released on atomic bomb over the Japanese city of Hiroshima, the White House released this statement by President Harry Truman. It is an extraordinary document, full of the twists and turns that were perhaps inevitable at this moment when the public was first introduced to the atomic bomb, told about its use at Hiroshima, and informed of its atomic future. How did Truman justify the use of this weapon? What aspects of the atomic bomb did Truman emphasize? What should or might he have said that he did not?*

Sixteen hours ago an American airplane dropped one bomb on Hiroshima, an important Japanese Army base. That bomb had more power than 20,000 tons of T.N.T. It had more than two thousand times the blast power of the British "Grand Slam" which is the largest bomb ever yet used in the history of warfare.

The Japanese began the war from the air at Pearl Harbor. They have been repaid many fold. And the end is not yet. With this bomb we have now added a new and revolutionary increase in destruction to supplement the growing

Foreign Relations of the United States, Potsdam, vol. 2, Washington, D.C., 1960, pp. 1380–1381.

power of our armed forces. In their present form these bombs are now in production and even more powerful forms are in development.

It is an atomic bomb. It is a harnessing of the basic power of the universe. The force from which the sun draws its power has been loosed against those who brought war to the Far East.

Before 1939, it was the accepted belief of scientists that it was theoretically possible to release atomic energy. But no one knew any practical method of doing it. By 1942, however, we knew that the Germans were working feverishly to find a way to add atomic energy to the other engines of war with which they hoped to enslave the world. But they failed. We may be grateful to Providence that the Germans got the V-1s and the V-2s late and in limited quantities and even more grateful that they did not get the atomic bomb at all.

The battle of the laboratories held fateful risks for us as well as the battles of the air, land and sea, and we have now won the battle of the laboratories as we have won the other battles.

Beginning in 1940, before Pearl Harbor, scientific knowledge useful in war was pooled between the United States and Great Britain, and many priceless helps to our victories have come from that arrangement. Under that general policy the research on the atomic bomb was begun. With American and British scientists working together we entered the race of discovery against the Germans.

The United States had available the large number of scientists of distinction in the many needed areas of knowledge. It had the tremendous industrial and financial resources necessary for the project and they could be devoted to it without undue impairment of other vital war work. In the United States the laboratory work and the production plants, on which a substantial start had already been made, would be out of reach of enemy bombing, while at that time Britain was exposed to constant air attack and was still threatened with the possibility of invasion. For these reasons Prime Minister Churchill and President Roosevelt agreed that it was wise to carry on the project here. We now have two great plants and many lesser works devoted to the production of atomic power. Employment during peak construction numbered 125,000 and over 65,000 individuals are even now engaged in operating the plants. Many have worked there for two and a half years. Few know what they have been producing. They see great quantities of material going in and they see nothing coming out of these plants, for the physical size of the explosive charge is exceedingly small. We have spent two billion dollars on the greatest scientific gamble in history—we won.

But the greatest marvel is not the size of the enterprise, its secrecy, nor its cost, but the achievement of scientific brains in putting together infinitely complex pieces of knowledge held by many men in different fields of science into a workable plan. And hardly less marvelous has been the capacity of industry to design, and of labor to operate, the machines and methods to do things never done before so that the brain child of many minds came forth in physical shape and performed as it was supposed to do. Both science and industry worked under the direction of the United States Army, which achieved a unique success in managing so diverse a problem in the advancement of knowledge in an amazingly short time. It is doubtful if such another combination could be got together in the world. What has been done is the greatest achievement of organized science in history. It was done under high pressure and without failure.

We are now prepared to obliterate more rapidly and completely every productive enterprise the Japanese have above ground in any city. We shall destroy their docks, their factories, and their communications. Let there be no mistake; we shall completely destroy Japan's power to make war.

It was to spare the Japanese people from utter destruction that the ultimatum of July 26 was issued at Potsdam. Their leaders promptly rejected that ultimatum. If they do not now accept our terms they may expect a rain of ruin from the air, the like of which has never been seen on this earth. Behind this air attack will follow sea and land forces in such numbers and power as they have not yet seen and with the fighting skill of which they are already well aware.

The secretary of war, who has kept in personal touch with all phases of this project, will immediately make public a statement giving further details.

His statement will give facts concerning the sites of Oak Ridge near Knoxville, Tennessee, and at Richland near Pasco, Washington, and an installation near Santa Fe, New Mexico. Although the workers at the sites have been making materials to be used in producing the greatest of destructive force in history they have not themselves been in danger beyond that of many other occupations, for the utmost care has been taken of their safety.

The fact that we can release atomic energy ushers in a new era in man's understanding of nature's forces. Atomic energy may in the future supplement the power that now comes from coal, oil, and falling water, but at present it cannot be produced on a basis to compete with them commercially. Before that comes there must be a long period of intensive research.

It has never been the habit of the scientists of this country or the policy of this government to withhold from the world scientific knowledge. Normally, therefore, everything about the work with atomic energy would be made public.

But under present circumstances it is not intended to divulge the technical processes of production or all the military applications, pending further examination of possible methods of protecting us and the rest of the world from the danger of sudden destruction.

I shall recommend that the Congress of the United States consider promptly the establishment of an appropriate commission to control the production and use of atomic power within the United States. I shall give further consideration and make further recommendations to the Congress as to how atomic power can become a powerful and forceful influence towards the maintenance of world peace.

Mickey Spillane

I, the Jury

To a reading public enthralled with detectives and detective stories, Mickey Spillane's 1947 best-seller, I, the Jury, introduced one of the most famous fictional detectives of all: Mike Hammer. Hammer was different. Though he was no dummy, his methods were not those of science (like Sherlock Holmes) or of advanced technology (like the comic strip figure Dick Tracy, who debuted in the 1940s). In reading the opening chapter to the novel, use the Hammer character to help shape your understanding of the 1940s. What were Hammer's methods? Why might readers have responded enthusiastically to Hammer's ways of doing things? In addition, pay close attention to the circumstances that bring Hammer into the case and make him want to solve it. How is Hammer affected by the war? Do you see any similarity between Hammer's style and values and those of Harry Truman, expressed in the previous document? Or between Hammer and Joe McCarthy (see chapter 10)?

I shook the rain from my hat and walked into the room. Nobody said a word. They stepped back politely and I could feel their eyes on me. Pat Chambers was standing by the door to the bedroom trying to steady Myrna. The girl's body was racking with dry sobs. I walked over and put my arms around her.

"Take it easy, kid," I told her. "Come on over here and lie down." I led her to a studio couch that was against the far wall and sat her down. She was in pretty bad shape. One of the uniformed cops put a pillow down for her and she stretched out.

Pat motioned me over to him and pointed to the bedroom. "In there, Mike," he said.

In there. The words hit me hard. In there was my best friend lying on the floor dead. The body. Now I could call it that. Yesterday it was Jack Williams, the guy that shared the same mud bed with me through two years of warfare in the stinking slime of the jungle. Jack, the guy who said he'd give his right arm for a friend and did when he stopped a bastard of a Jap from slitting me in two. He caught the bayonet in the biceps, and they amputated his arm.

Pat didn't say a word. He let me uncover the body and feel the cold face. For the first time in my life I felt like crying. "Where did he get it, Pat?"

"In the stomach. Better not look at it. The killer carved the nose off a forty-five and gave it to him low."

I threw back the sheet anyway, and a curse caught in my throat. Jack was in shorts, his one hand still clutching his belly in agony. The bullet went in clean, but where it came out left a hole big enough to cram a fist into.

Very gently I pulled the sheet back and stood up. It wasn't a complicated setup. A trail of blood led from the table beside the bed to where Jack's artificial arm lay. Under him the throw rug was ruffled and twisted. He had tried to drag himself along with his one arm, but never reached what he was after.

His police positive, still in the holster, was looped over the back of the chair. That was what he wanted. With a slug in his gut he never gave up.

I pointed to the rocker, overbalanced under the weight of the .38. "Did you move the chair, Pat?"

"No, why?"

"It doesn't belong there. Don't you see?"

Pat looked puzzled. "What are you getting at?"

"That chair was over there by the bed. I've been here often enough to remember that much. After the killer shot Jack, he pulled himself toward the chair. But the killer didn't leave after the shooting. He stood here and watched him grovel on the floor in agony. Jack was after that gun, but he never reached it. He could have if the killer didn't move it. The trigger-happy bastard must have stood by the door laughing while Jack tried to make his last play. He kept pulling the chair back, inch by inch, until Jack gave up. Tormenting a guy who's been through all sorts of hell. Laughing. This was no ordinary murder, Pat. It's as cold-blooded and as deliberate as I ever saw one. I'm going to get the one that did this."

"You dealing yourself in, Mike?"

"I'm in. What did you expect?"

"You're going to have to go easy."

"Uh-uh. Fast, Pat. From now on it's a race. I want the killer for myself. We'll work together as usual, but in the homestretch, I'm going to pull the trigger."

"No, Mike, it can't be that way. You know it."

"Okay, Pat," I told him. "You have a job to do, but so have I. Jack was about the best friend I ever had. We lived together and fought together. And by Christ, I'm not letting the killer go through the tedious process of the law. You know what happens, damn it. They get the best lawyer there is and screw up the whole thing and wind up a hero! The dead can't speak for themselves. They can't tell what happened. How could Jack tell a jury what it was like to have his insides ripped out by a dumdum? Nobody in the box would know how it felt to be dying or have your own killer laugh in your face. One arm. Hell, what does that mean? So he has the Purple Heart. But did they ever try dragging themselves across a floor to a gun with that one arm, their insides filling up with blood, so goddamn mad to be shot they'd do anything to reach the killer. No, damn it. A jury is cold and impartial like they're supposed to be, while some snotty lawyer makes them pour tears as he tells how his client was insane at the moment or had to shoot in self-defense. Swell. The law is fine. But this time I'm the law and I'm not going to be cold and impartial. I'm going to remember all those things."

I reached out and grabbed the lapels of his coat. "And something more, Pat. I want you to hear every word I say. I want you to tell it to everyone you know. And when you tell it, tell it strong, because I mean every word of it. There are ten thousand mugs that hate me and you know it. They hate me because if they mess with me I shoot their damn heads off. I've done it and I'll do it again."

There was so much hate welled up inside me I was ready to blow up, but I turned and looked down at what was once Jack. Right then I felt like saying a prayer, but I was too mad.

"Jack, you're dead now. You can't hear me any more. Maybe you can. I hope so. I want you to hear what I'm about to say. You've known me a long time, Jack. My word is good just as long as I live. I'm going to get the louse that killed you. He won't sit in the chair. He won't hang. He will die exactly as you died, with a .45 slug in the gut, just a little below the belly button. No matter who it is, Jack, I'll get the one. Remember, no matter who it is, I promise."

When I looked up, Pat was staring at me strangely. He shook his head. I knew what he was thinking. "Mike, lay off. For God's sake don't go off half-cocked about this. I know you too well. You'll start shooting up anyone connected with this and get in a jam you'll never get out of."

"I'm over it now, Pat. Don't get excited. From now on I'm after one thing, the killer. You're a cop, Pat. You're tied down by rules and regulations. There's someone over you. I'm alone. I can slap someone in the puss and they can't do a damn thing. No one can kick me out of my job. Maybe there's nobody to put up a huge fuss if I get gunned down, but then I still have a private cop's license with the privilege to pack a rod, and they're afraid of me. I hate hard, Pat. When I latch on to the one behind this they're going to wish they hadn't started it. Some day, before long, I'm going to have my rod in my mitt and the killer in front of me. I'm going to watch the killer's face. I'm going to plunk one right in his gut, and when he's dying on the floor I may kick his teeth out.

"You couldn't do that. You have to follow the book because you're a Captain of Homicide. Maybe the killer will wind up in the chair. You'd be satisfied, but I wouldn't. It's too easy. That killer is going down like Jack did."

There was nothing more to say. I could see by the set of Pat's jaw that he wasn't going to try to talk me out of it. All he could do was to try to beat me to him and take it from there. We walked out of the room together. The coroner's men had arrived and were ready to carry the body away.

I didn't want Myrna to see that. I sat down on the couch beside her and let her sob on my shoulder. That way I managed to shield her from the sight of her fiancé being carted off in a wicker basket. She was a good kid. Four years ago, when Jack was on the force, he had grabbed her as she was about to do a Dutch over the Brooklyn Bridge. She was a wreck then. Dope had eaten her nerve ends raw. But he had taken her to his house and paid for a full treatment until she was normal. For the both of them it had been a love that blossomed into a beautiful thing. If it weren't for the war they would have been married long ago.

When Jack came back with one arm it had made no difference. He no longer was a cop, but his heart was with the force. She had loved him before, and she still loved him. Jack wanted her to give up her job, but Myrna persuaded him to let her hold it until he really got settled. It was tough for a man with one arm to find employment, but he had many friends.

Before long he was part of the investigating staff of an insurance company. It had to be police work. For Jack there was nothing else. Then they were happy. Then they were going to be married. Now this.

Pat tapped me on the shoulder. "There's a car waiting downstairs to take her home."

I rose and took her by the hand. "Come on, kid. There's no more you can do. Let's go."

She didn't say a word, but stood up silently and let a cop steer her out the door. I turned to Pat. "Where do we start?" I asked him.

"Well, I'll give you as much as I know. See what you can add to it. You and Jack were great buddies. It might be that you can add something that will make some sense."

Inwardly I wondered. Jack was such a straight guy that he never made an enemy. Even while on the force. Since he'd gotten back, his work with the insurance company was pretty routine. But maybe an angle there, though.

"Jack threw a party last night," Pat went on. "Not much of an affair."

"I know," I cut in, "he called me and asked me over, but I was pretty well knocked out. I hit the sack early. Just a group of old friends he knew before the army."

"Yeah. We got their names from Myrna. The boys are checking on them now."

"Who found the body?" I asked.

"Myrna did. She and Jack were driving out to the country today to pick a building site for their cottage. She got here at eight A.M. or a little after. When Jack didn't answer, she got worried. His arm had been giving him trouble lately and she thought it might have been that. She called the super. He knew her and let her in. When she screamed the super came running back and called us. Right after I got the story about the party from her, she broke down completely. Then I called you."

"What time did the shooting occur?"

"The coroner places it about five hours before I got here. That would make it about three fifteen. When I get an autopsy report we may be able to narrow it down ever further."

"Anyone hear a shot?"

"Nope. It probably was a silenced gun."

"Even with a muffler, a .45 makes a good-sized noise."

"I know, but there was a party going on down the hall. Not loud enough to cause complaints, but enough to cover up any racket that might have been made here."

"What about those that were here?" Pat reached in his pocket and pulled out a pad. He ripped a leaf loose and handed it to me.

"Here's a list Myrna gave me. She was the first to arrive. Got here at eight thirty last night. She acted as hostess, meeting the others at the door. The last one came about eleven. They spent the evening doing some light drinking and dancing, then left as a group about one."

I looked at the names Pat gave me. A few of them I knew well enough, while a couple of the others were people of whom Jack had spoken, but I had never met.

"Where did they go after the party, Pat?"

"They took two cars. The one Myrna went in belonged to Hal Kines. They drove straight up to Westchester, dropping Myrna off on the way. I haven't heard from any of the others yet."

Both of us were silent for a moment, then Pat asked, "What about a motive, Mike?"

I shook my head. "I don't see any yet. But I will. He wasn't killed for nothing. I'll bet this much, whatever it was, was big. There's a lot here that's screwy. You got anything?"

"Nothing more than I gave you, Mike. I was hoping you could supply some answers."

I grinned at him, but I wasn't trying to be funny. "Not yet. Not yet. They'll come though. And I'll relay them on to you, but by that time I'll be working on the next step."

"The cops aren't exactly dumb, you know. We can get our own answers."

"Not like I can. That's why you buzzed me so fast. You can figure things out as quickly as I can, but you haven't got the ways and means of doing the dirty work. That's where I come in. You'll be right behind me every inch of the way, but when the pinch comes I'll get shoved aside and you slap the cuffs on. That is, if you can shove me aside. I don't think you can."

"Okay, Mike, call it your own way. I want you in all right. But I want the killer, too. Don't forget that. I'll be trying to beat you to him. We have every scientific facility at our disposal and a lot of men to do the leg work. We're not short in brains, either," he reminded me.

"Don't worry, I don't underrate the cops. But cops can't break a guy's arm to make him talk, and they can't shove his teeth in with the muzzle of a .45 to remind him that you aren't fooling. I do my own leg work, and there are a lot of guys who will tell me what I want to know because they know what I'll do to them if they don't. My staff is strictly ex officio, but very practical."

That ended the conversation. We walked out into the hall where Pat put a patrolman on the door to make sure things stayed as they were. We took the self-operated elevator down four flights to the lobby and I waited while Pat gave a brief report to some reporters.

My car stood at the curb behind the squad car. I shook hands with Pat and climbed into my jalopy and headed for the Hackard Building, where I held down a two-room suite to use for operation.

Dark Victory: A Visual Essay

Three of the illustrations in this grouping feature Americans dealing in ordinary ways with the fact of World War II. The fourth is an illustration from a high school yearbook for 1946 (a year of transition: the war was over, the cold war not yet recognizable). What does each illustration reveal about the era? About the war? About relations between men and women?

Soldier home on furlough, Brown Summit, North Carolina, May 1944.
Standard Oil Collection, University of Louisville Photographic Archives, Louisville, Kentucky.

The Tanner Family—Velma, Jimmie, and their son—at home in the Humble Oil Company "Poor Boy" Camp, Tomball, Texas, 1945.
Standard Oil Collection, University of Louisville Photographic Archives, Louisville, Kentucky.

A barmaid in Great Falls, Montana, 1944.
Standard Oil Collection, University of Louisville Photographic Archives, Louisville, Kentucky.

Riverside High School *Skipper,* Buffalo, New York, 1946.

CHAPTER 10

Cold War, Cold War at Home

The end of World War II marked a clear American military and economic success. But it also created a power vacuum in Europe and a sense of insecurity about the immediate future in Washington. Some prominent Americans, like Henry Luce, the publisher of *Life* magazine, welcomed the opportunity to inaugurate an "American Century," an era where the United States was challenged to embrace world leadership and create an environment conducive to American commercial growth and development. Should the nation fail to grasp this opportunity, Luce argued, it might find itself, as it had after World War I, hostage to the fortunes of fascist, totalitarian, or Communist nations that were less keen on peace, commercial development, and democracy.

Throughout World War II, Washington's major policies were consistent with Luce's vision of an American Century. At the Bretton Woods Conference in April 1944, the World Bank, the International Monetary Fund, and a system of currency exchange were created, all aimed at facilitating and stabilizing the free flow of trade. A further American diplomatic priority was world stability, addressed through the renewed commitment to collective security as defined by the United Nations, another agency given new life by the allies' military success.

America held one other high card in its hand, in addition to its immense military and economic and financial establishments. In August 1945, American technology and science were proved superior when the first atomic bomb was exploded over Hiroshima. In sole possession of a startling new weapon that redefined warfare, Americans felt they had a sure winner. It was, however, frustratingly difficult to find combat situations where the bomb could be profitably employed, especially since it took months to build each one. The preponderance of the American contribution in funding the war, in ending the conflict in the Pacific, and in creating the monetary environment of the future seemed to indicate that the American Century had commenced.

Yet August 1945 did not immediately usher in a secure, stable world for American workers. The problems inherent in converting the American economy to peacetime production, the demobilization of millions of servicemen, and the shift in the labor force as returning servicemen displaced recently hired women and minorities, meant a period of inflation and insecurity for a nation only too familiar with the economic hardships of the recent depression. Americans became aware, once again, that they could win the war and lose the peace. The clear military victory of 1945 was followed by inconclusive diplomacy, as the allies were unable to agree on the structure of postwar Germany; American factories were in danger of cutting production for lack of clients; and the shared goals and ideals of wartime were giving way to socialism and state economies among the allies.

As these concerns grew and multiplied, President Truman took action. In March 1947, he boldly asked Congress for $400 million in aid to Greece and Turkey. The general anxiety and sense of crisis among the American public regarding recent world events coalesced into active fear of the Soviet Union and Communist regimes. The cold war had officially begun.

Within two months, the Truman administration would call for the largest foreign aid program in the history of the United States: the Marshall Plan. The intent was to save the economies of Europe and indirectly to provide markets to sustain America's production. In 1948, the first arguments for American defense of Europe were heard; in 1949, the North Atlantic Treaty Organization was formed, and military containment was born. The American decision to reconstruct western Europe led the Soviet Union to retaliate by forming its own east European bloc. Truman's response to the crisis of 1947 institutionalized a military, economic, and diplomatic contest between the United States and the Soviet Union.

The 1952 election of Dwight D. Eisenhower redefined the problem. Republicans accused Truman of misunderstanding the nature of the fight; what Democrats called a relatively short-term crisis was, the Republicans argued, a long-term, ideological struggle between the forces of communism and capitalism—a struggle that threatened, if not dealt with correctly, to destroy the very foundations of American society. In this contest to the death, America's future lay in maintaining budgetary balance, military superiority, and a clear moral definition of its goals. If a "clear and present danger" existed in America's future, then all of America's promises of freedom, democracy, and individualism had to be placed on hold until security was won.

The acute insecurity expressed in the elections of 1950 and 1952 blurred the lines between foreign policy and domestic policy. Once the concept of America under siege became political consensus, dissension in actions or thoughts could easily be seen as treason, offering aid and comfort to the enemy, deeds worthy of prosecution and punishment. This was the climate that led to the growth of McCarthyism and its excesses.

INTERPRETIVE ESSAY

Walter LaFeber

Two Halves of the Same Walnut
(1947–1948)

The origins of the cold war have been widely debated by historians and politicians. A central controversial question remains: who was to blame? The Soviet Union, for its aggressive, imperial, military activities in eastern Europe after World War II? Or, the United States, anxious about its economic future and insecure about Soviet ideology, seeking to preemptively contain Soviet power? Were both countries driven by domestic imperatives, each blind to the security and economic needs of the other?

The enunciation of the Truman Doctrine stands as the opening salvo and the defining ethos of the cold war. Alone, it defines an altruistic American response to Soviet aggression "to support free peoples who are resisting attempted subjugation by armed minorities or by outside pressures." But, when Walter LaFeber, an eminent historian of the revisionist school, analyzes the Truman Doctrine in combination with the Marshall Plan, the overall intent of the policy is less humanitarian, more economically self-interested, and infinitely more complicated. Although criticized by many as a great giveaway program, the Marshall Plan provided huge markets for American products, especially munitions.

America's economic picture in 1945 was muddled. The sudden, early end of the war brought about by the atomic explosions at Hiroshima and Nagasaki ended all chances of a gradual conversion to a peacetime economy. Instead, policies originally expected to develop over months were approved over a weekend. The Office of War Mobilization and Reconversion reported that unemployment might reach 8 million by 1946. Demobilization ran at a precipitous rate, as Truman himself announced that 2 million men would be home by Christmas 1945. The biggest economic problem of all was inflation, which reached 18.2 percent in 1946. America's gross national product was growing, but American workers could not afford to purchase American products. American exports in 1947 accounted for one-third of the world's exports, and many worried that unless trade continued to expand, another depression would descend. But Europe, America's best customer and historic trading partner, was not recovering, and some governments were actually espousing socialist and communist programs. Was it time for America to stake out a new policy and take on responsibility for Europe's economic health? And if so, how could Congress and the people be convinced to indulge such a expensive, entangling endeavor?

America, Russia, and the Cold War: 1945–1972, 7th edition, McGraw-Hill, Inc., New York, 1993, pp. 49–73. © 1993. Used with the permission of McGraw-Hill.

On March 12, 1947, President Truman finally issued his own declaration of cold war. Dramatically presenting the Truman Doctrine to Congress, he asked Americans to join in a global commitment against communism. The nation responded. A quarter of a century later, Senator J. William Fulbright declared, "More by far than any other factor the anti-communism of the Truman Doctrine has been the guiding spirit of American foreign policy since World War II."

An odd circumstance, however, must be explained if the Truman Doctrine is to be understood. The Soviet Union had been less aggressive in the months before the president's pronouncement than at any time in the postwar period. Stalin consolidated his hold over Rumania and Poland through manipulated elections, and at home Soviet propagandists encouraged Western socialists and other "proletarians" to undertake revolutionary action. But throughout the winter of 1946–1947, the Soviet [leaders] acted cautiously. State Department officials privately believed that "the USSR is undergoing serious economic difficulties," which have led to "the less aggressive international attitude taken by Soviet authorities in recent weeks." This policy was only "a temporary retreat." Nonetheless, the problems seemed so great that the Russians gave military discharges to "hundreds of thousands of young men [who] will now become available for labor force in industry, agriculture and construction." Stalin reduced his 12 million military men of 1945 to between 3 and 4 million in 1947. (American forces dropped from 10 million to 1.4 million, but Americans enjoyed a monopoly of atomic weapons.) Russian military levels would go no lower, for the Red Army was Stalin's counter to Truman's atomic bomb. Poised in Eastern Europe, the troops threatened to take the continent hostage in case of atomic attack on Russia. Stalin had no navy capable of long-range offensive strikes. The fleet depended on 300 submarines geared for defensive purposes.

Truman's immediate problem was not the threat of a Russian invasion. As Dean Acheson privately remarked, the Russians would not make war with the United States "unless they are absolutely out of their minds."* The greater danger was that Stalin might be proven correct when he indicated the Communists could bide their time since a "general crisis" was becoming so "acute" in the West that it would sweep away "atom-dollar" diplomacy. Communist party power rose steeply in Europe, particularly in France, where the first cabinet of the new Fourth Republican contained four Communists, including the minister of defense. Chaotic conditions in former colonial areas also opened exceptional opportunities to revolutionaries. The two gems of the British crown, India and Egypt, shattered the empire with drives for independence. They were soon joined by Pakistan, Burma, Ceylon [Sri Lanka], and Nepal. France began a long, futile, eight-year war to regain Indochina. The Dutch faced full-scale revolution in Indonesia. The Middle East was in turmoil over the determination of a half-dozen countries to be totally independent, as well as over the influx of 100,000 Jews who hoped to establish a homeland in Palestine.

In late 1946 and early 1947, American officials gave increasing attention to these newly emerging areas. Europe could not be fully stabilized until England,

---

*Undersecretary Dean Acheson would be secretary of state from 1949 to 1953.

France, and the Netherlands settled their colonial problems. The State Department also assumed that the American economy, as well as the economy of the western community, which depended upon American prosperity, demanded a proper settlement of these conflicts. In a speech in November 1946, [Assistant Secretary of State] Will Clayton explained that the expansion in the domestic economy and the "depletion of our natural resources" would make the United States much more dependent on the importation of raw materials and minerals. Many of these came from the newly emerging areas. "No nation in modern times," the assistant secretary of state warned, "can long expect to enjoy a rising standard of living without increased foreign trade." Adolf Berle, economist, adviser to Roosevelt and Truman, and State Department official, declared in late 1946 that the Soviet [Union] and the United States had begun a battle for the allegiance of the less industrialized nations. "Within four years the world [will] be faced with an apparent surplus in production beyond any previously known," Berle explained. If American surpluses were used to "take the lead in material reconstruction" of the newly emerging countries, the United States could level off those "cycles of 'boom and bust' which disfigured our prewar economy."

"Boom and bust" already threatened. The American economy sagged, and unemployment rose in early 1946 before some expansion began. State Department experts worried that the improvement was temporary, for it rested on a $15 billion American export trade, nearly four times the level of the 1930s. Most of these exports were rebuilding western Europe, but the Europeans were rapidly running out of dollars to pay for the goods. When its remaining dollars and gold were spent, Europe would stagnate, then perhaps grasp at socialism to save itself. Americans would face the loss of their most vital market and probably the return of the 1930s with all the attendant political consequences. Truman understood this by early 1947, but a tax-cutting Republican Congress and his own low popularity seemed to block any action.

The turn came on Saturday morning, February 21, 1947, when a British embassy official drove to the near-deserted State Department building. He informed Acheson that because of its own economic crisis (more than half its industry was quiet), England could not provide the $250 million of military and economic support needed by Greece and Turkey. As Secretary of State George Marshall later observed, "It was tantamount to British abdication from the Middle East with obvious implications as to their successor."

American officials were not taken by surprise. From 1944 until early 1947 they had closely watched the British attempt to regain control of Greece become bogged down in a Greek civil war. On one side was a conservative-monarchical group supported by London. On the other was the National Liberation Front (NLF), with Communist leadership, which had gained popularity and power by leading resistance efforts against the Nazis. By 1947 the NLF received support from Yugoslav Communist leader Josep Broz (Marshal Tito). The Yugoslav was not motivated by affection for his fellow Communists in Greece. Rather, he hoped to annex parts of Greece to a large Yugoslav federation. Stalin was not directly involved and indeed developed a strong dislike for Tito's ambitions.

But as NLF strength grew, the United States did become involved. Throughout 1946 it sent special missions, poured in $260 million of aid, and sided with the British. Drawing on this experience, the State Department was able to work out a detailed proposal for assistance within a week after Acheson received the British message. After only nineteen days, Truman could appear before Congress with a complete program. Clearly, the president's request on March 12 for $400 million in Greek and Turkish aid (the Truman Doctrine speech) was not a sudden, drastic departure in American foreign policy.

But the reasoning in Truman's speech was radically new. That reasoning was worked out by American officials who had long been waiting for this opportunity. As they developed the speech, "they found release from the professional frustrations of years," as one later declared. "It seemed to those present that a new chapter in world history had opened and they were the most privileged of men." Those words help explain why the officials made certain choices. For example, they could have determined simply that Greece was in a civil war and therefore the United States had no business intervening. Or they could quietly have asked Congress to continue aid to Greece and Turkey while transferring to those nations weapons left from the war. The administration, however, rejected those alternatives, choosing instead to appear dramatically before Congress to request support for a global battle against communism. A White House adviser remarked that the message would be "the opening gun in a campaign to bring people up to [the] realization that the war isn't over by any means."

As State Department officials prepared drafts of the speech, Truman, Secretary of State Marshall, and Acheson met with congressional leaders. It was not a warm audience. The Republicans were busily cutting taxes 20 percent and chopping $6 billion from Truman's already tight budget. The legislators remained unmoved until Acheson swung into the argument that the threat was not a Greek civil war but Russian communism; its aim was the control of the Middle East, South Asia, and Africa; and this control was part of a communist plan to encircle and capture the ultimate objective, Germany and Europe. It was a struggle between liberty and dictatorship. By defending Greece and Turkey, therefore, Americans were defending their own freedoms. "The Soviet Union was playing one of the greatest gambles in history at minimal cost," Acheson concluded. "We and we alone are in a position to break up the play."

The congressmen were stunned. Silence followed until Arthur Vandenberg (now chairman of the Senate Foreign Relations Committee) told Truman that the message must include Acheson's explanation. As the senator advised, the president "scared hell" out of the American people. Insofar as public opinion was concerned, this tactic worked well for Truman (at least until three years later when Senator Joseph McCarthy and others turned the argument around and accused the administration of too gently handling such a horrible danger). The president also won over Congress with assurances that the United States would not only control every penny of America's aid to Greece but run the Greek economy by controlling foreign exchange, budget, taxes, currency, and credit.

Inside the State Department, however, Acheson ran into opposition. George Kennan, the top expert on Soviet affairs, objected bitterly to sending military assistance to nations such as Turkey that had no internal Communist problems and bordered the Soviet Union. Unlike economic help, military aid could be provocative. Acheson rejected the argument. The opportunity to build Turkey's military strength was too good to miss. Thus in the words of one official, "Turkey was slipped into the oven with Greece because that seemed the surest way to cook a tough bird." Kennan also protested against the harsh ideological tone and open-ended American commitment in the speech drafts. He was joined by Secretary of State Marshall and Charles Bohlen, another expert on Russia, who told Acheson that "there was a little too much flamboyant anti-communism in the speech." Acheson stood his ground. Marshall was informed that Truman believed the Senate would not approve the doctrine "without the emphasis on the Communist danger."

Acheson, however, carefully kept the central economic factors out of the speech. He and Truman wanted a simple ideological call to action that all could understand, not a message that might trigger arguments over American oil holdings in the Middle East. The economic interests were nevertheless crucial. As State Department official Joseph Jones noted, if Greece and similar key areas "spiral downwards into economic anarchy, then at best they will drop out of the United States orbit and try an independent nationalistic policy; at worst they will swing into the Russian orbit," and the result would be a depression worse than that of the 1930s.

Jones's insight was incorporated into a major speech made by Truman at Baylor University on March 6. The address provided the economic dimension to the Truman Doctrine pronounced six days later. The president frankly declared that if the expansion of state-controlled economies (such as the Communists') was not stopped, and an open world marketplace restored for private businessmen, depression would occur and the government would have to intervene massively in the society. Americans could then bid farewell to both their traditional economic and personal freedoms. "Freedom of worship—freedom of speech—freedom of enterprise," Truman observed. "It must be true that the first two of these freedoms are related to the third." For "Peace, freedom and world trade are indivisible." He concluded, "We must not go through the thirties again." The president had given the economic reasons for pronouncing the Truman Doctrine. The Baylor speech (written by Acheson and Will Clayton) explained why Americans, if they hoped to preserve their personal freedom, had to rebuild the areas west of the iron curtain before these lands collapsed into anarchy, radical governments, or even communism.

The Truman Doctrine speech itself laid out the ideological and political reasons for the commitment. The president requested $400 million for military and economic aid, but he also asked for something else. Truman warned Congress that the world must now "choose between alternative ways of life." He urged Americans to commit themselves to helping "free peoples" and to opposing "totalitarian regimes." This request, plus Truman's failure to place any geographical limits on where Americans must commit themselves (Africa as well as Germany? Southeast Asia as well as western Europe?), raised criticism.

Robert Taft of Ohio, the Senate's Republican leader, accused Truman of dividing the world into communist and anticommunist zones, then said flatly, "I do not want war with Russia." On the left, Henry Wallace, traveling in Europe, accused Truman of "reckless adventury" that would cost the world "a century of fear." Senator Vandenberg rushed to the president's defense by calling Wallace an "itinerant saboteur." But such fear was not only on Taft's and Wallace's minds. Shortly before the speech, Acheson told J. Robert Oppenheimer, a leading scientist in the atomic weapons field, "We are entering an adversary relationship with the Soviet [Union]," and "we should bear that in mind" while making atomic plans.

Congress wriggled uncomfortably. As Senator Vandenberg began closed door hearings on what he called "the most fundamental thing that has been presented to Congress in my time," Acheson hedged on whether the Truman Doctrine had any limitations. "If there are situations where we can do something effective, then I think we must certainly do it." But he was clear on one issue: "I think it is a mistake to believe that you can, at any time, sit down with the Russians and solve questions." Only when the West built insuperable bastions of strength would Stalin listen to American terms. Acheson assumed Russia was primarily responsible for the Greek revolution. After all, said Lincoln MacVeagh, United States ambassador to Greece, "Any empire that bases itself on revolution always has expansionist tendencies." (The ambassador was alluding to the revolution of 1917, not 1776.) This view of Soviet involvement was wrong. The Greek problem was caused by internal forces and fueled by Tito for his own purposes. But this point made little difference. The administration asked for a commitment against communism anywhere, not just against the Soviet [Union].

That caused a special problem in Greece, for as MacVeagh admitted, "the best men" in Greece "are the heads of the Communist movement. . . . That is the sad part of it." But Americans had to keep on "trying to make bricks without straw . . . or you are going to lose the country." The Greek government became so brutal that the State Department privately warned it must stop torturing its political prisoners or "the president's program" would be damaged. When criticized for helping the Greek and Turkish right-wing parties, however, Truman could simply ask Americans whether they preferred "totalitarianism" or "imperfect democracies." This settled that question.

The president and Acheson mousetrapped those in Congress who wanted to be both anticommunist and penny pinchers. As a leading Democrat chuckled privately, of course the Republicans "didn't want to be smoked out. . . . They don't like Communism but still they don't want to do anything to stop it. But they are all put on the spot now and they all have to come clean." The president, moreover, had moved so quickly that Congress had no choice but to give him increased powers. "Here we sit," mourned Vandenberg, "not as free agents," but dealing with something "almost like a Presidential request for a declaration of war." "There is precious little we can do," the senator concluded, "except say 'yes.'" Vandenberg was correct. Congress's acceptance of Truman's definition of crisis marked the point in the cold war when power in foreign policy formulation began shifting rapidly from Capitol Hill to the White House.

Nine days after his speech, Truman helped ensure his victory by announc-
ing a loyalty program to ferret out security risks in government. The first such
peacetime program in American history, it was so vaguely defined that political
ideas and long-past associations were suddenly made suspect. Most ominously,
the accused would not have the right to confront the accuser. Truman thus strikingly dramatized the communist issue, exerting new pressure on Congress to
support his doctrine. By mid-May Congress had passed his request by large
margins.

The Truman Doctrine was a milestone in American history for at least four
reasons. First, it marked the point at which Truman used the American fear of
communism both at home and abroad to convince Americans they must embark
upon a cold war foreign policy. This consensus would not break apart for a
quarter of a century. Second, as Vandenberg knew, Congress was giving the
president great powers to wage this cold war as he saw fit. Truman's personal
popularity began spiraling upward after his speech. Third, for the first time in
the postwar era, Americans massively intervened in another nation's civil war.
Intervention was justified on the basis of anticommunism. In the future, Americans would intervene in similar wars for supposedly the same reason and with
less happy results. Even Greek affairs went badly at first, so badly that in late
1947 Washington officials discussed sending as many as two divisions of Americans to save the situation. That proved unnecessary, for when Yugoslavia left
the Communist bloc in early 1948, Tito turned inward and stopped aiding the
rebels. Deprived of aid, the Greek left wing quickly lost ground. But it had been
close, and Americans were nearly involved massively in a civil war two decades
before their Vietnam involvement. As it was, the success in Greece seemed to
prove that Americans could, if they wished, control such conflicts by defining
the problem as "Communist" and helping conservatives remain in power.

Finally, and perhaps most important, Truman used the doctrine to justify a
gigantic aid program to prevent a collapse of the European and American
economies. Later such programs were expanded globally. The president's arguments about anticommunism were confusing, for the western economies would
have been in grave difficulties whether or not communism existed. The complicated problems of reconstruction and the United States dependence on world
trade were not well understood by Americans, but they easily comprehended
anticommunism. So Americans embarked upon the cold war for the good reasons given in the Truman Doctrine, which they understood, and for real reasons,
which they did not understand. Thus, as Truman and Acheson intended, the
doctrine became an ideological shield behind which the United States marched
to rebuild the western political-economic system and counter the radical left.
From 1947 on, therefore, any threats to that western system could be easily explained as communist inspired, not as problems that arose from difficulties
within the system itself. That was the most lasting and tragic result of the Truman Doctrine.

The president's program evolved naturally into the Marshall Plan. Although the speech did not limit American effort, Secretary of State Marshall did

by concentrating the administration's attention on Europe. Returning badly shaken from a foreign ministers conference in Moscow, the secretary of state insisted in a nationwide broadcast that western Europe required immediate help. "The patient is sinking," he declared, "while the doctors deliberate." Personal conversations with Stalin had convinced Marshall that the Russians believed Europe would collapse. Assuming that the United States must lead in restoring Europe, Marshall appointed a policy planning staff under the direction of George Kennan to draw up policies.

Kennan later explained the basic assumption that underlay the Marshall Plan and, indeed, the entire range of America's postwar policies between 1947 and the mid-1950s. Excluding the United States, Kennan observed,

> there are only four aggregations which are major ones from the standpoint of strategic realities [that is, military and industrial potential] in the world. Two of those lie off the shores of the Eurasian land mass. Those are Japan and England, and two of them lie on the Eurasian land mass. One is the Soviet Union and the other is that of central Europe. . . .
>
> Viewed in absolute terms, I think the greatest danger that could confront the United States security would be a combination and working together for purposes hostile to us of the central European and the Russian military-industrial potentials. They would really create an entity . . . which could overshadow in a strategic sense even our own power. It is not anything, I think, which would be as easy of achievement as people often portray it as being here. I am not sure the Russians have the genius for holding all that together. . . . Still, they have the tendency of political thought, of Communist political expansion.

Building on this premise, round-the-clock conferences in May 1947 began to fashion the main features of the Marshall Plan. Kennan insisted that any aid, particularly military supplies, be limited and not given to just any area where Communists seemed to be enjoying some success. The all-important question then became how to handle the Russians. Ostensibly, Marshall accepted Kennan's advice to "play it straight" by inviting the Soviet bloc. In reality, the State Department made Russian acceptance improbable by demanding that economic records of each nation be open to scrutiny. For good measure Kennan also suggested that the [Soviet Union's] devastated economy, weakened by war and at that moment suffering from drought and famine, participate in the plan by shipping Soviet goods to Europe. Apparently no one in the State Department wanted the Soviet [Union] included. Russian participation would vastly multiply the costs of the program and eliminate any hope of its acceptance by a purse-watching Republican Congress, now increasingly convinced by Truman that Communists had to be fought, not fed.

Acheson's speech at Cleveland, Mississippi, in early May and Marshall's address at Harvard on June 5 revealed the motives and substance of the plan. In preparing for the earlier speech, Acheson's advisers concluded that American exports were rapidly approaching the $16 billion mark. Imports, however, amounted to only half that amount, and Europe did not have sufficient dollars to pay the difference. Either the United States would have to give credits to Europeans or they would be unable to buy American goods. The president's Council of Economic Advisers predicted a slight business recession, and if, in addition, exports dropped in any substantial amount, "the effect in the United States," as one official wrote, "might be most serious." Acheson underlined these facts in his Mississippi speech.

At Harvard, Marshall urged Europeans to create a long-term program that would "provide a cure rather than a mere palliative." On June 13 British Foreign Minister Ernest Bevin accepted Marshall's suggestion that Europeans take the initiative. Bevin traveled to Paris to talk with French Foreign Minister Georges Bidault. The question of Russian participation became uppermost in their discussions. *Pravda* had labeled Marshall's speech as a Truman Doctrine with dollars, a useless attempt to save the American economy by dominating European markets. Bidault ignored this; pressured by the powerful French Communist party and fearful that Russia's absence might compel France to join the Anglo-Saxons in a divided Europe dominated by a resurrected Germany, he decided to invite [Soviet Foreign Minister Vyacheslao] Molotov. The Russian line immediately moderated.

On June 26 Molotov arrived in Paris with eighty-nine economic experts and clerks, then spent much of the next three days conferring over the telephone with Moscow officials. The Russians were giving the plan serious consideration. Molotov finally proposed that each nation individually establish its own recovery program. The French and British proposed instead that Europe as a whole create the proposal for American consideration. Molotov angrily quit the conference, warning that the plan would undermine national sovereignty, revive Germany, allow Americans to control Europe, and, most ominously, divide "Europe into two groups of states . . . creating new difficulties in the relations between them." Within a week after his return to Moscow, the Soviet [Union] set [its] own "Molotov Plan" in motion. The Poles and the Czechs, who had expressed interest in Marshall's proposal, now informed the Paris conference that they could not attend because it "might be construed as an action against the Soviet Union."

As the remaining sixteen European nations hammered out a program for Marshall to consider, the United States moved on another front: it determined to revive Germany quickly. In late 1946 the Americans and British had overridden French opposition to merge economically the United States and British zones in Germany. Administrative duties were given to Germans. By mid-July 1947 Washington officials so rapidly rebuilt German industry that Bidault finally pleaded with Marshall to slow down or else the French government would never survive to carry through the economic recovery program. The United States nevertheless continued to rebuild German nonmilitary industry to the point where the country would be both self-sufficient and able to aid the remainder of western Europe. On September 22, the Paris meeting completed its work, pledging increased production, tariff reductions, and currency convertibility in return for American aid. The State Department could view its successes in Germany during the summer as icing on the cake.

The European request for a four-year program of $17 billion of American aid now had to run the gauntlet of a Republican Congress, which was dividing

its attention between slashing the budget and attacking Truman, both in anticipation of the presidential election only a year away. In committee hearings in
late 1947 and early 1948, the executive presented its case. Only large amounts of
government money that could restore basic facilities, provide convertibility of
local currency into dollars, and end the dollar shortage would stimulate private
investors to rebuild Europe, administration witnesses argued. Then a rejuve-
nated Europe could offer many advantages to the United States: eradicate the
threat of continued nationalization and socialism by releasing and stimulating
the investment of private capital; maintain demand for American exports; encourage Europeans to produce strategic goods, which the United States could
buy and stockpile; preserve European and American control over Middle Eastern oil supplies from militant nationalism, which might endanger the weakened
European holdings; and free Europeans from economic problems so they could
help the United States militarily. It would all be like magic.

George Kennan summarized the central problem in a note to Acheson.
"Communist activities" were not "the root of the difficulties of Western Europe"
but rather "the disruptive effects of the war on the economic, political, and social structure of Europe." So in the final plan Italy, with Europe's largest Communist party, received less aid than other, more economically important nations. In this sense the plan revolved around a rebuilt and autonomous
Germany. As Secretary of State Marshall told Congress, "The restoration of Europe involved the restoration of Germany. Without a revival of German production there can be no revival of Europe's economy. But we must be very careful to see that a revived Germany can not again threaten the European
community." The Marshall Plan offered a way to circumvent allied restrictions
on German development, for it tied the Germans to a general European program and then offered vast sums to such nations as France that might otherwise
be reluctant to support reconstructing Germany.

The Marshall Plan served as an all-purpose weapon for Truman's foreign
policy. It charmed those who feared a slump in American exports and who believed, communist threat or no communist threat, that American and world
prosperity rested on a vigorous export trade. A spokesman for the National Association of Manufacturers, for example, appeared considerably more moderate
toward communism than some government officials when he argued that Europe suffered not from "this so-called communistic surge," but from a "production problem" that only the Marshall Plan could solve. Appropriately, Truman
named as administrator of the plan Paul Hoffman, a proven entrepreneur who,
as Acheson once observed, preached a "doctrine of salvation by exports with all
the passion of an economic Savonarola." The plan also attracted a group, including Reinhold Niebuhr, which placed more emphasis upon the containment
of communism. The plan offered all things to all people. Or almost all, for Henry
Wallace decided to oppose it in late 1947 on the grounds that only by channel-
ing aid through the United Nations could calamitous relations between the
United States and the Soviet Union be avoided.

The Marshall Plan now appears not the beginning but the end of an era. It
marked the last phase in the administration's use of economic tactics as the pri-

mary means of tying together the Western world. The plan's approach, that peaceful and positive approach which Niebuhr applauded, soon evolved into military alliances. Truman proved to be correct in saying that the Truman Doctrine and the Marshall Plan "are two halves of the same walnut." Americans willingly acquiesced as the military aspects of the doctrine developed into quite the larger part.

Why such programs could so easily be transformed into military commitments was explained by George Kennan in a well-timed article appearing in July 1947 under the mysterious pseudonym Mr. "X." Washington's most respected expert on Soviet affairs, Kennan (who once called Niebuhr "the father of us all") had warned throughout the early 1940s against any hope of close postwar cooperation with Stalin. In early 1946 he sent a long dispatch to Washington from Moscow suggesting that at the "bottom of the Kremlin's neurotic view of world affairs is the traditional and instinctive Russian sense of insecurity." In post-1917 Russia, this became highly explosive when mixed with Communist ideology and "Oriental secretiveness and conspiracy." This dispatch brought Kennan to the attention of Secretary of the Navy James Forrestal, who helped bring the diplomat back to Washington and then strongly influenced Kennan's decision to publish the "X" article.

The article gave the administration's view of what made the Russians act like Communists. The analysis began not by emphasizing "the traditional Russian sense of insecurity" but by assuming that Stalin's policy was shaped by a combination of Marxist-Leninist ideology, which advocated revolution to defeat the capitalist forces in the outside world, and the dictator's determination to use "capitalist encirclement" as a rationale to regiment the Soviet masses so that he could consolidate his own political power. Kennan belittled such supposed "encirclement," although he recognized Nazi-Japanese hatred of the Soviet [Union] during the 1930s. (He omitted mentioning specifically the American and Japanese intervention in Russia between 1918 and 1920 and the United States attempt to isolate the Soviet [Union] politically through the 1920s.) Mr. "X" believed Stalin would not moderate communist determination to overthrow the western governments. Any softening of the Russian line would be a diversionary tactic designed to lull the west. For in the final analysis Soviet diplomacy "moves along the prescribed path, like a persistent toy automobile wound up and headed in a given direction, stopping only when it meets some unanswerable force." Endemic Soviet aggression could thus be "contained by the adroit and vigilant application of counterforce at a series of constantly shifting geographical and political points." The United States would have to undertake this containment alone and unilaterally, but if it could do so without weakening its prosperity and political stability, the Soviet party structure would undergo a period of immense strain climaxing in "either the break-up or the gradual mellowing of Soviet power."

The publication of this article triggered one of the more interesting debates of the cold war. Walter Lippmann was the dean of American journalists and one of those who did not accept the "two halves of the same walnut" argument. He condemned the military aspects of the Truman Doctrine while applauding the Marshall Plan because he disagreed with Kennan's assessment of Soviet motivation. And that, of course, was a crucial point in any argument over American policy. In a series of newspaper articles later collected in a book entitled *The Cold War,* Lippmann argued that Soviet policy was molded more by traditional Russian expansion than by Communist ideology. "Stalin is not only the heir of Marx and of Lenin but of Peter the Great, and the Czars of all the Russians." Because of the victorious sweep of the Red Army into Central Europe in 1945, Stalin could accomplish what the czars for centuries had only hoped to obtain. This approach enabled Lippmann to view the Soviet advance as a traditional quest for national security and, in turn, allowed him to argue that Russia would be amenable to an offer of withdrawal of both Russian and American power from central Europe. The fuses would thus be pulled from that explosive area.

Lippmann outlined the grave consequences of the alternative, the Mr. "X"-Truman Doctrine policy: "unending intervention in all the countries that are supposed to 'contain' the Soviet Union"; futile and costly efforts to make "Jeffersonian democrats" out of eastern European peasants and Middle Eastern and Asian warlords; either the destruction of the United Nations or its transformation into a useless anti-Soviet coalition; and such a tremendous strain on the American people that their economy would have to be increasingly regimented and their men sent to fight on the perimeter of the Soviet bloc. The columnist warned that if Mr. "X" succeeded in applying counterforce to the "constantly shifting geographical and political points," the Soviet [Union] would perforce be allowed to take the initiative in the cold war by choosing the grounds and weapons for combat. Finally, Lippmann, like the administration, emphasized Germany's importance, but he differed by observing that Russia, which controlled eastern Germany, could, at its leisure, outmaneuver the west and repeat the 1939 Nazi-Soviet pact of offering the ultimate reward of reunification for German cooperation. "The idea that we can foster the sentiment of German unity, and make a truncated Germany economically strong," Lippmann wrote, "can keep her disarmed, and can use her in the anti-Soviet coalition is like trying to square the circle."

Lippmann was profound, but he had no chance of being persuasive. By the end of August 1947, the State Department rejected Lippmann's proposals for disengagement in Germany. American officials instead assumed that the "one world" of the United Nations was "no longer valid and that we are in political fact facing a division into two worlds." The "X" article also indicated the administration was operating on another assumption: economic development could not occur until "security" was established. This increasing concern with things military became evident in late 1947 when Kennan suggested that the United States change its long-standing hostility to Franco's government in Spain in order to cast proper military security over the Mediterranean area. A year earlier the United States had joined with Britain and France in asking the Spanish people to overthrow Franco by political means because his government was pro-Nazi and totalitarian. Kennan's suggestion marked the turn in Spanish-American relations, which ended in close military cooperation after 1950.

The quest for military security also transformed American policy in Asia. With Chiang Kai-shek's decline, the State Department searched for a new partner who could help stabilize the far east. The obvious candidate was Japan, which from the 1890s until 1931 had worked closely with Washington. It was also the potential industrial powerhouse of the area, the Germany of the Orient. Since 1945 the United States had single-handedly controlled Japan. The Soviet [Union] had been carefully excluded. Even Australia was allowed to send occupation forces only after promising not to interfere with the authority of General Douglas MacArthur, head of the American government in Japan. MacArthur instituted a new constitution (in which Japan renounced war for all time), then conducted elections that allowed him to claim that the Japanese had overwhelmingly repudiated communism. To the general, as to Washington officials, this was fundamental. In 1946 MacArthur privately compared America in its fight against communism to the agony of Christ at Gethsemane, for "Christ, even though crucified, nevertheless prevailed."

He added that Japan was becoming "the western outpost of our defenses." In 1947–1948 Japan received the "two halves of the same walnut" treatment. The State Department decided to rebuild Japanese industry and develop a sound export economy. At the same time, American bases on the islands were to be expanded and maintained until, in one official's words, "the at present disarmed soldiers of Japan are provided with arms and training to qualify them to preserve the peace." As in Europe, economic development and security moved hand in hand as Americans buttressed the Pacific portion of their system. . . .

Of special importance to Truman's "security" effort, the president transformed what he termed "the antiquated defense setup of the United States" by passing the National Security Act through Congress in July 1947. This bill provided for a single Department of Defense to replace the three independently run services, statutory establishment of the Joint Chiefs of Staff, a National Security Council to advise the president, and a Central Intelligence Agency to correlate and evaluate intelligence activities. James Forrestal, the stepfather of Mr. "X" and the leading advocate among presidential advisers of a tough military approach to cold war problems, became the first secretary of defense. Forrestal remained until he resigned in early spring 1949. Two months later on the night of May 22, Forrestal, suffering from mental and physical illness, jumped or accidentally fell to his death from the twelfth floor of the Bethesda Naval Hospital.

The military and personal costs of the Truman Doctrine–Mr. "X" policy would be higher than expected. And the cost became more apparent as Truman and J. Edgar Hoover (director of the Federal Bureau of Investigation) carried out the president's Security Loyalty program. Their search for subversives accelerated after Canadians uncovered a Soviet spy ring. During hearings in the Senate on the appointment of David E. Lilienthal as chairman of the Atomic Energy Commission, the first major charges of "soft on communism" were hurled by Robert Taft [in part] because of Lilienthal's New Deal background. . . .

Since the Iranian and Turkish crises of 1946, the Soviet [Union] had not been active in world affairs. But Molotov's departure from the Marshall Plan conference in Paris during July 1947 marked the turn. Russian attention was riveted on Germany. The Politburo interpreted the Marshall Plan to mean the American "intention to restore the economy of Germany and Japan on the old basis [of pre-1941] provided it is subordinated to interests of American capital." Rebuilding Europe through the plan and tying it closer to American economic power threatened Stalin's hope of influencing west European policies. Incomparably worse, however, was linking that Europe to a restored western Germany. This not only undercut Soviet determination to keep this ancient enemy weak, as well as divided, but vastly increased the potential of that enemy, tied it to the forces of "capitalist encirclement," and revived the memories of two world wars.

Molotov quickly initiated a series of moves to tighten Soviet control of the bloc. A program of bilateral trade agreements, the so-called Molotov Plan, began to link the bloc countries and Russia in July 1947. The final step came in January 1949, when the Council for Mutual Economic Assistance (COMECON) provided the Soviet answer to the Marshall Plan by creating a centralized agency for stimulating and controlling bloc development. As a result of these moves, Soviet trade with the east European bloc, which had declined in 1947 to $380 million, doubled in 1948, quadrupled by 1950, and exceeded $2.5 billion in 1952. Seventy percent of east European trade was carried on with either the Soviet Union or elsewhere within the bloc.

Four days after his return from Paris, Molotov announced the establishment of the Communist Information Bureau (Cominform). Including Communists from Russia, Yugoslavia, France, Italy, Poland, Bulgaria, Czechoslovakia, Hungary, and Rumania, the Cominform provided another instrument for increasing Stalin's control. This was his answer to the Czech and Polish interest in joining the Marshall Plan. In late August, a month before the first Cominform meeting, Soviet actions in Hungary indicated the line that would be followed. After a purge of left-wing anticommunist political leaders, the Soviet [Union] directly intervened by rigging elections. All anticommunist opposition disappeared. Three weeks later at the Cominform meeting in Warsaw, [Cominform leader Andrei] Zhdanov formally announced new Soviet policies in a speech that ranks next to Stalin's February 9, 1946, address as a Russian call to cold war.

Zhdanov's analysis of recent international developments climaxed with the announcement that American economic power, fattened by the war, was organizing western Europe and "countries politically and economically dependent on the United States, such as the Near-Eastern and South-American countries and China" into an anticommunist bloc. The Russians and the "new democracies" in eastern Europe, Finland, Indonesia, and Vietnam meanwhile formed another bloc, which "has the sympathy of India, Egypt and Syria." In this way, Zhdanov again announced the rebirth of the "two-camp" view of the world, an attitude that had dominated Russian policy between 1927 and 1934 when Stalin bitterly attacked the west, and a central theme in the dictator's speech of February 1946. In some respects Zhdanov's announcement resembled the "two-world" attitude in the United States. The mirror image was especially striking when Zhdanov admonished the socialist camp not to lower its guard. "Just as in the past the Munich policy united the hands of the Nazi aggressors, so today concessions to the new course of the United States and the imperialist camp may encourage its inspirers to be even more insolent and aggressive."

Following Zhdanov's call to action, the Cominform delegates sharply criticized French and Italian Communists, who seemed to want a more pacific approach, and, once again following the disastrous practices of the 1927–1934 era, ordered all members to foment the necessary strikes and internal disorder for the elimination of independent socialist, labor, and peasant parties in their countries. The meeting was the high-water mark of the tough Zhdanov line in Soviet foreign policy. Its effect was soon felt not only in bloc and west European countries but inside Russia as well. Stalin cleansed Soviet economic thinking by discrediting and removing from public view Eugene Varga, a leading Russian economist who had angered the Politburo by warning that Marxists were wrong in thinking that the western economies would soon collapse.

American officials fully understood why the Soviet [Union was] trying these new policies. As Secretary of State Marshall told Truman's cabinet in November 1947, "The advance of Communism has been stemmed and the Russians have been compelled to make a reevaluation of their position." America was winning its eight-month cold war. But the [Soviet Union's] difficulties provided an excuse for Congress, which was not anxious to send billions of dollars of Marshall Plan aid to Europe if the Russians posed no threat. Congress dawdled as the plan came under increased criticism. Taft urged that good money not be poured into a "European TVA." On the other side of the political spectrum, Henry Wallace labeled it a "Martial Plan." In speeches around the country, Marshall tried to sell the program for its long-term economic and political benefits. His arguments fell on deaf ears. The American economy seemed to be doing well. Just weeks before the 1948 presidential campaign was to begin, Truman faced a major political and diplomatic defeat.

And then came the fall of Czechoslovakia. The Czechs had uneasily coexisted with Russia by trying not to offend the Soviet [Union] while keeping doors open to the west. This policy had started in late 1943, when Czech leaders signed a treaty with Stalin that, in the view of most observers, obligated Czechoslovakia to become a part of the Russian bloc. President Eduard Beneš and Foreign Minister Jan Masaryk, one of the foremost diplomatic figures in Europe, had nevertheless successfully resisted complete communist control. Nor had Stalin moved to consolidate his power in 1946 after the Czech Communist party emerged from the parliamentary elections with 38 percent of the vote, the largest total of any party. By late 1947 the lure of western aid and internal political changes began to pull the Czech government away from the Soviet [Union]. At this point Stalin, who like Truman recalled the pivotal role of Czechoslovakia in 1938, decided to put the 1943 treaty into effect. Klement Gottwald, the Czech Communist party leader, demanded the elimination of independent parties. In mid-February 1948 Soviet armies camped on the border as Gottwald ordered the formation of a wholly new government. A Soviet mission of top officials flew to Prague to demand Beneš's surrender. The Communist assumed full control on February 25. Two weeks later Masaryk either committed suicide or, as Truman believed, was the victim of "foul play."

Truman correctly observed that the coup "sent a shock throughout the civilized world." He privately believed, "We are faced with exactly the same situation with which Britain and France was faced in 1938–9 with Hitler." In late 1947 Hungary had been the victim of a similar if less dramatic squeeze. Within two months, new opportunities would beckon to the Cominform when the Italian election was held. On March 5 a telegram arrived from General Clay in Germany. Although "I have felt and held that war was unlikely for at least ten years," Clay began, "within the last few weeks, I have felt a subtle change in Soviet attitude which . . . gives me a feeling that it may come with dramatic suddenness." For ten days, government intelligence worked furiously investigating Clay's warnings and on March 16 gave Truman the grim assurance that war was not probable within sixty days. Two days before, on March 14, the Senate had endorsed the Marshall Plan by a vote of 69 to 17. As it went to the House for consideration, Truman, fearing the "grave events in Europe [which] were moving so swiftly," decided to appear before Congress.

In a speech remarkable for its repeated emphasis on the "increasing threat" to the very "survival of freedom," the president proclaimed the Marshall Plan "not enough." Europe must have "some measure of protection against internal and external aggression." He asked for Universal Military Training, the resumption of Selective Service (which he had allowed to lapse a year earlier), and speedy passage of the Marshall Plan. Within twelve days the House approved authorization of the plan's money.

With perfect timing and somber rhetoric, Truman's March 17 speech not only galvanized passage of the plan but accelerated a change in American foreign policy that had been heralded the previous summer. Congress stamped its approval on this new military emphasis by passing a Selective Service bill. Although Universal Military Training, one of Forrestal's pet projects, found little favor, a supposedly penny-proud Congress replaced it with funds to begin a seventy-group Air Force, 25 percent larger than even Forrestal had requested.

Perhaps the most crucial effect of the new policy, however, appeared in the administration's determination to create great systems that would not only encourage military development but would also compel the western world to accept political realignments as well. The first of these efforts had been the Rio Pact and the new policies toward Japan. The next, somewhat different, and vastly more important effort would be the North Atlantic Treaty Organization (NATO).

SOURCES

Cold War at Home

During the Army-McCarthy hearings of 1954, McCarthy (far right) blocked an attempt by Army Counsel Joseph Welch (far left) to obtain names of McCarthy's office staff. McCarthy charged "a smear campaign" was under way against "anyone working with exposing communists." District of Columbia Public Library.

Tail Gunner Joe: The Wheeling Address

Joseph McCarthy

McCarthyism is the name applied to the second Red Scare, a period of political repression in America, epitomized by the career of Senator Joseph McCarthy. "Tail gunner Joe" was elected as the junior senator from Wisconsin in 1946 and received little recognition until his speech in Wheeling, West Virginia, in Feb-

From U.S., Congress, Senate, *Congressional Record*, 81st Cong., 2d sess., 1950, 96, 1954, 1946, 1957.

ruary 1950. For the next four years, he chaired Senate committee meetings where he accused first the Truman administration, and later the Eisenhower administration, of harboring known Communists and probable spies in the government. He was censured by his colleagues in the Senate in 1954 and faded into obscurity.

McCarthy did not create the atmosphere of suspicion and anticommunism given his name. Indeed, years before McCarthy came on the scene, the Truman administration had instituted its own loyalty-security program (1947) and stepped up the use of the Smith Act throughout 1948 to prosecute Americans suspected of subversive thinking. Congress also contributed with the hearings of the House Un-American Activities Committee (HUAC) and the Alger Hiss investigation and trials (1948). Yet McCarthy was surely the most notorious opportunist of the era. His tactics of demagoguery, insinuation, and guilt by association defined the means by which thousands of Americans were denied their civil rights. Worse still, a public insecure about the postwar world accepted his vision of conspiracy and sanctioned his attacks.

The following is a sample of McCarthy's tactics against the State Department. How does Senator McCarthy define the threat to American security? What proof does he offer that the State Department is filled with known Communists? What were the elements of his success? Was his failure inevitable? Or could he have become more powerful than he was?

Ladies and gentlemen, tonight as we celebrate the one hundred and forty-first birthday of one of the greatest men in American history, I would like to be able to talk about what a glorious day today is in the history of the world. As we celebrate the birth of this man who with his whole heart and soul hated war, I would like to be able to speak of peace in our time, of war being outlawed, and of worldwide disarmament. These would be truly appropriate things to be able to mention as we celebrate the birthday of Abraham Lincoln.

Five years after a world war has been won, men's hearts should anticipate a long peace, and men's minds should be free from the heavy weight that comes with war. But this is not such a period—for this is not a period of peace. This is a time of the "cold war." This is a time when all the world is split into two vast, increasingly hostile armed camps—a time of a great armaments race.

Today we can almost physically hear the mutterings and rumblings of an invigorated god of war. You can see it, feel it, and hear it all the way from the hills of Indochina, from the shores of Formosa, right over into the very heart of Europe itself.

The one encouraging thing is that the "mad moment" has not yet arrived for the firing of the gun or the exploding of the bomb which will set civilization about the final task of destroying itself. There is still a hope for peace if we finally decide that no longer can we safely blind our eyes and close our ears to those facts which are shaping up more and more clearly. And that is that we are now engaged in a showdown fight—not the usual war between nations for land areas or other material gains, but a war between two diametrically opposed ideologies.

The great difference between our western Christian world and the atheistic Communist world is not political, ladies and gentlemen, it is moral. There are other differences, of course, but those could be reconciled. For instance, the Marxian idea of confiscating the land and factories and running the entire economy as a single enterprise is momentous. Likewise, Lenin's invention of the one-party police state as a way to make Marx's idea work is hardly less momentous.

Stalin's resolute putting across of these two ideas, of course, did much to divide the world. With only those differences, however, the east and the west could most certainly still live in peace.

The real, basic difference, however, lies in the religion of immoralism—invented by Marx, preached feverishly by Lenin, and carried to unimaginable extremes by Stalin. This religion of immoralism, if the Red half of the world wins—and well it may—this religion of immoralism will more deeply wound and damage mankind than any conceivable economic or political system. . . .

Today we are engaged in a final, all-out battle between communistic atheism and Christianity. The modern champions of communism have selected this as the time. And, ladies and gentlemen, the chips are down—they are truly down. . . .

Ladies and gentlemen, can there be anyone here tonight who is so blind as to say that the war is not on? Can there be anyone who fails to realize that the Communist world has said, "The time is now"—that this is the time for the showdown between the democratic Christian world and the Communist atheistic world?

Unless we face this fact, we shall pay the price that must be paid by those who wait too long.

Six years ago, at the time of the first conference to map out the peace—Dumbarton Oaks—there was within the Soviet orbit 180 million people. Lined up on the antitotalitarian side there were in the world at that time roughly 1,625,000,000 people. Today, only six years later, there are 800 million people under the absolute domination of Soviet Russia—an increase of over 400 percent. On our side, the figure has shrunk to around 500 million. In other words, in less than six years the odds have changed from 9 to 1 in our favor to 8 to 5 against us. This indicates the swiftness of the tempo of Communist victories and American defeats in the cold war. As one of our outstanding historical figures once said, "When a great democracy is destroyed, it will not be because of enemies from without, but rather because of enemies from within."

The truth of this statement is becoming terrifyingly clear as we see this country each day losing on every front.

At war's end we were physically the strongest nation on earth and, at least potentially, the most powerful intellectually and morally. Ours could have been the honor of being a beacon in the desert of destruction, a shining living proof that civilization was not yet ready to destroy itself. Unfortunately, we have failed miserably and tragically to arise to the opportunity.

The reason why we find ourselves in a position of impotency is not because our only powerful potential enemy has sent men to invade our shores, but rather because of the traitorous actions of those who have been treated so well by this nation. It has not been the less fortunate or members of minority groups who have been selling this nation out, but rather those who have had all the benefits that the wealthiest nation on earth has had to offer—the finest homes, the finest college education, and the finest jobs in government we can give.

This is glaringly true in the State Department. There the bright young men who are born with silver spoons in their mouths are the ones who have been worst.

Now I know it is very easy for anyone to condemn a particular bureau or department in general terms. Therefore, I would like to cite one rather unusual case—the case of a man who has done much to shape our foreign policy.

When Chiang Kai-shek was fighting our war, the State Department had in China a young man named John S. Service. His task, obviously, was not to work for the communization of China. Strangely, however, he sent official reports back to the State Department urging that we torpedo our ally Chiang Kai-shek and stating, in effect, that communism was the best hope of China.

Later, this man—John Service—was picked up by the Federal Bureau of Investigation for turning over to the Communists secret State Department information. Strangely, however, he was never prosecuted. However, Joseph Grew, the under secretary of state, who insisted on his prosecution, was forced to resign. Two days after Grew's successor, Dean Acheson, took over as under secretary of state, this man—John Service—who had been picked up by the FBI and who had previously urged that communism was the best hope of China, was not only reinstated in the State Department but promoted. And finally, under Acheson, placed in charge of all placements and promotions.

Today, ladies and gentlemen, this man Service is on his way to represent the State Department and Acheson in Calcutta—by far and away the most important listening post in the far east. . . .

This, ladies and gentlemen, gives you somewhat of a picture of the type of individuals who have been helping to shape our foreign policy. In my opinion the State Department, which is one of the most important government departments, is thoroughly infested with Communists.

I have in my hand fifty-seven cases of individuals who would appear to be either card-carrying members or certainly loyal to the Communist party, but who nevertheless are still helping to shape our foreign policy. . . .

This brings us down to the case of one Alger Hiss who is important not as an individual any more, but rather because he is so representative of a group in the State Department. It is unnecessary to go over the sordid events showing how he sold out the nation which had given him so much. Those are rather fresh in all of our minds.

However, it should be remembered that the facts in regard to his connection with this international Communist spy ring were made known to the then Under Secretary of State Berle three days after Hitler and Stalin signed the Russo-German alliance pact. At that time one Whittaker Chambers—who was also part of the spy ring—apparently decided that with Russia on Hitler's side, he could no longer betray our nation to Russia. He gave Under Secretary of State Berle—and this is all a matter of record—practically all, if not more, of the facts upon which Hiss's conviction was based.

Under Secretary Berle promptly contacted Dean Acheson and received word in return that Acheson (and I quote) "could vouch for Hiss absolutely"—at which time the matter was dropped. And this, you understand, was at a time when Russia was an ally of Germany. This condition existed while Russia and Germany were invading and dismembering Poland, and while the Communist groups here were screaming "warmonger" at the United States for their support of the allied nations.

Again in 1943, the FBI had occasion to investigate the facts surrounding Hiss's contacts with the Russia spy ring. But even after that FBI report was submitted, nothing was done.

Then late in 1948—on August 5—when the Un-American Activities Committee called Alger Hiss to give an accounting, President Truman at once issued a presidential directive ordering all government agencies to refuse to turn over any information whatsoever in regard to the Communist activities of any government employee to a congressional committee.

Incidentally, even after Hiss was convicted—it is interesting to note that the president still labeled the exposé of Hiss as a "red herring."

If time permitted, it might be well to go into detail about the fact that Hiss was Roosevelt's chief advisor at Yalta when Roosevelt was admittedly in ill health and tired physically and mentally. . . .

Of the results of this conference, Arthur Bliss Lane of the State Department had this to say: "As I glanced over the document, I could not believe my eyes. To me, almost every line spoke of a surrender to Stalin."

As you hear this story of high treason, I know that you are saying to yourself, "Well, why doesn't the Congress do something about it?" Actually, ladies and gentlemen, one of the important reasons for the graft, the corruption, the dishonesty, the disloyalty, the treason in high government positions—one of the most important reasons why this continues is a lack of moral uprising on the part of the 140 million American people. In the light of history, however, this is not hard to explain.

It is the result of an emotional hangover and a temporary moral lapse which follows every war. It is the apathy to evil which people who have been subjected to the tremendous evils of war feel. As the people of the world see mass murder, the destruction of defenseless and innocent people, and all of the crime and lack of morals which go with war, they become numb and apathetic. It has always been thus after war.

However, the morals of our people have not been destroyed. They still exist. This cloak of numbness and apathy has only needed a spark to rekindle them. Happily, this spark has finally been supplied.

As you know, very recently the secretary of state proclaimed his loyalty to a man guilty of what has always been considered as the most abominable of all crimes—of being a traitor to the people who gave him a position of great trust. The secretary of state in attempting to justify his continued devotion to the man who sold out the Christian world to the atheistic world, referred to Christ's Sermon on the Mount as a justification and reason therefor, and the reaction of the American people to this would have made the heart of Abraham Lincoln happy.

When this pompous diplomat in striped pants, with a phony British accent, proclaimed to the American people that Christ on the Mount endorsed communism, high treason, and betrayal of a sacred trust, the blasphemy was so great that it awakened the dormant indignation of the American people.

He has lighted the spark which is resulting in a moral uprising and will end only when the whole sorry mess of twisted, warped thinkers are swept from the national scene so that we may have a new birth of national honesty and decency in government.

The Kitchen Debate, 1959

In July 1959, Vice President Richard Nixon was officially invited to Moscow to open the first American National Exhibition, held as part of a cultural exchange program initiated at Geneva in 1955. The central exhibit was a full-scale model of a six-room ranch-style house, with labor-saving appliances and devices meant to represent the typical American home.

Nixon intended to use the exhibition's picture of domestic affluence to demonstrate the stability and endurance of the American way of life. The exhibit offered an argument: that it was capitalism, not the ideology of socialism, that would improve the condition of working people everywhere.

Unofficially, the vice president was to let Soviet Premier Nikita Khrushchev know that Washington expected some movement on the Berlin discussions before the premier would receive an invitation to the United States. Behind the vice president's visit was the Soviet threat to reach a separate peace with East Germany in order to evict the allies from Berlin. West Berlin's prosperity and economic development were proving both an embarrassment to the Soviet system and a personal embarrassment to its leader.

Once again, the separation between foreign policy and domestic politics was blurred. The kitchen debate exemplified how affluence and mass consumption were all grist for the mill of American cold war politics: the ideology of capitalism, the American way of life, could win the cold war. After twelve years of pursuing containment, Nixon showed the American public that the diplomatic issues separating the United States and the Soviet Union could be easily understood in terms of dishwashers, toasters, and televisions.

Did the kitchen debate come to grips with differences between the two systems? What do you make of Khrushchev's comment that the Soviet Union does not have the "capitalist attitude toward women"?

Following is an account of the informal exchanges in Moscow yesterday between Vice President Richard M. Nixon and Premier Nikita S. Khrushchev. It was compiled from dispatches of the *New York Times*, the Associated Press, United Press International and Reuters. . . .

A TRADE OF GIBES ABOUT TRADE

On arriving at the gate of the American National Exhibition later in the morning, Mr. Khrushchev voiced a gibe about the United States ban on the shipment of strategic goods to the Soviet Union.

KHRUSHCHEV: "Americans have lost their ability to trade. Now you have grown older and you don't trade the way you used to. You need to be invigorated."
NIXON: "You need to have goods to trade."

The statesmen went on to look at equipment for playing back recordings. Mr. Nixon took a cue from it.

NIXON: "There must be a free exchange of ideas."

Mr. Khrushchev responded with a remark touching on the reporting of his speeches on his recent Polish tour.

Mr. Nixon said he was certain that Mr. Khrushchev's speeches and those of Frol R. Kozlov, a first deputy premier, had been fully reported in the West.

Khrushchev (indicating cameras, recording the scene on videotape): "Then what about this tape?" (smiling). "If it is shown in the United States it will be shown in English and I would like a guarantee that there will be a full translation of my remarks."

Mr. Nixon said there would be an English translation of Mr. Khrushchev's remarks and added his hope that all his own remarks in the Soviet Union would be given with full translations in that country.

KHRUSHCHEV: "We want to live in peace and friendship with Americans because we are the two most powerful countries, and if we live in friendship then other countries will also live in friendship. But if there is a country that is too war-minded we could pull its ears a little and say: Don't you dare; fighting is not allowed now; this is a period of atomic armament; some foolish one could start a war and then even a wise one couldn't finish the war. Therefore, we are governed by this idea in our policy—internal and foreign. How long has America existed? Three hundreds years?"
NIXON: "One hundred and fifty years."

THEY WILL WAVE AS THEY PASS U.S.

KHRUSHCHEV: "One hundred and fifty years? Well, then, we will say America has been in existence for 150 years and this is the level she has reached. We have existed not quite forty-two years and in another seven years we will be on the same level as America.

"When we catch you up, in passing you by, we will wave to you. Then if you wish we can stop and say: Please follow us. Plainly speaking, if you want capitalism you can live that way. That is your own affair and doesn't concern us. We can still feel sorry for you but since you don't understand us—live as you do understand.

"We are all glad to be here at the exhibition with Vice President Nixon. . . . I think you will be satisfied with your visit and if—I cannot go without saying it—if you would not take such a decision [proclamation by the United States Government of Captive Nations Week, a week of prayer for peoples enslaved by the Soviet Union] which has not been thought out thoroughly, as was approved by Congress, your trip would be excellent. But you have churned the water yourselves—why this was necessary God only knows.

"What happened? What black cat crossed your path and confused you? But that is your affair, we do not interfere with your problems. [Wrapping his arms about a Soviet workman] Does this man look like a slave laborer? [Waving at others] With men with such spirit how can we lose?"

EXCHANGE OF IDEAS URGED BY NIXON

NIXON (POINTING TO AMERICAN WORKMEN): "With men like that we are strong. But these men, Soviet and American, work together well for peace, even as they have worked together in building this exhibition. This is the way it should be.

"Your remarks are in the tradition of what we have come to expect—sweeping and extemporaneous. Later on we will both have an opportunity to speak and consequently I will not comment on the various points that you raised, except to say this—this color television is one of the most advanced developments in communications that we have.

"I can only say that if this competition in which you plan to outstrip us is to do the best for both of our peoples and for peoples everywhere there must be exchange of ideas. After all, you don't know everything—"

KHRUSHCHEV: "If I don't know everything, you don't known anything about communism except fear of it."

NIXON: "There are some instances where you may be ahead of us, for example in the development of the thrust of your rockets for the investigation of outer space; there may be some instances in which we are ahead of you—in color television, for instance."

KHRUSHCHEV: "No, we are up with you on this, too. We have bested you in one technique and also in the other."

NIXON: "You see, you never concede anything."

KHRUSHCHEV: "I do not give up."

APPEARANCES ON TV ARE SUGGESTED

NIXON: "Wait till you see the picture. Let's have far more communication and exchange in this very area that we speak of. We should hear you more on our television. You should hear us more on yours."

KHRUSHCHEV: "That's a good idea. Let's do it like this. You appear before our people. We will appear before your people. People will see and appreciate this."

NIXON: "There is not a day in the United States when we cannot read what you say. When Kozlov was speaking in California about peace, you were talking here in somewhat different terms. This was reported extensively in the American press. Never make a statement here if you don't want it to be read in the United States. I can promise you every word you say will be translated into English."

KHRUSHCHEV: "I doubt it. I want you to give your word that this speech of mine will be heard by the American people."

NIXON (SHAKING HANDS ON IT): "By the same token, everything I say will be translated and heard all over the Soviet Union?"

KHRUSHCHEV: "That's agreed."

NIXON: "You must not be afraid of ideas."

KHRUSHCHEV: "We are telling you not to be afraid of ideas. We have no reason to be afraid. We have already broken free from such a situation."

NIXON: "Well, then, let's have more exchange of them. We are all agreed on that. All right? All right?"

KHRUSHCHEV: "Fine. [Aside] Agree to what? All right, I am in agreement. But I want to stress what I am in agreement with. I know that I am dealing with a very good lawyer, I also want to uphold my own miner's flag so that the coal miners can say, 'Our man does not concede.'"

NIXON: "No question about that."

KHRUSHCHEV: "You are a lawyer for capitalism and I am a lawyer for communism. Let's compete."

VICE PRESIDENT PROTESTS FILIBUSTER

NIXON: "The way you dominate the conversation you would make a good lawyer yourself. If you were in the United States Senate you would be accused of filibustering."

NIXON (HALTING KHRUSHCHEV AT MODEL KITCHEN IN MODEL HOUSE): "You had a very nice house in your exhibition in New York. My wife and I saw and enjoyed it very much. I want to show you this kitchen. It is like those of our houses in California."

KHRUSHCHEV (AFTER NIXON CALLED ATTENTION TO A BUILT-IN PANEL-CONTROLLED WASHING MACHINE): "We have such things."

NIXON: "This is the newest model. This is the kind which is built in thousands of units for direct installation in the houses."

He added that Americans were interested in making life easier for their women. Mr. Khrushchev remarked that in the Soviet Union they did not have "the capitalist attitude toward women."

NIXON: "I think that this attitude toward women is universal. What we want to do is make easier the life of our housewives."

He explained that the house could be built for $14,000 and that most veterans had bought houses for between $10,000 and $15,000.

NIXON: "Let me give you an example you can appreciate. Our steel workers, as you know, are on strike. But any steel worker could buy this house. They earn $3 an hour. This house costs about $100 a month to buy on a contract running twenty-five to thirty years."

KHRUSHCHEV: "We have steel workers and we have peasants who also can afford to spend $14,000 for a house." He said American houses were built to last only twenty years, so builders could sell new houses at the end of that period. "We build firmly. We build for our children and grandchildren."

Mr. Nixon said he thought American houses would last more than twenty years, but even so, after twenty years many Americans want a new home or a new kitchen, which would be obsolete then. The American system is designed to take advantage of new inventions and new techniques, he said.

KHRUSHCHEV: "This theory does not hold water."

He said some things never got out of date—furniture and furnishings, perhaps, but not houses. He said he did not think that what Americans had written about their houses was all strictly accurate.

GADGETRY DERIDED BY KHRUSHCHEV

NIXON (POINTING TO TELEVISION SCREEN): "We can see here what is happening in other parts of the home."

KHRUSHCHEV: "This is probably always out of order."

NIXON: "Da [yes]."

KHRUSHCHEV: "Don't you have a machine that puts food into the mouth and pushes it down? Many things you've shown us are interesting but they are not needed in life. They have no useful purpose. They are merely gadgets. We have a saying, if you have bedbugs you have to catch one and pour boiling water into the ear." . . .

NIXON (HEARING JAZZ MUSIC): "I don't like jazz music."

KHRUSHCHEV: "I don't like it either."

NIXON: "But my girls like it." . . .

RUSSIANS HAVE IT TOO, PREMIER ASSERTS

KHRUSHCHEV: "The Americans have created their own image of the Soviet man and think he is as you want him to be. But he is not as you think. You think the Russian people will be dumbfounded to see these things, but the fact is that newly built Russian houses have all this equipment right now. Moreover, all you have to do to get a house is to be born in the Soviet Union. You are entitled to housing. I was born in the Soviet Union. So I have a right to a house. In America if you don't have a dollar—you have the right to choose between sleeping in a house or on the pavement. Yet you say that we are slaves of communism." ...

NIXON: "To us, diversity, the right to choose, the fact that we have 1,000 builders building 1,000 different houses, is the most important thing. We don't have one decision made at the top by one government official. This is the difference."

Selling America

The two photographs that follow are idealizations of American life, created by the United States Information Agency, the international propaganda arm of the American government. In a sense, they were weapons in the cold war. As you look at them, try to think of connections between them and the "kitchen debate" between Richard Nixon and Nikita Khrushchev. According to the first photograph, what apparent relationship exists between technology and domestic bliss and harmony? What idealized notions of youth culture are present in the second photograph? Is there some connection between this photograph and Nixon's and Khrushchev's disavowal of jazz in the "kitchen debate"? between the photograph and the emergence of rock 'n' roll (Chapter 11)?

Original caption: "Takoma Park, Maryland—In the living room of their home, the A. Jackson Cory family and some friends watch a television program. Some sociologists claim the growing popularity of television will tend to make family life stronger and make the home the center of the family's recreation. 1950."
United States Information Agency photo, National Archives.

Original caption: "Washington, D.C.—Brennan Jacques, a typical American teenager, has his own orchestra, the 'Fabulous Esquires,' composed of youngsters aware of what their schoolmates like and do not like in current music. Here, young Jacques plays the piano for a group of young people, who have gathered around him. 1957."
United States Information Agency photo, National Archives.

CHAPTER 11

The Eisenhower Consensus

Reason, objectivity, dispassion—these were the qualities and values that twice elected Dwight Eisenhower to the presidency. His appeal was bipartisan. In 1948 and 1952, politicians of both major parties sought to nominate this man with the "leaping and effortless smile" who promised the electorate a "constitutional presidency"—immune from the ideological harangues of European dictators, American demagogues, and New Deal presidents—and a secure economy—immune from major dislocations.

To replace the disjointed and unpredictable insecurity of depression, war, and ideological struggle, he offered Americans a society based on consensus. In the consensual society, major disagreements over important issues such as race, class, and gender were presumed not to exist. Conflict—serious conflict, about who had power and who did not—was considered almost un-American.

By 1960, it was clear that Eisenhower, and the nation at large, had not sought to create or maintain the consensual society through any radical departures from the past. The cold war, anticommunism, the welfare state—all inherited from his Democratic predecessor, Harry Truman—were not so much thrown aside as modulated or refined.

Anticommunism was central to the consensus, for the existence of a powerful enemy helped define the consensus and to deflect attention from the economic and social issues on which there could be no easy agreement. Joseph McCarthy would cease to be a factor after 1954, but otherwise, anticommunism was almost as much a part of the Eisenhower years as it had been of Truman's. The purges that cleansed most labor unions of Communist influence were completed when Ike took office, but cold war attitudes permeated the labor movement throughout the decade. The Committee on Un-American Activities of the House of Representatives (HUAC) would never know the acclaim it had mustered in the late 1940s, but each year it received more money from Congress and continued to function. In 1959, the Supreme Court refused to declare HUAC in violation of the First Amendment. New Organizations—Robert Welch's John

Birch Society and the Christian Anti-Communist Crusade, for example—emerged to carry on the struggle against internal subversion. Welch labeled Eisenhower a "dedicated, conscious agent of the Communist conspiracy."

Those who feared that the first Republican president since Herbert Hoover would grasp the opportunity to dismantle the welfare state had misunderstood both Eisenhower and the function of government at mid-century. If only intuitively, Eisenhower knew that what was left of the New Deal could not be eliminated without risking serious social and economic disruption. Countercyclical programs like old-age insurance and unemployment insurance were maintained or expanded; the Council of Economic Advisers, created in the Employment Act of 1946 to provide the president with his own planning staff, remained; spending for military hardware and interstate highways was expected to create jobs. Republicans did manage a rollback of New Deal policies in the areas of taxation and agriculture.

There was in much of this a pervasive element of acceptance—acceptance of American institutions as they were or as Americans wished they were. The power of the large corporation was accepted, its influence invited. Many agreed with General Motors president Charles E. Wilson, who during Senate hearings to confirm his nomination as secretary of defense said, "I thought what was good for our country was good for General Motors, and vice versa." Effective government was often conceptualized as the product of big business, big labor, and big government, each checking and balancing the others. The antitrust emphasis of the later New Deal was all but forgotten. Instead, Americans took comfort in John Kenneth Galbraith's theory of countervailing power, which postulated a self-regulating economy in which some big businesses (such as Sears, Roebuck) countervailed others (such as General Electric), leaving government the limited task of fine-tuning an economic system whose basic structure was virtually guaranteed to be competitive.

It followed that a wide variety of social problems—racism, unemployment, poverty, urban life, and the cult of domesticity, which suffocated women—were ignored, denied, accepted, or left in abeyance to be handled by some future generation. Throughout the 1950s, social commentators affirmed that America's central problems were ones of boredom, affluence, and classlessness. *The Midas Plague*, a science-fiction novel, described a world in which goods were so easily produced and so widely available that consuming had become a personal duty, a social responsibility, and an enormous and endless burden. David Riesman's *Lonely Crowd*, an influential study published in 1950, argued that the age of scarcity had ended; Americans would henceforth be concerned with leisure, play, and the "art of living." For many analysts of American society, the new conditions of life had eliminated the old conflicts between capital and labor and ushered in the "end of ideology." Economic growth—so the theory went—would increase the size of the total product to be distributed and soon result in a society consisting mainly of white-collar workers.

Beneath the surface of the consensual society, there were some currents that disturbed many Americans. Despite a landmark Supreme Court decision in 1954 ordering the racial integration of public schools with "all deliberate speed," black Americans remained outside the American system, gathering energies for a spectacular assault on the traditions of prejudice and exploitation. Women did not resist so overtly, but a growing body of scholarly literature suggests that many women were at best ambivalent about the June Cleaver ("Leave it to Beaver") and Margaret Anderson ("Father Knows Best") images that were television's contribution to the consensual society. Everyone was concerned about an apparent alienation among many young people, an alienation that expressed itself sometimes frighteningly as juvenile delinquency, sometimes just as a mystifying lack of energetic affirmation, most often in an affinity for a new music called rock 'n' roll. Following the launch of the Soviet satellite *Sputnik* in 1957, Americans began to ask whether this technological defeat reflected a general withering of national purpose (a theme taken up by Eisenhower's successor, John Kennedy). As the decade wore on, it became obvious, too, that millions of Americans were not participating in the prosperity the administration proclaimed. Eisenhower's farewell address would be silent on most of these issues; but its discussion of the military-industrial complex was perhaps Eisenhower's way of acknowledging that the consensus he had tried so hard to preserve—indeed, to create—was fundamentally unstable. If so, the next decade would prove him right.

Rebels Without a Cause? Teenagers in the 1950s

261

INTERPRETIVE ESSAY

Beth Bailey

Rebels Without a Cause? Teenagers in the 1950s

Against images of Elvis Presley's contorted torso, of Little Richard's screaming black sexuality, of Cleveland disc jockey Alan Freed introducing a generation of eager young people to the erotic pleasures of rhythm and blues, Beth Bailey offers a very different perspective on American youth in the 1950s. Using dating behavior to understand the emerging postwar youth culture, Bailey suggests that young people were responding to a climate of insecurity that had deep historical roots. Furthermore, she identifies the quest for security with a revised, "50s" version of the American dream that also encompassed family and suburbia. In short, Bailey seems to suggest that the youth of the 1950s were as attuned to consensual values as any other group.

While reading the essay, consider some of these questions: Does Bailey's argument apply to most American youths, or only to those who were white and middle class? What did parents find objectionable in this youth behavior, and why? Might "going steady" be understood as both a form of acquiescence in dominant values and a kind of resistance? And how can one square Bailey's perspective with the Presley, Little Richard, and Freed images mentioned above?

The United States emerged from the Second World War the most powerful and affluent nation in the world. This statement, bald but essentially accurate, is the given foundation for understanding matters foreign and domestic, the cold war and the age of abundance in America. Yet the sense of confidence and triumph suggested by that firm phrasing and by our images of soldiers embracing women as confetti swirled through downtown streets obscures another postwar reality. Underlying and sometimes overwhelming both bravado and complacency were voices of uncertainty. America at war's end was not naively optimistic.

The Great War had planted the seeds of the great depression. Americans wondered if hard times would return as the war boom ended. (They wouldn't.) The First World War had not ended all wars. Would war come again? (It would, both cold and hot.) And the fundamental question that plagued postwar America was, would American citizens have the strength and the character to meet the demands of this new world?

Postwar America appears in stereotype as the age of conformity—smug, materialistic, complacent, a soulless era peopled by organization men and their

Beth Bailey, "Rebels Without a Cause? Teenagers in the 1950s," *History Today* vol. 40, February 1990, pp. 25–31, without photographs.

(house)wives. But this portrait of conformity exists only because Americans created it. Throughout the postwar era Americans indulged in feverish self-examination. Experts proclaimed crises, limned the American character, poked and prodded into the recesses of the American psyche. Writing in scholarly journals and for an attentive general public, theorists and social critics suggested that America's very success was destroying the values that had made success possible. Success, they claimed, was eroding the ethic that had propelled America to military and industrial supremacy and had lifted American society (with significant exceptions seen clearly in hindsight) to undreamed-of heights of prosperity.

At issue was the meaning of the American dream. Did the American dream mean success through individual competition in a wide-open free marketplace? Or was the dream only of the abundance the American marketplace had made possible—the suburban American dream of two cars in every garage and a refrigerator-freezer in every kitchen? One dream was of competition and the resulting rewards. The *making* of the self-made man—the process of entrepreneurial struggle—was the stuff of that dream. Fulfillment, in this vision, was not only through material comforts, but through the prominence, social standing, and influence in the public sphere one achieved in the struggle for success.

The new-style postwar American dream seemed to look to the private as the sphere of fulfillment, of self-definition and self-realization. Struggle was not desired, but stasis. The dream was of a private life—a family, secure, stable, and comfortable—that compensated for one's public (work) life. One vision highlighted risk; the other security. Many contemporary observers feared that the desire for security was overwhelming the "traditional" American ethic. In the dangerous postwar world, they asserted, the rejection of the public, of work and of risk would soon destroy America's prosperity and security.

The focus for much of the fear over what America was becoming was, not surprisingly, youth. Adult obsession with the new postwar generation took diverse forms—from the overheated rhetoric about the new epidemic of juvenile delinquency (too many rebels without causes) to astringent attacks on the conformity of contemporary youth. These critiques, though seemingly diametrically opposed, were based on the shared assumption that young people lacked the discipline and get-up-and-go that had made America great.

Perhaps nowhere in American culture do we find a richer statement of concern about American youth and the new American dream than in the debates that raged over "going steady," an old name for a new practice that was reportedly more popular among postwar teenagers than "bop, progressive jazz, hot rods and curiosity (slight) about atomic energy." The crisis over the "national problem" of going steady is not merely emblematic—an amusing way into a serious question. "Going steady" seemed to many adults the very essence of the problem, a kind of leading indicator of the privatization of the American dream. Social scientists and social critics saw in the new security-first courtship patterns a paradigm for an emerging American character that, while prizing affluence, did not relish the risks and hard work that made it possible.

Certainly the change in courtship patterns was dramatic. And it was not hard to make a connection between the primary characteristics of teenagers' love lives and what they hoped to get out of American life in general. Before the Second World War, American youth had prized a promiscuous popularity, demonstrating competitive success through the number and variety of dates they commanded. Sociologist Willard Waller, in his 1937 study of American dating, gave this competitive system a name. "the campus rating complex." His study of Pennsylvania State University detailed a "dating and rating" system based on a model of public competition in which popularity was the currency. To be popular, men needed outward, material signs: an automobile, proper clothing, the right fraternity membership, money. Women's popularity depended on building and maintaining a reputation for popularity. They had to *be seen* with popular men in the "right" places, indignantly turn down requests for dates made at the "last minute," and cultivate the impression they were greatly in demand.

In *Mademoiselle*'s 1938 college issue, for example, a Smith college senior advised incoming freshmen to "cultivate an image of popularity" if they wanted dates. "During your first term," she wrote, "get 'home talent' to ply you with letters, invitations, telegrams. College men will think, 'She must be attractive if she can rate all that attention.' " And at Northwestern University in the 1920s, competitive pressure was so intense that co-eds made a pact not to date on certain nights of the week. That way they could preserve some time to study, secure in the knowledge they were not losing ground in the competitive race for success by staying home.

In 1935, the Massachusetts *Collegian* (the Massachusetts State College student newspaper) ran an editorial against using the library for "datemaking." The editors proclaimed: "The library is the place for the improvement of the mind and not the social standing of the student." Social standing, not social life: on one word turns the meaning of the dating system. That "standing" probably wasn't even a conscious choice shows how completely these college students took for granted that dating was primarily concerned with competition and popularity. As one North Carolina teenager summed it up:

> Going steady with one date
> Is okay, if that's all you rate.

Rating, dating, popularity, competition: catchwords hammered home, reinforced from all sides until they seemed a natural vocabulary. You had to rate in order to date, to date in order to rate. By successfully maintaining this cycle, you became popular. To stay popular, you competed. There was no end; the competitive process defined dating. Competition was the key term in the formula— remove it and there was no rating, dating, or popularity.

In the 1930s and 1940s, this competition was enacted most visibly on the dance floor. There, success was a dizzying popularity that kept girls whirling from escort to escort, "cut in" on by a host of popular men. Advice columns, etiquette books, even student handbooks told girls to strive to be "once-arounders," to never be left with the same partner for more than one turn around the dance floor. On the dance floor, success and failure were easily measured. Wallflowers were dismissed out of hand. But getting stuck—not being "cut in" on—was taken quite seriously as a sign of social failure. Everyone noticed, and everyone judged.

This form of competitive courtship would change dramatically. By the early 1950s, "cutting in" had almost completely disappeared outside the deep south. In 1955, a student at Texas Christian University reported, "To cut in is almost an insult." A girl in Green Bay, Wisconsin, said that her parents were "astonished" when they discovered that she hadn't danced with anyone but her escort at a "formal." "The truth was," she admitted, "that I wasn't aware that we were supposed to."

This 180-degree reversal took place quickly—during the years of the Second World War—and was so complete by the early 1950s that people under eighteen could be totally unaware of the formerly powerful convention. It signaled not simply a change in dancing etiquette but a complete transformation of the dating system as well. Definitions of social success as promiscuous popularity based on strenuous competition had given way to new definitions, which located success in the security of a dependable escort.

By the 1950s, early marriage had become the goal for young adults. In 1959, 47 percent of all brides married before they turned nineteen, and up to 25 percent of students at many large state universities were married. The average age at marriage had risen to 26.7 for men and 23.3 for women during the lingering depression, but by 1951 the average age at marriage had fallen to 22.6 for men, 20.4 for women. And younger teens had developed their own version of early marriage.

As early as 1950, going steady had completely supplanted the dating-rating complex as the criterion for popularity among youth. A best-selling study of American teenagers, *Profile of Youth* (1949) reported that in most high schools the "mere fact" of going steady was a sign of popularity "as long as you don't get tied up with an impossible gook." The *Ladies' Home Journal* reported in 1949 that "every high school student . . . must be prepared to fit into a high-school pattern in which popularity, social acceptance and emotional security are often determined by the single question: does he or she go steady?" A 1959 poll found that 57 percent of American teens had gone or were going steady. And, according to *Cosmopolitan* in 1960, if you didn't go steady, you were "square."

The new protocol of going steady was every bit as strict as the old protocol of rating and dating. To go steady, the boy gave the girl some visible token, such as a class ring or letter sweater. In Portland, Oregon, steadies favored rings (costing from $17 to $20). In Birmingham, Michigan, the girl wore the boy's identity bracelet, but never his letter sweater. In rural Iowa, the couple wore matching corduroy "steady jackets," although any couple wearing matching clothing in California would be laughed at.

As long as they went steady, the boy had to call the girl a certain number of times a week and take her on a certain number of dates a week (both numbers were subject to local convention). Neither boy nor girl could date anyone else or pay too much attention to anyone of the opposite sex. While either could go out with friends of the same sex, each must always know where the other was and what he or she was doing. Going steady meant a guaranteed date for special events, and it implied greater sexual intimacy—either more "necking" or "going further."

In spite of the intense monogamy of these steady relationships, teenagers viewed them as temporary. A 1950 study of 565 seniors in an eastern suburban high school found that 80 percent had gone or were going steady. Out of that number, only eleven said they planned to marry their steady. In New Haven, Connecticut, high school girls wore "obit bracelets." Each time they broke up with a boy, they added a disc engraved with his name or initials to the chain. In Louisiana, a girl would embroider her sneakers with the name of her current steady. When they broke up, she would clip off his name and sew an X over the spot. An advice book from the mid-1950s advised girls to get a "Puppy Love Anklet." Wearing it on the right ankle meant that you were available, on the left that you were going steady. The author advised having "Going Steady" engraved on one side, "Ready, Willing 'n Waiting" on the other—just in case the boys could not remember the code. All these conventions, cheerfully reported in teenager columns in national magazines, show how much teenagers took it for granted that going steady was a temporary, if intense, arrangement.

Harmless as this system sounds today, especially compared to the rigors of rating and dating, the rush to go steady precipitated an intense generational battle. Clearly some adult opposition was over sex: going steady was widely accepted as a justification for greater physical intimacy. But more fundamentally, the battle over going steady came down to a confrontation between two generations over the meaning of the American dream. Security versus competition. Teenagers in the 1950s were trying to do the unthinkable—to eliminate competition from the popularity equation. Adults were appalled. To them, going steady, with its extreme rejection of competition in favor of temporary security, represented all the faults of the new generation.

Adults, uncomfortable with the "cult of happiness" that rejected competition for security, attacked the teenage desire for security with no holds barred. As one writer advised boys, "To be sure of anything is to cripple one's powers of growth." She continued, "To have your girl always assured at the end of a telephone line without having to work for her, to beat the other fellows to her is bound to lessen your powers of personal achievement." A male adviser, campaigning against going steady, argued: "Competition will be good for you. It sharpens your wits, teaches you how to get along well in spite of difficulties." And another, writing in *Esquire*, explained the going steady phenomenon this way: "She wants a mate; he being a modern youth doesn't relish competition."

As for girls, the argument went: "She's afraid of competition. She isn't sure she can compete for male attention in the open market: 'going steady' frees her from fear of further failures." The author of *Jackson's Guide to Dating* tells the story of "Judith Thompson," a not-especially-attractive girl with family problems, who has been going steady with "Jim" since she was fourteen. Lest we think that poor Judith deserves someone to care for her or see Jim as a small success in her life, the author stresses that going steady is one more failure for Judith. "Now that Judith is sixteen and old enough to earn money and help herself in other ways to recover from her unfortunate childhood, she has taken on the additionally crippling circumstance of a steady boyfriend. How pathetic. The love and attention of her steady boyfriend are a substitute for other more normal kinds of success." What should Judith be doing? "A good deal of the time she spends going steady with Jim could be used to make herself more attractive so that other boys would ask her for dates."

There is nothing subtle in these critiques of going steady. The value of competition is presumed as a clear standard against which to judge modern youth. But there is more here. There is a tinge of anger in these judgments, an anger that may well stem from the differing experiences of two generations of Americans. The competitive system that had emerged in the flush years of the 1920s was strained by events of the 1930s and 1940s. The elders had come of age during decades of depression and world war, times when the competitive struggle was, for many, inescapable. Much was at stake, the cost of failure all too clear. While youth in the period between the wars embraced a competitive dating system, even gloried in it, as adults they sought the security they had lacked in their youth.

Young people and their advocates made much of the lack of security of the postwar world, self-consciously pointing to the "general anxiety of the times" as a justification for both early marriage and going steady. But the lives of these young people were clearly more secure than those of their parents. That was the gift their parents tried to give them. Though the cold war raged it had little immediate impact on the emerging teenage culture (for those too young to fight in Korea, of course). Cushioned by unprecedented affluence, allowed more years of freedom within the protected youth culture of high school and ever-more-frequently college, young people did not have to struggle so hard, compete so ferociously as their parents had.

And by and large, both young people and their parents knew it and were genuinely not sure what that meant for America's future. What did it mean—that a general affluence, at least for a broad spectrum of America's burgeoning middle class, was possible without a dog-eat-dog ferocity? What did *that* mean for the American Dream of success? One answer was given in the runaway best seller of the decade, *The Man in the Gray Flannel Suit*, which despite the title was not so much about the deadening impact of conformity but about what Americans should and could dream in the postwar world.

The protagonist of the novel, Tom Rath (the not-so-subtle naming made more explicit by the appearance of the word "vengeful" in the sentence following Tom's introduction), has been through the Second World War, and the shadow of war hangs over his life. Tom wants to provide well for his family, and feels a nagging need to succeed. But when he is offered the chance at an old-style American dream—to be taken on as the protégé of his business-wise, driven boss, he says no. In a passage that cuts to the heart of postwar American culture, Tom tells his boss:

> I don't think I'm the kind of guy who should try to be a big executive. I'll say it frankly: I don't think I have the willingness to make the sacrifices. . . . I'm try-

ing to be honest about this. I want the money. Nobody likes money better than I do. But I'm not the kind of guy who can work evenings and weekends and all the rest of it forever. . . . I've been through one war. Maybe another one's coming. If one is, I want to be able to look back and figure I spent the time between wars with my family, the way it should have been spent. Regardless of war, I want to get the most out of the years I've got left. Maybe that sounds silly. It's just that if I have to bury myself in a job every minute of my life, I don't see any point to it.

Tom's privatized dream—of comfort without sacrifice, of family and personal fulfillment—might seem the author's attempt to resolve the tensions of the novel (and of postwar American society). But the vision is more complex than simply affirmative. Tom's boss responds with sympathy and understanding, then suddenly loses control. "Somebody has to do the big jobs!" he says passionately. "This world was built by men like me! To really do a job, you have to live it, body and soul! You people who just give half your mind to your work are riding on our backs!" And Tom responds: "I know it."

The new American Dream had not yet triumphed. The ambivalence and even guilt implicit in Tom Rath's answer to his boss pervaded American culture in the 1950s—in the flood of social criticism and also in parents' critiques of teenage courtship rituals. The attacks on youth's desire for security are revealing, for it was in many ways the parents who embraced security—moving to the suburbs, focusing on the family. The strong ambivalence many felt about their lives appears in the critiques of youth. This same generation would find even more to criticize in the 1960s, as the "steadies" of the 1950s became the sexual revolutionaries of the 1960s. Many of the children of these parents came to recognize the tensions within the dream. The baby-boom generation accepted wholeheartedly the doctrine of self-fulfillment, but rejected the guilt and fear that had linked fulfillment and security. In the turbulence of the 1960s, young people were not rejecting the new American Dream of easy affluence and personal fulfillment, but only jettisoning the fears that had hung over a generation raised with depression and war. It turns out the 1950s family was not the new American Dream, but only its nurturing home.

SOURCES

The Suburbs

Photographs like this one, of a housing development called Levittown, on Long Island, appear in most history textbooks, usually to offer evidence of the inherent sterility of life in the new American suburbs. Yet there are those who argue that this is only a superficial impression and that up-close investigation of particular houses would reveal the effort most homeowners made to customize their homes and distinguish their properties from those of their neighbors. What do you think?

UPI.

Teen Culture
Rock 'n' Roll

The musical style called "rock 'n' roll" dates from the early 1950s. It is usually considered a sign of revolt, musical evidence that the generational rebellion that would sweep the 1960s was already under way even as Dwight Eisenhower was serving his first term. It was this. But rock 'n' roll was also essentially a white music, and a white music that was developed almost entirely from black musical styles.

The verses below—from the rock 'n' roll classic "Shake, Rattle and Roll" (1954)—allow us to inquire into the historical meaning of this new music. The verses on the left are from the original version, written by Charles Calhoun and recorded by Joe Turner for the black market. The verses on the right are from the more popular "cover" version by Bill Haley and the Comets. Both versions were hits in 1954.

Why did Haley change the words? Was rock 'n' roll part of the Eisenhower consensus, or its antithesis?

"SHAKE, RATTLE AND ROLL" (1954)

The Charles Calhoun / Joe Turner version

The Bill Haley version

The Charles Calhoun / Joe Turner version	The Bill Haley version
Get out of that bed, And wash your face and hands. (twice)	Get out in that kitchen, And rattle those pots and pans. (twice)
Get into the kitchen Make some noise with the pots and pans.	Roll my breakfast 'Cause I'm a hungry man.
Well you wear those dresses, The sun comes shinin' through. (twice)	You wear those dresses, Your hair done up so nice. (twice)
I can't believe my eyes, That all of this belongs to you.	You look so warm, But your heart is cold as ice.
I said over the hill, And way down underneath. (twice)	(the third verse of the Calhoun/Turner version is not part of the Haley version)
You make me roll my eyes, And then you make me grit my teeth.	

Dress Right

Parents, school officials, and other adult authorities carefully monitored the behavior of 1950s youth. The Catholic church published a list of films considered morally objectionable, and many radio stations refused to play rhythm and blues or rock 'n' roll. The schools had regulations too numerous to mention, among them dress codes like the one below. Called "Dress Right," this code was designed in part by student representatives from various schools. It was in force in Buffalo in the late 1950s and emulated nationally as The Buffalo Plan. What were the purposes of the code? On what assumptions was it based? What accounts for the distinction between academic and vocational schools? From the accompanying photograph of the lunchroom at one of the city's vocational schools (with a summary of the code on the wall), what can one conclude about student attitudes toward the code?

Board of Education
Buffalo, New York
School-Community Coordination
Recommendations of the Inter High School Student Council
for Appropriate Dress of Students in High School

BOYS
ACADEMIC HIGH SCHOOLS AND
HUTCHINSON-TECHNICAL HIGH SCHOOL

Recommended:

1. Dress shirt and tie or conservative sport shirt and tie with suit jacket, jacket, sport coat, or sweater
2. Standard trousers or khakis; clean and neatly pressed
3. Shoes, clean and polished; white bucks acceptable

Not Recommended:

1. Dungarees or soiled, unpressed khakis
2. T-shirts, sweat shirts
3. Extreme styles of shoes, including hobnail or "motorcycle boots"

VOCATIONAL HIGH SCHOOLS

Recommended:

1. Shirt and tie or sport shirt and tie
2. Sport shirt with sweater or jacket

3. Standard trousers or khakis; clean and neatly pressed
4. Shoes, clean and polished; white bucks acceptable

Not Recommended:

1. Dungarees or soiled, unpressed khakis
2. T-shirts, sweat shirts
3. Extreme styles of shoes, including hobnail or "motorcycle boots"

Note. The apparel recommended for boys should be worn in standard fashion with shirts tucked in and buttoned, and ties tied at the neck. Standard of dress for boys, while in school shops or laboratories, should be determined by the school.

GIRLS
ACADEMIC AND VOCATIONAL HIGH SCHOOLS

Recommended:

1. Blouses, sweaters, blouse and sweater, jacket with blouse or sweater
2. Skirts, jumpers, suits or conservative dresses
3. Shoes appropriate to the rest of the costume

Not Recommended:

1. V-neck sweaters without blouse
2. Bermuda shorts, kilts, party-type dresses, slacks of any kind
3. Ornate jewelry
4. T-shirts, sweat shirts

Note: All recommended wear for girls should fit appropriately and modestly. Standard of dress for girls, while in school shops or laboratories, should be determined by the school.

January 24, 1956

The cafeteria at Buffalo's Burgard Vocational High School, with the Dress Right code on the wall.
Burgard Craftsman, 1958.

School Sampler: An Essay in Words and Images

The items on these pages come from Buffalo, New York, school yearbooks. What does each tell us about coming of age in the 1950s—and, in the case of one of the photographs, in the early 1960s?

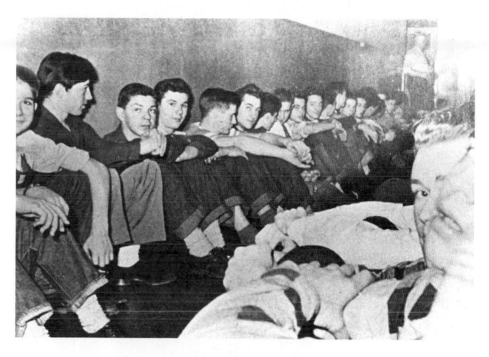

Bombs Away!

Seneca Vocational
Chieftain, 1952.

"We can't all be captains, we've got to be crew,
There's something for all of us here.
There's big work to do and there's lesser to do,
And the task we must do is the near.

If you can't be a highway then just be a trail,
If you can't be the sun be a star;
It isn't by size that you win or you fail--
Be the best of whatever you are !"

--Douglas Malloch

Riverside
Skipper, 1950.

The board of the Buffalo Seminary yearbook, *The Seminaria,* **beneath the image of the school's former headmistress.**
The Seminaria, 1950.

A home economics class at newly integrated East High, 1954.
Eastonian.

Bishop Timon Seniors, enjoying their smoking privilege in the school
cafeteria.
Talisman, 1962.

Joyce Johnson

Challenge to Consensus: The Beats

The consensus of the 1950s was maintained only with difficulty, if at all. One could theorize about the "American character," as many scholars did in the 1950s, but it was all too obvious that the blacks of Montgomery, Alabama were in some important sense outside America. One could make the American family into a bastion of strength and stability, but that would not make the new American working woman disappear. One could write, as John Kenneth Galbraith did, about a self-regulating economy of countervailing powers, but even Dwight Eisenhower could see that what he called the "military-industrial complex" was not self-regulating.

The beat phenomenon goes back to the late 1940s, when Jack Kerouac and Allen Ginsberg were students at Columbia University, and it reached its peak a decade later, when Ginsberg's poetry and Kerouac's novels (On the Road was published in 1957) brought the movement to the attention of the mass media. Even then, the beats, or "beatniks" as they were sometimes called, were always a tiny minority of the population, with much less presence and influence as a group than the hippies of the 1960s.

In the following passage, Joyce Johnson, a self-styled "minor character" in the story, describes something of the spirit of the Beat Generation and recalls her first encounter with Kerouac. How, and to what extent, did the beats challenge the dominant culture? In what sense could this challenge be described as "political"?

Jack Kerouac went on the road in the summer of 1947—from Ozone Park, Queens, of all places, to the Pacific, stopping off in Denver to see a new friend, Neal Cassady. As the saying goes, he was traveling light. None of the specialized equipment of latterday hitchhikers and wanderers. He had about fifty dollars in his pocket saved from veteran's benefits, a canvas bag "in which a few fundamental things were packed," and was wearing the wrong shoes—Mexican *huaraches*, the mark of the New York Bohemian intellectual back then.

It seems to have been a journey undertaken empirically, in mingled hope and desperation—an attempt to seek out a brand-new reality to match fantasy. He was looking, he said, for "girls, visions, everything; somewhere along the line the pearl would be handed to me."

It's strange, come to think of it, to go looking for visions. It seems more in the nature of visions to come upon you, seizing you unawares. If you look for them, they tend to recede, lead you a little further on. As for girls, there was uneasy flippancy in putting them at the head of his list—although looking for girls, in that sense, is not so much looking for love as for experience. The "everything," of course, was not to be found. Jack would find something out there, though. Sheer, joyous movement. If it had been possible to remain in motion for-

ever, never tiring, speeding away from each new encounter while it was still un-
sullied by the flagging of the first excitement, he might have been happy. As
happy as Neal Cassady,* who'd recently blown through the dragged-out end of
the Columbia scene like a fresh wind from the west. A joy-riding car thief, a yea-
saying delinquent, a guiltless, ravenous consumer of philosophy, literature,
women—all varieties of sexuality, in fact. An undecadent alter ego, Neal
seemed. He even uncannily looked like Jack—Jack the dark one, Neal golden
like Lucien, but so different from him or any of the Columbia crowd. He seemed
as familiar to Jack as the boys he'd grown up with in Lowell before he ever came
to the city: "I heard again the voices of old companions and brothers under the
bridge, among the motorcycles, along the wash-lined neighborhood and
drowsy doorsteps of afternoon where boys played guitar while their older
brothers worked in the mills."

Jack spent the months preceding his departure holed up in his mother's
house—a retreat foreshadowing other retreats to come, in other houses to which
he'd move Memere and all her pots and pans and furniture, as if home could be
pitched like a tent—in Denver, Colorado; Orlando, Florida; Rocky Mount,
North Carolina; Berkeley, California; Northport, Long Island; even Lowell
again. In Ozone Park, the evenings were as drowsy as his memories of boyhood.
In the eternal, spotless order of his mother's kitchen, a long subway ride from
the all-night haunts of Times Square, he spread maps out on the table after the
dishes were cleared, and like a navigator plotted the route of his contemplated
journey. The western place names were magic words of incantation. Cimarron,
Council Bluffs, Platte, Cheyenne. Thoughts of Neal stirred in him, merged with
romantic images of plainsmen and pioneers. Cassady loomed in Jack's mind as
archetypal, both his long-lost brother and the very spirit of the west in his root-
lessness and energy. . . .

Fifteen years later kids went on the road in droves, in the context Kerouac
and others had supplied for them. But in 1947, to be a college-educated hitch-
hiker was to be anachronistic. The depression decade, when millions of the hungry, homeless, and unemployed had roamed the U.S. landscape, hopped
freights, slept in open fields, was still grimly, unnostalgically alive in people's
memories. Status and security had been so recently won and still seemed tenu-
ously held. People did not walk the highways unless the cars they drove—
preferably the latest models—had flats or ran out of gas. In Council Bluffs,
where great wagon trains had gathered in the nineteenth century, Jack came
upon a depressing vista of "cute cottages of one damn kind and another." In
Cheyenne, he found Wild West Week being celebrated by "fat businessmen in
boots and ten-gallon hats," in whose eyes it would have been an act of incom-
prehensible perversity for a young man to become deliberately classless if he
had other options; in another few years, they would see it as positively un-
American.

---

*Neal Cassady would reappear in the 1960s as the bus driver for the Merry Pranksters, a colorful
and bizarre collection of antiauthoritarian performance-oriented California hippies, led (or not led)
by novelist Ken Kesey.—*Ed.*

Already what was left of the true west, as envisioned by Jack in Ozone Park, could no longer be found in the places with the legendary names, but in the open, empty spaces in between—a spirit to be grasped fleetingly from the back of a truck filled with migrant workers speeding across the prairies at midnight.

In the fall of '56, having narrowly survived my twentieth year, I was just turning twenty-one. My crash course in the depths of human experience sometimes made me feel extremely old. This was not entirely an unpleasant feeling but new and strange, like walking around in an exotic garment that suddenly made you impervious to everything but didn't connect you to most of the people you knew in your everyday life. Once you'd touched bottom, what was there to be afraid of anymore? I was continually lonely, but very fearless. Life seemed gray but not impossible.

I found a new job at another literary agency and got a little more money. I moved into a new apartment of my own that happened to be around the corner from Alex's. I worked on the novel about Barnard I'd begun in Hiram Haydn's workshop. Elise and Alex were characters in it. By making Alex into a character, I took away his power to hurt me. Just like me, my heroine would have an affair with the Alex character and end up alone. But in my fictional rearrangement of life, it was she who was going to leave him after their one and only night together. I rewarded her with a trip to Paris. I typed forty letters a day and dreamed of taking off myself.

"Hello. I'm Jack. Allen [Ginsberg] tells me you're very nice. Would you like to come down to Howard Johnson's on Eighth Street? I'll be sitting at the counter. I have black hair and I'll be wearing a red and black checked shirt."

I'm standing in Elise's kitchen, holding the phone Allen has just handed me. It's a Saturday night shortly after New Year's.

"Sure," I say.

I put on a lot of eye shadow and my coat and take the subway down to Astor Place and begin walking westward, cross-town, passing under the bridge between the two buildings of Wanamaker's Department Store and the eye of the giant illuminated clock. It's a dark, bitter January night with ice all over the pavements, so you have to be careful, but I'm flying along, it's an adventure as opposed to a misadventure—under which category so far I've had to put most of the risky occurrences in my life.

The windows of Howard Johnson's are running with steam so you can't see in. I push open the heavy glass door, and there is, sure enough, a black-haired man at the counter in a flannel lumberjack shirt slightly the worse for wear. He looks up and stares at me hard with blue eyes, amazingly blue. And the skin of his face is so brown. He's the only person in Howard Johnson's in color. I feel a little scared as I walk up to him. "Jack?" I say.

There's an empty stool next to his. I sit down on it and he asks me whether I want anything. "Just coffee." He's awfully quiet. We both lack conversation, but then we don't know each other, so what can we say? He asks after Allen, Lafcadio, that kind of thing. I'd like to tell him I've read his book, if that wouldn't sound gauche, obvious, and uncool.

When the coffee arrives, Jack looks glum. He can't pay for it. He has no money, none at all. That morning he'd handed his last ten dollars to a cashier in a grocery store and received change for a five. He's waiting for a check from a publisher, he says angrily.

I say, "Look, that's all right. I have money. Do you want me to buy you something to eat?"

"Yeah," he says. "Frankfurters. I'll pay you back. I always pay people back, you know."

I've never bought a man dinner before. It makes me feel very competent and womanly.

He has frankfurters, home fries, and baked beans with Heinz ketchup on them. I keep stealing looks at him because he's beautiful. You're not supposed to say a man is beautiful, but he is. He catches me at it and grins, then mugs it up, putting on one goofy face after another; a whole succession of old-time ridiculous movie-comedian faces flashes before me until I'm laughing too at the absurdity of this blind date Allen has arranged. (The notion of Allen Ginsberg arranging blind dates will crack people up years later when they ask me how on earth I met Kerouac.) . . .

I see the blue, bruised eye of Kerouac and construe his melancholy as the look of a man needing love because I'm, among other things, twenty-one years old. I believe in the curative powers of love as the English believe in tea or Catholics believe in the Miracle of Lourdes.

He tells me he's spent sixty-three days on a mountaintop without anyone. He made pea soup and wrote in his journal and sang Sinatra songs to keep himself company.

Some warning to me in all this. "You really liked being alone like that?" I ask.

"I wish I was there now. I should've stayed up there."

He could somehow cancel you out and make you feel sad for him at the same time. But I'm sure any mountaintop would be preferable to where he's staying—the Marlton Hotel on Eighth Street, with the dirty shades over the windows and the winos lounging on the steps.

"And where do you live?" Jack asks. He likes it that it's up near Columbia and the West End Bar where he used to hang out. Was Johnny the bartender still there? Johnny the bartender would remember him from the days he was a football hero at Columbia but he broke his leg in his sophomore year and stayed in his room reading Céline and Shakespeare and never went back to football again—thus losing his scholarship at Columbia, but he's always had affection for the neighborhood. "Why don't you let me stay at your place?" he says.

"If you wish," I say in *Desolation Angels*, deciding fast. And I know how I said it, too. As if it was of no great moment, as if I had no wishes of my own— in keeping with my current philosophy of nothing-to-lose, try anything. . . .

When we got in the door, he didn't ask to see my manuscript. He pulled me against him and kissed me before I even turned on the light. I kissed him back, and he acted surprised. He said I was even quieter than he was, he had no idea quiet girls liked kissing so much, and he undid the buttons on my coat and put both his hands up my back under my sweater. "The trouble is," Jack said with his voice against my ear, "I don't . . . like . . . blondes."

I remember laughing and saying, "Well, in that case I'll just dye my hair"— wondering all the same if it was true.

In the morning Jack left to get his stuff out of the Marlton. He returned with a sleeping bag and a knapsack in which there were jeans and a few old shirts like the one he was already wearing and some notebooks he'd bought in Mexico City. That was all he owned. Not even a typewriter—he'd been borrowing other people's typewriters, he said. I'd never seen such foreign-looking notebooks, long and narrow with shiny black covers and thin, bluish paper on which Jack's slanted penciled printing sped across page after page, interrupted here and there by little sketches. One notebook was just for dreams. He wrote in it every morning.

There was something heartbreakingly attractive in these few essentials to which Jack had reduced his needs. He reminded me of a sailor—not that I knew any sailors—something too about the way he looked coming out of the shower, gleaming and vigorous and ruddy with a white towel around his neck.

Very quickly it didn't seem strange to have him with me, we were somehow like very old friends—"buddies," Jack said, squeezing me affectionately, making me feel both proud and a little disappointed. Crazy as it was, I sometimes really wished I was dark—like this Virginia I felt jealous of for making him so wild. Or the girl named Esmeralda who lived in Mexico City and whom he'd loved tragically for a long time and written an entire novel about in one of his notebooks, calling her Tristessa. But he'd slept with her only once. She was a whore and a saint, so beautiful and lost—one of his mysterious *fellaheen* women, primeval and of the earth.

I was unprimeval and distinctly of the city. I was everydayness, bacon and eggs in the morning or the middle of the night, which I learned to cook just the way he liked—sunny-side up in the black iron frying pan. I'd buy slab bacon in the grocery store, like he'd always had in Lowell—not the skinny kind in packages—and add canned applesauce (a refinement I'd learned from Bickford's Cafeteria), which Jack had never thought of as anything that might enhance eggs. He took extraordinary pleasure in small things like that.

As a lover he wasn't fierce but oddly brotherly and somewhat reticent. I'd listen in amazement to his stories of Berkeley parties where everyone was naked and men and women engaged in some exotic Japanese practice called *yabyum* (but Jack, fully clothed, had sat apart brooding over his bottle of port, something he didn't tell me). In my memories of Jack in the good times we had together, I'm lying with my head on his chest, his heart pulsing against my ear. His smooth hard powerful arms are around me and I'm burying my face into them because I like them so much, making him laugh, "What are you doing there, Joycey?" And there's always music on the radio. Symphony Sid, whom he taught me to find on the dial, who always comes on at the stroke of midnight, bringing you the sounds of Charlie Parker, Lester Young, Miles Davis, and Stan

Getz, and who, according to Jack, is a subterranean himself—you can hear it in his gravel voice smoked down to a rasp by innumerable weird cigarettes. "And now—after a few words about that fan-tastic Mo-gen David wine—the great Lady Day . . ." In the darkness of the room we drift together as Billie Holiday bewails lost loves.

But then Jack leaves me. He goes into the small back bedroom where I never sleep because there's no radiator there. He pulls the window all the way up, closes the door, and lies down on the floor in his sleeping bag alone. This is the cure for the cough he brought with him from Mexico City. In the morning he'll do headstands with his feet against the wall, to reverse the flow of blood in his body. He tells me a frightening thing about himself. He's known for eight years that a blood clot could finish him off at any minute.

How can you bear living, I wonder, knowing death could be so close? Little by little I'm letting go of what I learned on the abortionist's table in the white upstairs room in Canarsie.

I'm good for him, Jack tells me. I don't mind anything he does. I don't mind about the sleeping bag, do I?

I didn't really mind, that was the strange part. Everything seemed so odd, so charmed, so transformed. . . .

I hate Jack's woman-hatred, hate it, mourn it, understand, and finally forgive.

CHAPTER 12

Coming Apart:
The 1960s

For a time, the decade of the 1960s looked very much like its predecessor. John F. Kennedy, elected by a narrow margin over Richard Nixon in 1960, sought to pump up the nation with rhetoric while practicing a brand of consensus politics designed to avoid overt conflict. The problems of the 1960s, said Kennedy at Yale University's commencement in 1962, presented "subtle challenges, for which technical answers, not political answers, must be provided." Because he believed that basic problems of adequate food, clothing, and employment had been solved through economic growth and the evolution of the welfare state, Kennedy was not the reform activist that many expected him to be. Several of his policies and programs—the commitment to space exploration, the Peace Corps, the rollback of prices in the steel industry—were essentially symbolic gestures. In foreign affairs, Kennedy carried on the cold war in grand fashion— deeper involvement in Vietnam; a CIA-sponsored invasion of Cuba in an attempt to depose Fidel Castro; a blockade to force the Soviet Union to remove its missiles from Cuba, when less bellicose but less satisfying alternatives were available.

There were signs of change and protents of turmoil in the early years of the decade—the gathering of political youth at Port Huron, Michigan, in 1962, to write and debate a manifesto; the assassination of John F. Kennedy; the assertive youth culture fostered by the English rock 'n' roll band the Beatles; the Berkeley Free Speech Movement in 1964. Yet the Eisenhower consensus was not irrevocably shattered until mid-decade. The cause was race. During the 1950s, black efforts to achieve integration had followed mainly legal channels. Gradually, though, black activists adopted the tactics of direct action. In February 1960, black and white college students conducted sit-ins at the segregated lunch counters of Woolworth dime stores in Durham and Greensboro, North Carolina; in 1961 and 1962, "freedom" rides took activists into segregated bus terminals across the deep south. In August 1963, Martin Luther King, Jr., brought the civil rights movement north and sharpened its political content with an enormous march on the nation's capital.

Then, in 1965, a minor summer incident involving police in Watts, a black section of Los Angeles, set off five days of looting and rioting that left thirty-four people dead. Within two years, there were over a hundred major urban riots, all centered in black ghettos in cities like Newark and Detroit. It was in this setting that young black leaders began to question whether integration was an appropriate goal. They began to talk of black power. It was in this setting, too, that two of the most charismatic black leaders, Malcolm X and Martin Luther King, Jr., were shot to death.

The urban ghetto riots of the mid-1960s occurred during times of relatively low national rates of unemployment and inflation and within the context of Lyndon Johnson's Great Society—a liberal reform program that included the Voting Rights Act of 1965 and the war on poverty. While the voting-rights legislation had immediate results that went well beyond what the civil rights movement had been able to accomplish in the early 1960s, the war on poverty as well as other Johnson programs were severely limited by a growing backlash against social unrest and the president's own policy of escalation in Vietnam. When Kennedy was killed in 1963, there were fewer than 20,000 American personnel in Vietnam; in 1968, there were more than 500,000. For Johnson, each new American commitment was absolutely necessary. Defeat or withdrawal, he believed, would only bring more aggression, new tests of the national and presidential will. Others, however, saw the conflict in Vietnam largely as a civil war and American involvement as an immoral and/or unlawful interference in a domestic dispute.

Protests against the war, centered on the college campuses and utilizing the tactics of the civil rights movement, began in earnest in early 1965 and grew in number and intensity through the decade. Almost every major campus in the United States was torn by rallies, teach-ins, and riots. One climax of the youth revolt was the massive demonstration—and the violent police response to it—centered on the Democratic National Convention in Chicago in 1968. The "protesters," as they had come to be called, could not prevent the nomination of the party's establishment candidate, Hubert Humphrey, but the event so clouded his candidacy that it almost ensured his defeat by Richard Nixon.

Nixon's widening of the Vietnam War in 1970, with an invasion of Cambodia, touched off the last major round of protest on the campuses. On May 4, panicky National Guardsmen, sent to quell a protest at Kent State University in Ohio, killed four students. Ten days later, two black youths were shot by police at Jackson State College in Mississippi.

By the end of the decade, the antiwar and civil rights movements had been joined and fueled by women seeking liberation from confining social roles and by a new group of environmental and consumer activists who saw that the nation had pursued economic growth at great cost to the quantity and quality of its remaining resources and the health of its citizens. Portions on this counterculture of protest were nonpolitical (Ken Kesey's San Francisco–based Merry Pranksters, for example, painted their faces with Day-Glo and inveigled protesters to "drop acid" and simply turn their backs on the war). But protest movements of the 1960s were by and large committed to making existing political frameworks responsive. Many believed that the Great Society could reconstruct the nation's cities, force corporations to clean up the air and water, provide for genuine equality of opportunity for all races, and even eliminate poverty. Others had faith that Ralph Nader and his "raiders" could mount and sustain a meaningful consumer movement and that Common Cause, an extensive liberal lobby established by former Department of Health, Education, and Welfare Secretary John Gardner, would significantly redress the balance in Congress. Not since the 1930s had Americans believed so mightily in the possibilities of change.

INTERPRETIVE ESSAY

Kenneth J. Heineman

Campus Wars

More than twenty years after they ended, the campus protests of the 1960s remain at the center of how Americans understand their recent history. For some, these protests were the last best hope of turning the country off the path of imperialism and militarism and reclaiming the American nation for democratic and moral purposes. For others, the same protests were just so much chaos and disorder, but with tragic consequences: the beginning of the decline of the United States as a world economic and political power, and a pervasive and irreparable fracturing of the sense of community.

Kenneth J. Heineman's analyzis of these "campus wars" offers us a way to enter this larger debate. Who, he asks, were the campus protesters? Who was likely to belong to SDS (Students for a Democratic Society), and who was not? Were the campus activists, as the Nixon administration liked to claim, just pampered rich kids used to having their own way in the affluent society of the 1950s or, just as bad, trying to end the war so that they would not have to serve in it? Having determined who they were, what conclusions can one draw about why they chose to become campus activists?

As late as 1940, just 16 percent of American college-aged youth could afford to attend an institution of higher education and prestigious private and public universities restricted the admission of Catholics and Jews. Liberals, from Franklin Roosevelt to Congressman Lyndon Johnson, believed that higher education, if made financially accessible and less culturally exclusive, would enable less-privileged citizens, particularly the New Deal's core constituency of industrial workers and ethnic Catholics and Jews, to achieve upward social mobility. Therefore, the federal government began in the 1930s to provide students with education grants and exerted some moral, and later legal, pressure on universities to abolish religious quotas.

Once the United States found itself engaged in the cold war, liberals came up with additional reasons to educate larger numbers of youth. As Clark Kerr and Harlan Hatcher argued in the 1950s and early 1960s, the demands placed upon the nation by the emerging American-centered global economy, as well as by an escalating nuclear arms race, required the creation of a technologically proficient, college-educated, society. Additionally, cold war liberal intellectuals such as Arthur Schlesinger, Jr., and Daniel Bell came to view higher education as a means to create a politically centrist, classless society. Ideally, educated cit-

Kenneth J. Heineman, *Campus Wars: The Peace Movement at American State Universities in the Vietnam Era,* New York University Press, New York, 1993, pp. 76–95, 124–125. Reprinted with the permission of New York University Press.

izens would cease to identify themselves by their class and cultural backgrounds. This loss of identity was necessary for, to a nation locked in struggle with international communism, class and cultural consciousness served only to promote disunity and lay bare America's historic class, ethnic, religious, and racial divisiveness. In any event, cold war liberals reasoned, the end of ethnic, religious, and racial discrimination in higher education, and the fact that more youths could obtain government education aid, signaled that class and cultural distinctions among Americans were disappearing.

Guided by a cold war liberal vision of the world, in which divisive class and cultural consciousness, and radical left and right political doctrines were ideologically repugnant, the federal government successfully promoted mass education. University enrollment expanded dramatically: from two million in 1950 to nearly four million in 1960 and further to seven million in 1968. By 1970, 50 percent of all college-aged youths attended an institution of higher education. With greater numbers of youths entering the universities in the 1960s, the title "student" began to take on the connotation of an occupation, albeit a temporary one. Intellectuals ranging from psychologist Kenneth Keniston to Michigan student activist Tom Hayden, ironically mirroring their cold war counterparts, described students as part of a new social class, a class that was neither blue nor white collar and which stood apart from the larger society. Moreover, this new class had personal and political concerns that were quite different from those of workers and professionals.

In many regards, students by the 1960s did represent a new social group. Escape from parental supervision, the mounting popularity among youth of vaguely antiauthoritarian rock 'n' roll music, and the increased prevalence on the campus of marijuana and psychedelics, combined to define a student lifestyle that was distinct from mainstream society. But despite those developments, it would be misleading to categorize students only by their lifestyle. Even though cold war liberal intellectuals proclaimed the end of class and cultural differences in America, such distinctions had not disappeared. In the 1960s, students' class and cultural backgrounds helped to determine which ideas they studied and adopted and which type of lifestyle they embraced.

Ironically, students who became involved in peace protest and the New Left in the 1960s were the beneficiaries of the expansion of higher education after World War II, an expansion ideologically justified in part by the intensifying cold war. With the military escalation of the Vietnam War, many sons and daughters of blue-collar workers and ethnic Catholics and Jews revolted against the political system that had made possible their entrance into the universities. Antiwar student activists, particularly those from middle- and upper-middle-class secularized Protestant backgrounds, championed the notion of student power. Such activists considered American youth to represent a new community that had, as cold war liberals predicted, become declassed. On the other hand, there were a number of antiwar students, generally working- and lower-middle-class and often Catholic, who, while accepting in part the idea of students as a new, declassed social group, acknowledged that their class and cultural heritages informed their politics.

White student activism of the 1960s owed much to the crusading reformist spirit of the New Frontier and the civil rights movement. Activism received further stimulus with the military escalation of the Vietnam War and the subsequent loss of the universities' scholarly neutrality as it became increasingly apparent to students that American institutions of higher education, through military research projects, were tied to the defense establishment. Alienation from the impersonal "multiversity," which stressed administrative form over intellectual content, and rejection of intrusive *in loco parentis*, also contributed to the political mobilization of students. Additionally, the federal government's conflicting educational policies, bound up with the draft and the war, promoted student rebellion. Citing a desperate shortage of primary and secondary school teachers and citizens schooled in the humanities, the federal government exhorted students to go into the fields of education and the arts. At the same time, the federal government awarded student draft deferments based upon a system that ranked education and humanities majors as least essential to national security and, therefore, least worthy of military service exemptions.

University administrators unwittingly set the stage for student disaffection by placing an increased emphasis upon liberal arts and social science programs. Large numbers of college students in the 1960s pursued studies in the humanities and social sciences. Significantly, liberal arts and social science majors predominated in the ranks of protestors. This may be explained by the nature of the social sciences and the humanities, which encourage critical approaches toward analyzing authority (and attract critical students), offer no specific avenues to jobs, and require sensitivity to, and reflection on, social problems. Science and business majors primarily deal with specific problems that have absolute answers and are not accustomed to dealing with social problems whose solutions are debatable. In addition, such majors often have specific jobs open to them and, since they typically work for corporations benefiting from defense contracts, are not inclined to be critical of the government.

Contrary to contemporary stereotypes, students who became involved in anti–Vietnam War protest were not all middle class and privileged. Indeed, student peace activists came from a variety of class and cultural backgrounds. One reason that the stereotype of the affluent student antiwar activists arose was the great news media attention that privileged, secularized Protestant and Jewish, radical youths received. Such activists did exist in number at elite schools and were considered newsworthy because they represented, figuratively and literally, the children of the Establishment. Culturally secure, and the products of elite university educations, these activists operated comfortably from a position of privilege and, since economic factors did not constrict their horizons, their idealism and expectations were accordingly great. They did not have to work while in college in order to pay for tuition and, further, could afford the luxury of not being career-oriented; their parents could support them indefinitely. This privileged cultural and class background led some upper-middle-class Jewish and Protestant activists to believe that all whites were similarly advantaged and all blacks conversely disadvantaged. Convinced that they constituted the most intellectually and morally advanced segment of society, well-to-do student activists such as Bill Ayers, Diana Oughton, and Terry Robbins issued secularized jeremiads against "American imperialism," which exploited their black, brown, and yellow comrades at home and abroad. This was the class and cultural milieu that produced the most violence-prone faction of the 1960s New Left: the Weathermen.

The 1960s academic and activist melting pot also included culturally insecure and less privileged groups, particularly working- and lower-middle-class Jews and Catholics. Jewish student activists, regardless of their degree of secularization and assimilation, absorbed from their backgrounds a propensity toward political awareness and liberalism. Once uprooted from eastern Europe in the early twentieth century, Jewish immigrants confronted a culturally ambiguous environment in America. Unlike other cultural groups, which, upon gaining upward social mobility, increasingly adopted more conservative politics, Jews did not tend to forsake their commitment to civil rights, civil liberties, and trade unionism. According to a 1970 Louis Harris survey, 23 percent of Jewish students termed themselves leftist, compared to 4 percent of Protestant students.

One possible explanation for Jewish political exceptionalism lies in part in their persistent cultural anxiety expressed by the image of the outsider who cannot accept that he has been accepted. There was some substance to Jewish cultural anxiety, given the fact that their economic success has been achieved largely in the independent professions of law, medicine, and teaching. Up to the 1970s, Protestant corporate America closed its doors to Jews and Catholics. It also must not be forgotten that for 1960s red diaper babies, 1950s McCarthyism underscored perceptions of vulnerability as well as injustice. Red diaper babies grew up with FBI harassment [and] economic hardship if their parents were blacklisted and lived in fear that their parents would be arrested and executed like Julius and Ethel Rosenberg. For these reasons, Jewish youths often interacted only with one another until entering college. Richard Flacks and Steve Max, both red diaper babies and founders of [the] SDS, were surprised to discover the existence of Midwestern Christian radicals at the 1962 Port Huron SDS convention. Indeed, Max did not meet his first Catholic until the Port Huron convention.

Catholic student activists were at once similar to, and greatly different from, Jewish student activists. Ideologically, Catholics tended to absorb from their church a reflexive distrust of communism. However, the Catholic church also taught its followers the need for community, mutual assistance, and social justice. Culturally, the parents of Catholic activists had experienced discrimination similar to that which had confronted the parents of Jewish student activists. Catholic student activists were also just as culturally insecure and insular as their Jewish counterparts. Mary Verala, a Hispanic Catholic student activist, expressed wonderment at the 1962 Port Huron convention upon meeting "my first Communist, Steve Max." In part this was because their upward mobility was largely, like that of Jews, the product of the New Deal. In addition, it is important to keep in mind that it was not until 1960 that even a Harvard-educated and wealthy Catholic could get elected president of the United States.

A final group of student activists may be broadly characterized as working and lower middle class, frequently Catholic or brought up in what Vance Packard called "low-status" Protestant denominations, Methodist, Baptist, and Lutheran. Scholars of the 1960s, as well as journalists at the time, have given short shrift to this group since they overwhelmingly attended state, rather than private, schools. For example, in 1967, 34 percent of entering Penn State students identified their parents as unskilled or skilled laborers. Nationally, just 17 percent of college students in 1966 came from working- and lower-middle-class families.

According to Richard Sennett and Jonathan Cobb, working- and lower-middle-class students whom they studied in the 1960s frequently developed feelings of cultural and intellectual inferiority vis-à-vis more economically privileged and culturally secure undergraduates. In New Left circles, these activists often found themselves condescended to and ridiculed because they were unfamiliar with the jargon employed, and authorities cited, by middle- and upper-middle-class students. Raised in a cultural milieu that placed a premium upon clear and direct discourse, less privileged activists became frustrated with the upper-middle-class students' opaque language.

Working- and lower-middle-class student activists experienced enormous psychic tensions. Not infrequently, these activists' parents did not support their decision to go to college, considering it a wasteful endeavor and an indication that they were too lazy to work. If supportive, working- and lower-middle-class parents wanted their children to concentrate on studying, not protesting, which would alienate future employers and get them in trouble with the government. Less privileged student activists, in contrast to middle- and upper-middle-class radicals, also had to concern themselves with paying for their educations since their parents had little disposable income and often opposed their enrollment in the university in the first place. This imposed limits on their degree of activism, giving rise to feelings that they were not doing enough to stop the war.

Finally, less privileged student activists, whose parents were frequently anticommunist New Deal Democrats, found themselves choosing between their new political orientation and their upbringing. Jewish student activists, at least, had generally liberal to left-of-center parents who supported their children's activism. This was not the case for working- and lower-middle-class activists who, as Texas SDS organizer Jeff Shero bitterly noted, often had to break with their past.

> If you were a New York student and became a member of SDS, it was essentially joining a political organization, which was a common experience. In Texas to join SDS meant breaking with your family, it meant being cut off—it was like in early Rome joining a Christian sect—and the break was so much more total, getting involved with something like SDS you had to be much more highly committed, and you were in a sense freed, 'cause you'd get written off. If you were from Texas, in SDS, you were a bad motherfucker, you couldn't go home for Christmas. Your mother didn't say, "Oh, isn't that nice, you're involved. We supported the republicans in the Spanish Civil War, and now you're in SDS and I'm glad to see you're socially concerned." In most of those places it meant, *"You Goddamn Communist."*

In Shero's terminology, "New York student" is to be understood as Jewish, while a "Texas student" is a stand-in for working- and lower-middle-class Catholic, Baptist, or Methodist. This quotation encompasses far more cultural tensions than just those represented by regional differences.

Student activists, their political values shaped by their varied class and cultural backgrounds, also dwelled in separate realities; there really never was one antiwar movement, or one New Left. Instead, there were in the 1960s many movements and any number of New Lefts, linked by their opposition to the Vietnam War or by their affiliation with [the] SDS, a national organization only in name. After Tom Hayden, joined by Michigan and Oberlin College students, had completed the 1962 *Port Huron Statement*, SDS's manifesto, the privileged activists were able to get an audience with the historian and Kennedy administration adviser, Arthur Schlesinger, Jr. At this meeting they proclaimed the birth of a new social reform movement. Similarly, Todd Gitlin, an early SDS president, and the Harvard peace group TOCSIN, had a back channel into the White House at the beginning of the 1960s. Such access was not extended to most university activists. Indeed, state university student activists never dreamed that such access was possible. Moreover, such student radicals had their energies consumed at their own campuses in simply trying to gain the right to be politically active. Securing this basic right, one that state university administrators did not consider to be a right at all, involved a great deal of effort. The possibility of meeting with a White House representative, then, was so remote as to be ludicrous; they often could not even get an appointment with the dean of student affairs. Further, the ideological struggles within the SDS National Office in Chicago were of little concern to the rank-and-file activists; their attentions were focused on the local struggle for peace and social justice.

MICHIGAN STATE UNIVERSITY

Born in the Bronx to working-class German-Polish Jewish parents, Edward Gewirts (later anglicized to Garrett) entered Michigan State College in 1937. With an uncle serving as an official in the then militant American Federation of Labor, Gewirts gravitated toward campus leftist groups. Although an associate of several East Lansing radicals, Gewirts never joined the Communist party and broke off all relations with Moscow-oriented campus organizations after the 1939 Stalin-Hitler Pact—a decision he mentioned to a dean who noted his break and which subsequently saved him from "the worse ravages of the McCarthyite inquisition of the early Fifties." Eventually, Gewirts married a Methodist school teacher who supported Henry Wallace's 1948 presidential candidacy and settled in Kalamazoo, Michigan. The Garretts became active in local Democratic party politics and were frightened by the televised Army-McCarthy hearings.

The Garretts' liberalism and ties to Michigan State influenced their son's politics and led him to East Lansing in 1961. Excited by the Cuban revolution and exposed to the cold war dissent of such liberal magazines as the *Nation* and the *New Republic*, Jan Garrett, a scholarship student, joined the university's model United Nations (UN), which attracted the most socially aware students on campus. Garrett subsequently refused to participate in compulsory ROTC [Reserve Officer Training Corps], involved himself with free speech issues on the campus, and helped to revive the Young Socialist Club (YSC).

At least as early as 1961, [MSU president John Hannah] had authorized the university's Department of Public Safety (DPS) to spy upon and infiltrate activist campus organizations, sending names and photographs of student protestors to the Michigan Red Squad. One student informant infiltrated the YSC and incorrectly identified Al Meyers, a political science professor and anticommunist social democrat, as its faculty sponsor. The university also employed as informants *State News'* reporters who provided photographs and phone tips that enabled the DPS to collect several file drawers of data on student groups by the early 1960s. Garrett's efforts to revive the YSC, and invite a Communist, Robert Thompson, to speak at MSU in 1962–1963, elicited overt university hostility.

The *State News* dramatically headlined the YSC's invitation, "Young Socialists Sponsor Red." Livid, Hannah denied university facilities to Thompson, exerted pressure on the student government president to revoke the YSC's charter, and met with, and chastised, two YSC members. At that meeting, the MSU president read to the students excerpts from [the House Un-American Activities Committee's] "100 Things to Know about Communism." The MSU board of trustees, belatedly informed by Hannah that he had banned Thompson from the campus, divided, with a large minority affirming the right of a Communist to speak at the university. Trustee Don Stevens, noting that his anticommunist credentials dated from the 1930s as an activist in the Congress of Industrial Organizations (CIO), supported the YSC invitation. The Lansing ACLU [American Civil Liberties Union] and faculty activists Larrowe and Repas joined the fight to uphold free speech, as did MSU Humanist Society leader Peter Werbe, who later became an editor of the Detroit-based underground newspaper, *Fifth Estate*. Ultimately, the Delta Sigma Phi fraternity offered its backyard to Thompson and a thousand curious people gathered there, a considerable number coming to heckle his speech.

While the YSC-Hannah confrontation radicalized few students, it did serve to underscore MSU's changing political environment. Larry Lack, a Goldwater supporter who grew up in a working-class Baltimore, Maryland, neighborhood, came to MSU in 1961 and participated in the university's model UN. Partly as a result of associating in the model UN with "the sons and daughters of African revolutionaries" who had been recruited to the university by the school's aggressive international affairs programs, Lack became interested in American race relations and informally affiliated with the MSU Friends of the Student Non-Violent Coordinating Committee (SNCC). After listening to Ivanhoe Donaldson speak at MSU, Lack went south with the civil rights activist to deliver textbooks to a black college. While driving through Georgia, they were arrested and Donaldson severely beaten. Appalled, Lack moved to the left and after graduating from MSU in 1963 became a reporter for the underground newspaper, the Los Angeles *Free Press*.

Lack's radicalization was the product of an increasingly assertive civil rights movement, and part of a national as well as local process that swept up larger and larger numbers of students. In East Lansing, the MSU Friends of [the] SNCC initiated the picketing of local businesses that discriminated against the university's burgeoning African, Asian, and Latin American student population. Picketing gave way to marches on behalf of open housing in the city, culminating in the largest mass arrest in East Lansing's history in 1965. Fifty-nine students marched on city hall and wound up in the county prison. Against this backdrop of escalated protest, dozens of student volunteers took part in the Student Tutorial Education Project (STEP) and spent their summers teaching economically deprived blacks at Rust College in Holly Springs, Mississippi. In that intensely hostile and racist environment, MSU students learned how to form support networks and to sustain commitment. When such students returned to East Lansing, their experiences had prepared them to challenge the university administration and the Vietnam War.

Immediately after the march on city hall, the *State News* published the names of the students who had been arrested and "tarnished" the image of the university. Although not noted by the *State News,* at least eight of the students were members of the then straight-laced campus SDS chapter. Established in 1963 by a handful of discontented history, political science, and sociology graduate students, [the] SDS sharply criticized American cold war foreign policy and a variety of university rules and regulations. Unlike its sister chapter in Ann Arbor, [the] MSU SDS claimed a good share of working- and lower-middle-class students. Jack Sattel, a MSU SDS leader, came from a working-class, German immigrant family. In high school, Sattel "had some sense of being an outsider . . . since the majority of my friends were solidly middle class and college-bound." Upon graduation from high school, Sattel enlisted in the air force. Trained in electronics and the operation of nuclear weapons, which "scared the hell out of" him, he began "to read seriously about politics and history" and developed a new view of the nation's foreign policy. His political consciousness was heightened as a result of witnessing Japanese student peace demonstrations and developing friendships with black soldiers who were excited by the Freedom Rides. By the time Sattel left the air force in 1961 to go to MSU, he considered himself a radical.

Noticing the existence of the Young Socialist Club in the fall 1961 MSU catalogue, Sattel indicated his interest in the group on his application to the university, a fact subsequently noted in his Michigan Red Squad file. "The size and anonymity of MSU," Sattel recalled, did not distrub him "after four years in the Air Force . . . although it clearly seemed to bewilder a lot of the undergraduates and seemed to anger them." He reserved his anger "for things *outside* the university: nuclear war; racial injustice; poverty."

In 1962–1963, Sattel started to attend YSC meetings, which he came to view as:

arcane and frustrating—arguments about sectarian left-political issues . . . however, the group did some support work for the Southern student movement,

brought in some trade-unionists, began demonstrating against racial discrimination in off-campus housing, etc. It served as a way of connecting people and
issues—it gave me a sense of purpose/direction while also pursuing my degree.
At the same time, I always had one or two friends who were *not* political . . .
with whom it was more fun to go out and raise hell. . . . Most of this group was
too serious to have much fun with. I saw politics as a way to *transform* society in
more open, satisfying ways; they tended to see politics as an end to itself.

It was the serious politicos of the YSC, Ed and Sheri Lessin, Paul Schiff, Brian
Keleher, Harvey Goldman—a 15-year-old scholarship student—and Stu and
Janet (Goldwasser) Dowty—frequent travelers to Ann Arbor and friends of Al
Haber—who founded [the] MSU SDS.

In its early days, [the] MSU SDS was very much a family affair, with members frequently entering into relationships that culminated in marriage. Sue Van
Eyck, whose lower-middle-class parents lived in Royal Oak, Michigan, came
from a conservative Republican background, offset somewhat by the influence
of her neighbor and rebellious schoolmate, Tom Hayden. The prohibitive costs
of attending Michigan, and realization that she would not fit in socially with the
more affluent students at Ann Arbor, led her to MSU in 1961. At the university,
she was exposed to activist guest speakers and met and married Jack Sattel.
Both became heavily involved in the antiwar movement: Jack as president of
[the] MSU SDS and Sue as president of the East Lansing chapter of the Women's
International League for Peace and Freedom.

The Sattels deeply believed in nonviolent protest and identified with community and labor union organizing. Sue had no patience for those in the MSU
and the national SDS who advocated "rock throwing," describing such activists
as the "sons and daughters of the ruling class" who "wanted 'to win this' and to
win (bring revolution) soon . . . due to their being used to getting what they
wanted if they wanted it bad enough." Jack also did not care for the upper-middle-class Columbia and Michigan SDSers who came to East Lansing in the late
1960s to sow discord within [the] MSU SDS and urge violent confrontations
with the university administration. Similarly, MSU SDS member George Fish, a
scholarship student from an Indianapolis, Indiana, lower-middle-class German
Catholic family, railed against the elitist Michigan and National Office
(Chicago) SDS travelers. Fish viewed them as "patronizing colonizers" bringing
light to economically and intellectually inferior MSU SDSers. Class antagonisms
between the MSU and Michigan SDS, and among MSU SDSers, mounted
throughout the 1960s and contributed to the factionalism of the East Lansing
chapter after upper-middle-class Columbia and Michigan SDSers seized control
of the National Office in 1969.

While class conflict divided [the] MSU SDS, the East Lansing chapter was
largely spared the discord resulting from overt male chauvinism. At the outset,
female MSU SDSers such as Sue Sattel, Sheri Lessin, Denise Ryan, Kaye Bradley
(who became a regional traveler in the south), and Carlie Tanner (later a National Office organizer) played key roles in formulating chapter policies and tactics. Initially, these women, heirs to a tradition of female subordination, had to
force themselves "to speak up at meetings" and to "be taken seriously and not

just get the coffee." Their efforts to influence the direction of the chapter succeeded, and they received the support of "enlightened" male SDSers who were not threatened by female assertiveness. The MSU SDS's relatively egalitarian relationship between the sexes was exceptional. In general, sexism pervaded the New Left.

An important religious-left alternative to the secular-left SDS, the University Christian Movement (UCM) emerged in East Lansing in the mid-1960s. The UCM, founded in September 1966, evolved from the religious, apolitical National Student Christian Federation. UCM's founders proclaimed that God acted on earth only through political modes; fundamental social change could be realized by activist humans working toward "community dialogue, diversity, freedom, and the abolition of bourgeois complacency through radical education." MSU UCM members, thirty in number by the fall of 1966, came from rural, moderate-to-conservative, white, evangelical Protestant families. Seemingly, their backgrounds precluded radical political activism, but their rooted home-grown religious convictions, most of all their belief that all human life was sacred, led them to disavow the war. Further, they argued that if Christian Americans truly believed in God and democracy, they could not fight on behalf of an undemocratic, immoral South Vietnamese government.

The UCM's emphasis upon social issues, and its evangelical zeal for converting students to the cause of peace, served to bring together Catholics, Jews, Methodists, and Quakers, surmounting theological differences. This united religious front, however, had a price. UCM advisers Lynn Jondahl and Keith Pohl became the subjects of intense police surveillance, and Michigan Red Squad agents broke into the University Methodist Church to copy documents pertaining to local clergy-faculty draft counseling efforts. Moreover, older hawkish faculty and residents at the University Methodist Church resented the younger Methodists' unpatriotic, morally self-righteous opposition to the war. Methodist UCM activists found the generation gap too great to bridge and proceeded to drop out of the church. In October 1966, the University Methodist Church held three services every Sunday for eight hundred students. By 1968, only fifty students showed up for the one remaining service.

[The] MSU UCM organized students on three levels. At the first level, students formed support networks and discussed their problems in adjusting to the impersonal multiversity. Students in the first level who became interested in civil rights and peace issues graduated to the second level and joined Depth Education Groups (DEGs). Those students in the DEGs who had studied a particular social issue and had become convinced that political action was required flowed into the third level, where activist cadres were spawned. These cadres organized teach-ins, rallies, and formulated strategies with the SDS. It was through this intense, politicizing indoctrination in social interaction that a once conservative religion major from western Michigan, Dave Stockman (later President Reagan's director of the Office of Management and Budget), became a MSU antiwar leader.

Given Stockman's subsequent, controversial political career, it is necessary to point out that he in no way later set aside his commitment to social reform.

The bright and energetic child of solid, conservative farmers, whether as anti-war organizer or as Reagan's budget director, possessed an ingrained distrust of the federal government, particularly of the [Defense Department]. He also consistently championed the cause of civil rights and risked his congressional seat in the 1970s by denouncing racists in his district. Sue Sattel, who worked with Stockman on the 1967 Vietnam Summer program, praised him as a committed and enthusiastic peace worker, as did Jondahl and Pohl. When a hawkish student in April 1967 denounced [the] MSU SDS as unAmerican, Stockman defended the radicals who had pledged to resist the draft as America's true patriots:

> A nation is not defined by the particular policy, of a particular administration, in power at a particular point in time. Rather, the genius of a nation is expressed in those lofty ideals and broad spiritual currents which have threaded their way through the fabric of its history. In our country these ideals are embodied in concepts like: distributive justice, limited government; individual freedom of speech, assembly and worship; and the rights to life, liberty and the pursuit of happiness. . . . Many of us feel that American intervention in Vietnam runs contrary to the spirit of this historical tradition. Therefore, our commitment to the real core values and ideals that have made this nation great, demands that we oppose the war.
>
> There have been many expressions of this opposition. One of them being the SDS anti-draft union. . . . I think the action of many of those . . . is motivated by a broader courage than simple, blind obedience, and by a sense of responsibility to values higher than the shallow rhetoric of the present administration.

Stockman never repudiated the sentiments he expressed on behalf of [the] SDS; the Methodist populist did, however, come to loathe the organization after it became committed to violence in 1969.

A disproportionate number of students in the MSU SDS, the UCM, and the campus antiwar movement in general were National Merit Scholarship recipients. In 1963, in order to enhance the university's national prominence, MSU began a campaign to recruit greater numbers of scholarship students and to create special honors programs with close student-faculty interaction. Hundreds of highly motivated, sensitive, intelligent Merit Scholars flocked to East Lansing. Here they were soon disenchanted with the large, impersonal, bureaucratic nature of the university and with Hannah's insistence upon *in loco parentis*, which cast a shadow across every aspect of their social lives. These alienated scholars, soured by an administration promising more than it could deliver, formed mutual support groups, developed close relationships, and became reform-minded activists. In 1965, when MSU's enrollment of Merit Scholars surpassed the number attending Harvard, *Look* magazine profiled the university's academic superstars. Within a year, MSU's academic superstars had acquired a new collective label: "John Hannah's Worst Nightmares."

Hannah's nightmares filled the ranks of the Committee for Student Rights and [the] SDS and founded, in 1965, the first campus-based underground newspaper in the nation, *The Paper*. Merit Scholar-SDS reporters for *The Paper* honored Hannah with a comic strip, "Land Grant Man." Inspired by "Batman," scholarship student Steve Badrich, the product of a working-class, Yugoslavian immigrant family, conceived the idea of the comic strip. With dialogue by Jane Munn, the scrappy daughter of legendary MSU football coach and athletic director Clarence "Biggie" Munn, President "Palindrome" (Hannah), once he thumped a hoe on the floor and shouted the magic word "Poultry!" became the inept caped crusader, "Land Grant Man." Gleefully, the comic strip writers subjected Hannah's alter ego to acid trips, gang rape by sexually repressed coeds, and assault by his wife, who did not recognize him in the "Land Grant Man" costume.

The lèse-majesté explicit in "Land Grant Man" reflected the impact of events, chiefly the escalation of the Vietnam War, on activists' attitudes toward authority. It also signaled a transforming cultural-political style on the left. Activist students who entered the university in 1965 were prepared to act upon the philosophy Jack Sattel had embraced in 1962—the belief that humor and fun were integral to, and not mutually exclusive of, politics. One MSU SDSer, acting upon this idea, acquired legendary status following his summons to report for induction into the military. During his physical examination, the medical doctor ordered the SDSer to drop his pants and to bend over. The doctor noticed something protruding from the student's anus and, shocked, asked "what the hell" it was. Nonchalantly, the SDSer replied, "Oh, that's my pet rat." He was not drafted. Humor and politics were also deployed against the local news media. A group of MSU SDSers, living off-campus in the facetiously dubbed "Lenin House," learned that a news reporter was coming over to investigate rumors that [the] SDS was recruiting volunteers to fight in the North Vietnamese Army. The gullible reporter subsequently witnessed students performing military drills.

MSU student antiwar activists were overwhelmingly of northern and western European (72 percent), or Jewish (19 percent), stock, as well as male (75 percent). (See Table 12.1.) They largely majored in the liberal arts and the social sciences (76 percent) and were undergraduates (87 percent). A significant minority came from metropolitan areas (43 percent), and (46 percent) were not Michigan residents. Further, a disproportionate number were National Merit Scholarship-Honors College students (12 percent), and enrolled in the humanities and social science residential colleges (9 percent).

The significant characteristics of the MSU student antiwar movement become evident when they are compared to those of the overall student body. In 1969, 17 percent of MSU students were from out of state, while 46 percent of antiwar activists were not Michigan residents; Jews were 10 percent of the student body but 19 percent of activists; National Merit Scholarship-Honors College and residential college students constituted, respectively, 2 and 3 percent of the student body, compared to 12 and 9 percent of antiwar activists. Finally, business and science majors were underrepresented in the antiwar movement; 46 percent of the student body, and just 24 percent of peace activists.

Contrasts between the overall student body and members of [the] MSU SDS

TABLE 12-1 MSU Antiwar Student Activists, 1965–1972 (N = 263*)

	North-West European	South-East European	Jewish		
Ethnicity	72%	9%	19%		
Gender	Female 25%	Male 75%			
Major	Liberal Arts/ Social Science 76%	Business/ Science 24%			
Residence I	Metropolitan Area 43%	Large City 5%	Medium City 9%	Small City 14%	Small Town 30%
Residence II	In-state 54%	Out-of-state 46%			
Status	Undergraduate 87%	Graduate 13%			
Specific Academic Characteristics	National Merit Scholar/ Honors College 12%	Humanities and Social Science Residential College 9%			

*Of 349 names collected, I identified 263 (75%) as to majors, residence, and status. Figures reported for ethnicity and gender are derived from the entire data base.

are particularly striking. (See Table 12.2.) Compared to the student body at large and non-SDS antiwar students, [the] MSU SDS had fewer south and east European Catholics, disproportionately more Jews (24 percent), and somewhat greater numbers of females, although they were underrepresented given their campus total. By contrasting *just* liberal-dovish antiwar students to radicals, we learn that fewer SDSers (16 percent) majored in business and science than [did] non SDS antiwar students (29 percent), while a majority of the former (53 percent) came from metropolitan areas as opposed to a minority of the latter (35 percent). More SDSers claimed out-of-state residences (52 percent) than [did] non-SDS activists (42 percent), and were disproportionately National Merit Scholarship-Honors College (16 percent), and residential college (10 percent), students. [The] MSU SDS attracted to its ranks people who considered themselves culturally disfranchised from American society and the university: Jews, intellectuals, women, and urbanites transplanted into an alien environment that caused them to suffer culture shock.

To an extent, certain social characteristics of student antiwar activists and

TABLE 12-2 The MSU SDS, 1965–1970 (N = 109*)

	NORTH-WEST EUROPEAN	SOUTH-EAST EUROPEAN	JEWISH		
Ethnicity	71%	5%	24%		
	Female	Male			
Gender	29%	71%			
	Liberal Arts/ Social Science	Business/ Science			
Major	84%	16%			
	Metropolitan Area	Large City	Medium City	Small City	Small Town
Residence I	53%	4%	6%	12%	25%
	In-state	Out-of-state			
Residence II	48%	52%			
	Undergraduate	Graduate			
Status	89%	11%			
	National Merit Scholar/ Honors College	Humanities and Social Science Residential College			
Specific Academic Characteristics	16%	10%			

*Of 145 names collected, I identified 109 (75%) as to majors, residence, and status. Figures reported for ethnicity and gender are derived from the entire data base.

SDSers differed only slightly from those of prowar students. (See Table 12.3.) A caveat is in order. By taking a public stand in favor of military intervention in Indochina, prowar activists set themselves apart from the apathetic or anticommunist majority on campus. If we accept the fact that liberal arts and social science majors are more prone to speak out and be engaged in the political process than their career-oriented business and science counterparts, then it should be no surprise that they comprise the majority of *prowar,* as well as antiwar, activists. Nonetheless, business and science majors have a greater propensity to make a prowar, rather than antiwar, stand.

Prowar activists differed slightly from the overall MSU student body, at least in terms of majors and representation in the honors and residential colleges. On the other hand, a third of MSU prowar student activists came from out of state, nearly twice the norm, although 9 percent were Jews, nearly their proportional representation on campus. It is when prowar students are compared to non-SDS antiwar students and SDSers, in terms of gender, residential status, and enrollment in the honors and residential colleges, that contrasts become striking. Female students, if inclined to become activists, gravitated more fre-

TABLE 12-3 MSU Prowar Student Activists, 1965–1972 (N = 112*)

	NORTH-WEST EUROPEAN	SOUTH-EAST EUROPEAN	JEWISH		
Ethnicity	82%	9%	9%		
	Female	Male			
Gender	15%	85%			
	Liberal Arts/ Social Science	Business/ Science			
Major	57%	43%			
	Metropolitan Area	Large City	Medium City	Small City	Small Town
Residence I	35%	6%	11%	12%	36%
	In-state	Out-of-state			
Residence II	67%	33%			
	Undergraduate	Graduate			
Status	87%	13%			
	National Merit Scholar/ Honors College	Residential College			
Specific Academic Characteristics	2%	2%			

*Of 148 names collected, I identified 112 (76%) as to majors, residence, and status. Figures reported for ethnicity and gender are derived from the entire data base.

quently to the left than to the anticommunist center or right. Further, antiwar students, SDS and non-SDS alike, were more often from out of state than prowar students. Although there is no difference between non-SDS antiwar students and prowar students as far as metropolitan residence is concerned, there is a sharp divergence between MSU SDSers and prowar students who came from such locales: 53 percent as opposed to 35 percent. Finally, honors college and residential college students were disproportionately antiwar, rather than prowar.

While the locus of student antiwar protest and organization was largely confined to the "Old Campus," where the liberal arts and social science departments were situated, gaining few business and science majors on the "New Campus" across the Red Cedar River, prowar students after 1966 exercised little negative influence in shaping antiwar protest. MSU student peace activists had momentum and went on the offensive in 1966, reasonably assured that prowar student resistance would be sporadic and of little political consequence. Antiwar activists were also aided, ironically, by the outspokenness of anticommunist Vietnam Project veterans and President Hannah who, inadvertently, demonstrated the university's considerable role in creating the Indochinese conflict. Also, Hannah's zealous anticommunism, as well as his strong ties to the defense establishment, made him a perfect foil for SDSers. He was their best recruiter. Consequently, antiwar activists found that the MSU student body was relatively easy to mobilize and radicalize. . . .

The emergence of student political activism at state schools predated the 1964 uprising at Berkeley, which, according to various scholars, spawned white student activism. Student activists at Kent State, Michigan State, and SUNY-Buffalo, their numbers varying from campus to campus, were involved in free speech protests several months prior to the Berkeley Free Speech movement. In addition, student activists at Kent State, Michigan State, and Penn State had established antiwar organizations months, if not years, before the military escalation of the Vietnam War and the founding of the famous Berkeley Vietnam Day Committee.

Moreover, contrary to scholars who have contended that state university student activists were less articulate, intelligent, and effective than their elite-educated counterparts, the fact remains that eloquent, bright, and dynamic, as well as nationally prominent, antiwar student leaders emerged from less well-regarded universities: Carl Davidson, Clinton Deveaux, Howie Emmer, Carl Oglesby, and Andy Stapp, to list only a few. These activists contributed a moral and political approach to the peace movement, an approach shaped by their class and cultural values. Set forth by particular activists were possibilities for CIO-inspired student syndicalism and Old Testament–influenced Marxist liberation theology. However, class and cultural differences among activists, and between activists and community residents, ultimately undermined such sweeping visions, leaving in their wake political fragmentation and bitter conflict.

The influence of the local environment on the development of each campus' antiwar movement was significant. Students did react to national events and the ebb and flow of the civil rights and anti–Vietnam War movements. At the same time, though, students' tactics and perceptions of American society reflected their immediate cultural and political environment. The type of relationship antiwar students had with university administrators, prowar students, law enforcement agencies, and community residents determined the mode of dissent as well as the ways in which confrontation unfolded. Each campus was quite different from the others in such regards and bore little semblance to the so-called activist schools: Berkeley, Columbia, Harvard, and Michigan.

State university student activists greatly differed from elite university protestors as far as class and cultural origins are concerned. Activists from the less prestigious universities drew upon a diverse membership of red diaper babies, upper-middle-class secularized Protestants, and working- and lower-middle-class Catholics and Protestants. At the elite schools, student activists were overwhelmingly middle and upper middle class. Moreover, even though Jewish students represented a significant part of [the] SDS and the New Left at the state universities, their numbers, with the exception of SUNY-Buffalo, were much greater at schools such as Columbia and Michigan (anywhere from 50 to 75 percent). Finally, the state universities claimed far more Catholic student activists than the heavily WASP [White, Anglo-Saxon Protestant] elite schools.

SOURCES

Vietnam

For more than two decades, the United States tried, and failed, to create a Vietnam suitable to its own vision of the postwar world. This failure became most apparent in the 1960s, when the fighting of the war divided Americans into bitter factions. Apologists for John Kennedy believed that he would have avoided full-scale involvement. But Kennedy had remarked that a withdrawal from Vietnam would mean collapse in Southeast Asia; and by 1963 he had sent 15,000 advisers to the country, more than fifteen times Dwight Eisenhower's commitment. Lyndon Johnson also believed in the domino theory and defined the Vietnam problem as simple Communist aggression, and in 1964, he inaugurated systematic air attacks on North Vietnam. But neither the air war nor an additional half-million American troops were sufficient to bring anything resembling victory. Even before the January 1968 Tet offensive, when Viet Cong and North Vietnamese attacks on major South Vietnamese cities made clear that the American claim to be winning the war was a sham, many Americans had come to question the war in moral terms. Over 200,000 marched against the war in Washington, D.C., in 1967. When Richard Nixon in 1970 moved ground troops into Cambodia, students closed down many colleges and universities in protest. By 1973, as Nixon withdrew the last of the nation's ground troops, the Eisenhower consensus lay in ruins.

To illustrate the polarization that the Vietnam War produced, and to offer some sense of how reasonable people could find themselves at loggerheads over this conflict, we have assembled two disparate views on the war. The first, a 1965 address by President Lyndon Johnson, reveals how a socially engaged, activist president could see the war as a high priority and, indeed, allow the war to interfere with his domestic agenda. The second, a 1967 speech by the Reverend Martin Luther King, Jr., announced his opposition to the war. It was a courageous decision, for it set King apart from his own political party and identified him in certain respects with the radical, "black power" side of the civil rights movement.

How did Johnson defend the war in Vietnam? Can you find flaws or weaknesses in his argument? How did King justify his new stance of opposition? Do you find his arguments convincing?

Lyndon Johnson

Pattern for Peace in Southeast Asia
(1965)

Last week seventeen nations sent their views to some two dozen countries having an interest in Southeast Asia. We are joining those seventeen countries and
stating our American policy tonight, which we believe will contribute toward
peace in this area of the world.

I have come here to review once again with my own people the views of the
American government.

Tonight Americans and Asians are dying for a world where each people
may choose its own path to change. This is the principle for which our ancestors
fought in the valleys of Pennsylvania. It is a principle for which our sons fight
tonight in the jungles of Vietnam.

Vietnam is far away from this quiet campus. We have no territory there, nor
do we seek any. The war is dirty and brutal and difficult. And some 400 young
men, born into an America that is bursting with opportunity and promise, have
ended their lives on Vietnam's steaming soil.

Why must we take this painful road? Why must this nation hazard its ease,
its interest, and its power for the sake of a people so far away?

We fight because we must fight if we are to live in a world where every
country can shape its own destiny, and only in such a world will our own freedom be finally secure.

This kind of world will never be built by bombs or bullets. Yet the infirmi-
ties of man are such that force must often precede reason and the waste of war,
the works of peace. We wish that this were not so. But we must deal with the
world as it is, if it is ever to be as we wish.

The world as it is in Asia is not a serene or peaceful place.

The first reality is that North Vietnam has attacked the independent nation
of South Vietnam. Its object is total conquest. Of course, some of the people of
South Vietnam are participating in attack on their own government. But trained
men and supplies, orders and arms, flow in a constant stream from north to
south.

This support is the heartbeat of the war.

And it is a war of unparalleled brutality. Simple farmers are the targets of
assassination and kidnaping. Women and children are strangled in the night because their men are loyal to their government. And helpless villages are ravaged
by sneak attacks. Large-scale raids are conducted on towns, and terror strikes in
the heart of cities.

The confused nature of this conflict cannot mask the fact that it is the new
face of an old enemy.

Speech made at Johns Hopkins University, Baltimore, Maryland, April 17, 1965, Department of State
Bulletin, April 26, 1965, pp. 606–610.

Over this war—and all Asia—is another reality: the deepening shadow of Communist China. The rulers in Hanoi are urged on by Beijing. This is a regime that has destroyed freedom in Tibet, attacked India, and has been condemned by the United Nations for aggression in Korea. It is a nation that is helping the forces of violence in almost every continent. The contest in Vietnam is part of a wider pattern of aggressive purposes.

WHY ARE WE IN SOUTH VIETNAM?

Why are these realities our concern? Why are we in South Vietnam?

We are there because we have a promise to keep. Since 1954 every American president has offered support to the people of South Vietnam. We have helped to build, and we have helped to defend. Thus, over many years, we have made a national pledge to help South Vietnam defend its independence.

And I intend to keep that promise.

To dishonor that pledge, to abandon this small and brave nation to its enemies, and to the terror that must follow, would be an unforgivable wrong.

We are also there to strengthen world order. Around the globe, from Berlin to Thailand, are people whose well-being rests in part on the belief that they can count on us if they are attacked. To leave Vietnam to its fate would shake the confidence of all these people in the value of an American commitment and in the value of America's word. The result would be increased unrest and instability, and even wider war.

We are also there because there are great stakes in the balance. Let no one think for a moment that retreat from Vietnam would bring an end to conflict. The battle would be renewed in one country and then another. The central lesson of our time is that the appetite of aggression is never satisfied. To withdraw from one battlefield means only to prepare for the next. We must say in Southeast Asia—as we did in Europe—in the words of the Bible: "Hitherto shalt thou come, but no further."

There are those who say that all our effort there will be futile—that China's power is such that it is bound to dominate all Southeast Asia. But there is no end to that argument until all the nations of Asia are swallowed up.

There are those who wonder why we have a responsibility there. Well, we have it there for the same reason that we have a responsibility for the defense of Europe. World War II was fought in both Europe and Asia, and when it ended we found ourselves with continued responsibility for the defense of freedom.

Our objective is the independence of South Vietnam and its freedom from attack. We want nothing for ourselves—only that the people of South Vietnam be allowed to guide their own country in their own way. We will do everything necessary to reach that objective, and we will do only what is absolutely necessary.

In recent months attacks on South Vietnam were stepped up. Thus it became necessary for us to increase our response and to make attacks by air. This is not a change of purpose. It is a change in what we believe that purpose requires.

We do this in order to slow down aggression.

We do this to increase the confidence of the brave people of South Vietnam who have bravely borne this brutal battle for so many years with so many casualties.

And we do this to convince the leaders of North Vietnam—and all who seek to share their conquest—of a simple fact:

We will not be defeated.

We will not grow tired.

We will not withdraw, either openly or under the cloak of a meaningless agreement.

We know that air attacks alone will not accomplish all these purposes. But it is our best and prayerful judgment that they are a necessary part of the surest road to peace.

THE PATH OF PEACEFUL SETTLEMENT

We hope that peace will come swiftly. But that is in the hands of others besides ourselves. And we must be prepared for a long continued conflict. It will require patience as well as bravery—the will to endure as well as the will to resist.

I wish it were possible to convince others with words of what we now find it necessary to say with guns and planes: armed hostility is futile—our resources are equal to any challenge—because we fight for values and we fight for principle, rather than territory or colonies, our patience and our determination are unending.

Once this is clear, then it should also be clear that the only path for reasonable men is the path of peaceful settlement. Such peace demands an independent South Vietnam—securely guaranteed and able to shape its own relationships to all others—free from outside interference—tied to no alliance—a military base for no other country.

These are the essentials of any final settlement.

We will never be second in the search for such a peaceful settlement in Vietnam.

There may be many ways to this kind of peace: in discussion or negotiation with the governments concerned; in large groups or in small ones; in the reaffirmation of old agreements or their strengthening with new ones.

We have stated this position over and over again fifty times and more to friend and foe alike. And we remain ready with this purpose for unconditional discussions.

And until that bright and necessary day of peace we will try to keep conflict from spreading. We have no desire to see thousands die in battle—Asians or Americans. We have no desire to devastate that which the people of North Vietnam have built with toil and sacrifice. We will use our power with restraint and with all the wisdom that we can command.

But we will use it.

A COOPERATIVE EFFORT FOR DEVELOPMENT

This war, like most wars, is filled with terrible irony. For what do the people of North Vietnam want? They want what their neighbors also desire—food for their hunger, health for their bodies, a chance to learn, progress for their country, and an end to the bondage of material misery. And they would find all these things far more readily in peaceful association with others than in the endless course of battle.

These countries of Southeast Asia are homes for millions of impoverished people. Each day these people rise at dawn and struggle through until the night to wrest existence from the soil. They are often wracked by diseases, plagued by hunger, and death comes at the early age of forty.

Stability and peace do not come easily in such a land. Neither independence nor human dignity will ever be won, though, by arms alone. It also requires the works of peace. The American people have helped generously in times past in these works, and now there must be a much more massive effort to improve the life of man in that conflict-torn corner of our world.

The first step is for the countries of Southeast Asia to associate themselves in a greatly expanded cooperative effort for development. We would hope that North Vietnam would take its place in the common effort just as soon as peaceful cooperation is possible.

The United Nations is already actively engaged in development in this area, and as far back as 1961 I conferred with our authorities in Vietnam in connection with their work there. And I would hope tonight that the secretary-general of the United Nations could use the prestige of his great office and his deep knowledge of Asia to initiate, as soon as possible, with the countries of that area, a plan for cooperation in increased development.

For our part I will ask the Congress to join in a billion-dollar American investment in this effort as soon as it is under way. And I would hope that all other industrialized countries, including the Soviet Union, will join in this effort to replace despair with hope and terror with progress.

The task is nothing less than to enrich the hopes and existence of more than a hundred million people. And there is much to be done.

The vast Mekong River can provide food and water and power on a scale to dwarf even our own TVA [Tennessee Valley Authority]. The wonders of modern medicine can be spread through villages where thousands die every year from lack of care. Schools can be established to train people in the skills needed to manage the process of development. And these objectives, and more, are within the reach of a cooperative and determined effort.

I also intend to expand and speed up a program to make available our farm surpluses to assist in feeding and clothing the needy in Asia. We should not allow people to go hungry and wear rags while our own warehouses overflow with an abundance of wheat and corn and rice and cotton.

So I will very shortly name a special team of outstanding, patriotic, and distinguished Americans to inaugurate our participation in these programs. This team will be headed by Mr. Eugene Black, the very able former president of the World Bank.

THE DREAM OF OUR GENERATION

This will be a disorderly planet for a long time. In Asia, and elsewhere, the forces of the modern world are shaking old ways and uprooting ancient civilizations. There will be turbulence and struggle and even violence. Great social change—as we see in our own country—does not always come without conflict.

We must also expect that nations will on occasion be in dispute with us. It may be because we are rich, or powerful, or because we have made some mistakes, or because they honestly fear our intentions. However, no nation need ever fear that we desire their land, or to impose our will, or to dictate their institutions.

But we will always oppose the effort of one nation to conquer another nation.

We will do this because our own security is at stake.

But there is more to it than that. For our generation has a dream. It is a very old dream. But we have the power, and now we have the opportunity to make that dream come true.

For centuries nations have struggled among each other. But we dream of a world where disputes are settled by law and reason. And we will try to make it so.

For most of history men have hated and killed one another in battle. But we dream of an end to war. And we will try to make it so.

For all existence most men have lived in poverty, threatened by hunger. But we dream of a world where all are fed and charged with hope. And we will help to make it so.

The ordinary men and women of North Vietnam and South Vietnam, of China and India, of Russia and America, are brave people. They are filled with the same proportions of hate and fear, of love and hope. Most of them want the same things for themselves and their families. Most of them do not want their sons to ever die in battle, or to see their homes, or the homes of others, destroyed.

Well, this can be their world yet. Man now has the knowledge—always before denied—to make this planet serve the real needs of the people who live on it.

I know this will not be easy. I know how difficult it is for reason to guide passion, and love to master hate. The complexities of this world do not bow easily to pure and consistent answers.

But the simple truths are there just the same. We must all try to follow them as best we can.

POWER, WITNESS TO HUMAN FOLLY

We often say how impressive power is. But I do not find it impressive at all. The guns and the bombs, the rockets and the warships, are all symbols of human failure. They are necessary symbols. They protect what we cherish. But they are witness to human folly.

A dam built across a great river is impressive.

In the countryside where I was born, and where I live, I have seen the night illuminated, and the kitchen warmed, and the home heated, where once the cheerless night and the ceaseless cold held sway. And all this happened because electricity came to our area along the humming wires of the REA [Rural Electrification Administration]. Electrification of the countryside—yes, that, too, is impressive.

A rich harvest in a hungry land is impressive.

The sight of healthy children in a classroom is impressive.

These—not mighty arms—are the achievements that the American nation believes to be impressive. And if we are steadfast, the time may come when all other nations will also find it so.

Every night before I turn out the lights to sleep I ask myself this question: Have I done everything that I can do to unite this country? Have I done everything I can to help unite the world, to try to bring peace and hope to all the peoples of the world? Have I done enough?

Ask yourselves that question in your homes—and in this hall tonight. Have we, each of us, all done all we can do? Have we done enough?

We may well be living in the time foretold many years ago when it was said: "I call heaven and earth to record this day against you, that I have set before you life and death, blessing and cursing: therefore choose life, that both thou and thy seed may live."

This generation of the world must choose: destroy or build, kill or aid, hate or understand. We can do all these things on a scale that has never been dreamed of before.

Well, we will choose life. And so doing, we will prevail over the enemies within man, and over the natural enemies of all mankind.

Martin Luther King, Jr.

Declaration of Independence from the War in Vietnam (1967)

Over the past two years, as I have moved to break the betrayal of my own si-
lences and to speak from the burnings of my own heart, as I have called for radical departures from the destruction of Vietnam, many persons have questioned
me about the wisdom of my path. At the heart of their concerns this query has
often loomed large and loud: Why are *you* speaking about the war, Dr. King?
Why are *you* joining the voices of dissent? Peace and civil rights don't mix, they
say. Aren't you hurting the cause of your people, they ask. And when I hear
them, though I often understand the source of their concern, I am nevertheless
greatly saddened, for such questions mean that the inquirers have not really
known me, my commitment or my calling. Indeed, their questions suggest that
they do not know the world in which they live.

In the light of such tragic misunderstanding, I deem it of signal importance
to try to state clearly why I believe that the path from Dexter Avenue Baptist
Church—the church in Montgomery, Alabama, where I began my pastorage—
leads clearly to this sanctuary tonight.

I come to this platform to make a passionate plea to my beloved nation. This
speech is not addressed to Hanoi or to the National Liberation Front. It is not addressed to China or to Russia.

Nor is it an attempt to overlook the ambiguity of the total situation and the
need for a collective solution to the tragedy of Vietnam. Neither is it an attempt
to make North Vietnam or the National Liberation Front paragons of virtue, nor
to overlook the role they can play in a successful resolution of the problem.
While they both may have justifiable reasons to be suspicious of the good faith
of the United States, life and history give eloquent testimony to the fact that conflicts are never resolved without trustful give and take on both sides.

Tonight, however, I wish not to speak with Hanoi and the NLF, but rather
to my fellow Americans who, with me, bear the greatest responsibility in ending a conflict that has exacted a heavy price on both continents.

Since I am a preacher by trade, I suppose it is not surprising that I have
seven major reasons for bringing Vietnam into the field of my moral vision.
There is at the outset a very obvious and almost facile connection between the
war in Vietnam and the struggle I, and others, have been waging in America. A
few years ago there was a shining moment in that struggle. It seemed as if there
was a real promise of hope for the poor—both black and white—through the
Poverty Program. Then came the buildup in Vietnam, and I watched the program broken and eviscerated as if it were some idle political plaything of a society gone mad on war, and I knew that America would never invest in the necessary funds or energies in rehabilitation of its poor so long as Vietnam
continued to draw men and skills and money like some demonic, destructive

suction tube. So I was increasingly compelled to see the war as an enemy of the poor and to attack it as such.

Perhaps the more tragic recognition of reality took place when it became clear to me that the war was doing far more than devastating the hopes of the poor at home. It was sending their sons and their brothers and their husbands to fight and to die in extraordinarily high proportions relative to the rest of the population. We were taking the young black men who had been crippled by our society and sending them 8000 miles away to guarantee liberties in Southeast Asia that they had not found in Southwest Georgia and East Harlem. So we have been repeatedly faced with the cruel irony of watching Negro and white boys on TV screens as they kill and die together for a nation that has been unable to seat them together in the same schools. So we watch them in brutal solidarity burning the huts of a poor village, but we realize that they would never live on the same block in Detroit. I could not be silent in the face of such cruel manipulation of the poor.

My third reason grows out of my experience in the ghettos of the north over the last three years—especially the last three summers. As I have walked among the desperate, rejected, and angry young men, I have told them that Molotov cocktails and rifles would not solve their problems. I have tried to offer them my deepest compassion while maintaining my conviction that social change comes most meaningfully through nonviolent action. But, they asked, what about Vietnam? They asked if our own nation wasn't using massive doses of violence to solve its problems, to bring about the changes it wanted. Their questions hit home, and I knew that I could never again raise my voice against the violence of the oppressed in the ghettos without having first spoken clearly to the greatest purveyor of violence in the world today—my own government. . . .

And as I ponder the madness of Vietnam, my mind goes constantly to the people of that peninsula. I speak now not of the soldiers of each side, not of the junta in Saigon, but simply of the people who have been living under the curse of war for almost three continuous decades. I think of them, too, because it is clear to me that there will be no meaningful solution there until some attempt is made to know them and their broken cries.

They must see Americans as strange liberators. The Vietnamese proclaimed their own independence in 1945 after a combined French and Japanese occupation and before the Communist revolution in China. Even though they quoted the American Declaration of Independence in their own document of freedom, we refused to recognize them. Instead, we decided to support France in its reconquest of her former colony.

Our government felt then that the Vietnamese people were not "ready" for independence, and we again fell victim to the deadly western arrogance that has poisoned the international atmosphere for so long. With that tragic decision, we rejected a revolutionary government seeking self-determination, and a government that had been established not by China (for whom the Vietnamese have no great love) but by clearly indigenous forces that included some Communists. For the peasants, this new government meant real land reform, one of the most important needs in their lives.

For nine years following 1945 we denied the people of Vietnam the right of independence. For nine years we vigorously supported the French in their abortive effort to recolonize Vietnam.

Before the end of the war we were meeting 80 percent of the French war costs. Even before the French were defeated at Dien Bien Phu, they began to despair of their reckless action, but we did not. We encouraged them with our huge financial and military supplies to continue the war even after they had lost the will to do so.

After the French were defeated it looked as if independence and land reform would come again through the Geneva agreements. But instead there came the United States, determined that Ho [Chi Minh] should not unify the temporarily divided nation, and the peasants watched again as we supported one of the most vicious modern dictators—our chosen man, Premier [Ngo Dinh] Diem. The peasants watched and cringed as Diem ruthlessly routed out all opposition, supported their extortionist landlords and refused even to discuss reunification with the north. The peasants watched as all this was presided over by U.S. influence and then by increasing numbers of U.S. troops who came to help quell the insurgency that Diem's methods had aroused. When Diem was overthrown they may have been happy, but the long line of military dictatorships seemed to offer no real change—especially in terms of their need for land and peace.

The only change came from America as we increased our troop commitments in support of governments that were singularly corrupt, inept, and without popular support. All the while, the people read our leaflets and received regular promises of peace and democracy—and land reform. Now they languish under our bombs and consider us—not their fellow Vietnamese—the real enemy. They move sadly and apathetically as we herd them off the land of their fathers into concentration camps where minimal social needs are rarely met. They know they must move or be destroyed by our bombs. So they go.

They watch as we poison their water, as we kill a million acres of their crops. They must weep as the bulldozers destroy their precious trees. They wander into the hospitals, with at least twenty casualties from American firepower for each Viet Cong-inflicted injury. So far we may have killed a million of them— mostly children.

What do the peasants think as we ally ourselves with the landlords and as we refuse to put any action into our many words concerning land reform? What do they think as we test out our latest weapons on them, just as the Germans tested out new medicine and new tortures in the concentration camps of Europe? Where are the roots of the independent Vietnam we claim to be building?

Now there is little left to build on—save bitterness. Soon the only solid physical foundations remaining will be found at our military bases and in the concrete of the concentration camps we call "fortified hamlets." The peasants may well wonder if we plan to build our new Vietnam on such grounds as these. Could we blame them for such thoughts? We must speak for them and raise the questions they cannot raise. These too are our brothers.

Perhaps the more difficult but no less necessary task is to speak for those who have been designated as our enemies. What of the NLF—that strangely anonymous group we call VC or Communists? What must they think of us in America when they realize that we permitted the repression and cruelty of Diem that helped to bring them into being as a resistance group in the south? How can they believe in our integrity when now we speak of "aggression from the north" as if there were nothing more essential to the war? How can they trust us when now we charge *them* with violence after the murderous reign of Diem, and charge *them* with violence while we pour new weapons of death into their land?

How do they judge us when our officials know that their membership is less than 25 percent Communist and yet insist on giving them the blanket name? What must they be thinking when they know that we are aware of their control of major sections of Vietnam and yet we appear ready to allow national elections in which this highly organized political parallel government will have no part? They ask how we can speak of free elections when the Saigon press is censored and controlled by the military junta. And they are surely right to wonder what kind of new government we plan to help form without them—the only party in real touch with the peasants. They question our political goals, and they deny the reality of a peace settlement from which they will be excluded. Their questions are frighteningly relevant.

Here is the true meaning and value of compassion and nonviolence—when it helps us to see the enemy's point of view, to hear his questions, to know of his assessment of ourselves. For from his view we may indeed see the basic weaknesses of our own condition, and if we are mature, we may learn and grow and profit from the wisdom of the brothers who are called the opposition.

So, too, with Hanoi. In the north, where our bombs now pummel the land, and our mines endanger the waterways, we are met by a deep but understandable mistrust. In Hanoi are the men who led the nation to independence against the Japanese and the French, the men who sought membership in the French commonwealth and were betrayed by the weakness of Paris and the willfulness of the colonial armies. It was they who led a second struggle against French domination at tremendous costs, and then were persuaded at Geneva to give up, as a temporary measure, the land they controlled between the thirteenth and seventeenth parallels. After 1954 they watched us conspire with Diem to prevent elections that would have surely brought Ho Chi Minh to power over a united Vietnam, and they realized they had been betrayed again.

When we ask why they do not leap to negotiate, these things must be remembered. Also, it must be clear that the leaders of Hanoi considered the presence of American troops in support of the Diem regime to have been the initial military breach of the Geneva agreements concerning foreign troops, and they remind us that they did not begin to send in any large number of supplies or men until American forces had moved into the tens of thousands.

Hanoi remembers how our leaders refused to tell us the truth about the earlier North Vietnamese overtures for peace, how the president claimed that none existed when they had clearly been made. Ho Chi Minh has watched as America has spoken of peace and built up its forces, and now he has surely heard the increasing international rumors of American plans for an invasion of the north. Perhaps only his sense of humor and irony can save him when he hears the most powerful nation of the world speaking of aggression as it drops thousands of bombs on a poor, weak nation more than 8000 miles from its shores.

At this point, I should make it clear that while I have tried here to give a voice to the voiceless of Vietnam and to understand the arguments of those who are called enemy, I am as deeply concerned about our own troops there as any- thing else. For it occurs to me that what we are submitting them to in Vietnam is not simply the brutalizing process that goes on in any war where armies face each other and seek to destroy. We are adding cynicism to the process of death, for our troops must know after a short period there that none of the things we claim to be fighting for are really involved. Before long they must know that their government has sent them into a struggle among Vietnamese, and the more sophisticated surely realize that we are on the side of the wealthy and the secure while we create a hell for the poor.

Somehow this madness must cease. I speak as a child of God and brother to the suffering poor of Vietnam and the poor of America who are paying the dou- ble price of smashed hopes at home and death and corruption in Vietnam. I speak as a citizen of the world, for the world as it stands aghast at the path we have taken. I speak as an American to the leaders of my own nation. The great initiative in this war is ours. The initiative to stop must be ours. . . .

If we continue, there will be no doubt in my mind and in the mind of the world that we have no honorable intentions in Vietnam. It will become clear that our minimal expectation is to occupy it as an American colony, and men will not refrain from thinking that our maximum hope is to goad China into a war so that we may bomb her nuclear installations.

The world now demands a maturity of America that we may not be able to achieve. It demands that we admit that we have been wrong from the beginning of our adventure in Vietnam, that we have been detrimental to the life of her people. . . .

There is something seductively tempting about stopping there and sending us all off on what in some circles has become a popular crusade against the war in Vietnam. I say we must enter that struggle, but I wish to go on now to say something even more disturbing. The war in Vietnam is but a symptom of a far deeper malady within the American spirit, and if we ignore this sobering real- ity we will find ourselves organizing clergy- and laymen-concerned committees for the next generation. We will be marching and attending rallies without end unless there is a significant and profound change in American life and policy.

In 1957 a sensitive American official overseas said that it seemed to him that our nation was on the wrong side of a world revolution. During the past ten years we have seen emerge a pattern of suppression which now has justified the presence of U.S. military "advisers" in Venezuela. The need to maintain social stability for our investments accounts for the counterrevolutionary action of American forces in Guatemala. It tells why American helicopters are being used against guerrillas in Colombia and why American napalm and green beret forces have already been active against rebels in Peru. With such activity in mind, the words of John F. Kennedy come back to haunt us. Five years ago he said, "Those who make peaceful revolution impossible will make violent revolution inevitable."

Increasingly, by choice or by accident, this is the role our nation has taken— by refusing to give up the privileges and the pleasures that come from the immense profits of overseas investment.

I am convinced that if we are to get on the right side of the world revolution, we as a nation must undergo a radical revolution of values. When machines and computers, profit and property rights are considered more important than people, the giant triplets of racism, materialism, and militarism are incapable of being conquered.

A true revolution of values will soon cause us to question the fairness and justice of many of our past and present policies. True compassion is more than flinging a coin to a beggar; it is not haphazard and superficial. It comes to see that an edifice that produces beggars needs restructuring. A true revolution of values will soon look easily on the glaring contrast of poverty and wealth. With righteous indignation, it will look across the seas and see individual capitalists of the west investing huge sums of money in Asia, Africa, and South America, only to take the profits out with no concern for the social betterment of the countries, and say: "This is not just." It will look at our alliance with the landed gentry of Latin America and say: "This is not just." The western arrogance of feeling that it has everything to teach others and nothing to learn from them is not just. A true revolution of values will lay hands on the world order and say of war: "This way of settling differences is not just." This business of burning human beings with napalm, of filling our nation's homes with orphans and widows, of injecting poisonous drugs of hate into the veins of peoples normally humane, of sending men home from dark and bloody battlefields physically handicapped and psychologically deranged, cannot be reconciled with wisdom, justice, and love. A nation that continues year after year to spend more money on military defense than on programs of social uplift is approaching spiritual death.

Legacies: The Monument Controversy

A decade after the last American soldiers left Vietnam in 1973, Americans quarreled again over Vietnam—this time over the shape of a monument to commemorate the war dead. The two most prominent proposals were for a sunken wall, inscribed with the names of the dead, and a statue of combat soldiers. The upshot was a memorial incorporating both designs; the statue is positioned a short distance from the wall. What was at stake in the monument controversy? What, in your opinion, is the message or theme of each design, and how might each represent a distinct understanding of the war?

The Wall Portion of the Vietnam Memorial. The design by Yale University architecture student Maya Ying Lin was the winning entry in an open competition. *National Park Service.*

The Statue Portion of the Vietnam Memorial. Sculpted by Frederick Hart.
National Park Service.

CHAPTER 13

America Under Siege

Whether understood as an era of destructive social upheaval or of productive social reformism, the "sixties" had a number of hard and bitter endings. Politically, the sixties began to end in 1968, when many union and working-class voters, long the mainstay of the Democratic party, helped elect Richard Nixon, and definitively terminated in 1972, when Nixon thrashed the liberal Democratic candidate, George McGovern, whose nomination had been made possible by internal changes in the party (motivated by the reformist energies of the sixties) that had given blacks and women larger roles in the political process. Economically, the sixties may have ended in 1971, when the United States experienced its first international trade deficit since 1893. Or they may have ended on October 16, 1973, when the Arab-dominated Organization of Petroleum Exporting Companies (OPEC) responded to American intervention in the Arab-Israeli war by cutting off oil shipments to the United States, Japan, and western Europe. By early 1974 the stock market was in free fall and problems of inflation and economic stagnation had surfaced that would last nearly another decade. Culturally, one might mark the end of the 1960s by the breakup of the Beatles in 1970, an event that brought to an end the band's effort to produce creative music in a framework of group cooperation—and ushered in an era focusing on self and family, typified by Paul McCartney's self-conscious anthem to his wife, "Lovely Linda" (1971), in which McCartney played all the parts himself.

For those who would like to see the "fall" of the 1970s as a product of the excesses of the 1960s, consider the event known as Watergate. Watergate had its origins in 1969, when the Nixon administration embarked on a campaign to isolate and discredit the peace movement. By 1971 the people charged with this responsibility had moved to the Committee for the Reelection of the President (CREEP), where they were working with former Attorney General John Mitchell on an illegal effort to gather information on political opponents. In June 1972, five CREEP operatives were apprehended at Democratic National Committee headquarters in Washington's Watergate apartment complex. Two years later, when the president's own tape recordings revealed that he had conspired to cover up the break-in, a humiliated Nixon resigned. His legacy (although it also owed something to Lyndon Johnson's lack of candor in handling the war in Vietnam) focused on a new and troublesome attitude toward politics: credibility. He didn't have any. Simply put, many Americans no longer believed what the politicians told them.

Given the depressed economic conditions of the decade, the crisis of confidence in politics, and the working-class-led backlash against the social reform energies of the sixties, it is not surprising that there was little progress made on "reform" fronts in the seventies. To be sure, powerful lobbies of the elderly were able to bring their constituents tangible gains: a new system that indexed social security to changes in the cost of living and a 1978 law that abolished mandatory retirement in most employment. Campaigns for gay rights and women's rights also remained vital through the 1970s. And environmental issues proved able to generate an ongoing consensus for continued government action. But on the critical issues that the sixties had courageously and optimistically raised to prominence—poverty, racism, the decaying inner cities—the consensus was washing away. What was left was a new and mistaken reliance on forced busing as the solution to all these ills. It was a solution that relied too much on the sacrifices of the white working class and on schools that were inadequate no matter who attended them. It was a solution bound to fail.

Above all it was an age of survival, of getting by until things got better, of coming to terms with limited opportunities. Hence the quintessential movie star of the day was John Travolta, whose characters were ordinary guys whose main task was to achieve a modicum of self-respect, and whose triumphs were limited ones—learning to ride a mechanical bull, or winning a dance contest—won in bars and discos. As for disco, there was no more consensus over the music than over anything else in the 1970s, and its origins in the gay and black communities in the early part of the decade did not endear it to the white working class. Yet disco was enormously popular because it spoke so clearly to the question of survival, with the darkened disco a haven of refuge from a difficult world and the pulsating, irrepressible beat a pacemaker for the walking (or dancing) wounded. In the words of the Bee Gees' 1977 hit, it all came down to "stayin' alive."

Jimmy Carter spoke this language, too, and for four years he ministered to the needs of the population like Mom with a bowl of chicken soup. He worked at labeling the nation's illness—a "malaise" in one speech, a "crisis of purpose" in another. And he patiently explained to Americans how they could survive the new regime of limits by conserving energy and living simpler lives. It was not bad advice at all, and for a time Americans responded enthusiastically to a president that at least seemed honest and credible. But Carter could not solve the riddle of "stagflation"—high rates of inflation and unemployment at the same time. Nor could he do anything much about the Iranian militants who in 1979 took 52 American hostages and held them for 444 days—for many Americans, the last in a long series of national humiliations. By 1980, Americans wanted more than survival, and they were willing to listen to anyone who promised to give them back the nation they had lost.

INTERPRETIVE ESSAY

Samuel P. Hays

Environmental Politics

In the following essay, historian Samuel P. Hays outlines the transition from a turn-of-the-century "conservation" approach to natural resources, to a post-1960 "environmental era." This broad historical overview makes it possible to understand environmental concerns not just as another 1960s issue that happened to survive into the 1970s, but also as a product of major and ongoing changes in the lives of most Americans. Why, then, did environmental matters remain potent issues in the 1980s, whereas public housing, urban "renewal," and other ingredients of Lyndon Johnson's Great Society had virtually disappeared from the political agenda? What great historical forces underpinned the environmental era? In what other ways have those forces changed today's world?

The historical significance of the rise of environmental affairs in the United States in recent decades lies in the changes that have taken place in American society since World War II. Important antecedants of those changes, to be sure, can be identified in earlier years as "background" conditions on the order of historical forerunners. But the intensity and force, and most of the substantive direction of the new environmental social and political phenomenon can be understood only through the massive changes that occurred after the end of the war—and not just in the United States but throughout advanced industrial societies. . . .

THE CONSERVATION AND
ENVIRONMENTAL IMPULSES

Prior to World War II, before the term "environment" was hardly used, the dominant theme in conservation emphasized physical resources, their more efficient use and development. The range of emphasis evolved from water and forests in the late nineteenth and early twentieth centuries, to grass and soils and game in the 1930s. In all these fields of endeavor there was a common concern for the loss of physical productivity represented by waste. The threat to the future that that "misuse" implied could be corrected through "sound" or efficient management. Hence in each field there arose a management system that emphasized a balancing of immediate in favor of more long-run production, the coordination

From Samuel P. Hayes, "From Conservation to Environment: Environmental Politics in the United States Since World War Two," *Environmental Review,* vol. 6, no. 2, fall 1982, pp. 14–41. First published in *Environmental Review.* Reprinted with permission of the publisher.

of factors of production under central management schemes for the greatest efficiency. All this is a chapter in the history of production rather than of consumption, and of the way in which managers organized production rather than the way in which consumers evolved ideas and action amid the general public.

Enough has already been written about the evolution of multiple-purpose river development and sustained-yield forestry to establish their role in this context of efficient management for commodity production. But perhaps a few more words could be added for those resources that came to public attention after World War I. Amid the concern about soil erosion, from both rain and wind, the major stress lay in warnings about the loss of agricultural productivity. What had taken years to build up over geologic time now was threatened with destruction by short-term practices. The soil conservation program inaugurated in 1933 gave rise to a full-scale attack on erosion problems that was carried out amid almost inspired religious fervor. . . .

Perhaps the most significant vantage point from which to observe the common processes at work in these varied resource affairs was the degree to which resource managers thought of themselves as engaged in a common venture. It was not difficult to bring into the overall concept of "natural resources" the management of forests and waters, of soils and grazing lands, and of game. State departments of natural resources emerged, such as in Michigan, Wisconsin, and Minnesota, and some university departments of forestry became departments of natural resources—all this as the new emphases on soils and game were added to the older ones on forests and waters. By the time of World War II a complex of professionals had come into being, with a strong focus on management as their common task, on the organization of applied knowledge about physical resources so as to sustain output for given investments of input under centralized management direction. This entailed a common conception of "conservation" and a common focus on "renewable reasources," often within the rubric of advocating "wise use" under the direction of professional experts.

During these years another and altogether different strand of activity also drew upon the term "conservation" to clash with the thrust of efficient commodity management. Today we frequently label it *preservation* as we seek to distinguish between the themes of efficient development symbolized by Gifford Pinchot and natural environment management symbolized by John Muir. Those concerned with national parks and the later wilderness activities often used the term *conservation* to describe what they were about. In the Sierra Club the "conservation committees" took up the organization's political action in contrast with its outings. And those who formed the National Parks Association and later the Wilderness Society could readily think of themselves as conservationists, struggling to define the term quite differently than did those in the realm of efficient management. . . .

Prior to World War II the natural environment movement made some significant gains. One thinks especially of the way in which Pinchot was blocked from absorbing the national parks under his direction in the first decade of the century and then, over his objections, advocates of natural environment values succeeded in establishing the National Park Service in 1916. Then there was the ensuing struggle of several decades in which an aggressive Park Service was able to engage the Forest Service in a contest for control of land and on many occasions won. . . .

After the war a massive turnabout of historical forces took place. The complex of specialized fields of efficient management of physical resources increasingly came under attack amid a new "environmental" thrust. It contained varied components. One was the further elaboration of the outdoor recreation and natural environment movements of prewar, as reflected in the Wilderness Act of 1964, the Wild and Scenic Rivers Act of 1968, and the National Trails Act of the same year, and further legislation and administrative action on through the 1970s. But there were other strands even less rooted in the past. The most extensive was the concern for environmental pollution, or *environmental protection* as it came to be called in technical and managerial circles. While smoldering in varied and diverse ways in this or that setting from many years before, this concern burst forth to national prominence in the mid-1960s and especially in air and water pollution. And there was the decentralist thrust, the search for technologies of smaller and more human scale, which complement rather than dwarf the more immediate human setting. . . . The search for a "sense of place," for a context that is more manageable intellectually and emotionally amid the escalating pace of size and scale had not made its mark in earlier years as it did in the 1970s to shape broad patterns of human thought and action.

One of the most striking differences between these postwar environmental activities, in contrast to the earlier conservation affairs, was their social roots. Earlier one can find little in the way of broad popular support for the substantive objectives of conservation, little "movement" organization, and scanty evidence of broadly shared conservation values. The drive came from the top down, from technical and managerial leaders. . . . [I]n sharp contrast, the environmental era displayed demands from the grass-roots, demands that are well charted by the innumerable citizen organizations and studies of public attitudes. One of the major themes of these later years, in fact, was the tension that evolved between the environmental public and the environmental managers, as impulses arising from the public clashed with impulses arising from management. This was not a new stage of public activity per se, but of new values as well. The widespread expression of social values in environmental action marks off the environmental era from the conservation years.

It is useful to think about this as the interaction between two sets of historical forces, one older that was associated with large-scale management and technology, and the other newer that reflected new types of public values and demands. The term *environment* in contrast with the earlier term *conservation* reflects more precisely the innovations in values. The technologies with which those values clashed in the postwar years, however, were closely aligned in spirit and historical roots with earlier conservation tendencies, with new stages in the evolution from the earlier spirit of scientific management of which conservation had been an integral part. A significant element of the historical analysis, therefore, is to identify the points of tension in the environmental era between the new stages of conservation as efficient management as it became more highly elaborated, and the newly evolving environmental concerns, which displayed an altogether different thrust. . . .

There was, for example, the changing public conception of the role and meaning of forests. The U.S. Forest Service, and the entire community of professional foresters, continued to elaborate the details of scientific management of wood production, it took the form of increasing input for higher yields, and came to emphasize especially even-aged management. But an increasing number of Americans thought of forests as environments for home, work, and play, as an environmental rather than as a commodity resource, and hence to be protected from incompatible crop-oriented strategies. Many of them bought woodlands for their environmental rather than their wood production potential. But the forestry profession did not seem to be able to accept the new values. The Forest Service was never able to "get on top" of the wilderness movement to incorporate it in "leading edge" fashion into its own strategies. As the movement evolved from stage to stage the Service seemed to be trapped by its own internal value commitments and hence relegated to playing a rear-guard role to protect wood production. . . .

There was one notable exception to these almost irreconcilable tensions between the old and the new in which a far smoother transition occurred—the realm of wildlife. In this case the old emphasis on game was faced with a new one on nature observation or what came to be called a *nongame* or *appreciative* use of wildlife. Between these two impulses there were many potential arenas for deep controversy. But there was also common ground in their joint interest in wildlife habitat. The same forest that served as a place for hunting also served as a place for nature observation. . . . As a result of this shared interest in wildlife habitat it was relatively easy for many "game managers" to shift in their self-conceptions to become "wildlife managers." . . .

If we examine the values and ideas, then, the activities and programs, the directions of impulses in the political arena, we can observe a marked transition from the pre–World War II conservation themes of efficient management of physical resources, to the post–world war environmental themes of environmental amenities, environmental protection, and human-scale technology. Something new was happening in American society, arising out of the social changes and transformation in human values in the postwar years. These were associated more with the advanced consumer society of those years than with the industrial manufacturing society of the late nineteenth and the first half of the twentieth centuries. Let me now root these environmental values in these social and value changes.

THE ROOTS OF NEW ENVIRONMENTAL VALUES

The most immediate image of the "environmental movement" consists of its "protests," its objections to the extent and manner of development and the shape of technology. From the media evidence one has a sense of environmentalists blocking "needed" energy projects, dams, highways, and industrial plants, and of complaints of the environmental harm generated by pollution. Environmental action seems to be negative, a protest affair. This impression is also heavily shaped by the "environmental impact" mode of analysis, which identifies the "adverse effects" of development and presumably seeks to avoid or mitigate them. The question is one of how development can proceed with the "least" adverse effect to the "environment." From this context of thinking about environmental affairs one is tempted to formulate an environmental history based upon the way in which technology and development have created "problems" for society to be followed by ways in which action has been taken to cope with those problems.

This is superficial analysis. For environmental impulses are rooted in deep-seated changes in recent America, which should be understood primarily in terms of new positive directions. We are at a stage in history when new values and new ways of looking at ourselves have emerged to give rise to new preferences. These are characteristic of advanced industrial societies throughout the world, not just in the United States. They reflect two major and widespread social changes. One is associated with the search for standards of living beyond necessities and conveniences to include amenities made possible by considerable increases in personal and social "real income." The other arises from advancing levels of education, which have generated values associated with personal creativity and self-development, involvement with natural environments, physical and mental fitness and wellness and political autonomy and efficacy. Environmental values and objectives are an integral part of these changes. . . .

The "environmental impulse" . . . reflects a desire for a better "quality of life," which is another phase of the continual search by the American people throughout their history for a higher standard of living. Environmental values are widespread in American society, extending throughout income and occupational levels, areas of the nation, and racial groups, somewhat stronger in the middle sectors and a bit weaker in the very high and very low groupings. There are identifiable "leading sectors" of change with which they are associated as well as "lagging sectors." They tend to be stronger with younger people and increasing levels of education and move into the larger society from those centers of innovation. They are also more associated with particular geographical regions such as New England, the Upper Lakes states, the Upper Rocky Mountain region, and the far west, while the south, the Plains states, and the lower Rockies constitute "lagging" regions. Hence one can argue that environmental values have expanded steadily in American society, associated with demographic sectors that are growing rather than with those that are more stable or declining.

Within this general context one can identify several distinctive sets of environmental tendencies. One was the way in which an increasing portion of the American people came to value natural environments as an integral part of their rising standard of living. They sought out many types of such places to experience, explore, enjoy, and protect; high mountains and forests, wetlands, ocean shores, swamplands, wild and scenic rivers, deserts, pine barrens, remnants of the original prairies, places of relatively clean air and water, more limited "natural areas." Interest in such places was not a throwback to the primitive, but an integral part of the modern standard of living as people sought to add new "amenity" and "aesthetic" goals and desires to their earlier preoccupation with necessities and conveniences. These new consumer wants were closely associated with many others of a similar kind such as in the creative arts, recreation and leisure in general, crafts, indoor and household decoration, hi-fi sets, the care of yards and gardens as living space, and amenity components of necessities and conveniences. Americans experienced natural environments both emotionally and intellectually, sought them out for direct personal experience in recreation, studied them as objects of scientific and intellectual interest, and desired to have them within their community, their region, and their nation as symbols of a society with a high degree of civic consciousness and pride.

A new view of health constituted an equally significant innovation in environmental values, health less as freedom from illness and more as physical and mental fitness, of feeling well, of optimal capability for exercising one's physical and mental powers. The control of infectious diseases by antibiotics brought to the fore new types of health problems associated with slow, cumulative changes in physical condition, symbolized most strikingly by cancer, but by the 1980s ranging into many other conditions such as genetic and reproductive problems, degenerative changes such as heart disease and deteriorating immune systems. All this put more emphasis on the nonbacterial environmental causes of illness but, more importantly, brought into health matters an emphasis on the positive conditions of wellness and fitness. There was an increasing tendency to adopt personal habits that promoted rather than threatened health, to engage in physical exercise, to quit smoking, to eat more nutritiously, and to reduce environmental threats in the air and water that might also weaken one's wellness. [One] result of this concern [was] the rapid increase in the business of health food stores, which reached $1.5 billion in 1979. . . .

These new aesthetic and health values constituted much of the roots of environmental concern. They came into play in personal life and led to new types of consumption in the private market, but they also led to demands for public action both to enhance opportunities, such as to make natural environments more available and to ward off threats to values. The threats constituted some of the most celebrated environmental battles: power and petrochemical plant siting, hardrock mining and strip mining, chemicals in the workplace and in underground drinking water supplies, energy transmission lines and pipelines. Many a local community found itself faced with a threat imposed from the outside and sought to protect itself through "environmental action." But the incidence and intensity of reaction against these threats arose at a particular time in history because of the underlying changes in values and aspirations. People had new preferences and new personal and family values that they did not have before. . . .

Still another concern began to play a more significant role in environmental affairs in the 1970s—an assertion of the desirability of more personal family and community autonomy in the face of the larger institutional world of corporate industry and government, an affirmation of smaller in the face of larger contexts of organization and power. This constituted a "self-help" movement. It was re-

flected in numerous publications about the possibilities of self-reliance in production of food and clothing, design and construction of homes, recreation and
leisure, recycling of wastes and materials, and use of energy through such decentralized forms as wind and solar. These tendencies were far more widespread than institutional and thought leaders of the nation recognized since
their world of perception and management was far removed from community
and grass-roots ideas and action. The debate between "soft" and "hard" energy
paths seemed to focus much of the controversy over the possibilities of decentralization. But it should also be stressed that the American economy, while
tending toward more centralized control and management, also generated
products that made individual choices toward decentralized living more possible and hence stimulated this phase of environmental affairs. While radical
change had produced large-scale systems of management it had also reinvigo-
rated the more traditional Yankee tinkerer who now found a significant niche in
the new environmental scheme of things.

Several significant historical tendencies are integral parts of these changes.
One involves consumption and the role of environmental values as part of
evolving consumer values. At one time, perhaps as late as 1900, the primary
focus in consumption was on necessities. By the 1920s a new stage had emerged,
which emphasized conveniences in which the emerging consumer durables,
such as the automobile and household appliances were the most visible elements. This change meant that a larger portion of personal income, and hence
of social income and production facilities were now being devoted to a new type
of demand and supply. By the late 1940s a new stage in the history of consumption had come into view. Many began to find that both their necessities and conveniences had been met and an increasing share of their income could be devoted to amenities. The shorter work week and increasing availability of
vacations provided opportunities for more leisure and recreation. Hence personal and family time and income could be spent on amenities. Economists
were inclined to describe this as *discretionary income*. The implications of this observation about the larger context of environmental values is that it is a part of
the history of consumption rather than of production. That in itself involves a
departure from traditional emphases in historical analysis.

Another way of looking at these historical changes is to observe the shift in
focus in daily living from a preoccupation with work in earlier years to a greater
role for home, family and leisure in the postwar period. Public opinion surveys
indicate a persistent shift in which of these activities respondents felt were more
important, a steady decline in a dominant emphasis on work and a steady rise
in those activities associated with home, family, and leisure. One of the most significant aspects of this shift was a divorce in the physical location of work and
home. For most people in the rapidly developing manufacturing cities of the
nineteenth century the location of home was dictated by the location of work.
But the widespread use of the automobile, beginning in the 1920s, enabled an
increasing number of people, factory workers as well as white-collar workers,
to live in one place and to work in another. The environmental context of home,
therefore, came to be an increasingly separate and distinctive focus for their

choices. Much of the environmental movement arose from this physical separation of the environments of home and work.

One can identify in all this a historical shift in the wider realm of politics as well. Prior to World War II the most persistent larger context of national political debate involved the balance among sectors of production. From the late nineteenth century on the evolution of organized extra-party political activity, in the form of "interest groups," was overwhelmingly devoted to occupational affairs, and the persistent policy issues involved the balance of the shares of production that were to be received by business, agriculture, and labor, and subsectors within them. Against this array of political forces consumer objectives were woefully weak. But the evolution of new types of consumption in recreation, leisure, and amenities generated quite a different setting. By providing new focal points of organized activity in common leisure and recreational interest groups, and by emphasizing community organization to protect community environmental values against threats from external developmental pressures, consumer impulses went through a degree of mobilization and activity that they had not previously enjoyed. In many an instance they were able to confront developmentalists with considerable success. Hence environmental action reflects the emergence in American politics of a new effectiveness for consumer action not known in the years before the war.

One of the distinctive aspects of the history of consumption is the degree to which what once were luxuries, enjoyed by only a few, over the years became enjoyed by many—articles of mass consumption. . . . And so it was with environmental amenities. What only a few could enjoy in the nineteenth century came to be mass activities in the mid-twentieth , as many purchased homes with a higher level of amenities around them and could participate in outdoor recreation beyond the city. Amid the tendency for the more affluent to seek out and acquire as private property the more valued natural amenity sites, the public lands came to be places where the opportunity for such activities remained far more accessible to a wide segment of the social order.

A major element of the older, pre–World War II "conservation movement," efficiency in the use of resources, also became revived in the 1970s around the concern for energy supply. It led to a restatement of rather traditional options, as to whether or not natural resources were limited, and hence one had to emphasize efficiency and frugality, or whether or not they were unlimited and could be developed with unabated vigor. Environmentalists stressed the former. It was especially clear that the "natural environments" of air, water, and land were finite, and that increasing demand for these amid a fixed supply led to considerable inflation in price for those that were bought and sold in the private market. Pressures of growing demand on limited supply of material resources appeared to most people initially in the form of inflation; this trend of affairs in energy was the major cause of inflation in the entire economy. The great energy debates of the 1970s gave special focus to a wide range of issues pertaining to the "limits to growth." Environmentalists stressed the possibilities of "conservation supplies" through greater energy productivity and while energy producing companies objected to this as a major policy alternative, industrial consumers of energy joined with household consumers in taking up efficiency as the major alternative. In the short run the "least cost" option in energy supply in the private market enabled the nation greatly to reduce its energy use and carried out the environmental option.

In accounting for the historical timing of the environmental movement one should emphasize changes in the "threats" as well as in the values. Much of the shape and timing of environmental debate arose from changes in the magnitude and form of these threats from modern technology. That technology was applied in increasing scale and scope, from enormous drag-lines in strip mining, to 1000-megawatt electric generating plants and "energy parks," to superports and large-scale petrochemical plants, to 765-kilovolt energy transmission lines. And there was the vast increase in the use and release into the environment of chemicals, relatively contained and generating a chemical "sea around us" that many people consider to be a long-run hazard that was out of control. The view of these technological changes as threats seemed to come primarily from their size and scale, the enormity of their range of impact, in contrast to the more human scale of daily affairs. New technologies appeared to constitute radical influences, disruptive of settled community and personal life, of a scope that was often beyond comprehension, and promoted and carried through by influences "out there" from the wider corporate and governmental world. All this brought to environmental issues the problem of "control," of how one could shape more limited personal and community circumstance in the face of large-scale and radical change impinging from afar upon daily life.

STAGES IN THE EVOLUTION OF
ENVIRONMENTAL ACTION

Emerging environmental values did not make themselves felt all in the same way or at the same time. Within the context of our concern here for patterns of historical change, therefore, it might be well to secure some sense of stages of development within the post–World War II years. The most prevalent notion is to identify Earth Day in 1970 as the dividing line. There are other candidate events, such as the publication of Rachel Carson's *Silent Spring* in 1962 and the Santa Barbara oil blowout in 1969. But in any event definition of change in these matters seems to be inadequate. Earth Day was as much a result as a cause. It came after a decade or more of underlying evolution in attitudes and action without which it would not have been possible. Many environmental organizations, established earlier, experienced considerable growth in membership during the 1960s, reflecting an expanding concern. The regulatory mechanisms and issues in such fields as air and water pollution were shaped then; for example the Clean Air Act of 1967 established the character of the air quality program more than did that of 1970. General public awareness and interest were expressed extensively in a variety of public forums and in the mass media. Evolving public values could be observed in the growth of the outdoor recreation movement that reached back into the 1950s and the search for amenities in quieter and more natural settings, in the increasing number of people who engaged in hiking and camping or purchased recreational lands and homes on the seashore, by lakes and in woodlands. This is not to say that the entire scope of environmental concerns emerged fully in the 1960s. It did not. But one can observe a gradual evolution rather than a sudden outburst at the turn of the decade, a cumulative social and political change that came to be expressed vigorously even long before Earth Day.

We might identify three distinct stages of evolution. Each stage brought a new set of issues to the fore without eliminating the previous ones, in a set of historical layers. Old issues persisted to be joined by new ones, creating over the years an increasingly complex and varied world of environmental controversy and debate. The initial complex of issues that arrived on the scene of national politics emphasized natural environment values in such matters as outdoor recreation, wildlands, and open space. These shaped debate between 1957 and 1965 and constituted the initial thrust of environmental action. After World War II the American people, with increased income and leisure time, sought out the nation's forests and parks, its wildlife refuges, its state and federal public lands, for recreation and enjoyment. Recognition of this growing interest and the demands upon public policy that it generated, led Congress in 1958 to establish the National Outdoor Recreational Review Commission, which completed its report in 1962. Its recommendations heavily influenced public policy during the Johnson administration. . . .

During the 1950s many in urban areas had developed a concern for urban overdevelopment and the need for open space in their communities. . . . The concern for open space extended to regional as well as community projects, involving a host of natural environment areas ranging from pine barrens to wetlands to swamps to creeks and streams to remnants of the original prairies. Throughout the 1960s there were attempts to add to the national park system, which gave rise to new parks such as Canyonlands in Utah, new national lakeshores and seashores, and new national recreation areas.

These matters set the dominant tone of the initial phase of environmental concern until the mid-1960s. They did not decline in importance, but continued to shape administrative and legislative action as specific proposals for wilderness, scenic rivers, or other natural areas emerged to be hotly debated. Such general measures as the Eastern Wilderness Act of 1974 . . . and the Alaska National Interest Lands Act of 1980 testified to the perennial public concern for natural environmental areas. . . . One might argue that these were the most enduring and fundamental environmental issues throughout the two decades. While other citizen concerns might ebb and flow, interest in natural environment areas persisted steadily. That interest was the dominant reason for membership growth in the largest environmental organizations. The Nature Conservancy, a private group that emphasized acquisition of natural environment lands, grew in activity in the latter 1970s and reached 100,000 members in 1981. . . .

Amid this initial stage of environmental politics there evolved a new and different concern for the adverse impact of industrial development with a special focus on air and water pollution. This had long evolved slowly on a local and piecemeal basis, but emerged with national force only in the mid-1960s. In the early part of the decade air and water pollution began to take on significance as national issues, and by 1965 they had become highly visible. The first national public opinion poll on such questions was taken in that year, and the president's annual message in 1965 reflected, for the first time, a full-fledged concern for pollution problems. Throughout the rest of the decade and on into the 1970s these issues evolved continually. Federal legislation to stimulate remedial action was shaped over the course of these seven years, from 1965 to 1972, a distinct period that constituted the second phase in the evolution of environmental politics, taking its place alongside the previously developing concern for natural environment areas.

The legislative results were manifold. Air pollution was the subject of new laws in 1967 and 1970; water pollution in 1965, 1970, and 1972. The evolving concern about pesticides led to revision of the existing law in the Pesticides Act of 1972. The growing public interest in natural environment values in the coastal zone, and threats to them by dredging and filling, industrial siting, and offshore oil development first made its mark on Congress in 1965 and over the next few years shaped the course of legislation, which finally emerged in the Coastal Zone Management Act of 1972. Earth Day in the spring of 1970 lay in the middle of this phase of historical development, both a result of the previous half-decade of activity and concern and a new influence to accelerate action. . . .

Yet this new phase was shaped heavily by the previous period in that it gave primary emphasis to the harmful impact of pollution on ecological systems rather than on human health—a concern that was to come later. In the years between 1965 and 1972 the interest in "ecology" came to the fore to indicate the intense public interest in potential harm to the natural environment and in protection against disruptive threats. The impacts of highway construction, electric power plants, and industrial siting on wildlife, on aquatic ecosystems, and on natural environments in general played a major role in the evolution of this concern. . . . The major concern for the adverse effect of nuclear energy generation in the late 1960s involved its potential disruption of acquatic ecosystems from thermal pollution rather than the effect of radiation on people. The rapidly growing ecological concern was an extension of the natural environment interests of the years 1957 to 1965 into the problem of the adverse impacts of industrial growth.

Beginning in the early 1970s still a third phase of environmental politics arose, which brought three other sets of issues into public debate: toxic chemicals, energy, and the possibilities of social, economic, and political decentralization. These did not obliterate earlier issues, but as some natural environment matters and concern over the adverse effects of industrialization shifted from legislative to administrative politics, and thus become less visible to the general public, these new issues emerged often to dominate the scene. They were influenced heavily by the seemingly endless series of toxic chemical episodes, from PBBs in Michigan to kepone in Virginia to PCBs on the Hudson River, to the discovery of abandoned chemical dumps at Love Canal and near Louisville, Kentucky. These events, however, were only the more sensational aspects of a more deep-seated new twist in public concern for human health. Interest in personal health and especially in preventive health action took a major leap forward in the 1970s. It seemed to focus especially on such matters as cancer and environmental pollutants responsible for a variety of health problems, on food and diet on the one hand and exercise on the other. From these interests arose a central concern for toxic threats in the workplace, in the air and water, and in food and personal habits that came to shape some of the overriding issues of the 1970s on the environmental front. It shifted the earlier emphasis on the ecological effects of toxic pollutants to one more on human health effects. Thus, while proceedings against DDT in the late 1960s had emphasized adverse ecological impacts, similar proceedings in the 1970s focused primarily on human health.

The energy crisis of the winter of 1973–1974 brought a new issue to the fore. Not that energy matters had gone unnoticed earlier, but their salience had been far more limited. After that winter they became more central. They shaped environmental politics in at least two ways. First, energy problems brought material shortages more forcefully into the realm of substantive environmental concerns and emphasized more strongly the problem of limits that these shortages imposed upon material growth. The physical shortages of energy sources such as oil in the United States, the impact of shortages on rising prices, the continued emphasis on the need for energy conservation all helped to etch into the experience and thinking of Americans the "limits" to which human appetite for consumption could go. Second, the intense demand for development of new energy sources increased significantly the political influence of developmental advocates in governmental, corporate, and technical institutions that had long chafed under both natural environment and pollution control programs. This greatly overweighted the balance of political forces so that environmental leaders had far greater difficulty in being heard. . . .

Lifestyle issues also injected a new dimension into environmental affairs during the course of the 1970s. They became especially visible in the energy debates, as the contrast emerged between highly centralized technologies on the one hand and decentralized systems on the other. Behind these debates lay the evolution of new ideas about organizing one's daily life, one's home, community, and leisure activities and even work—all of which had grown out of the changing lifestyles of younger Americans. It placed considerable emphasis on more personal, family, and community autonomy in the face of the forces of larger social, economic, and political organization. The impact and role of this change was not always clear, but it emerged forcefully in the energy debate as decentralized solar systems and conservation seemed to be appropriate to decisions made personally and locally—on a more human scale—contrasting markedly with high-technology systems that leaders of technical, corporate, and governmental institutions seemed to prefer. Issues pertaining to the centralization of political control played an increasing role in environmental politics as the 1970s came to a close. . . .

From the beginning of [the Reagan] administration, the new governmental leaders made clear their conviction that the "environmental movement" had spent itself, was no longer viable, and could readily be dismissed and ignored.

During the campaign the Reagan entourage had often refused to meet with citizen environmental groups, and in late November it made clear that it would not even accept the views of its own "transition team," which was made up of former Republican administration environmentalists who were thought to be far too extreme. Hence environmentalists of all these varied hues faced a hostile government that was not prone to be evasive or deceptive about that hostility. Its antienvironmental views were expressed with enormous vigor and clarity.

We can well look upon that challenge as an historical experiment that tested the extent and permanence of the changes in social values that lay at the root of environmental interest. By its opposition the Reagan administration could be thought of as challenging citizen environmental activity to prove itself. And the response, in turn, indicated a degree of depth and persistence that makes clear that environmental affairs stem from the extensive and deep-seated changes we have been describing. Most striking perhaps have been the public opinion polls during 1981 pertaining to revision of the Clean Air Act. On two occasions, in April and in September, the Harris poll found that some 80 percent of the American people favor at least maintaining that act or making it stricter, levels of positive environmental opinion on air quality higher than for polls in the 1960s or 1970. . . .

We might take this response to the Reagan administration challenge, therefore, as evidence of the degree to which we can assess the environmental activities of the past three decades as associated with fundamental and persistent change, not a temporary display of sentiment, which causes environmental values to be injected into public affairs continuously and even more vigorously in the face of political adversity. The most striking aspect of this for the historian lies in the way in which it identifies more sharply the social roots of environmental values, perception, and action. Something is there, in a broad segment of the American people that shapes the course of public policy in these decades after World War II that was far different from the case earlier. One observes not rise and fall, but persistent evolution, changes rooted in personal circumstance, which added up to broad social changes out of which "movements" and political action arise and are sustained. Environmental affairs take on meaning as integral parts of a "new society" that is an integral element of the advanced consumer and industrial order of the last half of the twentieth century.

SOURCES

New-Style Feminism

*Modern feminism emerged in the early 1960s, with John Kennedy's Commis-
sion on the Status of Women, the Equal Pay Act of 1963, and the publication
that year of Betty Friedan's* The Feminine Mystique. *During the 1960s, feminists emphasized their exclusion from the mainstream — from politics, from the
professions, from Princeton and Yale, from ordinary good jobs. Through the
National Organization for Women (NOW) and other organizations, they demanded equality in the workplace and assailed the idea, captured in the phrase
"the feminine mystique," that women could live full, rich lives in purely domestic roles. By the 1970s, vocal critics of this position had emerged. Some believed that there could be no equality that did not involve significant changes
in the family and domestic relations. Others rejected the assumption, implicit
in the earlier view, that women should strive to be like men. This new-style feminism emphasized that feminists should understand, value, and utilize their
qualities as* women.

*Our Bodies, Ourselves (1971) was part of this new brand of feminism.
What kinds of information did the book contain? Why did the women who
wrote the book think it was necessary? What connection is there between its
publication and the* Roe v. Wade *decision, handed down by the Supreme Court
in 1973, which made invalid all laws prohibiting abortion during the first three
months of pregnancy?*

Our Bodies, Ourselves
The Boston Women's Health Book Collective

PREFACE

A Good Story

The history of this book, *Our Bodies, Ourselves*, is lengthy and satisfying.

It began at a small discussion group on "women and their bodies" that was
part of a women's conference held in Boston in the spring of 1969. These were
the early days of the women's movement, one of the first gatherings of women
meeting specifically to talk with other women. For many of us it was the very
first time we got together with other women to talk and think about our lives

and what we could do about them. Before the conference was over some of us decided to keep on meeting as a group to continue the discussion, and so we did.

In the beginning we called the group "the doctor's group." We had all experienced similar feelings of frustration and anger toward specific doctors and the medical maze in general, and initially we wanted to do something about those doctors who were condescending, paternalistic, judgmental, and noninformative. As we talked and shared our experiences with one another, we realized just how much we had to learn about our bodies. So we decided on a summer project—to research those topics that we felt were particularly pertinent to learning about our bodies, to discuss in the group what we had learned, then to write papers individually or in small groups of two or three, and finally to present the results in the fall as a course for women on women and their bodies.

As we developed the course we realized more and more that we were really capable of collecting, understanding, and evaluating medical information. Together we evaluated our reading of books and journals, our talks with doctors and friends who were medical students. We found we could discuss, question, and argue with each other in a new spirit of cooperation rather than competition. We were equally struck by how important it was for us to be able to open up with one another and share our feelings about our bodies. The process of talking was as crucial as the facts themselves. Over time the facts and feelings melted together in ways that touched us very deeply, and that is reflected in the changing titles of the course and then the book—from *Women and Their Bodies* to *Women and Our Bodies* to, finally, *Our Bodies, Ourselves*.

When we gave the course we met in any available free space we could get—in day schools, in nursery schools, in churches, in our homes. We expected the course to stimulate the same kind of talking and sharing that we who had prepared the course had experienced. We had something to say, but we had a lot to learn as well; we did not want a traditional teacher-student relationship. At the end of ten to twelve sessions—which roughly covered the material in the current book—we found that many women felt both eager and competent to get together in small groups and share what they had learned with other women. We saw it as a never-ending process always involving more and more women. . . .

You may want to know who we are. We are white, our ages range from twenty-four to forty, most of us are from middle-class backgrounds and have had at least some college education, and some of us have professional degrees. Some of us are married, some of us are separated, and some of us are single. Some of us have children of our own, some of us like spending time with children, and others of us are not sure we want to be with children. In short, we are both a very ordinary and a very special group, as women are everywhere. We are white middle-class women, and as such can describe only what life has been for us. But we do realize that poor women and nonwhite women have suffered far more from the kinds of misinformation and mistreatment that we are describing in this book. In some ways, learning about our womenhood from the inside out has allowed us to cross over the socially created barriers of race, color, income, and class, and to feel a sense of identity with all women in the experience of being female.

We are twelve individuals and we are a group. (The group has been ongoing for three years, and some of us have been together since the beginning. Others came in at later points. Our current collective has been together for one year.) We know each other well—our weaknesses as well as our strengths. We have learned through good times and bad how to work together (and how not to as well). We recognize our similarities and differences and are learning to respect each person for her uniqueness. We love each other.

Many, many other women have worked with us on the book. A group of gay women got together specifically to do the chapter on lesbianism. Other papers were done still differently. For instance, along with some friends the mother of one woman in the group volunteered to work on menopause with some of us who have not gone through that experience ourselves. Other women contributed thoughts, feelings, and comments as they passed through town or passed through our kitchens or workrooms. There are still other voices from letters, phone conversations, a variety of discussions, etc., that are included in the chapters as excerpts of personal experiences. Many women have spoken for themselves in this book, though we in the collective do not agree with all that has been written. Some of us are even uncomfortable with part of the material. We have included it anyway, because we give more weight to accepting that we differ than to our uneasiness. We have been asked why this is exclusively a book about women, why we have restricted our course to women. Our answer is that we are women and, as women, do not consider ourselves experts on men (as men through the centuries have presumed to be experts on us). We are not implying that we think most twentieth-century men are much less alienated from their bodies than women are. But we know it is up to men to explore that for themselves, to come together and share their sense of themselves as we have done. We would like to read a book about men and their bodies.

We are offering a book that can be used in many different ways—individually, in a group, for a course. Our book contains real material about our bodies and ourselves that isn't available elsewhere, and we have tried to present it in a new way—an honest, humane, and powerful way of thinking about ourselves and our lives. We want to share the knowledge and power that comes with this way of thinking, and we want to share the feelings we have for each other—supportive and loving feelings that show we can indeed help one another grow.

From the very beginning of working together, first on the course that led to this book and then on the book itself, we have felt exhilarated and energized by our new knowledge. Finding out about our bodies and our bodies' needs, starting to take control over that area of our life, has released for us an energy that has overflowed into our work, our friendships, our relationships with men and women, for some of us our marriages and our parenthood. In trying to figure out why this has had such a life-changing effect on us, we have come up with several important ways in which this kind of body education has been liberating for us and may be a starting point for the liberation of many other women.

First, we learned what we learned equally from professional sources—textbooks, medical journals, doctors, nurses—and from our own experiences. The facts were important, and we did careful research to get the information we had not had in the past. As we brought the facts to one another we learned a good deal, but in sharing our personal experiences relating to those facts we learned still more. Once we had learned what the "experts" had to tell us, we found that we still had a lot to teach and to learn from one another. For instance, many of us had "learned" about the menstrual cycle in science or biology classes—we had perhaps even memorized the names of the menstrual hormones and what they did. But most of us did not remember much of what we had learned. This time when we read in a text that the onset of menstruation is a normal and universal occurrence in young girls from ages ten to eighteen, we started to talk about our first menstrual periods. We found that, for many of us, beginning to menstruate had not felt normal at all, but scary, embarrassing, mysterious. We realized that what we had been told about menstruation and what we had not been told, even the tone of voice it had been told in—all had had an effect on our feelings about being female. . . .

Learning about our bodies in this way really turned us on. This is an exciting kind of learning, where information and feelings are allowed to interact. It has made the difference between rote memorization and relevant learning, between fragmented pieces of a puzzle and the integrated picture, between abstractions and real knowledge. We discovered that you don't learn very much when you are just a passive recipient of information. We found that each individual's response to information is valid and useful, and that by sharing our responses we can develop a base on which to be critical of what the experts tell us. Whatever we need to learn now, in whatever area of our life, we know more how to go about it.

A second important result of this kind of learning has been that we are better prepared to evaluate the institutions that are supposed to meet our health needs—the hospitals, clinics, doctors, medical schools, nursing schools, public health departments, Medicaid bureaucracies, and so on. For some of us it was the first time we had looked critically, and with strength, at the existing institutions serving us. The experience of learning just how little control we had over our lives and bodies, the coming together out of isolation to learn from each other in order to define what we needed, and the experience of supporting one another in demanding the changes that grew out of our developing critique— all were crucial and formative political experiences for us. We have felt our potential power as a force for political and social change.

The learning we have done while working on *Our Bodies, Ourselves* has been such a good basis for growth in other areas of life for still another reason. For women throughout the centuries, ignorance about our bodies has had one major consequence—pregnancy. Until very recently pregnancies were all but inevitable, biology *was* our destiny—that is, because our bodies are designed to get pregnant and give birth and lactate, that is what all or most of us did. The courageous and dedicated work of people like Margaret Sanger started in the early twentieth century to spread and make available birth control methods that women could use, thereby freeing us from the traditional lifetime of pregnancies. But the societal expectation that a woman above all else will have babies does not die easily. When we first started talking to each other about this we found that that old expectation had nudged most of us into a fairly rigid role of wife and motherhood from the moment we were born female. Even in 1969 when we first started the work that led to this book, we found that many of us were still getting pregnant when we didn't want to. It was not until we researched carefully and learned more about our reproductive systems, about birth-control methods and abortion, about laws governing birth control and abortion, not until we put all this information together with what it meant to us to be female, did we begin to feel that we could truly set out to control whether and when we would have babies.

This knowledge has freed us to a certain extent from the constant, energy-draining anxiety about becoming pregnant. It has made our pregnancies better, because they no longer happen to us; we actively choose them and enthusiastically participate in them. It has made our parenthood better, because it is our choice rather than our destiny. This knowledge has freed us from playing the role of mother if it is not a role that fits us. It has given us a sense of a larger life space to work in, an invigorating and challenging sense of time and room to discover the energies and talents that are in us, to do the work we want to do. And one of the things we most want to do is to help make this freedom of choice, this life space, available to every woman. That is why people in the women's movement have been so active in fighting against the inhumane legal restrictions, the imperfections of available contraceptives, the poor sex education, the highly priced and poorly administered health care that keeps too many women from having this crucial control over their bodies.

There is a fourth reason why knowledge about our bodies has generated so much new energy. For us, body education is core education. Our bodies are the physical bases from which we move out into the world; ignorance, uncertainty—even, at worst, shame—about our physical selves create in us an alienation from ourselves that keeps us from being the whole people that we could be. Picture a woman trying to do work and to enter into equal and satisfying relationships with other people—when she feels physically weak because she has never tried to be strong; when she drains her energy trying to change her face, her figure, her hair, her smells, to match some ideal norm set by magazines, movies, and TV; when she feels confused and ashamed of the menstrual blood that every month appears from some dark place in her body; when her internal body processes are a mystery to her and surface only to cause her trouble (an unplanned pregnancy, or cervical cancer); when she does not understand nor enjoy sex and concentrates her sexual drives into aimless romantic fantasies, perverting and misusing a potential energy because she has been brought up to deny it. Learning to understand, accept, and be responsible for our physical selves, we are freed of some of these pre-occupations and can start to use our untapped energies. Our image of ourselves is on a firmer base, we can be better friends and better lovers, better *people*, more self-confident, more autonomous, stronger, and more whole.

1. OUR CHANGING SENSE OF SELF

Changing Our Internalized Sexist Values

When we started talking to each other we came to realize how deeply ingrained was our sense of being less valuable than men.

> In my home I always had a sense that my father and brother were more important than my mother and myself. My mother and I shopped, talked to each other, and had friends over—this was considered silly. My father was considered more important—he did the real work of the world.

Rediscovering Activity

Talking to each other, we realized that many of us shared a common perception of men—that they all seemed to be able to turn themselves on and to do things for themselves. We tended to feel passive and helpless and to expect and need men to do things for us. We were trained to give our power over to men. We had reduced ourselves to objects. We remained children, helpless and giving other people power to define us and objectify us.

As we talked together we realized that one of our central fantasies was our wish to find a man who could turn us on, to do for us what we could not do for ourselves, to make us feel alive and affirm our existence. It was as if we were made of clay and man would mold us, shape us, and bring us to life. This was the material of our childhood dreams: "Someday my prince will come." We were always disappointed when men did not accomplish this impossible task for us. And we began to see our passive helpless ways of handing power over to others as crippling to us. What became clear to us was that we had to change our expectations for ourselves. There was no factual reason why we could not assert and affirm our own existence and do and act for ourselves.

There were many factors that affected our capacity to act. For one, the ideal woman does less and less as her class status rises. Most of us, being middle class, were brought up not to do very much. Also, the kind of activity that is built into the traditional female role is different in quality from masculine activity. Masculine activity (repairing a window, building a house) tends to be sporadic, concrete, and have a finished product. Feminine activity (comforting a crying child, preparing a meal, washing laundry) tends to be repetitive, less tangible, and have no final durable product. Here again our sense of inferiority came into play. We had come to think of our activity as doing nothing—although essential for maintaining life—and of male activity as superior. We began to value our activity in a new way. We and what we did were as valuable as men and what they did.

On the other hand, we tried to incorporate within us the capacity to do more "male" product-oriented activity. . . .

We have also come to enjoy physical activity as well as mental and emotional activity. Again, the realm of physical strength is traditionally male. Once again we realized that we were active in our own ways, but we did not value

them. As we looked at the details of our lives—the shopping and the cleaning—
we realized that we used up a lot of physical energy every day but that we had
taken it for granted and thought of it as nothing. We did avoid heavy, strenuous
activity. . . .

We are learning to do new things—mountain climbing, canoeing, karate,
auto mechanics.

Rediscovering Our Separateness

. . . During this period of building up our own sense of ourselves we tried to find
out what we were like on our own, what we could do on our own. We discovered resources we never thought we had. Either because we had been dependent on men to do certain things for us or because we had been so used to thinking of ourselves as helpless and dependent, we had never tried.

It is hard. We are forever fighting a constant, inner struggle to give up and
become weak, dependent, and helpless again. . . .

As we have come to feel separate we try to change old relationships and/or
try to enter new relationships in new ways. We now also feel positive about our
needs to be dependent and connect with others. We have come to value long-
term commitments, which we find increasingly rare in such a changing society,
just as we value our new separateness.

Visualizing Feminism

The photographs on this page illustrate the enormous changes that occurred in feminism between 1945 and 1975. The first photograph, of a display celebrating the one hundredth anniversary of the Women's Rights Convention at

National Archives, Women's Bureau.

Photo by Dennis Brack from Black Star.

Seneca Falls, New York, reflects the ambivalence of women's position at mid-century. The second, of a 1971 rally in Washington, D.C., reveals no ambivalence at all. Look at the photographs carefully. What can be learned from each of them?

Graduating Seniors

To come of age in the 1970s was often to feel cheated, deprived not only of the economic opportunities that one's older brothers and sisters had had, but of the sense of adventure, of open-ended possibilities, that was part of life for the previous generation. Some social critics have argued that the diminished expectations that characterized the era produced a population of narcissists, committed only to their own lives and divorced from social commitment.

Transcribed below are the mid-decade commencement addresses of two bright and concerned graduating seniors of rural high schools in western New York, south of Buffalo. How does each speaker understand the climate of the era? Are the speeches optimistic or pessimistic? Do you hear evidence of narcissism in either address?

Dorothy L. Rowan

Valedictory Address, Clymer Central, 1975 "March to the Beating of Your Own Drums"

Mr. Swan, Reverend Sellers, Reverend DeGerlando, Mr. Fergus, Mr. Jaeger, Members of the Board of Education, Faculty, Parents and Relatives, Fellow Graduates:

Most of us feel a great accomplishment at being here tonight. We have spent the last twelve years of our lives in school, and for most of us, in this school. This accomplishment is shadowed, though, by the thought that this is the last time any of us will be active members of Clymer Central School.

None of us could have made it here tonight without the help and encouragement of our families, teachers, and friends. They all influenced the decisions we have made and have tried to guide us with their knowledge and experience.

Each of us is a separate individual with a mind and will of our own.

Archives, SUNY, College at Fredonia. Reprinted with permission of Dorothy R. Babcock.

Through all time each person has been created differently with the specific intention of individuality. Sometimes, however, it seems that instead of emphasizing individuality, our society encourages conformity.

A person's goal in life should not be to keep up with the "Joneses," and therefore be a success, but to be totally himself and to succeed in being himself. Success should not be a goal, but the result of developing and exercising qualities of character. Success is not what we do, but what we are; not what our actions are, but what our attitudes are. Those who seem to have success did not seek it, and those who make it their life's aim never seem to hit target.

We should all aim for our own personal success; a goal we set for ourselves, not one set by someone else.

Seniors, especially, should be encouraged to think for themselves, not to decide what they think someone else wants them to decide, although sometimes that is easier. It is hard to make decisions because you always risk making the wrong choice.

But there never seems to be enough time even to sit down and think. Americans have been justly accused of always rushing around in order to "save" time, but you wonder if in the end you are not actually wasting more time than you are saving.

A comparison was made between an *Alice in Wonderland* character and time. The Red Queen, rushing through the Looking-Glass Wonderland with Alice in hand kept crying, "Faster! Faster! Don't try to talk. Faster!" Maybe the Red Queen is another name for our time. We ought to try to catch our breath long enough to ask ourselves if all this activity indicates achievement.

Also, there is an example of a certain pilot who, in answer to a passenger's question, "How're we doing?" he replied, "We're lost, but we're making good time!"

Time is a very precious thing and should never be taken for granted; you may realize, too late, how much you could have done with the time you have wasted. Time can never be brought back, so each minute should be spent carefully and wisely. Kipling's poem "If" stated how personal success could be achieved and that the main way to do this is to strive for individuality. He says a person can mature only if he lives his life according to his own mind and morals, not of those around him, he must see life in perspective and learn to live among all the conformities and immoralities he may see, but yet not let his own life be touched by it. He must keep his individuality, not just to be different, but because he should live according to his own mind.

If a man can do all this, then as Kipling says in the last line of his poem, "Yours is the Earth and everything that's in it. And, which is more—you'll be a man, my son."

Thoreau once said, "Everyone marches to the beating of his own drums." He said it a long time ago, but it really applies to all men, no matter when they lived. And it is especially important for us to listen to what he said because with our standard of living and all the rush for fame and fortune we sometimes forget we are individuals. And we tend to think of ourselves along with a group of other persons instead of just an individual. We should sit down and think for a few minutes about where we are really going and what we are really doing.

The most important thing today is for everyone to "march to the beating of his own drums."

Dorothy L. Rowan
Clymer Central School

Carson J. Leikam

Valedictory Address, Pine Valley Central, 1976

For quite some time now, especially in the last couple of years, our parents, teachers, and others who are already wise to the ways of the world, have been telling us that it's going to be tough once we get out there. They aren't going to have to tell us much longer—we're going to find out soon. Once we get out there it's not going to become "our world"; we're going to have to compete with everybody else, making it just that much tougher.

Here we are—the class of '76, all fairly confident that we're going to succeed in the world. How many of us are going to be able to keep that confidence when every place we go employers tell us that they have no openings for employment. Sociologists tell us that the strain of many jobs is almost unbearable. Is it as unbearable as having bills come in with no money to pay them off? Is it as unbearable as having a Ph.D. and being unable to get a job because of too much specialization? I can't number the times I've looked in the job section of the paper and found that I must have experience before an employer will hire me. How does one get experience without first getting hired?

I'm not pessimistic, but I won't say that the world isn't. The class of '76 knows it's tough out there, but that by itself isn't going to stop us! Probably some of you are thinking: "How can he stand up there and talk about how tough the world is? Only after he's been out there and really felt the pressure and the competition, only then will he know just how tough it is!" Well, people who think like that haven't had a son or daughter in high school for a while, because the pressure and competition in high school can be quite phenomenal. Hopefully, our years at Pine Valley have been more than just taking notes, reading books, and writing papers. If that's it, then our education to date has been totally worthless. But if our education has stressed competition, recognition for novel ideas, praise for excellent work, discussions and assignments that relate to the "world out there," then it has been very beneficial. Our education will have prepared us even more for the trials to come if all these things have been combined in a manner that makes the student feel the need to succeed.

Someone might think that that's a pretty brutal way to assess one's years in

Archives, SUNY-College at Fredonia. Reprinted with permission of Carson J. Leikam.

school. Well, if it wasn't tough, if we didn't have to think for ourselves, if we didn't have to get in there and really dig to stay on top, then that brutal world out there is going to chew us to pieces.

Our attitude toward reality, toward the way things are, is going to have to much to do with our success or failure. Sure, it's a tough world to make a living in, but we can't go out into the world with the attitude that since those who came before us made the world the way it is, then it's their responsibility to fix it up. "To err is human." Therefore we should remember that we're all capable of error. If we tackle life with the attitude that we're here now, and if we get in gear, then maybe we can shift things in the right direction. It's going to have to be a team effort, with everybody giving his utmost to put this world back on course. If we don't, the finger won't be pointed at any certain person or group as being to blame for creating the mess that we seem to be headed for right now. If we don't, it's not going to be much of a world by the time people start pointing those accusing fingers.

There are people starving to death, people living in run-down apartments with paper-thin walls and having only the bare necessities. Some don't even have that much. It's not just in Africa, underdeveloped countries of Europe, sections of Asia and South America—it's right here in the good ole USA. Let's get our country back on its feet—let's aid our own poor and deprived. Once we're strong again, we can put out our hand and help the less fortunate countries of the world. But we aren't going to be able to extend that helping hand if it turns into a mass of accusing fingers—pointing at us and the slow deterioration of our country, economically, socially, physically, and maybe most important of all—morally. The weak cannot help the weak. It is my belief that we should make ourselves strong again—the definite number one of the world. Then, we will be ready to help the other people and nations of our troubled world.

How can we do this? By exercising the qualities that I know the class of '76 has—an attitude of working together and pulling toward that common goal; to use that attitude to get out and do our part in a team effort. We need to get that nationalistic feeling—not as a show-off in the world of nations, but that feeling of unity and solidarity. Everybody forward, all at once.

I can't say "Never fear! The world is now in the hands of the class of '76!," because it's not. Even if it were in our hands I don't think I could say "Never fear." But I can say that if this country gets it together and makes a genuine effort like the class of '76 has made to attain its goals—that's going to help. With the attitude of our class of '76, the ability and desire to work together, the diligence, the high moral standard, and a real trust in our Lord, we can help steer this world right back on course.

They say that history repeats itself and goes in a pattern; that no great civilization has lasted for much more than two hundred years. There's no doubt that this country is definitely great. But, there also is no doubt that the bicentennial class of '76 with the help of the other people of this magnificent land, will not allow the death of our American civilization, but will struggle to ensure a more secure, richer heritage for us and for our descendants.

Film and Culture

In an era of VCRs, movie rentals, and cable television, students increasingly carry with them substantial knowledge of the history of film—enough, we hope, to have some fun with the lists that follow. Do the films on the 1970s list reflect some of the seventies themes discussed in this chapter, such as survival, narcissism, environmentalism, and the retreat from social reformism? What other themes might one suggest? The original Superman *was a product of the 1930s. How do you explain the reemergence of the character in the 1970s? Can you see any difference between the films of the 1960s and those of the 1970s?*

TOP TEN MONEYMAKING FILMS FROM THE SEVENTIES

1. *Star Wars* (1977)
2. *Jaws* (1975)
3. *Grease* (1978)
4. *The Exorcist* (1973)
5. *The Godfather* (1972)
6. *Superman* (1978)
7. *The Sting* (1973)
8. *Close Encounters* (1977)
9. *Saturday Night Fever* (1977)
10. *National Lampoon Animal House* (1978)

Runners-up

1. *Smokey and the Bandit* (1977)
2. *One Flew Over the Cuckoo's Nest* (1975)
3. *American Graffiti* (1973)
4. *Rocky* (1976)
5. *Jaws II* (1978)
6. *Love Story* (1970)
   Towering Inferno (1975)
8. *Every Which Way But Loose* (1978)
9. *Heaven Can Wait* (1978)
10. *Airport* (1970)

Cobbett S. Steinberg, *Film Facts* (New York: Facts on File, 1980), pp. 13–14.

TOP TEN MONEYMAKING FILMS FROM
THE SIXTIES

1. *The Sound of Music* (1965)
2. *The Graduate* (1968)
3. *Doctor Zhivago* (1965)
4. *Butch Cassidy* (1969)
5. *Mary Poppins* (1964)
6. *Thunderball* (1965)
7. *Funny Girl* (1968)
8. *Cleopatra* (1963)
9. *Guess Who's Coming to Dinner?* (1968)
10. *The Jungle Book* (1967)

Runners-up

1. *2001* (1968)
2. *Goldfinger* (1964)
3. *Bonnie and Clyde* (1967)
4. *The Love Bug* (1969)
5. *It's a Mad, Mad, Mad, Mad World* (1963)
6. *Midnight Cowboy* (1969)
7. *The Dirty Dozen* (1967)
8. *The Valley of the Dolls* (1967)
   The Odd Couple (1968)
10. *West Side Story* (1961)

CHAPTER 14

Culture Wars

When he took office as president in 1981, Ronald Reagan had many constituencies. As the oldest man ever to assume the presidency, he was the candidate of the elderly. His promises to restore American "strength" and "pride" brought him the support of millions of working-class and middle-class Americans who could not understand or accept the defeat in Vietnam, humiliation at the hands of the Arab nations, or the nation's weakness in the international marketplace. Reagan appealed to the business community and to growing numbers of other Americans who believed that welfare, the welfare state, liberalism, big government, unions, or high taxes were responsible for the nation's ills. And he had the support of fundamentalist Christians, who interpreted the nation's troubles as a fall from grace and sought a remedy in the restoration of traditional values and practices: an end to abortion, prayer in the public schools, sexual abstinence before marriage, old-fashioned gender roles, censorship of the pornographic or salacious.

For twelve years Reagan and his successor, George Bush, held this curious coalition together. They did it partly with bravado and posturing, partly with American lives. Reagan did his best to revive a foundering cold war and to restore the Soviet Union as the "evil empire" that Americans loved to hate. He even imagined a technology, familiarly known as "Star Wars," that would miraculously protect Americans from missile attacks. Americans lapped it up, shelling out billions for Star Wars and celebrating the October 1983 invasion of the tiny Caribbean island of Grenada, with its Marxist government, as a sign of a reemerging America that once again had control of its destiny. Almost a decade later, when the cold war had ended, Bush found a new, and even worthy, enemy: Iraq's Saddam Hussein, who had invaded oil-rich Kuwait. Once again, the American public responded, greeting "Operation Desert Storm" with a frenzy of patriotism and, rather pointedly, offering returning troops (136 Americans were killed) the lavish homecomings that Vietnam veterans had been denied.

On the domestic front, Reagan and Bush appeared to have made some progress, especially in reconstructing the nation's faltering economy. The catastrophic inflation rates of the Carter years had been dramatically reduced. Unemployment, which had reached a post–World War II peak of 10 percent in the second year of Reagan's first term, had been reduced as well. The Reagan administration had found a remedy for "stagflation."

Yet problems remained. In the midst of the prosperity of the mid-1980s, unemployment stayed at a level more than twice that considered reasonable a generation earlier. Major industries, including machine tools, clothing, steel, and automobiles, remained at the mercy of foreign competition. The United States was losing its heavy industry and, increasingly, its light industry, too. Most of the new jobs—and there were millions of them—were in nonunion service industries that paid low wages and did not offer their employees health insurance or pension plans. More Americans were working, but poor, too—and frightened about the future. When Bush proved ineffectual at dealing with recession in 1992, the voters replaced him with Arkansas Governor Bill Clinton.

Facing the economic uncertainties that were part of the ordinary round of life, Americans turned mean, aggressive, and deadly. Violent crimes—assaults, murders, and rapes—became commonplace events in major cities, and the ghettos of some cities, where drug traffic was heavy, became zones of terror, where people were afraid to leave their homes. Despite Bush's call for a "kinder, gentler" nation, all manner of real and fictitious Americans—talk show hosts, comedians, rock stars, cartoon characters—seemed to revel in insults, abuse, and hate-mongering. The victims were predictable: blacks, women, Asians, Arabs, welfare recipients, Jews, homosexuals, and (for rap artists like N.W.A.) the police. It was—and is—an ugly age.

As the twenty-first century approached, the search for ways of understanding the nation's difficult recent history increasingly took the form of forays into the realm of culture. One set of conservative critics attacked the emerging "multicultural" focus of the high schools and universities, calling for a return to a traditional curriculum that emphasized the nation's European roots. Book-banning made a comeback when fundamentalist, "pro-family" groups went to court to prove that some school districts were using public-school textbooks to teach the "religion" of secular humanism. Under Reagan and Bush—but not Clinton—the National Endowment for the Arts withdrew its support from projects—usually ones with some erotic content—that did not have "the widest audience."

One of the more interesting cultural battles of the 1980s was waged by Tipper Gore, the wife of Albert Gore, Jr., the Tennessee senator who would become Clinton's vice president. Working through a variety of family groups, including her own Parents' Music Resource Center, Gore focused her criticism on heavy metal rock music, a genre she claimed was characterized by harmful images of sadism, brutality, and eroticism. After congressional hearings in 1985, the record industry agreed to a voluntary system of warning labels. Later in the decade and into the 1990s, cultural censors turned their guns on the misogynist lyrics of rap group 2 Live Crew and the violent lyrics of what had become known as "gangsta" rap. And the beat goes on.

Americans have always had a prudish streak, and perhaps the culture wars of the 1980s and 1990s were just another outbreak of the nation's obsession with morality. More likely they are the other face of the American postindustrial economy. One face—whether under Reagan, Bush, or Clinton seems to make no difference—looks outward toward a new, post-American world in which the United States is just another player in the international marketplace. The other face looks inward, contemplating the damage already wrought by these changes and anticipating problems to come. It is this face—the face of a pervasive anxiety about the future—that seeks some modicum of control in the "culture wars."

INTERPRETIVE ESSAY

James Davison Hunter

Culture Wars

In this thoughtful analysis of recent controversies over art, music, television, and other aspects of culture, James Davison Hunter offers us a picture of two cultural camps, one conservative and "orthodox," the other liberal and "progressivist." Because each camp has its own idea of what is vital and important, they appear in this story almost as shadowboxers, struggling furiously against their opponents yet somehow never landing a blow.

While reading Hunter's essay, look for evidence that would indicate the author's sympathies. Is Hunter consistently evenhanded, or does his account lean toward the orthodox or progressivist camp? Consider, too, the meaning of Hunter's overall analysis for American history in the late twentieth century. That is, what kind of society does Hunter describe? Is it healthy or sick? Furthermore, if the culture wars are, indeed, "the struggle to define America" (the words of the subtitle of Hunter's book), which definitions of America have been offered in this debate? Perhaps more significant, which definitions have been left out? In the end, can anything significant be accomplished through wars over culture?

One does not need to endure a thousand bleary-eyed evenings with Dan Rather or Tom Brokaw to understand how important a role the media of mass communications play in our lives. Television, radio, magazines, newspapers, news magazines, the popular press, as well as music, film, theater, visual arts, popular literature, do much more than passively reflect the social and political reality of our times. Like the institutions of public education . . . , these institutions actively define reality, shape the times, give meaning to the history we witness and experience as ordinary citizens. This outcome is unavoidable in many ways. In the very act of *selecting* the stories to cover, the books to publish and review, the film and music to air, and the art to exhibit, these institutions effectively define which topics are important and which issues are relevant—worthy of public consideration. Moreover, in the *substance* of the stories covered, books published and reviewed, art exhibited, and so on, the mass media act as a filter through which our perceptions of the world around us take shape. Thus, by virtue of the decisions made by those who control the mass media—seemingly innocuous decisions made day to day and year to year—those who work within these institutions cumulatively wield enormous power. In a good many situations, this power is exercised unwittingly, rooted in the best intentions to perform a task well, objectively, fairly. Increasingly, however, the effects of this power have become understood and deliberately manipulated. Is it not inevitable that the media and the arts would become a field of conflict in the contemporary culture war?

There are at least two matters to consider here. First, the contest to define reality, so central to the larger culture war, inevitably becomes a struggle to control the "instrumentality" of reality definition. This means that the battle over this symbolic territory has practically taken shape as a struggle to influence or even dominate the businesses and industries of public information, art, and entertainment—from the major television and radio networks to the National Endowment for the Arts; from the Hollywood film industry to the music recording industry, and so on. But there is more. At a more subtle and symbolic level, the tensions in this field of conflict point to a struggle over the meaning of "speech" or the meaning of "expression" that the First Amendment is supposed to protect. Underlying the conflict over this symbolic territory, in other words, are the questions "What constitutes art in our communities?" "Whose definition of entertainment and aesthetic appreciation do we accept?" "What version of the news is fair?" And so on.

TAKING ON THE ESTABLISHMENT

We begin by considering a brief vignette of an event that occurred at a pro-life march in Washington, D.C. The day was filled with speeches from politicians, religious leaders, pro-life leaders, and other luminaries. Several hundred thousand people listened attentively, cheered, chanted, prayed, and sang songs. Such are the rituals of modern political rallies. At one point during the rally, however, a number of pro-life advocates spontaneously turned toward a television news crew filming the event from atop a nearby platform and began to chant in unison, "Tell the truth!" "Tell the truth!" "Tell the truth!" What began as a rumble within a few moments had caught on within the crowd. Soon, tens of thousands of people were chanting "Tell the truth!" "Tell the truth!" "Tell the truth!" Of all the aspects of the rally covered in the newscast that evening or in the newspapers the following day, this brief and curious event was not among them.

The story highlights the conviction held by virtually everyone on the orthodox and conservative side of the new cultural divide that the media and arts establishment is unfairly prejudiced against the values they hold dear. They do not tell the truth, the voices of orthodoxy maintain, and what is worse, they do not even present opposing sides of the issues evenhandedly. . . .

Exaggerated [though] they may be, the general perceptions are not totally born out of illusion. Studies of the attitudes of media and entertainment elites, as well as of television news programming and newspaper coverage of various social issues and political events, have shown a fairly strong and consistent bias toward a liberal and progressivist point of view. The field over which these particular battles are waged, then, is uneven—and the contenders recognize it as such. One contender takes a position of defending territory already won; the other strives to reclaim it. There are three major ways in which traditionalists have sought to reclaim this symbolic (and institutional) territory.

One way has been in a direct assault against the media and arts establishment. Acquiring a large-circulation newspaper or a network was something that had been "a dream of conservatives for years," according to Howard Phillips of the Conservative Caucus. Early in 1985, such an assault was made. After years of frustration with what it called "the liberal bias" of CBS, a group called Fairness in Media (FIM) spearheaded a move to buy out the television network. . . . Ultimately, of course, the bid to take over the network failed, but those who supported the idea were not put off. "It may take a while to accomplish [this goal]," one editorialized, "but it's a goal well worth waiting—and striving—for."

The persistent effort of the orthodox alliance to hold the media establishment accountable for the content it presents is another strategy. Numerous national and local organizations are committed to this task, covering a wide range of media. Morality in Media, for example, is an interfaith organization founded in 1962 by three clergymen in order to stop traffic in pornography and to challenge "indecency in media" and to work "for a media based on love, truth and good taste." Accuracy in Media has, since 1969, sought to combat liberal bias by exposing cases where the media have not covered stories "fairly and accurately." The Parents' Music Resource Center, established in 1985, is concerned to raise the awareness of parents about the content of modern rock music, especially heavy metal music. Its specific focus is, according to one of its founders, "not the occasional sexy rock lyric . . . [but] the celebration of the most gruesome violence, coupled with explicit messages that sadomasochism is the essence of sex." One of the most visible of all media watchdog groups is the American Family Association and the affiliated CLeaR-TV, or Christian Leaders for Responsible Television. Founded by the Reverend Donald Wildmon, the American Family Association membership claims ordinary believers and religious leaders from all Christian faiths, Protestant, Catholic, and Orthodox, and together they propose to combat the "excessive, gratuitous sex, violence, profanity, [and] the negative stereotyping of Christians."

These organizations are joined by many others both national and local, including town and city councils around the country that share a similar concern about the content of public information and entertainment. They are effective because they are grass roots in orientation (or at least they pose as being locally connected to the grass roots), and they make use of proven techniques of popular political mobilization: letter writing, boycott, countermedia exposure, and the like.

As much a support structure for the various orthodox and conservative subcultures as a weapon in the culture war, communities within the orthodox alliance have created an entire network of alternative electronic media. These alternative media challenge the media and arts establishment a third way, then, through competition, offering programming that defines a fundamentally different and competing reality and vision of America. . . .

. . . Vigorous challenges have been made by the Evangelical-dominated television and radio industry. Within the Evangelical subculture alone there were over 1300 religious radio stations, over 200 religious television stations, and 3 religious television networks broadcasting in the United States by the early 1990s. The Catholic place in this industry is relatively small by comparison, but it does make an important contribution. The programming goes far beyond televised religious services or radio broadcasts of sacred music to include religious talk shows, soap operas, drama, Bible studies, and news commentary. In addition to these enterprises is a billion-dollar book industry (made up, within the Evangelical orbit alone, of over eighty publishing houses and over 6000 independent religious bookstores) that publish and market books on, for example, how to be a better Christian, how to raise children, how to cope with a mid-life crisis, not to mention a sizable literature on what is wrong about America and what you can do about it. And a multimillion-dollar music industry extends far beyond the latest rendition of "Blessed Assurance" by George Beverly Shea to Hasidic and Christian rock and roll, folk, heavy metal (groups called Vengeance, Petra, or Shout singing such releases as "In Your Face"), and even rap music.

THE POLITICS OF FREE SPEECH

What makes these battles over the media and arts especially interesting is that they reveal a conflict that is several layers deeper. The first layer of conflict concerns the nature and meaning of art and music, as well as the nature and meaning of information. Inevitably this conflict leads to the more philosophical and legal disputes over the nature of "speech" and "expression" protected by the First Amendment. There is no end to the number of "headline cases" in which these sorts of issues are worked out. The fact is that each dispute contains within it all the underlying philosophical and legal tensions as well. Collectively, they make the matter a crisis over which actors on both sides of the cultural divide urgently press for resolution.

To demonstrate how this conflict is played out at these different levels, it is necessary to get down to specific cases. . . .

The Avant-Garde and Its Discontents

It begins with the quest for novelty. This impulse is undeniably a driving force in the arts, entertainment, and news media. The quest is based on the premise that the new will somehow be better than the old, a premise that fits well with America's utilitarian demand for improvement. The expectation that the media and arts will continue to innovate keeps an audience coming back for more. Cultural tensions, of course, inhere within the quest and on occasion they erupt into full-blown controversy.

Art

Out of a budget of more than $150 million a year, the National Endowment for the Arts funds literally hundreds upon hundreds of projects in theater, ballet, music, photography, film, painting, and sculpture. In the late 1980s, however, it became widely publicized that the National Endowment for the Arts had indirectly funded two controversial photographic exhibits. One project, by Andres Serrano, included, among others, a photograph of a crucifix in a jar of Serrano's urine, entitled *Piss Christ;* the other project, by Robert Mapplethorpe, included, among many others, a photograph that turned an image of the Virgin Mary into a tie rack as well as a number of homoerotic photos (such as one showing Mapplethorpe with a bullwhip implanted in his anus and another showing a man urinating in another man's mouth). All of this was well publicized. Avant-garde? To say the least! But Serrano and Mapplethorpe are, their defenders maintained, "important American artists." One critic called the photograph *Piss Christ* "a darkly beautiful photographic image." Likewise, the director of the Institute of Contemporary Art in Boston concluded of Mapplethorpe's exhibit, "Mapplethorpe's work is art, and art belongs in an art museum."

For those in the various orthodox communities, the controversial aspects of the Serrano and Mapplethorpe exhibits were not art at all but obscenity. "This so-called piece of art is a deplorable, despicable display of vulgarity," said one critic. "Morally reprehensible trash," said another. Of Serrano himself, a third stated, "He is not an artist, he is a jerk. Let him be a jerk on his own time and with his own resources." The American Family Association responded with full-page advertisements in newspapers asking, "Is this how you want your tax dollars spent?"

These voices had a sympathetic hearing in the halls of government as well. In response to the National Endowment for the Arts funding of these projects and the likelihood that it would fund still other such projects in the future, Senator Jesse Helms introduced legislation that would forbid the endowment from supporting art that is "obscene or indecent." The National Endowment for the Arts agreed to make grants available only to those who pledge not to do anything of this nature. The endowment, a Helms ally argued in support of this proposal, should not showcase "artists whose forte is ridiculing the values . . . of Americans who are paying for it." Conservative columnist Doug Bandow argued similarly. "There's no justification for taxing lower-income Americans to support glitzy art shows and theater productions frequented primarily by the wealthy." Still others cited Thomas Jefferson's dictum that it is "sinful and tyrannical" to compel a person to contribute money for the propagation of opinions with which he or she disagrees.

Music

Rap is just one more innovation in youth-oriented music that began decades before with rock and roll. Serious questions were raised about the form and content of this innovation, however, with the 1989 release of *As Nasty As They Wanna Be* by the Miami-based rap group 2 Live Crew. On just one album, there were over 200 uses of the word *fuck*, over 100 uses of explicit terms for male and female genitalia, over 80 descriptions of oral sex, and the word *bitch* was used over 150 times. And what about the work of groups like Mötley Crüe, which in-

vokes images of satanism, and the rap group the Beastie Boys, who mime mas-
turbation on stage, or N.W.A., who sing about war against the police (in "Fuck
tha Police"), or Ozzy Osbourne, who sings of the "suicide solution"? Was this
really music?

The arts establishment responded with a resounding "yes." Its endorse-
ments were positive and sympathetic. Notwithstanding the violence and irrev-
erence, one essay in the *Washington Post* described rap in particular as "a vibrant
manifestation of the black oral tradition. . . . You cannot fully understand this
profane style of rapping if you disregard the larger folklore of the streets." A review of 2 Live Crew and rap in general in the *New York Times* claimed that this
form of musical expression "reveals the tensions of the communities it speaks
to: But with its humor, intelligence and fast-talking grace, it may also represent
a way to transcend those tensions." Even at its grossest, one critic wrote in *Time*,
this entire genre of music represents "a vital expression of the resentments felt
by a lot of people."

Needless to say, the opinions within the orthodox communities were less
enthusiastic. One American Family Association member called the work of the
rap poets of 2 Live Crew as well as other exemplars of popular music, such as
the heavy metal of Mötley Crüe, Twisted Sister, and the like, "mind pollution
and body pollution." An attorney involved in the controversy commented,
"This stuff is so toxic and so dangerous to anybody, that it shouldn't be allowed
to be sold to anybody or by anybody." Because this album was being sold to
children, he continued, the group's leader, Luther Campbell, was nothing less
than "a psychological child molester." Judges in Florida agreed with the sentiment, finding the lyrics to *As Nasty As They Wanna Be* to violate local obscenity
laws. Police arrested Campbell for performing the music in a nightclub after the
decree, as well as record store owners who continued to sell the album. In response, Campbell promised two things: a legal appeal and a new album—"this
one dirtier than the last."

Television

Every year during the ratings sweep, the major networks display their raciest
and most innovative programming. In years past, television shows like "Miami
Vice," "Dream Street," "Knots Landing," "thirty-something," "A Man Called
Hawk," "The Cosby Show," among many others have made strong showings
within the national television audience. These, in turn, become strong draws for
corporations wanting to advertise their products. Critics admit that the amount
of sexual intimacy outside marriage, violence, and profanity portrayed on some
of these shows is very high, yet they also have been quick to point out that many
of these shows are technically innovative and treat many issues such as homosexuality, child abuse and incest, and the ambiguities of ethical behavior in law
enforcement, marriage, student culture, and the like, with great sensitivity.

Sensitivity is the last thing these television shows display, in the view of
many with orthodox commitments. To the contrary, "television," claimed a letter from the American Family Association, "is undermining the Judeo-Christian

values you hold dear and work hard to teach your children." For this reason, leaders from CLeaR-TV visited with executives from the three major networks in order to express their concerns. According to Reverend Wildmon, "They used the same words that I used, but we certainly didn't mean the same thing by them." From this point on, the leaders decided to approach the advertisers rather than the networks. "Advertisers don't give you a cold shoulder. They want to be your friend." In line with this strategy, the American Family Association and CLeaR-TV began to approach advertisers. Sponsors who did not respond positively to their concerns very often faced the threat of a boycott. PepsiCo, for example, pulled a commercial featuring pop star, nude model, and actress Madonna and their promotion of her world tour; General Mills, Ralston Purina, and Domino's Pizza pulled advertising from "Saturday Night Live"; Mazda and Noxell were also influenced in this way; and of the 400 sponsors of prime-time television in the 1989 ratings sweeps, CLeaR-TV focused on the Mennon Company and the Clorox Corporation, pledging to boycott their products for a year for their sponsorship of programs containing sex, violence, and profanity. . . .

Decoding Art and the Avant-Garde

The preceding examples are but a few well-publicized illustrations of cultural warfare in various media and forms of public expression. The point of reviewing them was to demonstrate, across media, certain patterns of cultural conflict. Despite the variations of situation and media, one can trace a common and consistent thread of sentiment on each side of the new cultural divide.

On the progressivist side, there is a tendency to value novelty and the avant-garde for their own sake. This in itself is not controversial. What is controversial is *how* avant-garde is defined. Progressives implicitly define the "avant-garde" not so much as the presentation of classic social themes in new artistic forms, but rather as the symbolic presentation of behavior and ideas that test the limits of social acceptability. More often than not this means the embrace of what the prevailing social consensus would have called "perverse" or "irreverent," what Carol Iannone calls "the insistent and progressive artistic exploration of the forbidden frontiers of human experience." Lucy Lippard acknowledges as much in her review of the Serrano corpus in *Art in America:* "His work shows," she contends, "that the conventional notion of good taste with which we are raised and educated is based on an illusion of social order that is no longer possible (nor desirable) to believe in. We now look at art in the context of incoherence and disorder—a far more difficult task than following the prevailing rules." A similar theme can be found in each of the other cases reviewed. In rap music and in television programming, the boundaries of social consensus around human relationships are tested through excessive sex and violence. . . . In each case, an earlier consensus of what is "perverse" and what is "irreverent" is challenged, and as it is challenged, it inevitably disintegrates.

The issue is sharpened when considering the special case of art. Here too the underlying controversy is over how art is to be defined. In general, progressivists tend to start with the assumption that there is no objective method of determining what is art and what is obscene. Historical experience demonstrates time and again that even if a consensus declares that a work has no enduring artistic value, the consensus may change; the work could, over time, come to be viewed as art. For this reason one must recognize and at all times respect and defend the autonomy of the artist and of artistic effort. Artists should not be bound by legal constraints or inhibited by social conventions, for artistic genius may yet emerge, if it is not already evident. Indeed, modern criticism does regard art "as a 'sacred wood,' a separate universe, a self-contained sovereignty" and the artist, in writer Vladimir Nabokov's words, as responsible to no one but himself. One artist expressed this theme when he said, "It is extremely important that art be unjustifiable."

Out of this general perspective comes the implicit understanding that a work is art if "experts" are willing to call it art and if it symbolically expresses an individual's personal quest to understand and interpret one's experience in the world. Both themes were evident in the expert testimony given at the 1990 obscenity trial of the Contemporary Arts Center in Cincinnati where the question "What is art?" was posed directly in view of the Mapplethorpe retrospective. Jacquelynn Baas, director of the University Art Museum at the University of California at Berkeley, responded to the question of why one should consider Robert Mapplethorpe's work as art by declaring: "In the first place, they're great photographs. Secondly, in this work he dealt with issues that our society, modern society is grappling with . . . what it means to be a sexual being, and also race, that was an important part of the show." . . .

For the orthodox and their conservative allies, expert opinion is not a reliable measure of artistic achievement and the artist's intentions are completely irrelevant to determining whether a work is art. Rather, artistic achievement is measured by the extent to which it reflects the sublime. Critic Hilton Kramer endorses this view in speaking of federal funding for art that reflects "the highest achievements of our civilization." George F. Will similarly favors the view that art, at least art worthy of support, is recognized in its capacity to "elevate the public mind by bringing it into contact with beauty and even ameliorate social pathologies." Art worthy of government funding, therefore, should be justifiable on the grounds that it serves this high public purpose. Congressman Henry Hyde, in reflecting about his role in the public policy process, argues that "art detached from the quest for truth and goodness is simply self-expression and ultimately self-absorption." . . .

In sum, for the orthodox and their conservative allies artistic creativity is concerned to reflect a higher reality. For their opponents, art is concerned with the creation of reality itself. Art for the progressivist is, then, a statement of being. To express oneself is to declare one's existence. Hilton Kramer may be correct that the professional art world maintains a sentimental attachment to the idea that art is at its best when it is most extreme and disruptive, but he is probably wrong if he believes this to be its chief or only aim. More fundamentally, if only implicitly, the contemporary arts project is a statement about the meaning of life, namely that life is a process of self-creation. As this enterprise takes public form, however, contemporary art and the avant-garde come to represent nothing less than the besmearing of the highest ideals of the orthodox moral vision.

When all is said and done, however, the events taking place in each of the contexts mentioned earlier—the action and reaction of progressivists and cultural conservatives—represent only the first state in the development of a deeper debate about the limits of public expression in American society.

CENSORSHIP

Progressivist Accusations

The immediate reaction of the progressivists is that those who complain about art do so because they "do not know enough about art," or simply "do not care about art." All the protest demonstrates, as the *Washington Post* put it, "the danger of a cultural outsider passing judgement on something he doesn't understand." Such comments may sound elitist (and undoubtedly are), but their significance goes beyond implying that those who do not share progressive aesthetic taste are simple philistines. The real significance of such sentiments is that they reaffirm the basic characteristic of the contemporary culture war, namely the nigh complete disjunction of moral understanding between the orthodox and progressivist communities—in this case, on what constitutes art. The progressivist communities and the arts establishment display a certain arrogance in believing that their definitions of "serious artistic merit" should be accepted by all, and this leads them to categorize various cultural conservatives as "Know-Nothings," "yahoos," "neanderthals," "literary death squads," "fascists," and "cultural terrorists."

The response of progressivists to this situation, however, quickly evolves beyond this. In a way, what we hear after this initial response is less an argument than a symbolic call to arms, a "Banzai!" that reveals a spontaneous, unified, and passionate indignation every bit as deep as that expressed by the orthodox in reaction to tarnishing of their ideals. Irrespective of the circumstances or media, the orthodox protest evokes among progressives the cry of "censorship."

Nowhere has this alarm sounded more loudly than in the case of the protest against network television. People for the American Way, Americans for Constitutional Freedom, *Playboy,* and many others have viewed the boycotting of corporate advertisers of television programming as acts of "economic terrorism" that are tantamount to censorship. "What is more intrusive that the attempt by fundamentalist censors to dictate what we can watch in the privacy of our own homes?" asked the founder of Fundamentalists Anonymous. Donald Wildmon, whom *Playboy* called the "Tupelo Ayatollah," is nothing short of "dangerous." Said the executive director of Americans for Constitutional Freedom, "We intend to do everything to prevent him from setting himself up as a censor who can remake America in his own image."

Similar accusations are leveled in every other situation where the orthodox protest the content of public media. The music industry viewed the efforts of the Parents' Music Resource Center to have albums labeled "contains explicit lyrics" as an act of censorship. Frank Zappa called it a conspiracy to extort. . . . And, finally, efforts to prohibit flag burning have been called political censorship.

Implicit within this accusation, of course, is the legal judgment that the constitutionally guaranteed right to freedom of speech is either threatened or actually violated by conservative protest. For this reason, the Bill of Rights is almost always invoked by progressives or by artists themselves. When, for example, Nikki Sixx of Mötley Crüe was told in an interview that there were those who objected to the band stating on stage that their "only regret is that [they] couldn't eat all the pussy [they] saw here tonight, he responded, 'I say fuck 'em. It's freedom of speech; First Amendment!'" Thomas Jefferson himself might not have put it quite that way or even necessarily agreed with the application, but without fail, the legacy of Jefferson directly informs the content of the progressivist reply. Luther Campbell of 2 Live Crew echoed this sentiment when he said, "We give America what they want. Isn't there such a thing as free enterprise here? Isn't there such a thing as freedom of speech?" The record store owner in Florida arrested for selling *As Nasty As They Wanna Be* put the matter in a slightly larger context. "We tell the Lithuanians, you know, fight for freedom. . . . And yet, we're trying to censor our own country. . . . We don't need nobody to censor us and they're violating our civil rights and our freedom of speech. And next— what else will it be next?" . . .

The pounding repetition of this accusation is in accord with the general position taken by the People for the American Way, who believe that this brand of censorship is not only on the increase, it "has become more organized and more effective" with haunting implications. The very language employed by cultural conservatives when they insist it is time to "clean up our culture" or to "stop subsidizing decadence" is, as several writers contend, "chillingly reminiscent of Nazi cultural metaphors." Robert Brustein, writing in the *New Republic*, goes so far as to dismiss the distinction between censorship and the effort to influence the distribution of taxpayers' money (as in the effort to defund "offensive art" at the National Endowment for the Arts), insisting that defunding art is a form of censorship. He concludes that "only government—in a time when other funding has grown increasingly restrictive and programmatic—can guarantee free and innovative art. And that means acknowledging that, yes, every artist has a First Amendment right to subsidy."

The progressivist response to this blacklash has gone beyond rhetoric into direct political action as well. Full-page newspaper ads criticizing the censorious impulse have appeared. Individual artists, the ACLU [American Civil Liberties Union], Playboy Enterprises, *Penthouse*, the American Booksellers Association, and many other individuals and organizations have initiated litigation against a number of organizations, such as Concerned Women for America and the American Family Association. . . .

Orthodox Counteraccusations

To the accusation of censorship, the reply of cultural conservatives is "non-sense!" *Christianity Today* editorialized that the media and arts establishment

> use freedom of speech as a means to flout standards of common public decency.
> We must not throw in the towel. Christians must unite in mounting a coun-
> teroffensive through our families, churches, schools, and other institutions. The
> legal issues surrounding public standards may be complex, but the moral im-
> peratives are not. We must not abandon the ring of public debate to those who
> would use freedom of speech as an excuse to be as morally offensive as they
> "wanna" be.

Implicit here and in much of the orthodox and conservative rhetoric is the view
that communities have the right to decide for themselves what standards will be
used to discriminate between art and obscenity. If, through the democratic
process, standards are agreed upon, why should communities not be entitled to
uphold them through official means?

Donald Wildmon also rejects the idea that he and his compatriots are somehow violating the First Amendment protections of free speech, but he takes a
slightly different tack. He insists that artists do have the right to express themselves as they please but that he too has a right to speak out against them. This
posture is expressed paradigmatically in his rationale for acting against Pepsi
for its plans to fund the Madonna tour.

> Here is a pop singer who makes a video that's sacrilegious to the core. Here's a
> pop star that made a low-budget porn film. Here's a pop star who goes around
> in her concerts with sex oozing out, wearing a cross. Now Pepsi is saying to all
> the young people of the new generation, "Here is the person we want you to
> emulate and imitate." They can do that. They've got every right to give
> Madonna $10 million dollars, put it on television every night if they want to. All
> I'm saying is "Don't ask me to buy Pepsi if you do it." . . .

Tipper Gore of the Parents' Music Resource Center called the cry of censorship "a smoke screen," a dodge for taking corporate responsibility for their
product. In asking for labels on record albums, her group claimed, they were
asking for more information, not less. The group's approach, then, "was the direct opposite of censorship." Morality in Media takes the argument one step further in maintaining that "freedom of expression is not the exclusive right of pro-
ducers, publishers, authors or a handful of media executives. Freedom of
expression belongs . . . to the entire community. . . . [it is only a] vocal, unremit-
ting, organized community expression [that] will bring about a media based on
love, truth and good taste." . . .

Some complain that progressivists and a liberal educational establishment
censor, through exclusion, material on traditional religion in the public school
textbooks. . . . The same kind of de facto censoring occurs, it is maintained,
when major magazines and newspapers, through editorial edict, refuse to review books written and published by conservative Catholics or Evangelical
Protestants, or deny them the recognition they deserve by not including these

works on their best-seller lists. The Evangelical writer Francis Schaeffer, for example, sold over 3 million copies of his books in the United States, and yet his books were never reviewed in the *New York Times Book Review* or *Time* and never counted on any best-seller list. The same was true of Hal Lindsey's *Late Great Planet Earth,* a book that was the top nonfiction seller in America in the 1970s— for the entire decade. The book was not reviewed by the literary establishment nor did it appear on weekly best-seller lists until it was later published by a secular publishing house. For publishing elites to ignore this literature, for whatever reasons—even if they do not believe such works constitute "serious literature or scholarship"—is, they say, to "censor." . . .

Decoding Free Speech

Back and forth the arguments go. After a time, the details of this conflict become tediously predictable. One side claims that a work is "art"; the other claims it is not. One claims that a work has enduring aesthetic or literary appeal; the other claims it appeals only to the eccentric interests of a deviant subculture. At least on the face of it, one is tempted to agree with Justice John Marshall Harlan, who concluded that "one man's vulgarity is another's lyric." Such relativism may not be desirable but it seems to be the necessary outcome of the present cultural conflict. In this light, it is entirely predictable that each side would claim that the other side is not committed to free speech but to a systematic imposition of its values and perspectives on everyone else. Alas, one person's act of "censorship" has become another's "commitment to community standards."

Thus, in the contemporary culture war, regard for rights to the freedom of speech has become a matter of "whose ox is being gored" at the moment. The fact is, both sides make a big mistake when they confuse *censuring* (the legitimate mobilization of moral opprobrium) with *censoring* (the use of the state and other legal or official means to restrict speech). Censuring, say through economic boycott or letter-writing campaigns, is itself a form of political speech protected by the First Amendment and employed legally all the time whether in boycotts against South Africa, Nestle's, or California lettuce growers, or against the purveyors of sexually explicit or theologically controversial art. But the finer points of distinction are lost on many of the activists in this debate. Even when the protest is merely the expression of disapproval, what each side invariably hears are the footsteps of an approaching cadre of censors. In most cases, however, neither side presents a genuine threat to the rights of the other to free expression. The cry of censorship from both sides of the cultural divide, then, becomes an ideological weapon to silence legitimate dissent.

This being said, it must also be stated that real censorship *is* taking place and the voices of both cultural conservatism and progressivism perpetuate it in their own ways. Censorship, again, is the use of the state or other official means to restrict speech. In every case it is justified by the claim that "community standards" have been violated. The use of the police to arrest the members of 2 Live Crew in Florida and the use of law to shut down the Contemporary Arts Center in Cincinnati because they violated community standards of obscenity are, then, textbook cases of such censorship. Censorship is also perpetuated on the other side of the cultural divide. It is seen in the efforts of student groups and universities to prohibit, in the name of community standards, defamatory remarks and expressions against minorities, gays, and women. (Would progressives throw their support or legal weight behind a similar code that prohibited say, unpatriotic, irreligious, or sexually explicit "expressions" on the community campus?) Censorship is also seen, to give another example, in the suspension of Andy Rooney from his job at CBS in 1990 for making remarks against gays. On both sides of the cultural divide, the concept of "community standards" is invoked as an ideological weapon to silence unpopular voices. Understanding how the standards of one moral community can be so diametrically opposed to the standards of the other takes us back to the root of the culture war itself.

ART, EXPRESSION, AND THE SACRED

A critic quoted earlier warned of the danger of a cultural outsider passing judgment on something he does not understand. The reality of the culture war is that the cultural conservative and the progressivist are each outsiders to the other's cultural milieu. Accordingly, each regularly and often viciously passes judgment on the other. That judgment is not at all bad in itself. Such is the back and forth of democratic discourse. The danger is not in passing judgment but in the failure to understand why the other is so insulted by that judgment. *That* is the measure of their mutual outsiderness.

The orthodox, for example, demonstrate such a position when they view certain artistic work in isolation from the larger aesthetic project of an artist and label is obscene, pornographic, and prurient. Who are these people, progressivists ask, to label the life work of Serrano and Mapplethorpe as vulgarity? That they cannot see the "enduring artistic achievement" of an artist's oeuvre is a gauge of their alienation from "high art" discourse. The same kind of obtuseness is found among progressivists. Consider the controversy surrounding *The Last Temptation of Christ*. A *Washington Post* editorial stated with no equivocation that audiences would not find the film blasphemous. Another reviewer, from *Newsweek*, said, "One can think of hundreds of trashy, thrill-happy movies devout Christians could get upset about. Instead, they have taken to the airwaves to denounce *the one movie that could conceivably open a viewer's heart to the teachings of Jesus*." Still another reviewer, from Newhouse Newspapers, called the film, "The most realistic biblical film ever made." Who are these people, orthodox Christians ask, to proclaim universally that *The Last Temptation of Christ* was not blasphemous? For millions of Americans it certainly was, and it was a measure of progressives' outsiderness that they could not acknowledge it to be.

This kind of mutual misunderstanding reveals once more that the conflict over the media and the arts is not just a dispute among institutions and not just a disagreement over "speech" protected by the First Amendment. Ultimately the battle over this symbolic territory reveals a conflict over world views—over what standards our communities and our nation will live by; over what we consider to be "of enduring value" in our communities; over what we consider a fair representation of our times, and so on. As a bystander at the Contemporary Arts Center in Cincinnati observed during the controversy over the Mapplethorpe exhibit, "This isn't just an obscenity prosecution. This is a trial of a good part of American culture."

But even more, these battles again lay bare the tensions that exist between two fundamentally different conceptions of the sacred. For those of orthodox religious commitments, the sacred is obvious enough. It is an unchanging and everlasting God who ordained through Scripture, the church, or Torah, a manner of life and of social relationship that cannot be broached without incurring the displeasure of God. On the other side of the cultural divide, the sacred is a little more difficult to discern. Perhaps Tom Wolfe had it right when he observed that art itself was the religion of the educated classes. Maybe this is why Broadway producer Joseph Papp said as he observed the police coming into the Cincinnati Contemporary Arts Center to close the Mapplethorpe exhibit, "It's like an invasion. It's like they're coming into a church or coming into a synagogue, or coming into any place of worship. It's a violation." Such an insight makes sense if we see art as a symbol of conscience. To place any restrictions on the arts, therefore, is to place restrictions on the conscience itself; it is to place fetters on the symbol of being. Such an insight also makes sense if we see art as a symbol of immortality—of that which will outlive us all. To place restrictions on art is to place restrictions on the (secular) hope of eternity. Perhaps this is why the procedural guarantee of freedom of expression has also acquired a sacred quality in progressivist circles.

The idea that the battle over the arts is related to the tensions between two different conceptions of the sacred is not far-fetched. How else can one explain the passion and intensity on both sides of the cultural divide were it not that each side, by its very being and expression, profanes what the other holds most sublime? If this is true, we are again reminded of the reasons that the larger culture war will not subside any time soon.

SOURCES

The Battleground of History

Since the mid-1960s, a new generation of historians has been rewriting American history. What has emerged is less an account of politics, economics, the nation, big business, and presidents of the United States and more the story of ordinary people, minorities, local contexts, everyday lives, and popular culture. Although the people responsible see this new perspective as much more accurate and truthful than the old one, there are others who believe that the new emphases distort the American experience and encourage people to see themselves as African-Americans or Asian-Americans or women, rather than as simply "Americans."

The selections that follow feature two of the great speechmakers of the 1980s, Ronald Reagan and African-American leader Jesse Jackson, functioning here partly as historians, probing the American past in very different ways. Focus on the sections of each speech that deal with American history. What "history" does each speaker present? What kinds of people populate Reagan's version of the American past? Or Jackson's? Does one man's version of American history seem more accurate to you than the other?

Ronald Reagan

Second Inaugural Address, January 21, 1985

Senator Mathis, Chief Justice Burger, Vice President Bush, Speaker O'Neill, Senator Dole, Reverend Clergy and members of my family and friends, and my fellow citizens: This day has been made brighter with the presence here of one who for a time has been absent. Senator John Stennis, God bless you and welcome back.

There is, however, one who is not with us today. Representative Gillis Long of Louisiana left us last night. And I wonder if we could all join in a moment of silent prayer.

Amen.

There are no words to—adequate to express my thanks for the great honor that you've bestowed on me. I will do my utmost to be deserving of your trust.

This is, as Senator Mathias told us, the fiftieth time that we, the people, have celebrated this historic occasion. When the first president, George Washington, placed his hand upon the Bible, he stood less than a single day's journey by

Vital Speeches of the Day, February 1, 1985.

horseback from raw, untamed wilderness. There were four million Americans in a Union of thirteen states.

Today we are sixty times as many in a Union of fifty states. We've lighted the world with our inventions, gone to the aid of mankind wherever in the world there was a cry for help, journeyed to the moon and safely returned.

So much has changed. And yet we stand together as we did two centuries ago.

When I took this oath four years ago, I did so in a time of economic stress. Voices were raised saying that we had to look to our past greatness and glory. But we, the present-day Americans, are not given to looking backward. In this blessed land, there is always a better tomorrow.

Four years ago I spoke to you of a new beginning, and we have accomplished that. But in another sense, our new beginning is a continuation of that beginning created two centuries ago when, for the first time in history, government, the people said, was not our master. It is our servant; its only power that which we, the people, allow it to have.

That system has never failed us. But for a time we failed the system. We asked things of government that government was not equipped to give. We yielded authority to the national government that properly belonged to states or to local governments or to the people themselves. We allowed taxes and inflation to rob us of our earnings and savings and watched the great industrial machine that had made us the most productive people on earth slow down and the number of unemployed increase.

By 1980 we knew it was time to renew our faith, to strive with all our strength toward the ultimate in individual freedom consistent with an orderly society.

We believed then and now there are no limits to growth and human progress when men and women are free to follow their dreams. And we were right. And we were right to believe that. Tax rates have been reduced, inflation cut dramatically and more people are employed than ever before in our history.

We are creating a nation once again vibrant, robust and alive. But there are many mountains yet to climb. We will not rest until every American enjoys the fullness of freedom, dignity, and opportunity as our birthright. It is our birthright as citizens of this great republic.

And if we meet this challenge, these will be years when Americans have restored their confidence and tradition of progress; when our values of faith, family, work, and neighborhood were restated for a modern age; when our economy was finally freed from government's grip; when we made sincere efforts at meaningful arms reductions by rebuilding our defenses, our economy, and developing new technologies helped preserve peace in a troubled world; when America courageously supported the struggle for individual liberty, self-government, and free enterprise throughout the world and turned the tide of history away from totalitarian darkness and into the warm sunlight of human freedom.

My fellow citizens, our nation is poised for greatness. We must do what we know is right and do it with all our might. Let history say of us, these were golden years—when the American Revolution was reborn, when freedom gained new life and America reached for her best.

Our two-party system has solved us—served us, I should say, well over the years, but never better than in those times of great challenge, when we came together not as Democrats or Republicans but as Americans united in the common cause.

Two of our Founding Fathers, a Boston lawyer named Adams and a Virginia planter named Jefferson, members of that remarkable group who met in Independence Hall and dared to think they could start the world over again, left us an important lesson. They had become, in the years spent in government bitter political rivals. In the presidential election of 1800, then years later, when both were retired and age had softened their anger, they began to speak to each other again through letters.

A bond was reestablished between those two who had helped create this government of ours.

In 1826, the fiftieth anniversary of the Declaration of Independence, they both died. They died on the same day, within a few hours of each other. And that day was the Fourth of July.

In one of those letters exchanged in the sunset of their lives, Jefferson wrote, "It carries me back to the times when, beset with difficulties and dangers, we were fellow laborers in the same cause, struggling for what is most valuable to man, his right of self-government. Laboring always at the same oar, with some wave ever ahead threatening to overwhelm us, and yet passing harmless we rode through the storm with heart and hand." . . .

The time has come for a new American emancipation, a great national drive to tear down economic barriers and liberate the spirit of enterprise in the most distressed areas of our country. My friends, together we can do this, and do it we must, so help me God.

From new freedom will spring new opportunities for growth, a more productive, fulfilled and united people and a stronger America, an America that will lead the technological revolution and also open its mind and heart and soul to the treasures of literature, music and poetry, and the values of faith, courage, and love. . . .

Now there is another area where the federal government can play a part. As an older American, I remember a time when people of different race, creed, or ethnic origin in our land found hatred and prejudice installed in social custom and, yes, in law. There's no story more heartening in our history than the progress that we've made toward the brotherhood of man that God intended for us. Let us resolve: There will be no turning back or hesitation on the road to an America rich in dignity and abundant with opportunity for all our citizens.

Let us resolve that we, the people, will build an American opportunity society in which all of us—white and black, rich and poor, young and old—will go forward together, arm in arm. Again, let us remember that, though our heritage is one of blood lines from every corner of the earth, we are all Americans pledged to carry on this last best hope of man on earth.

And I have spoken of our domestic goals, and the limitations we should put on our national government. Now let me turn to a task that is the primary responsibility of national government—the safety and security of our people.

Today we utter no prayer more fervently than the ancient prayer for peace on earth. Yet history has shown that peace does not come, nor will our freedom be preserved, by good will alone. There are those in the world who scorn our vision of human dignity and freedom. One nation, the Soviet Union, has conducted the greatest military buildup in the history of man, building arsenals of awesome offensive weapons. . . .

I have approved a research program to find, if we can, a security shield that will destroy nuclear missiles before they reach their target. It wouldn't kill people, it would destroy weapons. It wouldn't militarize space, it would help demilitarize the arsenals of earth. It would render nuclear weapons obsolete. We will meet with the Soviet [leaders] hoping that we can agree on a way to rid the world of the threat of nuclear destruction.

We strive for peace and security, heartened by the changes all around us. Since the turn of the century, the number of democracies in the world has grown fourfold. Human freedom is on the march, and nowhere more so than in our own hemisphere. Freedom is one of the deepest and noblest aspirations of the human spirit. People worldwide hunger for the right of self-determination, for those inalienable rights that make for human dignity and progress.

America must remain freedom's staunchest friend, for freedom is our best ally, and it is the world's only hope to conquer poverty and preserve peace. Every blow we inflict against poverty will be a blow against its dark allies of oppression and war. Every victory for human freedom will be a victory for world peace. . . .

My friends, we, we live in a world that's lit by lightning. So much is changing and will change, but so much endures and transcends time.

History is a ribbon, always unfurling; history is a journey. And as we continue on our journey we think of those who traveled before us. We stand again at the steps of this symbol of our democracy, or we would've been standing at the steps if it hadn't gotten so cold. Now, we're standing inside this symbol of our democracy, and we see and hear again the echoes of our past.

A general falls to his knees in the hard snow of Valley Forge; a lonely president paces the darkened halls and powers, ponders his struggle to preserve the Union; the men of the Alamo call out encouragement to each other; a settler pushes west and sings a song, and the song echoes out forever and fills the unknowing air.

It is the American sound: It is hopeful, big-hearted, idealistic—daring, decent and fair. That's our heritage, that's our song. We sing it still. For all our problems, our differences, we are together as of old. We raise our voices to the God who is the author of this most tender music. And may he continue to hold us close as we fill the world with our sand, sound—in unity, affection and love. One people under God, dedicated to the dream of freedom that he has placed in the human heart, called upon now to pass that dream on to a waiting and a hopeful world.

God bless you and may God bless America.

Jesse Jackson

Address to the Democratic Convention, July 19, 1988

Thank you. Thank you. Thank you. Tonight, we pause and give praise and honor to God for being good enough to allow us to be at this place at this time. When I look out at this convention, I see the face of America, red, yellow, brown, black and white. We are all precious in God's sight—the real rainbow coalition. All of us—all of us who are here think that we are seated. But we're really standing on someone's shoulders. Ladies and gentlemen. Mrs. Rosa Parks. The mother of the civil rights movement. . . .

My right and my privilege to stand here before you has been won—won in my lifetime—by the blood and the sweat of the innocent. . . .

Dr. Martin Luther King Jr. lives only a few miles from us tonight. Tonight he must feel good as he looks down upon us. We sit here together, a rainbow coalition—the sons and daughters of slavemasters and the sons and daughters of slaves sitting together around a common table, to decide the direction of our party and our country. His heart would be full tonight.

As a testament to the struggles of those who have gone before; as a legacy for those who will come after; as a tribute to the endurance, the patience, the courage of our forefathers and mothers; as an assurance that their prayers are being answered, their work have not been in vain, and hope is eternal, tomorrow night my name will go into nomination for the Presidency of the United States of America.

HIGHER GROUND

We meet tonight at the crossroads, a point of decision.

Shall we expand, be inclusive, find unity and power; or suffer division and impotence.

We've come to Atlanta, the cradle of the old south, the crucible of the new south.

Tonight there is a sense of celebration because we are moved, fundamentally moved from racial battlegrounds by law, to economic common ground, with the moral challenge to move to higher ground.

Common ground! . . .

When people come together, flowers always flourish—the air is rich with the aroma of a new spring.

Take New York, the dynamic metropolis. What makes New York so special?

It's the invitation of the Statue of Liberty—give me your tired, your poor, your huddled masses who yearn to breathe free.

Not restricted to English only. . . .

Common ground!

That's the challenge of our party tonight.

Left wing. Right wing. Progress will not come through boundless liberalism nor static conservatism, but at the critical mass of mutual survival. . . .

SALUTE FOR DUKAKIS

When we divide, we cannot win. We must find common ground as a basis for survival and development and change and growth. The day when we debated, differed, deliberated, agreed to agree, agree to disagree, when we had the good judgment to argue a case and then not self-destruct, George Bush was just a little further away from the White House and a little closer to private life.

Tonight I salute Governor Michael Dukakis. He has run—He has run a well-managed and a dignified campaign.

No matter how tired or how tried, he always resisted the temptation to stoop to demagoguery. I have watched a good mind fast at work, with steel nerves, guiding his campaign out of the crowded field without appeal to the worst in us.

I have watched his perspective grow as his environment has expanded. I've seen his toughness and tenacity close up, knew his commitment to public service. . . .

His foreparents came to America on immigrant ships. My foreparents came to America on slave ships. But whatever the original ships, we are in the same boat tonight. . . .

Our choice? Full participation in a democratic government or more abandonment and neglect. And so this night, we choose not a false sense of independence, not our capacity to survive and endure. Tonight we choose interdependency, and our capacity to act and unite for the greater good.

SETTING AN AGENDA

Common good is finding commitment to new priorities to expansion and inclusion. A commitment to expanded participation in the Democratic Party at every level. A commitment to a shared national campaign strategy and involvement at every level.

A commitment to new priorities that insure that hope will be kept alive.

A common ground commitment to a legislative agenda for empowerment—for the John Conyers bill, universal, on-site, same-day registration everywhere. A commitment to D.C. statehood and empowerment, these we deserve, statehood. A commitment to economic set-asides. A commitment to the

Dellums bill for comprehensive sanctions against South Africa. A sad commitment to a common direction. . . .

We find common ground at the plant gate that closes on workers without
notice. We find common ground at the farm auction where a good farmer loses
his or her land to bad loans or diminishing markets. Common ground at the
school yard where teachers cannot get adequate pay, and students cannot get a
scholarship, and can't make a loan. Common ground at the hospital admitting
room, where somebody tonight is dying because they cannot afford to go upstairs to a bed that's empty waiting for someone with insurance to get sick.

We are a better nation than that. We must do better than that. . . .

A QUILT OF UNITY

Common ground. America is not a blanket, woven from one thread, one color,
one cloth. When I was a child growing up in Greenville, South Carolina, and
grandmomma could not afford a blanket, she didn't complain and we did not
freeze. Instead she took pieces of old cloth—patches—wool, silk, gaberdine,
crockersack—only patches, barely good enough to wipe off your shoes with.
But they didn't stay that way very long. With sturdy hands and a strong cord,
she sewed them together into a quilt, a thing of beauty and power and culture.
Now, Democrats, we must build such a quilt. . . .

Reaganomics. Based on the belief that the rich had too much money, too little money and the poor had too much. That's classic Reaganomics. They believe
that the poor had too much money and the rich had too little money so they engaged in reverse Robin Hood—took from the poor and gave to the rich, paid for
by the middle class. We cannot stand four more years of Reaganomics in any
version, in any disguise.

How'd I document that case.—Seven years later—the richest 1 percent of
our society pays 20 percent less in taxes. The poorest 10 percent pay 20 percent
more. Reaganomics.

Reagan gave the rich and the powerful a multibillion-dollar party. Now the
party's over, he expects the people to pay for the damage.

I take this principal position . . . let us not raise taxes on the poor and the
middle-class, but those who had the party, the rich and the powerful must pay
for the party. . . .

CHALLENGE OF OUR DAY

Leadership must meet the moral challenge of its day. What's the moral challenge of our day? We have public accommodations. We have the right to vote.
We have open housing. What's the fundamental challenge of our day? It is to
end economic violence. Plant closings without notice. Economic violence. . . .

Most poor people are not lazy. They're not black: They're not brown.

They're mostly white and female and young. But whether white, black or brown, a hungry baby's belly turned inside out is the same color. . . .

Most poor people are not on welfare. Some of them are illiterate and can't read the Want Ad section and when they can, they can't find a job that matches the address. They work hard everyday I know, I live amongst them. They catch the early bus. They work every day. They raise other people's children. They work every day. They clean the streets. They work every day. . . .

No, no, they're not lazy. Someone must defend them because it's right and they cannot speak for themselves. . . .

DRUG POLICY

We need a real war on drugs. You can't just say no. It's deeper than that. You can't just get a palm reader or an astrologer. It's more profound than that.

We are spending $150 billion on drugs a year. We've gone from ignoring it to focusing on the children. Children cannot buy $150 billion worth of drugs a year. A few high-profile athletes, athletes are not laundering $150 billion a year. Bankers are.

I met the children in Watts who unfortunately in their despair, their grapes of hope have become raisins of despair and they're turning on each other and they're-self-destructing. . . .

They say we don't have Saturday night specials anymore. They say, We buy AK47's and Uzis the latest make of weapons. We buy them across the counter on Long Beach Boulevard. You cannot fight a war on drugs unless until you're going to challenge the bankers and the gun sellers and those who grow them. Don't just focus on the children. Let's stop drugs at the level of supply and demand. . . .

REVERSE THE ARMS RACE

. . . Leadership must face the moral challenge of our day. In the nuclear age, buildup is irrational. Strong leadership cannot desire to look tough and let that stand in the way of the pursuit of peace.

Leadership must reverse the arms race. At least we should pledge no first use. Why? Because first use begets first retaliation. And that's mutual annihilation. That's not a rational way out. . . .

NEVER STOP DREAMING

I am often asked, Jesse, why do you take on these toughies? They're not very political. You can't win that way. If an issue is morally right, it will eventually be political. It may be political and never be right. . . .

We can win. We must not lose to the drugs, and violence, premature pregnancy, suicide, cynicism, pessimism and despair. We can win. Wherever you are tonight, now I challenge you to hope and to dream. Don't submerge your dreams. Exercise above all else—even on drugs, dream of the days you are drug free. Even in the gutter, dream of the day that you will be up on your feet again. You must never stop dreaming. . . .

Dream of peace. Peace is rational and reasonable. War is irrational . . . and unwinnable.

And I was not supposed to make it. You see, I was born of a teen-age mother, who was born of a teen-age mother. I understand. I know abandonment, and people being mean to you, and saying you're nothing and nobody and can never be anything. I understand. . . .

Wherever you are tonight, you can make it. Hold your head high. Stick your chest out. You can make it. It gets dark sometimes, but the morning comes. Don't you surrender. Suffering breeds character, character breeds faith, in the end faith will not disappoint.

You must not surrender. You may or may not get there but just know that you're qualified and you hold on and hold out. We must never surrender.

America will get better and better. Keep hope alive. Keep hope alive. Keep hope alive for tomorrow night and beyond. Keep hope alive. I love you very much. I love you very much.

Rap Wars

Rap music emerged in the South Bronx ghetto in the late 1960s and was first recorded in 1979. During the mid-1980s, rap entered the mainstream, and by 1988, white ten-year-olds in the suburbs were plugged into "wholesome" black rappers like Young MC or white rappers like Vanilla Ice. At the same time, however, a new generation of confrontational, hard-core rappers—among them Public Enemy, N.W.A., and 2 Live Crew—had begun to record forms of rap music that many thought were simply unacceptable. In 1990, 2 Live Crew's album As Nasty As They Wanna Be *was ruled obscene by a U.S. District Court in Florida, and the band was arrested and tried on obscenity charges for its performance at an adults-only concert in Hollywood, Florida.*

Concerned about the content and tone of rap music, Tipper Gore (see the introduction to this chapter) offered her thoughts in a January 1990 editorial in the Washington Post; *the piece was written before the controversy over 2 Live Crew erupted. Henry Louis Gates, Jr., professor of English at Duke University and an authority on African-American culture, joined the fray six months later, when 2 Live Crew was at the center of things, with a brief column for the* New York Times.

Is Gates's defense of 2 Live Crew convincing? Do his arguments address Tipper Gore's concerns?

Tipper Gore

Hate, Rape and Rap

Words like bitch and nigger are dangerous. Racial and sexual epithets, whether screamed across a street or camouflaged by the rhythms of a song, turn people into objects less than human—easier to degrade, easier to violate, easier to destroy. These words and epithets are becoming an accepted part of our lexicon. What's disturbing is that they are being endorsed by some of the very people they diminish, and our children are being sold a social dictionary that says racism, sexism, and antisemitism are okay.

As someone who strongly supports the First Amendment, I respect the freedom of every individual to label another as he likes. But speaking out against racism isn't endorsing censorship. No one should silently tolerate racism or sexism or antisemitism, or condone those who turn discrimination into a multimillion-dollar business justified because it's "real."

A few weeks ago television viewers saw a confrontation of depressing proportions on the Oprah Winfrey show. It was one I witnessed firsthand; I was there in the middle of it. Viewers heard some black American women say they didn't mind being called "bitches" and they weren't offended by the popular rap music artist Ice-T when he sang about "Evil E" who "f—ed the bitch with a flashlight/pulled it out, left the batteries in/so he could get a charge when he begins." There is more, and worse.

Ice-T, who was also on the show, said the song came from the heart and reflected his experiences. He said he doesn't mind other groups using the word nigger in their lyrics. That's how he described himself, he said.

Some in the audience questioned why we couldn't see the humor in such a song.

Will our kids get the joke? Do we want them describing themselves or each other as "niggers?" Do we want our daughters to think of themselves as "bitches" to be abused? Do we want our sons to measure success in gold guns hanging from thick neck chains? The women in the audience may understand the slang; Ice-T can try to justify it. But can our children?

One woman in the audience challenged Ice-T. She told him his song about the flashlight was about as funny as a song about lynching black men.

The difference is that sexism and violence against women are accepted as almost an institutionalized part of our entertainment. Racism is not—or at least, it hasn't been until recently. The fact is, neither racism, sexism nor antisemitism should be accepted.

Yet they are, and in some instances that acceptance has reached startling proportions. The racism expressed in the song "One In A Million" by Guns N' Roses, sparked nationwide discussion and disgust. But, an earlier album that featured a rape victim in the artwork and lyrics violently degrading to women created barely a whisper of protest. More than 9 million copies were sold, and it was played across the radio band. This is only one example where hundreds exist.

Rabbi Abraham Cooper of the Simon Wiesenthal Center, who also appeared on the Oprah Show, voiced his concerns about the antisemitic statements made by Professor Griff, a nonsinging member of the rap group Public Enemy; statements that gain added weight from the group's celebrity. "Jews are wicked." Professor Griff said in an interview with the *Washington Times*." . . . [Responsible for] a majority of wickedness that goes on across the globe."

The Simon Wiesenthal Center placed a full-page ad in *Daily Variety* calling for self-restraint from the music industry, a move that prompted hundreds of calls to the center. Yet Rabbi Cooper's concerns barely elicited a response from Oprah Winfrey's audience.

Alvin Poussaint, a Harvard psychiatrist who is black, believes that the widespread acceptance of such degrading and denigrating images may reflect low self-esteem among black men in today's society. There are few positive black male role models for young children, and such messages from existing role models are damaging. Ice-T defends his reality: "I grew up in the streets— I'm no Bryant Gumbel." He accuses his critics of fearing that reality and says the fear comes from an ignorance of the triumph of the street ethic.

A valid point, perhaps. But it is not the messenger that is so frightening, it is the perpetuation—almost glorification—of the cruel and violent reality of his "streets."

A young black mother in the front row rose to defend Ice-T. Her son, she said, was an A student who listened to Ice-T. In her opinion, as long as Ice-T made a profit, it didn't matter what he sang.

Cultural economics were a poor excuse for the south's continuation of slavery. Ice-T's financial success cannot excuse the vileness of his message. What does it mean when performers such as Ice-T, Axl Rose of Guns N' Roses and others can enrich themselves with racist and misogynist diatribes and defend it because it sells? Hitler's antisemitism sold in Nazi Germany. That didn't make it right.

In America, a woman is raped once every six minutes. A majority of children surveyed by a Rhode Island Rape Crisis Center thought rape was acceptable. In New York City, rape arrests of thirteen-year-old boys have increased 200 percent in the past two years. Children eighteen and younger now are responsible for 70 percent of the hate crime committed in the United States. No one is saying this happens solely because of rap or rock music, but certainly kids are influenced by the glorification of violence.

Children must be taught to hate. They are not born with ideas of bigotry— they learn from what they see in the world around them. If their reality consists of a street ethic that promotes and glorifies violence against women or discrimination against minorities—not only in everyday life, but in their entertainment—then ideas of bigotry and violence will flourish.

We must raise our voices in protest and put pressure on those who not only reflect this hatred but also package, polish, promote, and market it; those who would make words like nigger acceptable. Let's place a higher value on our children than on our profits and embark on a remedial civil rights course for children who are being taught to hate and a remedial nonviolence course for children who are being taught to destroy. Let's send the message loud and clear through our homes, our streets and our schools, as well as our art and our culture.

Henry Louis Gates, Jr.

2 Live Crew, Decoded

Durham, N.C.

The rap group 2 Live Crew and their controversial hit recording *As Nasty As They Wanna Be* may well earn a signal place in the history of First Amendment rights. But just as important is how these lyrics will be interpreted and by whom.

For centuries, African-Americans have been forced to develop coded ways of communicating to protect them from danger. Allegories and double meanings, words redefined to mean their opposites (*bad* meaning *good*, for instance), even neologisms (*bodacious*) have enabled blacks to share messages only the initiated understood.

Many blacks were amused by the transcripts of Marion Barry's sting operation, which reveals that he used the traditional black expression about one's *nose being opened.* This referred to a love affair and not, as Mr. Barry's prosecutors have suggested, to the inhalation of drugs. Understanding this phrase could very well spell the difference (for the Mayor) between prison and freedom.

2 Live Crew is engaged in heavy-handed parody, turning the stereotypes of black and white American culture on their heads. These young artists are acting out, to lively dance music, a parodic exaggeration of the age-old stereotypes of the oversexed black female and male. Their exuberant use of hyperbole (phantasmagoric sexual organs, for example) undermines—for anyone fluent in black cultural codes—a too literal-minded hearing of the lyrics.

This is the street tradition called *signifying* or *playing the dozens*, which has generally been risqué, and where the best signifier or "rapper" is the one who invents the most extravagant images, the biggest "lies," as the culture says. (H. "Rap" Brown earned his nickname in just this way.) In the face of racist stereotypes about black sexuality, you can do one of two things: you can disavow them or explode them with exaggeration.

2 Live Crew, like many "hip-hop" groups, is engaged in sexual carnivalesque. Parody reigns supreme, from a take-off of standard blues to a spoof of

the black power movement; their off-color nursery rhymes are part of a venerable western tradition. The group even satirizes the culture of commerce when it appropriates popular advertising slogans ("Tastes great!" "Less filling!") and puts them in a bawdy context.

2 Live Crew must be interpreted within the context of black culture generally and of signifying specifically. Their novelty, and that of other adventuresome rap groups, is that their defiant rejection of euphemism now voices for the mainstream what before existed largely in the "race record" market—where the records of Redd Foxx and Rudy Ray Moore once were forced to reside.

Rock songs have always been about sex but have used elaborate subterfuges to convey that fact. 2 Live Crew uses Anglo-Saxon words and is self-conscious about it: a parody of a white voice in one song refers to "private personal parts," as a coy counterpart to the group's bluntness.

Much more troubling than its so-called obscenity is the group's overt sexism. Their sexism is so flagrant, however, that it almost cancels itself out in a hyperbolic war between the sexes. In this it recalls the intersexual jousting in Zora Neale Hurston's novels. Still, many of us look toward the emergence of more female rappers to redress sexual stereotypes. And we must not allow ourselves to sentimentalize street culture: the appreciation of verbal virtuosity does not lessen one's obligation to critique bigotry in all its pernicious forms.

Is 2 Live Crew more "obscene" than, say, the comic Andrew Dice Clay? Clearly, this rap group is seen as more threatening than others that are just as sexually explicit. Can this be completely unrelated to the specter of the young black male as a figure of sexual and social disruption, the very stereotypes 2 Live Crew seems determined to undermine?

This question—and the very large question of obscenity and the First Amendment—cannot even be addressed until those who would answer them become literate in the vernacular traditions of African-Americans. To do less is to censor through the equivalent of intellectual prior restraint—and censorship is to art what lynching is to justice.

Generation X

A generation that had come of age in the great depression of the 1930s and fought World War II found itself well represented in the 1980s by Presidents Reagan and Bush. Then in 1992, the enormous generation of postwar baby-boomers, many of whom had come of age in the maelstrom of the 1960s, elected their first president in Bill Clinton. Yet, as the following letter reveals, another generation—the sons and daughters of the baby boom—had yet to be heard from.

Do you think the term **Generation X** *as used in the letter is useful and rea-*

Buffalo News, December 5, 1993. Used with permission of Mark Poloncarz.

sonably descriptive? According to the young man from Lackawanna, New York
(an economically depressed community south of Buffalo), who wrote this letter,
what are the characteristics of this younger generation?

Generation X: Struggling for R-E-S-P-E-C-T

Recently, there has been much written about the generation of which I am a member. As a twenty-six-year-old college graduate, I fall perfectly into the middle of "Generation X."

Our generation of young Americans has been characterized as being everything from hard-luck losers to lazy, good-for-nothing crybabies. Yet very few of the people describing my generation are actually from my generation or understand what we are thinking.

Many of my peers, including myself, believe that the reason we have not found ourselves or command any respect from others is not in our lack of ability, but in who we are. As the children of the "baby boomers," we are in the process of inheriting a nation that looks upon us with a disdain toward what it thinks we possess: an unbridled youth without a vision. We are the children of the generation that tried to change the world, and in many respects they did achieve this goal.

Our parents both fought in and fought against the Vietnam War. They changed a nation's attitudes toward how we live with and appreciate one race from another. It is the generation that has now assumed the reins of power in every facet of life. Yet this generation is now coming to realize it is losing the one thing that at one time mattered to them the most: their youth.

Is it not surprising then to see the "young at heart" criticizing the youth of today on their lack of vision or direction. Yet, it is not a lack of vision that we possess, but a lack of believing that the vision will ever come to any fruition. We still dream of a future in which we all will find good, high-paying jobs, one in which purchasing a house is an attainable goal. And one where our children will have a better life than we did.

While the vision of a better life is still there, the reality is that, even through hard work, nothing is guaranteed. I can remember being told, throughout my schooling, that a college education was the key to a better future. While this still is true, there is no longer any guarantee that the key will unlock any door.

Maybe my generation does not want to change the world. Yet, we have not stated that our goal is to fail. All we wish for is the same opportunity to prove ourselves as our parents were given twenty-five years ago.

It is not the lack of vision that we possess, but a feeling of not being given a chance to go after and grasp that vision. If given the opportunity, we can succeed at any task, for we possess all of the latest skills, knowledge, and, most importantly, youth.

The next time anyone hears of Generation X and its frustration with today's society, remember that we are not interested in changing the world—that was the last generation's goal. We just want to be allowed an opportunity to enter into and be a vital part of this society.

We are not asking for the silver platter to be given to us—just a chance to go after the platter and whatever it may hold.

MARK POLONCARZ
Lackawanna

Reprinted with permission of Tom Toles and the Buffalo and Erie County Historical Society.